# writers
## THEIR LIVES AND WORKS

# writers
## THEIR LIVES AND WORKS

Foreword by **JAMES NAUGHTIE**

Penguin Random House

**DK LONDON**

**Senior Editor** Angela Wilkes
**Senior Art Editor** Helen Spencer
**Managing Editor** Gareth Jones
**Senior Managing Art Editor** Lee Griffiths
**US Editors** Megan Douglass, Jane Perlmutter
**Jacket Designers** Surabhi Wadhwa-Gandhi,
Juhi Sheth
**Design Development Manager** Sophie MTT
**Jacket Editor** Claire Gell
**Pre-production Producer** Dave Almond
**Senior Producer** Mandy Inness
**Associate Publishing Director** Liz Wheeler
**Publishing Director** Jonathan Metcalf
**Art Director** Karen Self

Produced for DK by

**cobaltid**

www.cobaltid.co.uk

**Art Editors**
Paul Reid, Darren Bland, Rebecca Johns

**Editors**
Marek Walisiewicz, Diana Loxley,
Johnny Murray, Kirsty Seymour-Ure

First American Edition, 2018
Published in the United States by DK Publishing
345 Hudson Street, New York, New York 10014

Copyright © 2018 Dorling Kindersley Limited
DK, a Division of Penguin Random House LLC
18 19 20 21 22  10 9 8 7 6 5 4 3 2 1

001–305935–Sep/2018

ISBN: 978-1-4654-7477-3

DK books are available at special discounts when
purchased in bulk for sales promotions, premiums,
fund-raising, or educational use.
For details, contact: DK Publishing Special
Markets, 345 Hudson Street, New York,
New York 10014
SpecialSales@dk.com

Printed and bound in China

All images © Dorling Kindersley Limited
For further information see:
www.dkimages.com

A WORLD OF IDEAS:
SEE ALL THERE IS TO KNOW

**www.dk.com**

# CONTRIBUTORS

**Kay Celtel**
has a PhD in history and, after a career
spanning publishing, training, and the auction
business, now works as a writer, researcher,
and editor.

**Helen Cleary**
works from her home in rural South Wales,
writing, editing, and making fine-art prints. She
graduated in English literature from Cambridge
University and has an MA in creative writing.

**R. G. Grant**
has written extensively in the fields of history,
biography, and culture. He contributed to *1001
Books You Must Read Before You Die* (2006) and
*501 Great Writers* (2008).

**Ann Kramer**
is a writer and historian and has written
numerous books for the general reader on
subjects ranging from women's history to
art and literature.

**Diana Loxley**
is a freelance editor and writer, and a former
managing editor of a publishing company in
London. She has a doctorate in literature.

**Esther Ripley**
is a writer and editor who began her career in
journalism and was a managing editor at DK.
She studied literature with psychology and
writes on a range of cultural subjects.

**Kirsty Seymour-Ure**
has a degree in English literature and Italian
from Durham University. Now living in Italy, she
is an experienced freelance writer and editor.

**Bruno Vincent**
is an editor and author who lives in London.
In total he has written or contributed to nearly
30 books, including the *Enid Blyton for Grown
Ups* series.

**Marcus Weeks**
is a writer and musician. He has written and
contributed to many books on philosophy,
literature, and the arts, including several of
DK's "Big Ideas Simply Explained" series.

**Iain Zaczek**
studied French and History at Wadham College,
Oxford University. He has written more than 30
books on various aspects of literature, history,
and art.

**Content Consultant: Peter Hulme**
is Emeritus Professor in Literature at the
University of Essex, where he taught for 40
years. His books include *Colonial Encounters:
Europe and the Native Caribbean, 1492–1797*
(1986) and *Cuba's Wild East: A Literary
Geography of Oriente* (2011).

**FOREWORD**
**James Naughtie**
An award-winning radio host and broadcaster,
James Naughtie began his career as a
journalist before moving to radio broadcasting
in 1986. For over 20 years he cohosted on BBC
Radio 4's Today program, and he has chaired
Radio 4's monthly book club since it began in
1998. James Naughtie has chaired both the
Man Booker and Samuel Johnson judging
panels and written a number of nonfiction
books including *The Rivals: The Intimate Story
Of A Political Marriage, The Accidental American:
Tony Blair And The Presidency, The Making Of
Music,* and *The New Elizabethans* and two novels,
*The Madness of July* and *Paris Spring.*

PAGE 2  COLORED ENGRAVING OF
WILLIAM SHAKESPEARE FOLLOWING
EARLIER LIKENESSES, c.1750

PAGE 3  THE WRITING DESK OF HERMAN
MELVILLE AT ARROWHEAD, PITTSFIELD,
MASSACHUSETTS

▷ *JOHANN WOLFGANG VON GOETHE AND HIS
SECRETARY IN HIS STUDY,* J. J. SCHMELLER, 1851

CONTENTS

# Foreword

A celebrated author once apologized to me for having to disappear for a while from public view. "I've been arguing with a novel for six months," he said. No further explanation was necessary. He had to return to the fray because the argument couldn't be put aside and had to be settled one way or another. Pen in hand, he had to gaze once more at a blank page.

Imaginative writers—the novelists and poets in this volume and countless hordes of others—have all heard that insistent call pulling them away. They have also learned, with varying degrees of reluctance and joy, that the place to which they are taken is the one where they are meant to be. The first act of the writer is not so much to put the first word on the page, but to understand the obligation to listen when the call comes.

This is as true for writers driven by an urge to confront the world around them—a satirist like Jonathan Swift, a Dickens, or a Kafka— as for those who want to build a new and distant place for their imaginations. They are all aware of what some poets and novelists have characterized as a near-priestly function, as if they are the interpreters of a higher truth for those who require their intervention and guidance to see it and understand it for themselves.

A convenient belief, you might say, because it swathes the whole business in mystery and suggests there are secrets that can never be unraveled by outsiders. Yet it's true. Writers who don't accept that they are on a journey into the unknown will never produce work that lasts, because it will lack the magic that can infect a reader's mind. Even authors who are brutal about the day-to-day struggles of their trade come back, again and again, to the inexplicable character of the force that propels them. When George Orwell described writers as "vain, selfish, and lazy" he went on to say that it wasn't moral weakness of that kind that kept them at it—the business of producing a book was for him like enduring a long, painful illness—but the presence of a demon that they could neither resist nor understand.

Poets have the luxury of being more open about this than novelists, of course, because in every culture they have always been expected to be in touch with some muse, in a way denied to everyone else. In their own world. Long before the Romantics in early-nineteenth-century England put aside the mirror that poets before them had professed to hold up to nature, and replaced it with a lamp that would light up their own inner lives, the poem was the vehicle that could take you out of the world as surely as the tale-telling of an oral tradition that mingled history with mystery and fantasy when verses and stories were lovingly passed down the generations.

Seamus Heaney, a Nobel laureate in literature in the last decade of the twentieth century, returned to the *Aeneid* for his last published work, translating Book VI of Virgil's epic, which describes how the Trojan hero Aeneas descends into the underworld, having cut the golden bough to protect him as he goes—the mythic story that inspired poets from Dante Alighieri in the Italian Middle Ages, to the Anglo-American T.S. Eliot writing just after World War I nearly six centuries later. Like Heaney, they were drawn to the oldest and most enduring stories, the ones that we want to interpret over and over again to explain to ourselves who we are and why we behave as we do.

No writer of quality can escape that task. At the end of F. Scott Fitzgerald's *The Great Gatsby*, the narrator, Nick Carraway, says, "So we beat on, boats against the current, borne back ceaselessly into the past." This is much more than a cry of regret at the glitzy insubstantial world of wealth that first attracted Carraway and then repelled him—it is Fitzgerald's own profound feeling for a journey of his own that was destined never to end. It is as sharply relevant to the whole story of American life as the elemental struggle against the wild forces of nature in Herman Melville's *Moby-Dick*. Generations later, a novelist like John Updike was grappling with the same question in the same culture: what drives us on?

Whether in the particular preoccupations with power and individual responsibility that motivated European writers over centuries—and produced the most dominating poetic voice in the English language, in Shakespeare—or in Eastern literature with its vast sweep of historical and mythic sensibility, a writer in poetry or prose who doesn't confront that question is probably doomed to skate aimlessly across the surface and to vanish into the distance, there to be forgotten. None of the writers in this volume will disappear—be they treasured as gritty story-tellers, spinners of great fantasy, or angry young (and old) men and women—because somehow, with a flash of genius or a lifetime of careworn toil, they've left their readers with a character or a tragedy, a moment of exhilaration or an insistent question that will never pass away.

We all know we'll return to them. How many of us long to pick up a favorite book and absorb a memorable opening line, or meet an old friend in the first chapter, not because we're in search of a new experience, but because we want to relive something we can't forget? Or start to read a poem we can also hear in our head? Writers know it, too, and perhaps the mysterious urge that drives them on has at least one obvious component that we can all recognize. An insistent desire to give. They enlighten and entertain; trouble and perplex. Lift up.

That much we know. And perhaps the mystery that remains—the tantalizing, insoluble question of how it is done—is one we cherish, too, because we know that writers of quality are people apart. They do what we can't, which is why we need them, and most of the time we feel no envy.

How could we? They are bound on their own wheel of fire. Ernest Hemingway, in his curmudgeonly, macho way, once tried to make writing sound simple and succeeded in doing the opposite. He said, "All you have to do is to write one true sentence. Write the truest sentence that you know."

But that's when the difficulties begin.

*James Naughtie*

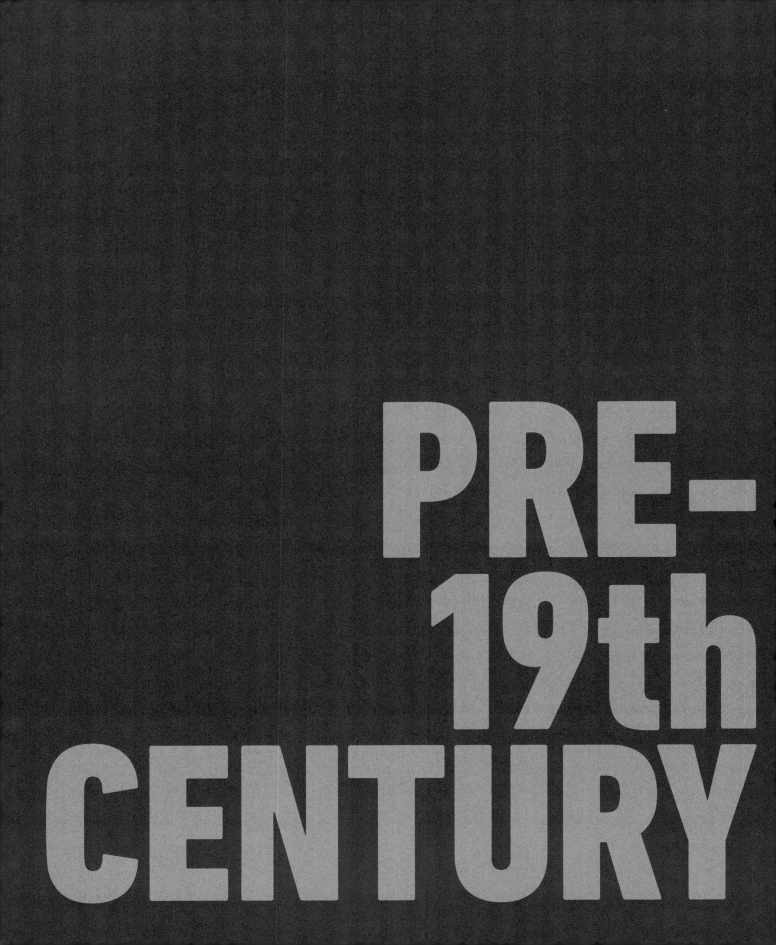

# PRE-19th CENTURY

CHAPTER 1

# Dante Alighieri

## 1265–1321, ITALIAN

Author of the epic poem *The Divine Comedy*, Dante is a towering figure in the history of literature. His dramatic vision of Hell, purgatory, and Heaven has inspired writers and artists up to the present day.

Dante Alighieri was born in Florence, Italy, probably in May 1265. At that time, Florence was an independent city-state of unrivaled wealth; the output of its workshops and the astuteness of its bankers attracted admiration and envy. It was also a place of political instability, with rival families competing, often violently, for control of the city's government.

Dante's father, a moneylender and lawyer, belonged to the political faction known as the Guelphs, and when Dante was 11 years old he was betrothed to Gemma Donati, a member of a powerful Guelph family. This arranged marriage was to last a lifetime and the couple would have at least three children. But Dante never wrote a word about his wife, Gemma. The woman who appeared as a love object in his writing was a Florentine neighbor, Beatrice Portinari.

Dante tells the strange story of his love for Beatrice in his early collection of poems and prose commentaries, *La Vita Nuova* (*The New Life*; 1294). By this account, he met Beatrice when he was just 9 years old (and she 10), and fell in love at first sight. He saw her just one more time, 9 years later, when they exchanged a brief greeting on the street. This contact was enough to make Beatrice the symbol of his highest spiritual aspirations. In

addition to inspiring his early lyric verse, she recurs in his final writings, the "Purgatory" and "Heaven" sections of *The Divine Comedy*.

### Early mentors

On the brink of the Renaissance, Florence was the center of innovation in the arts and philosophy, with the rediscovered writings of ancient Latin and Greek authors providing an alternative source of authority to the church. Dante's intellectual development was influenced by two Florentine mentors: the scholar Brunetto Latini (c.1220–1294), who introduced him to the latest humanist

△ **DANTE AND BEATRICE**
This scene, imagined by the 19th-century English artist Henry Holiday, was inspired by Dante's text *La Vita Nuova* (*The New Life*). It shows Dante and his love, Beatrice (in cream), with her companions near the Ponte Vecchio in Florence. Beatrice deliberately avoids Dante's gaze.

thinking; and the love poet Guido Cavalcanti (c.1250–1300), who served as his model for writing verse. Cavalcanti wrote in the *dolce stil novo* (sweet new style)—the culmination of the medieval tradition of "courtly love," in which the poet celebrated a pure love for an inaccessible woman seen from afar.

*LAST JUDGMENT* (DETAIL), GIOTTO, 1306

" There is no **greater sorrow** than to recall a **time of happiness** in **misery**. "

DANTE, "HELL" (CANTO 5, LINES 121–123)

▷ **PORTRAIT TRIBUTES**
Dante inspired much art in his native Florence. This 1475 portrait, showing him wearing a laurel wreath—a symbol of achievement—is by the renowned early Renaissance artist Sandro Botticelli.

The story of Dante's love for Beatrice so perfectly fits this template that many critics have suspected it of being a fiction invented by the poet to fulfill the stereotype—although Beatrice Portinari definitely did exist, and died at the age of 24.

### Civic strife

In Florence, Dante became known for his lyric poetry but also for his civic activities. As a member of the Guelph faction, he played an increasingly active role in the city's turbulent political life. He fought in a Guelph army that defeated their bitter rivals, the Ghibellines, at the battle of Campaldino in 1289, and starting in 1295 became an elected representative in Florence's complex republican system of government.

In the summer of 1300, Dante was elected to Florence's six-man ruling Council of Priors. Personal disaster soon followed. The Guelphs had traditionally supported the popes against their secular rivals for supreme power in Christendom—the Holy Roman Emperors—but had now split into pro-papal Black Guelphs and anti-papal White Guelphs, the group that Dante supported. As a city prior, he was sent as part of a deputation to Pope Boniface VIII at his residence

▽ **INFERNO**

Dante holds a copy of *The Divine Comedy* in this fresco painted by Domenico di Michelino in 1465. Behind the poet is a depiction of his Hell and the city of Florence, closed off to Dante.

▷ **BONIFACE VIII**

A marble statue on the facade of the Basilica di Santa Maria del Fiore in Florence commemorates Dante's enemy, Pope Boniface VIII. Dante took his revenge in the pages of *The Divine Comedy* by damning the pope—well before his death in 1303.

just outside Rome. There, he was detained by the pope and treated like a prisoner. In Florence, Black Guelphs seized control of the city at the pope's instigation and launched a wholesale persecution of White Guelphs. Dante was declared an exile and his property confiscated. He was later condemned to be burned alive should he ever set foot in Florence again.

### Exile from Florence

Dante found refuge in various other Italian cities, notably Verona, where he was welcomed by the ruling Scaliger family. Not a gentle, forgiving man, Dante raged against his Florentine enemies and joined other exiles in vain plots to wrest Florence from the Black Guelphs by force. However, his expulsion from his home city seems to have propelled his writing to a new level. It was in his early years of exile that he produced his influential essay *De Vulgari Eloquentia*. Written in Latin, the universal literary language of educated Europeans at the time, the essay argued paradoxically for giving vernacular Italian equal status with Latin as a literary language and discussed which version of the popular spoken tongue should be adopted for the purpose.

### *The Divine Comedy*

Dante appears to have begun writing his masterpiece, *The Divine Comedy*, in around 1307. A poem containing more than 14,000 lines of verse, it describes the narrator's journey through Hell

and purgatory to Heaven and a vision of God. In the first section, "Hell," Dante is led by the Latin poet Virgil; in the second and third sections, "Purgatory" and "Heaven," he follows his beloved Beatrice as a spiritual guide. Along the way he meets characters from contemporary life, history, and myth, each with a story to tell. "Hell" has always been the most widely read part of the poem, its vivid fresco of crimes

and punishments in the circles of Hell inspiring both horror and pity. Dante does not hesitate to avenge himself on his real-life enemies by condemning them to tortures, but he sympathizes with some of the damned—such as the lovers Paolo Malatesta and Francesca da Rimini, condemned for succumbing to lust; or his old mentor Brunetto Latini, who had been found guilty of sodomy. The mythological figure of Ulysses is in Hell (in part, for his ambush of the Trojan horse), but Dante's description of his restless quest for knowledge seems heroic rather than damnable.

In addition to a vision of the afterlife, *The Divine Comedy* presents Dante's interpretation of the failings of the contemporary political order. The ideal he embraced at the end of his life was one of a Christian world unified under the political leadership of the Holy Roman Emperor and the spiritual leadership of the pope, fulfilling God's purpose on Earth. He developed this concept in the treatise *De Monarchia* and in letters expressing support for Emperor Henry VII, who led an army into Italy in 1310. The emperor's death in 1313 ended Dante's hopes of any practical progress toward his ideal.

△ **DANTE'S FLORENCE**
Dante's life was inextricably tied to the city of Florence, which is shown in this aerial view. The great poet's image appears throughout the city in various frescoes, statues, and reliefs.

Dante never returned to Florence but spent his final years at the court of the Polenta family, the rulers of Ravenna. *The Divine Comedy* seems to have been completed there shortly before his death in 1321, at the age of 56. The final cantos of the poem were discovered concealed in his bedroom after he was buried.

## KEY WORKS

**c.1294**
*La Vita Nuova* is published— lyric poetry and prose passages explore Dante's idealized love for Beatrice.

**c.1303**
*De Vulgari Eloquentia* argues for the use of the Tuscan Italian vernacular as a literary language.

**c.1307–09**
The first section of *The Divine Comedy* describes Dante's journey through Hell, led by the poet Virgil.

**c.1308–12**
The second section of *The Divine Comedy* has Dante climb Mount Purgatory, where sinners purge their sins.

**c.1314**
In *Monarchia*, Dante argues for division of authority between the Holy Roman Emperor and the pope.

**c.1316–21**
The last section of *The Divine Comedy*, "Heaven," charts Dante's rise through the spheres of Heaven to a vision of God.

# Giovanni Boccaccio

## 1313–1375, ITALIAN

Boccaccio's magnificent stories of the everyday lives of ordinary people laid the literary foundations for prose narrative, providing inspiration for both the Renaissance and later generations of writers.

Giovanni Boccaccio was born in Italy in 1313, the illegitimate son of a wealthy Florentine banker, Boccaccino di Chellino. The boy was raised by his father and Margherita de' Mardoli, a woman of noble birth who became his stepmother. In 1327, the family moved from Florence to Naples, where it was hoped that Boccaccio would follow his father into business. But the young man had other ideas—he studied law for six years, then developed a love of literature, especially of Dante (whom Boccaccio described as "the first guide of my studies"). Turning away from commerce and the law, he devoted his energies to reading,

accruing a vast knowledge of culture, science, and literature. His was a life of privilege that allowed him many insights into the courtly world of Robert the Wise, King of Naples, which he would draw upon in his later writing.

### The little flame

It was in Naples that Boccaccio fell in love with a woman who some believe was a daughter of the king. Although her identity remains obscure, she appears as Fiammetta ("little flame") in his early prose and in *The Decameron*. She also appears in *The Elegy of Lady Fiammetta* (1343–1344), thought to be Western literature's first psychological novel, where she recounts the phases of an affair with a Panfilo—a loosely autobiographical character.

In 1341, Boccaccio reluctantly rejoined his widowed father in Florence—a city recently ravaged

by plague and beset by political turmoil. When his father died as a result of plague in 1348, Boccaccio inherited his estate and gained financial independence. His home became a meeting place for intellectuals, writers, and scholars. Over the next three years, he wrote his best known work, *The Decameron* (see box, right), in which he moved away from the medieval use of virtues and vices toward a more humanistic vision. His characters had real dimension, and through them he could reflect upon people's power to shape their own destiny, while gracefully accepting their human limitations.

### Late years

Boccaccio formed a close and lasting friendship with the poet Petrarch—the most famous writer of his generation. In the years after 1350, Boccaccio devoted himself increasingly to scholarship, writing several works in Latin, and he also undertook civic and diplomatic assignments for the city of Florence. He became deeply disillusioned and depressed in old age; the death of his friend Petrarch in 1374 provided the inspiration for one of his last works, a lyric poem. Boccaccio died the following year and was buried in the village of Certaldo, near Florence.

▽ **CERTALDO, TUSCANY**
In 1363, Boccaccio retired in poverty to the Tuscan hilltop town of Certaldo. He returned only briefly to Florence, in 1373, to give readings of Dante's *Divine Comedy*.

## ON FORM
### *The Decameron*

In Boccaccio's *The Decameron*, 10 young Florentines escape the black death ravaging their city by traveling to a villa deep in the countryside. They agree that every day, each of them will tell a tale. So the book is divided into 10 days of 10 stories, connected by the author's narrative. This device gave Boccaccio a framework within which he could explore a variety of themes (such as deception, unhappy love, and licentiousness) and could readily vary the tone of his work, from comic to bawdy to tragic.

A 19TH-CENTURY DEPICTION OF THE 10 NARRATORS OF *THE DECAMERON*

▷ **CLASSICAL SCHOLAR**
This anonymous portrait of Boccaccio presents him as a man of classical learning, wreathed in laurel.

" **Nothing is** so **indecent** that it cannot be said to another person **if the proper words are used** to convey it. "

BOCCACCIO, *THE DECAMERON*

# Geoffrey Chaucer

## c.1343–1400, ENGLISH

Chaucer was an early champion of the English vernacular in literature. His vivid characterizations of pilgrims in *The Canterbury Tales* have remained popular since the Middle Ages.

Chaucer was born in London, the son of a wine merchant. Although little is known of his early years and education, his professional life is well documented because he was a civil servant, bureaucrat, and diplomat, moving in court circles under Edward III and then Richard II. He found patronage under John of Gaunt, who later became his brother-in-law.

Chaucer's eventful career may have informed his writing, although his poetry is scarcely mentioned in contemporary accounts. Edward III did award Chaucer "a gallon of wine daily for the rest of his life" on St. George's Day 1374, a date when endeavors in the arts were celebrated.

### European influences
The life of a diplomat gave Chaucer experience abroad. He traveled on missions to France while employed by Lionel of Antwerp, the third son of Edward III. He was captured by the French in 1359, but freed on payment of a ransom by the king, who then sent him on further diplomatic missions to Flanders, Spain, and Italy. There, he

was exposed to the radical new ideas of the Italian Renaissance, probably including the writings of Dante and Boccaccio.

While the courtly stories of the medieval period had been populated by idealized figures and steeped in Christian dogma, the writers of the Italian Renaissance were influenced instead by classical civilization. From their humanist perspective, they wrote about ordinary characters and everyday concerns; moreover, they wrote in the vernacular to widen their readership. Following their example, Chaucer elected to write

in Middle English at a time when most writing in England was in Latin or French. After the Norman Conquest of Britain in 1066, the English language had no official status; French was the language of the nobility and of power. Middle English—the language of ordinary people—developed in response.

### Early poems
Chaucer published his first major poems around the age of 30. *The Book of the Duchess* is an elegy to Blanche, Duchess of Lancaster, that uses a game of chess as its central motif.

▷ **THE KELMSCOTT CHAUCER**
In 1896, the English writer and designer William Morris produced this highly ornate collection of Chaucer's works at his Kelmscott Press.

" This world **nys but a thurghfare** ful of wo, And we been **pilgrymes**, passynge **to and fro** "

GEOFFREY CHAUCER, *THE CANTERBURY TALES*

▷ *CHAUCER* (ARTIST UNKNOWN)
This portrait in the Bodleian Library, Oxford, is thought to have been painted after Chaucer died—the figure "1400" refers to the supposed year of his death.

Caucer 1400

△ **BECKET CASKET, c.1180**
On December 29, 1170, Archbishop Thomas Becket was killed in Canterbury Cathedral by four knights in the service of Henry II. The murder stunned Christians and led to Becket's canonization in 1173, making Canterbury the most important destination in England for pilgrims. This elaborate casket, which is decorated with scenes of his martyrdom, was made to house Becket's relics.

▽ **THE STARTING POINT**
An 1843 print from Edward Henry Corbould's painting depicts Chaucer's pilgrims at the Tabard Inn in Southwark, south London, where they began their journey to Canterbury.

Blanche was the first wife of Chaucer's patron, John of Gaunt, who probably commissioned the piece when she died. Other early writings include the shorter poems "Anelida and Arcite" and "The House of Fame," which openly references the Roman or Italian authors Ovid, Virgil, Boccaccio, and Dante. Chaucer's affinity with the Italians and the swift development of his literary skills places him ahead of the canon of Renaissance literature in England, most of which dates from the late 15th century.

## Official appointments
Around 1366, Chaucer married Philippa Roet, a lady-in-waiting in the queen's household, and the couple had at least three children. Philippa's sister later married John of Gaunt.

In 1374, Chaucer was appointed customs comptroller for London, a highly prestigious position because customs duties were a major source of the city's wealth. The post earned him enemies in influential positions, and when he lost the protection of his patron, London's mayor, he was

▷ **CANTERBURY CATHEDRAL**
Chaucer uses the pilgrimage to Canterbury as a framework to organize stories from a diverse cast of characters from different levels of society, who would have met only on such a journey.

denounced and forced to flee to the relative safety of Kent. In 1386, he became a member of parliament for Kent, and also served as a justice of the peace. Later, he held other royal posts, for Edward III and Richard II, including clerk of the king's works, with responsibility for the construction and repair of royal residences and parks as well as for walls, bridges, and sewers along the Thames river.

### *The Canterbury Tales*
During his 12 years of service as customs comptroller, Chaucer wrote prolifically, producing poems such as "The Legend of Good Women" and his much admired epic *Troilus and Cressida*, which tells in Middle English the story of the two lovers against the backdrop of the Siege of Troy. But his most celebrated work, *The Canterbury Tales*, was begun in the early 1380s.

The book is a collection of 24 vivid, naturalistic tales told in a storytelling contest by a group of "sondry folk"—pilgrims of diverse standing and occupations—during their journey to the shrine of St. Thomas Becket in Canterbury. Chaucer may have taken inspiration for his great work from Boccaccio's *Decameron* (1353), a series of 100 prose stories narrated by 10 ordinary people who gathered in a rural villa near Florence, in flight from the black death.

Chaucer almost certainly drew on real-life people for the cast of *The Canterbury Tales*: the innkeeper shares the name of a known contemporary from London, and scholars have also

suggested identities for the Wife of Bath, the Merchant, the Man of Law, and the Student. Chaucer ensured that the speech and mannerisms of each of his characters reflected their status and occupation, and their tales are further brought to life with witty references and colorful themes. He also proved his strength as a satirist, introducing a regional accent for the Reeve and exposing religious hypocrisy in the Pardoner's Tale.

The tales are loved for their earthy humor and bawdiness. In the Miller's Tale, the unlucky admirer of the Miller's wife is tricked into kissing her bottom. The Wife of Bath recounts with glee how she has manipulated

" The **lyf so short**, the craft so **long to lerne**. "

GEOFFREY CHAUCER, *THE PARLIAMENT OF FOWLS*

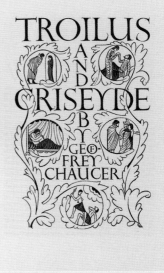

## ON FORM
### Rhyme royal

Chaucer is acknowledged for his metrical innovation and poetic invention. He created rhyme royal, a form in which each stanza has seven lines, usually in iambic pentameter, and was among the first poets to use the five-stress line in rhyming couplets. Rhyme royal is a feature of Chaucer's long poems *Troilus and Cressida* and *The Parliament of Fowls* and appears in four of the *Canterbury Tales*: the Man of Law's Tale, the Prioress's Tale, the Clerk's Tale, and the Second Nun's Tale. It later became a standard poetic form in English.

**FRONTISPIECE FOR A 1927 EDITION OF *TROILUS AND CRISEYDE* BY ERIC GILL**

five husbands and remained happily childless. Modern readers gain insight into the everyday lives and opinions of late 14th-century folk, who show little concern for their spiritual purity and far more interest in their social standing and physical satisfactions.

An important aspect of the tales is Chaucer's "General Prologue," in which the narrator introduces the pilgrims and explains how they met in the Tabard Inn, Southwark. The omniscient narrator becomes an "I" in line 20 and begs intimacy: he undermines the authority of his own story by stating that he intends to describe each pilgrim as he perceives them, hinting that the tales may be unreliable and influenced by personal opinion. Each of the characters is defined by his or her social standing, which seems to be the main focus of the poem.

### Declining fortunes
Chaucer's masterpiece was incomplete when he died in 1400, and not all of the pilgrims introduced in the Prologue tell their tales. It seems that Chaucer suffered financial hardship later in his life, for although he received a pension from Richard II, the new king, Henry IV (1367–1413), neglected to fulfill his predecessor's promise. One of Chaucer's last works, "The Complaint of Chaucer to His Purse," is a love poem to his purse and a plea to the king to renew his annuity.

Chaucer was the first poet to be interred in Poet's Corner at Westminster Abbey. The memorial erected there more than a century after his death suggests that he died on October 25, 1400, but—as with much of Chaucer's life—we cannot be entirely sure that this is true.

## KEY WORKS

**1379–80**
*The House of Fame*, a 2,000-line poem, is published. It recounts a dream vision in which the narrator is guided by an eagle.

**1381–82**
In *The Parliament of Fowls*, Chaucer makes the first reference in English to a special day commemorating love—Valentine's Day.

**Mid-1380s**
Chaucer writes *Troilus and Cressida*, taking his inspiration from Boccaccio's *Decameron*.

**1386–88**
"The Legend of Good Women" is published. It tells the stories of 10 virtuous women from the classical world.

**1387–1400**
*The Canterbury Tales* is published and becomes Chaucer's most popular work.

# François Rabelais

## 1493/4–1553, FRENCH

Writer, physician, scholar, and priest, Rabelais was an intellectual giant of 16th-century France. His name has become a byword for earthy, bawdy humor as a result of his masterpiece, *Gargantua and Pantagruel*.

◁ **LA DEVINIERE**
Rabelais was born and raised in this cottage near the village of Seuilly. The early battles in *Gargantua* are acted out in the surrounding countryside.

The son of a wealthy lawyer and landowner, François Rabelais was born late in the 15th century in Chinon in the wine region of Touraine. This landscape is described in full in the adventures of his giant, Gargantua, whose battle with his angry neighbor Picrochole is played out across the fields, streams, and great castles that surrounded Rabelais' childhood home.

Rabelais studied law in the early 1500s, but after joining a Franciscan convent at La Baumette and taking holy orders in Poitou, he ran afoul of the Franciscans' narrow-minded scholastic tradition. Drawn instead to Renaissance humanism (an intellectual approach founded on a resurgence of interest in classical ideas), Rabelais aligned himself with scholars who were using new translations of Latin and Greek manuscripts to underpin a broader, more enlightened philosophical education. Their analysis of text in ancient scrolls was also laying the foundation for the first modern translations of the Bible. However, in his French convent, Rabelais' passion for the Greek language was deemed heretical and likely to foster dangerous thoughts.

Rabelais was granted a dispensation from the pope to continue his studies as a Benedictine monk, but by 1530 he had broken his vows and moved to the University of Montpellier to study medicine. His two children by an unnamed widow were probably born during this period. Employed as a doctor at the Hôtel-Dieu hospital in Lyon, he based his treatments on his own translations of the works of Galen and Hippocrates and was noted for his care of victims of the black death.

### Renaissance agenda

Rabelais lived in turbulent times. France's lengthy war with the Holy Roman Emperor Charles V over French territories in Italy led to a humiliating defeat in 1525, when Francis I was captured and held for ransom. The rise of humanism also coincided with the spread of the Reformation from Germany. Posters in French streets that railed against church corruption and Catholic practices had violent repercussions as Lutherans were accused of heresy and burned at the stake.

**ENGRAVED FRONTISPIECE OF RABELAIS' *PANTAGRUEL*, 1532**

▷ **A PROSE INNOVATOR**
Rabelais is memorialized in this 17th-century portrait, which hangs in the Château de Versailles near Paris. His legacy was liberating prose writing from its medieval constraints.

> **"** My pen's to **laughs** not tears **assigned.**
> Laughter's the **property of Man.**
> **Live joyfully. "**

FRANÇOIS RABELAIS

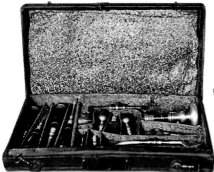

△ **RABELAIS' INSTRUMENT CASE**
In his time, Rabelais was a highly regarded physician. He presided over a lecture on anatomy that included the public dissection of a hanged man.

## IN PROFILE
### Erasmus

Rabelais counted the preeminent French humanists Pierre Amy, Guillaume Budé, and André Tiraqueau as allies, and the Dutch Renaissance humanist Erasmus as his guiding light. Rabelais was a dedicated follower of this man of learning, humanity, and wit, subscribing to his view that core human principles and a wealth of knowledge could be sourced from ancient Greek and Latin manuscripts. He corresponded with Erasmus, and modeled his life of intellectual pursuits, medicine, and humorous writing on that of his "spiritual father."

*ERASMUS*, QUENTIN METSYS, 1517

Standing on the threshold of this rapidly changing world, Rabelais began to write tales that had no precedent in medieval literature. His stories relate the adventures of two giants, Gargantua and his son Pantagruel. *Pantagruel* (fully titled *The Horrible and Terrifying Deeds and Words of the Renowned Pantagruel, King of the Dipsodes*) was published in 1532 under the pseudonym Alcofribas Nasier (an anagram of Rabelais' name) and was followed in 1535 by *Gargantua* (*The Inestimable Life of the Great Gargantua*).

The tales are packed with bawdy and often scatological humor: some chapters are filled with lists of vulgar insults; characters are given gross names (Captain Squit, Sieur de Slurp-ffart); and the chapter titles themselves signal Rabelais' comic taste ("How Grandgousier recognized the miraculous intelligence of Gargantua from his invention of a bum-wiper"). However, beneath their surface, the tales bubble with satire and philosophical insight.

### Giant steps

Rabelais was well versed in the traditions of medieval chivalric romance and filled his mock-heroic stories with wine-drinking, gluttony, debauchery, bodily functions, and bizarre reversals of expectation: for example, Gargantua awards his monk the sumptuous Abbey of Thélème, where nuns and monks live in luxury and marry well. Laughter is central to the book, but Rabelais invites readers to seek out the intellectual marrow in his tales as he ridicules futile warfare, religious dogma, and narrow-minded education. In their search for life's meaning, his giants and their

companions reveal an aptitude for law, science, philosophy, poetry, medicine, nature, and pacifism.

Rabelais borrowed from the poetry and prose of previous eras but laced them with modern wisdom, new words coined from Greek and Latin roots, and aphorisms such as "Ignorance is the mother of all evils" and "Nature abhors a vacuum," many of which are still in use today.

### Patronage and censorship

*Pantagruel* and *Gargantua* were hailed by the public but were condemned as obscene by the censors at the Collège de Sorbonne in Paris, who repeatedly petitioned the Supreme Court to have

△ *MARGUERITE OF NAVARRE*, c.1527
Rabelais benefited from the patronage of Marguerite of Navarre (the older sister of Francis I). She is pictured here in a portrait by Jean Clouet, court painter to Francis.

them banned for their political and heretical content. Rabelais, however, had influential friends. He enjoyed the protection of senior statesman Guillaume du Bellay and high-ranking liberal ecclesiastics Cardinal Jean du Bellay, Bishop Geoffroy d'Estissac, and Cardinal Odet de Châtillon. He was also part of a favored circle of poets and writers protected by Marguerite of Navarre, the sister of Francis I.

" **... a good deed** freely done to a **man of reason** grows from **noble thoughts** and **memories**. "

FRANÇOIS RABELAIS, *GARGANTUA*

The king and his successor, Henri II, granted Rabelais a royal privilege to publish his works, which lasted throughout his lifetime. In 1535, the author traveled to Rome as companion and physician to Cardinal Jean du Bellay, and was granted absolution by the pope for giving up his holy orders. He then returned to France, becoming a secular priest and practicing medicine, and in 1537 became a Doctor of Medicine in Montpellier.

### New volumes

More than 10 years passed before Rabelais picked up the story of Pantagruel and his down-and-out trickster companion Panurge in his *Third Book*. In the meantime, two of his most important patrons had died and, in France's increasingly dangerous climate of religious intolerance, Rabelais was forced to flee to the free German city of Metz. There, he worked as a physician, read the work of Martin Luther, and remained unrepentant about his writing.

The theologians who had savagely attacked his earlier writing found themselves mocked in the comedic *Fourth Book*, which Rabelais prepared during another stay in Italy with Cardinal Jean du Bellay. Thanks to his powerful patrons, these chapters of Pantagruel's deeds were published in spite of repeated condemnation and censorship by the Sorbonne and the Supreme Court.

After Rabelais returned to France he was given two benefices, the parishes of Medon and Saint-Christophe-de-Jambet, to support him in his old age but he never officiated in them. He died on the rue des Jardins, Paris in 1553. His last reported words reveal an open-minded readiness for the next big adventure: "I am going to seek a great perhaps ...."

## KEY WORKS

**1532**
Rabelais begins *Pantagruel* with gross details of the giant's birth and goes on to describe how he creates a race of tiny people by farting.

**1534**
*Gargantua* features the giant's inventive use of a well-downed goose as proto–toilet paper. Gargantua's father is drawn into a childish war over stolen cakes.

**1546**
*The Third Book* introduces Panurge, a trickster who seeks advice on whether to marry after it is prophesied that he will be cuckolded.

**1552**
*The Fourth Book* takes Pantagruel and Panurge on a sea voyage, and into battle with the chitterlings, who are half people and half sausage.

**1564**
*The Fifth Book*, published posthumously, features journeys to a collection of fantasy islands. It may not be the work of Rabelais.

▷ **GARGANTUA, DORE, 1873**
The French printmaker Gustave Doré brought Gargantua to grotesque life in his 19th-century wood-engraved illustrations. Here, men shovel mustard into the giant's mouth.

# Michel de Montaigne

**1533–1592, FRENCH**

Born into an aristocratic family, Montaigne enjoyed a successful career as a statesman before turning to writing. His magnum opus, the *Essays*, established the essay as a literary genre.

Michel de Montaigne was born in 1533 in Guienne, southwest France. A scion of minor nobility, he was first educated at home, in Latin. He was later sent to the Collège de Guienne in Bordeaux, which had gained a reputation for its teaching of the liberal arts. From there, he progressed to the University of Toulouse to study law and, after taking a seat in the Bordeaux parliament, the young man looked set to pursue a successful career in government. However, in 1568 Montaigne's father commissioned Michel to produce a translation of Raymond Sebond's 15th-century theological treatise *Theologia Naturali*—a task that fueled Montaigne's passion for literature and philosophy. That same year, his father died, and Michel inherited the title of Seigneur de Montaigne and the estate that went with it. He began to extricate himself from his responsibilities in Bordeaux, and in 1571 finally made the break, retiring from the parliament and moving permanently to Guienne.

## A place for thought

Montaigne devoted himself to writing, and chose the southern tower of the chateau as his workplace, redesigning it to house his study and library. Here, he embarked on the series of short, idiosyncratic pieces of prose that he called *essais* (see box, right), which covered a vast range of topics from politics and philosophy to love, sex, anger, cannibalism, and the art of conversation. His writings gave little respect to traditional theories; indeed he embraced uncertainty and often contradicted himself. The way in which he blended personal experience with philosophical inquiry made him one of the most original thinkers of his time. By 1580, he had written enough of these short pieces of prose to publish them as the two-volume first edition of the *Essays*.

## Final years

Soon after, Montaigne was troubled by kidney stones and traveled to Italy in search of a cure. While there, he discovered he had been elected Mayor of Bordeaux in his absence, and returned to France to take up his duties. Although this must have been a distraction from his writing—the job included the handling of the conflict between Catholics and Protestants in the area—he found time to continue revising and adding to his essays, publishing several more editions, culminating in the three-volume fifth edition featuring all his essays, three years before his death in 1592.

◁ **CHATEAU DE MONTAIGNE**
Built in the 14th century, this castle in Guienne, Périgord, was home to Michel de Montaigne. Most of the structure was rebuilt after a devastating fire in 1885.

## ON FORM
### The essay

Montaigne is regarded as the originator of what is today known as the essay—a short piece of prose expressing a personal point of view. He chose the word *essais* (attempts) to describe his experiments with the form; the term was later adopted for the genre of short pieces of writing presenting an argument or opinion (including the "formal" academic essay). It was his subjective approach that inspired the development of the essay as a genre, especially among English writers.

**TITLE PAGE OF THE FIFTH EDITION (1588) OF MONTAIGNE'S *ESSAYS***

◁ **WRITER AND STATESMAN**
This portrait of Michel de Montaigne, painted by an unknown French artist in the first quarter of the 17th century, hangs in the magnificent Château de Versailles just outside Paris.

" It is **myself** that **I portray ... I am myself** the **matter** of my **book.** "

MICHEL DE MONTAIGNE, *ESSAIS* (BOOK I)

# Miguel de Cervantes

## 1547–1616, SPANISH

Spain's most celebrated writer, Cervantes, was a 16th-century soldier, poet, playwright, and novelist. His landmark work, *Don Quixote*, is regarded as the first great novel of modern literature.

Miguel de Cervantes was 50 years old and in prison for the third time in his life when a story began to take shape in his imagination. In the years after his release, he set its hero loose on the page: Don Quixote, a would-be knight driven insane by reading chivalric romances, pursued his quests across La Mancha, Spain, mounted on his skeletal horse, Rocinante, and accompanied by his loyal squire, Sancho Panza. Published five years after Cervantes' release in 1605, *Don Quixote* was unlike anything that had come before in literary history, and it became the springboard for centuries of experimentation with the novel form. The book spawned its own adjective, "quixotic," to describe a certain hopeless idealism. Aptly, the word is a fitting description of Cervantes' own life, with its peaks and valleys of military heroics and capture, and storytelling that floats over a period of Spanish history that was fraught with conflict.

### Early life and learning

Born on St. Michael's Day (September 29) 1547 in Alcalá de Henares near Madrid, Miguel was the fourth of seven children born to Leonor de Cortinas, the daughter of a nobleman, and Rodrigo de Cervantes, an itinerant surgeon-cum-barber. Little is known

of Cervantes' early life, but at the age of 21 he was studying in Madrid under the tutorship of a humanist professor, Juan López de Hoyos, who described him as his "beloved pupil." By 1569, Cervantes had moved to Rome (possibly because he was wanted in Spain for wounding a rival in a duel) and was working as a manservant for a cardinal.

### Conflict and capture

In a struggle to wrest control of the Mediterranean from the Ottoman forces under Selim II, Spain had

LA MERAVIGLIOSA E GRAN VITTORIA, DATA DA DIO A CHRISTIANI CONTRA TVRCHI ALLI SCOGLI CVRZOLARI LANO 1571 A 7 01

△ **THE BATTLE OF LEPANTO**
Cervantes was badly injured in 1571 at the Battle of Lepanto, shown in this 16th-century painting, in which Christian naval forces defeated the Turks.

formed an alliance of Catholic forces with Venice and the papacy. In 1570, Cervantes and his brother Rodrigo embraced the cause, and joined the army in Spanish-controlled Naples. The two brothers sailed with the fleet on board the *Marquesa* and joined in the bloody battle of Lepanto near Corinth, which ended in a crushing

## ON FORM
### Fact and fantasy

Cervantes experimented with many literary forms over his lifetime, but in *Don Quixote* he created a hall of mirrors. The reader is drawn into the fantasies of its insane hero, who nonetheless travels in the real world with a sensible companion. Comedy, tragedy, and the social tensions of the time surface in this interplay between reality and illusion. The novel is episodic, with stories from multiple characters broadening the view, and playfully self-referential: characters are aware of their role in the book and the narrator makes regular appearances to discuss the subterfuge in his work and the beguiling effects of literature.

EL INGENIOSO
HIDALGO DON QVI-
xote de la Mancha.
*Compuesto por Miguel de Ceruantes Saauedra.*
DIRIGIDO AL DVQVE DE
Bejar, Marques de Gibraleon, Conde de henalcaçar, y Bañares, Vizconde dela Puebla de Alcozer, Señor de las villas de Capilla, Curiel, y Burguillos.

Impresso con licencia, en Valencia, en casa de Pedro Patricio Mey, 1605.

A costa de Iuſepe Ferrer mercader de libros, delante la Diputacion.

**TITLE PAGE OF THE FIRST PART OF**
***DON QUIXOTE*, PUBLISHED IN 1605**

" For me alone was **Don Quixote** born, and **I for him**. His was the **power** of **action**, mine of **writing**. "

MIGUEL DE CERVANTES, *DON QUIXOTE* (PART II)

△ FIVE YEARS A SLAVE
Cervantes was captured and sold as a slave. He drew on his experiences in the Captive's Tale in *Don Quixote* and in two plays that he set in Algiers.

▷ PRIDE OF PLACE
Cervantes and his creation Don Quixote have become symbolic of Spain itself. This statue of the writer stands in Cervantes Square in the author's hometown of Alcalá de Henares.

defeat for the Turks. Cervantes was shot twice in the chest, and his left hand was all but destroyed by a third gunshot, yet he recovered to fight in other battles. His experiences fueled his later stories, but his time on Italian soil was invaluable, too: as an avid reader, Cervantes was exposed to the Renaissance's philosophical and literary revolution in its birthplace.

The brothers were sailing back to Spain in 1575 when Barbary pirates attacked their ship, captured the crew, and sold them into slavery in Algiers, a Muslim center for Christian slave traffic. Cervantes was carrying letters of commendation from high command, in the hope of later securing a captaincy in Spain; these letters made him a prize captive, with

a large ransom on his head. Records from other slaves at the time describe Cervantes as a courageous leader who made four attempts to escape, but was protected from punishment and even death by the high regard of his captors. His status prolonged his imprisonment; he was incarcerated for five years and was on the point of being shipped to Constantinople and sold when his family, helped by an order of Trinitarian friars, raised 500 gold escudos to free him and bring him back to Madrid.

## A return to Spain

The one-armed man from Lepanto, as Cervantes came to be known, struggled to make a living in Spain; and so he turned to writing. Enriched by its American colonies, Spain was in the midst of its Golden Age—a period of intense artistic and literary creativity—and Cervantes made an impact with two of his early plays. *The Dungeons of Algiers* drew on his time as a Christian slave in Algiers, and *Numantia* told the story of a cruel siege of Numantia by the Romans.

Cervantes also wrote fiction. His pastoral romance, *La Galatea* (1585), was centered on the story of two shepherds who fall in love with the sea nymph Galatea.

Although he was paid for his writing, Cervantes did not earn enough to support himself and his complex family. At the age of 37, he had met the love of his life, a married woman

## IN CONTEXT
## Spain in retreat

At the time of Cervantes' birth, Habsburg Spain was a superpower with territories in the East Indies, the Low Countries, and Italy. Huge quantities of gold from the Americas were enriching the country, and Spain was a European center of art, literature, and philosophy. However, Cervantes' major works were all produced in a country that was in retreat. The reigns of both Philip II (1527–1598) and Philip III (1598–1621) were dogged by repression, the Inquisition's notorious religious fanaticism, the Catholic Counter-Reformation to stem the spread of Protestantism, and rapidly dwindling fortunes from Spain's colonies and from the defeat of the Armada.

*DAY SEVEN OF THE BATTLE WITH THE ARMADA*, HENDRICK CORNELISZ VROOM, 1601

named Ana Franca de Rojas, and fathered his only child, Isabel de Saavedra. He then married Catalina de Palacios Salazar from Esquivias but lived apart from her, traveling across Andalusia as a commissary for provisions for the Armada, the Spanish naval fleet.

The defeat of the Spanish Armada by the English in 1588 accelerated Spain's decline after its golden age of superpower status (see box, opposite). The monarchy tried to remedy the faltering economy by imposing punitive taxes on people who worked the land. In spite of many discrepancies in the ledgers from his earlier grain collecting, Cervantes was appointed a tax collector, but jailed in Seville for embezzlement for a brief period, and then again for a year. On his release, he continued to write sonnets and plays, and also the great story that he mapped out in prison.

### Don Quixote

In 1605, at the age of 57, Cervantes saw his masterpiece, *Don Quixote*, published and began his most productive period as a writer. The novel was both a parody of the medieval world of chivalric knights and their ladies and a satirical commentary on contemporary Spanish society. It was an instant success. The name of Cervantes became known in Spain as well as in England, France, and Italy, since his book was translated and published internationally. However, he enjoyed only temporary prosperity because he

## KEY WORKS

**1585**
*La Galatea*, Cervantes' first major work, is a pastoral romance, popular around this time. It ends abruptly, mid story, in Part II.

**1605**
*El Ingenioso Hidalgo Don Quijote de la Mancha*, the first volume of *Don Quixote*, is published and becomes an immediate success.

**1613**
*Exemplary Novels*, Cervantes' collection of 12 short stories typifying the problems of 17th-century Spain, is published.

**1616**
*Don Quixote* Part II is published after an unknown writer produces an unauthorized sequel.

**1617**
*Persiles* (*Los Trabajos de Persiles y Sigismunda*) is published. Cervantes finished the work just three days before his death.

had sold the rights. He moved to Madrid where he lived among writers and poets, and went on to write *Exemplary Novels* (1613) and *Journey to Parnassus* (1614). Incensed by the appearance of a counterfeit Part II of Don Quixote's adventures written by an anonymous author, he published his own sequel in 1615.

Cervantes died "old, a soldier, a gentleman and poor" on April 22, 1616, and was buried at the Convent of the Barefoot Trinitarians in Madrid. In 2015, fragments of his bones were recovered. Spain's greatest writer was then given a formal burial, and a monument was erected to him almost 400 years after his death.

▷ **TILTING AT WINDMILLS**
The everyday is transformed into the extraordinary in Cervantes' world; his eccentric hero, Don Quixote, famously tilts at windmills, which he believes to be giants crossing the plains of La Mancha.

# William Shakespeare

## 1564–1616, ENGLISH

The outstanding poet and dramatist of the English Renaissance, Shakespeare wrote more than 30 plays, as well as narrative poems and sonnets. As a master of tragedy and comedy, he has no equal in English literature.

◁ **CHILDHOOD HOME**
Shakespeare was born and grew up in this timber-framed house in Stratford-upon-Avon. The house was divided into two: one part served as a living space, the other as his father's business premises.

### Early life in Stratford

Shakespeare married Anne Hathaway, a Stratford woman eight years his senior. She was pregnant by the time they reached the altar and twins soon followed the first child—the boy twin was christened Hamnet. At the age of 23, Shakespeare was living in his father's house with a wife and three children. He then moved to London, leaving his family behind. According to some accounts, he was obliged to leave Stratford after being accused of poaching a deer; other sources suggest that he was fleeing the constraints of a loveless marriage. But it is possible that, being aware of possessing an exceptional talent for verse, he simply left to pursue a life of fame and fortune.

### A London debut

In 1587, when Shakespeare arrived in London, the city's theatrical scene was in its infancy. The few permanent theaters, built just outside the city, were

William Shakespeare was born in the market town of Stratford-upon-Avon, Warwickshire, in April 1564. The exact date of his birth is not known, but is usually given as April 23, St. George's Day. His father was a man of ambition, who had been born into a family of tenant farmers but left the land to become a glover in Stratford; he prospered in his business, and married a daughter of the landowning Arden family to whom the farming Shakespeares paid their rent. He played a prominent part in Stratford life and owned two houses.

The oldest of five children who survived infancy, William was sent to the local secondary school. He was later described by his fellow English dramatist Ben Jonson as having "small Latin and less Greek," but his schooling undoubtedly introduced him to the works of classical Latin authors, the essential grounding for any educated person at that time. Little is known of Shakespeare's progress from his provincial roots to success as an actor and dramatist in London—only the bare bones of this story have any certainty.

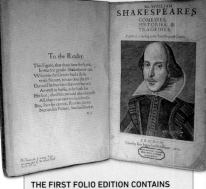

**THE FIRST FOLIO EDITION CONTAINS 36 OF SHAKESPEARE'S PLAYS**

> " We are **such stuff** / As **dreams** are made on, and **our little life** / Is **rounded** with a **sleep**. "

WILLIAM SHAKESPEARE, *THE TEMPEST*

▷ **THE COBBE PORTRAIT, c.1612**
Thought to be the only portrait of William Shakespeare painted during his lifetime, this work was commissioned from an unknown artist by the writer's patron, the Earl of Southampton. Its name comes from the Cobbe family, who owned it.

SHAKESPEARE'S GLOBE THEATRE AT BANKSIDE, LONDON

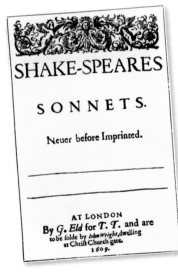

◁ **SONNETS, FIRST EDITION**
This 1609 edition of *Shakespeare's Sonnets* was probably compiled and ordered by Shakespeare himself. It contains some of the most famous verses in English literature.

hardly a decade old, and a handful of university-educated poets, including Thomas Nashe, Robert Greene, and Christopher Marlowe, were beginning to write original works for companies of actors to perform. Exactly how Shakespeare insinuated himself into this budding theatrical world is a matter for speculation. Legend has it that he started by taking care of the horses outside one of the playhouses, but it is known that by 1592 he had established himself as both an actor and a playwright.

Elizabethan theatrical productions were collaborative activities, and the earliest plays in the Shakespeare canon—including the three parts of *Henry VI* and *Richard III*—may have been written with contributions from other dramatists such as

Marlowe or Nashe. A tremendous popular success, these works made Shakespeare prominent enough to receive a bitter verbal broadside from rival playwright Robert Greene, who abused him as "an upstart Crow ... in his own conceit the only Shake-scene in the country."

## Plague and poetry
From 1592 to 1594, Shakespeare's career as a dramatist was interrupted by a major outbreak of the plague that decimated London's population. All the playhouses were closed for the duration, and it was during this fallow period for drama that Shakespeare's

first poetry appeared in print. *Venus and Adonis*, a narrative love poem, was issued in 1593 and dedicated to the 20-year-old Henry Wriothesley, Earl of Southampton. Shakespeare's second narrative poem, *The Rape of Lucrece*, published the following year, was also dedicated to the earl.

By this time, Shakespeare had begun writing a sonnet sequence—a poetic genre recently popularized by Edmund Spenser. Probably written between 1591 and 1603, and first published together in 1609, the 154 sonnets loosely narrate the poet's love for a "Fair Youth" and a "Dark Lady." Many scholars have attempted to identify these characters as real people in Shakespeare's life, as well as the mysterious "Mr. W. H." to whom the sonnets are dedicated. The poems suggest that Shakespeare may have been gay or bisexual, and some scholars argue that the "Fair Youth" can be identified as the Earl of Southampton or Shakespeare's later patron, the Earl of Pembroke. It is also possible that the poems are purely imaginative and bear little relationship to Shakespeare's private life. Either way, they are certainly among the finest poems in the English language.

## Stage successes
When the plague abated and the playhouses reopened in 1594, Shakespeare joined a company known

▷ **WILL KEMP**
The English actor and popular clown Will Kemp (died 1603) is shown dancing a jig in this woodcut, c.1600. Kemp was one of Shakespeare's original players, and his name is mentioned in the stage directions of some of the early quarto editions of the author's plays ("Enter Will Kemp").

as the Lord Chamberlain's Men (so called because its patron was Lord Hunsdon, the Queen's Lord High Chamberlain). The company included two of the finest actors of the time—comedian Will Kemp and tragedian Richard Burbage. Shakespeare also performed on stage, but his chief role was to create new material. Over the following 5 years he wrote 10 plays, including *Romeo and Juliet*,

the comedies *A Midsummer Night's Dream* and *As You Like It*, and the history plays *Richard II*, *Henry IV* (Parts One and Two) and *Henry V*. These works were an immediate success, both with popular London audiences and when they were performed for the queen at court.

Shakespeare did not invent his own stories—his plots were borrowed from a variety of sources—but

he breathed life into a vast range of characters with an unmatched vigor of language. His mixing of high tragedy and low comedy, romance and bawdiness, troubled some educated Elizabethans concerned with the classical rules of drama, but even they eventually succumbed to the power of his inventiveness and imagery. While other playwrights led checkered lives—Marlowe was

△ **OPHELIA**
In *Ophelia* (1851–1852), English artist Sir John Everett Millais depicts a scene from Shakespeare's tragedy *Hamlet*, c.1601 (Act IV, Scene VII). Ophelia—shown here floating in a brook—drowns herself over her deep distress upon hearing that Hamlet, her lover, has murdered her father.

" All the **world's a stage**, / And all the **men** and **women merely players**. "

WILLIAM SHAKESPEARE, *AS YOU LIKE IT*

ELIZABETH I, c.1588

killed in a pub brawl and Jonson was imprisoned twice for offending the authorities—Shakespeare kept out of trouble and accumulated modest wealth. He bought New Place, a substantial house in Stratford, and later acquired land outside the town. When the Chamberlain's company built the Globe Theatre in London in 1599, he was one of the co-owners who invested in the property. But public success was overshadowed by great private misfortune when Shakespeare's 12-year-old son, Hamnet, died in 1596.

### Darkening drama
Many critics have noted a darkening of Shakespeare's mood in the early years of the 17th century, which is reflected in the succession of tragedies that he wrote, from *Julius Caesar* (1599) and *Hamlet* (c.1601) to *Othello*, *King Lear*, and *Macbeth* (c.1604–1606), and *Antony and Cleopatra* and *Coriolanus* (1606–1607). There is also speculation that he may have contracted a venereal disease, which provoked violent expressions of revulsion at the sexual act in some of these plays. On the other hand, this is also the period when he wrote the mellifluous comedy *Twelfth Night*. Also, since tragedy was considered the highest form of drama, it is not surprising that a playwright at the peak of his powers should have turned to weighty tragic themes.

After the death of Elizabeth I in 1603, the Chamberlain's Men were accorded the patronage of the new Scottish occupant of the throne, James I. They became the King's Men and flourished on frequent, well-paid

△ *MACBETH*
This painting, *Macbeth* (c.1820), by English artist John Martin, depicts a scene from Shakespeare's play in which Macbeth and Banquo meet the three witches (shown on the left in the painting) on the heath.

performances for the court. In writing his Scottish play, *Macbeth*, Shakespeare was probably catering to James's interest in his home country, although the tragedy hardly presents a flattering view of political life north of the border.

### Changes in style
Shakespeare continued to write plays for performance at the Globe, with its healthily mixed audience of sophisticates and boisterous common people. However, the influence of the court gradually pushed him toward a more refined style of drama, in line with educated taste. This tendency was further encouraged when, starting in 1608, the company began also to perform at the smaller, covered Blackfriars Theatre, a venue that attracted a more exclusive audience.

Plays such as *Pericles* and *The Winter's Tale* exhibit a more ornate and less vigorous late Shakespearean style.

*The Tempest*, written around 1611, is probably the last play Shakespeare wrote on his own. Its final speech, in which the magician Prospero calls on the audience to "set me free," is often interpreted as Shakespeare's farewell to the theater. He continued to write for the King's Men's company, especially in partnership with John Fletcher. However, the first performance of Shakespeare and

## KEY WORKS

**c.1591–92**
*Henry VI, Parts 1 to 3*, is a trilogy of history plays that focuses on the Wars of the Roses.

**c.1596**
*A Midsummer Night's Dream*, a romantic comedy, includes country lore of the fairy world.

**1599**
*Julius Caesar*, a Roman tragedy, is one of the first plays performed at the Globe Theatre.

**c.1601**
*Hamlet*—a complex story of murder, madness, and revenge set in Denmark—is the longest of Shakespeare's plays.

**c.1604**
*Othello* is a tragedy in which the insane jealousy of the Moorish soldier Othello drives him to murder his innocent wife.

**1606**
*Macbeth* is one of Shakespeare's bleakest tragedies, and depicts the corrosive effects of guilt on the minds of a regicidal couple.

**1609**
*Sonnets* (the complete sequence) is published. It was probably written in the 1590s and early 1600s.

**1611**
*The Tempest* tells the story of the magician Prospero and his daughter; it is the last complete play written by Shakespeare.

# "Life's but a walking shadow, a poor player / That struts and frets his hour upon the stage ..."

WILLIAM SHAKESPEARE, *MACBETH*

Fletcher's play *King Henry VIII* in 1613 led to disaster, when a cannon shot used as a special effect set fire to the Globe's roof and burned down the building. Yet it was rebuilt and Shakespeare was still involved in the affairs of the acting company.

According to a well-established rumor, it was while traveling back to Stratford from London in rough weather after a hearty session with fellow poets in the Mermaid Tavern that Shakespeare contracted the fever that killed him. He died in April 1616, possibly on his 52nd birthday. He left a will that reflected a normal concern for the future of his family members; the only, much-noted, oddity being the bequest to his wife of his "second-best bed." It has been persuasively argued that the second-best bed would have been the marital bed, whereas the best bed was reserved for guests. Shakespeare's family erected a monument to him in Stratford's Holy Trinity Church, where he was buried.

▷ **BEN JONSON**
This portrait of Jonson, Shakespeare's friend and rival, is by Abraham van Blyenberch, c.1617. Jonson described Shakespeare's writings in a poem as such that "neither man nor muse can praise too much."

▽ **HOLY TRINITY CHURCH**
Shakespeare was buried (April 25, 1616) in the same church in which he was baptized (April 26, 1564). His wife and eldest daughter are buried with him.

# John Donne

## 1572–1631, ENGLISH

Donne had a rich and varied career—soldier, politician, courtier, diplomat, and clergyman—but he is remembered for his startlingly original verse and is recognized as one of the finest poets of the Renaissance.

John Donne was born in London. His father was an iron merchant, and mother the daughter of the playwright John Heywood. He studied at Oxford University but left without earning a degree and, in 1592, entered Lincoln's Inn (one of London's Inns of Court). He never practiced law, but his legal training had a significant impact on his writing.

Donne became a soldier in 1596, joining the Earl of Essex's expedition against Spain. The action that he saw there inspired two poems ("The Calme" and "The Storme"), and helped him to land his first important post, as secretary to Sir Thomas Egerton, the Lord Keeper of the Great Seal. In 1601, he became a member of parliament for Brackley, a seat that was in Egerton's gift.

### Love's troubles

Donne wrote much of his finest love poetry around this time but, ironically, love led to his professional undoing. In 1601, he secretly married Anne More, the 17-year-old niece of Lady Egerton. A storm of protest ensued. Anne's horrified father tried

◁ **PSEUDO-MARTYR**
The title page of the 1610 edition of John Donne's *Pseudo-Martyr* is shown here, with the poet's handwriting visible at the top and bottom of the page.

to have the marriage annulled, and Donne was fired from his post and briefly imprisoned. Jobless and homeless, the couple had to rely for a time on the generosity of friends. Donne used the opportunity to study and develop his writing, but his efforts to find another public post failed.

### Church career

Donne realized that his only hope of advancement lay with the church. But he had been raised a Catholic and these were difficult times for the faith, particularly after the Gunpowder Plot of 1605, when Catholic rebels tried to blow up the Houses of Parliament. Over time, Donne shifted allegiance to the Church of England, and even wrote a tract, *Pseudo-Martyr* (1610), urging others to follow his lead. He was ordained in 1615 and gained a series of promotions. He became a royal chaplain, a divinity reader at Lincoln's Inn, and, ultimately, dean of

St. Paul's. He preached before both James I and Charles I, and was chosen for a prestigious peacemaking mission to Germany (1619–1620).

Donne produced prose and verse, tackling both secular and religious themes, and also wrote verses to win favor with potential patrons. His love poetry is urgent, witty, and often racy. Much of it is conversational, as if addressed to an imagined mistress: "For Godsake hold your tongue, and let me love …" ("The Canonization"). It often revolves around ingenious puns or conceits, but it can also be disarmingly tender: "I wonder by my troth, what thou and I / Did, till we lov'd?…" ("The Good Morrow"). In later life, Donne concentrated on religious verse. The finest examples are his *Holy Sonnets*.

Donne was revered as a master when his poems were published, but fell out of favor in the 18th century. His star rose again in the 20th century, when T. S. Eliot hailed him as a major precursor of Modernist poetry.

**ANDREW MARVELL, ARTIST UNKNOWN, c.1655**

▽ **ACTION IN SPAIN**
As a soldier, Donne was involved in the Anglo-Spanish War, when English and Dutch forces attacked the city of Cádiz. This engraving from 1596 depicts the troops landing and the Spanish ships being attacked in the harbor.

◁ **JOHN DONNE, c.1695**
This portrait, by an unknown English artist, shows Donne as a brooding lover. The inscription reads "O Lady, lighten our darkness," suggesting that the cause of the writer's misery is a woman.

▷ **MILTON, c.1629**
This portrait (artist unknown) depicts Milton in his early 30s, possibly while studying at Cambridge University. The poet began writing when he was young and produced a number of major poems while he was still a student.

# John Milton
## 1608–1674, ENGLISH

Author of the epic poem *Paradise Lost*, John Milton was a politically engaged writer who advocated the execution of Charles I. The last 20 years of his life were affected by total blindness.

John Milton was born in London in 1608, the son of a prosperous scrivener (lawyer). A studious child, he became fluent in Latin, Hebrew, and Italian. He was sent to complete his education at Cambridge University, but found the teaching and company dull. At Christmas 1629, he wrote his first major poem, "On the Morning of Christ's Nativity." This was followed by *L'Allegro* and *Il Penseroso*, brilliant exercises in the pastoral style. He left Cambridge in 1632, convinced that his destiny lay in poetry.

Milton's early writings show a creative tension between his serious Protestant faith and the world of mythology, opened up to him by

> " The **mind** is its **own place**, and in itself Can make a **heaven** of **hell**, a **hell** of **heaven**. "

JOHN MILTON, *PARADISE LOST*

his reading of Latin classics. In 1634, he wrote *Comus*, a masque (a form of staged aristocratic entertainment) in which Christian virtue triumphs over debauched revelry. *Lycidas*, written in 1637 to mourn the death of a friend, combines an exuberant display of classical learning with an attack on the failings of the Anglican clergy.

### Republican pamphleteer
In the 1640s, still little known as a poet, Milton emerged as a prominent figure in the debate over England's form of government and religion. He supported the Parliamentary side in the civil war and served as a civil servant under the Republican government of Oliver Cromwell (see box, left). His famous prose polemic, the *Areopagitica* of 1644, was an impassioned argument for freedom of speech. Milton never renounced his republicanism and was fortunate to escape punishment when the monarchy was restored in 1660.

He experienced trouble and loss in his personal life. In 1642, he married Mary Powell, the 16-year-old daughter of a Royalist family. Although Milton regretted the marriage and became an advocate of divorce, the couple eventually lived together and had three surviving children. After Mary died in 1652, Milton remarried, but he was

widowed again in 1658. By that time he had totally lost his sight and had to dictate his works to an assistant. Milton wrote two deeply felt sonnets in reaction to his misfortunes, "On His Blindness," and "Methought I saw my late espoused saint," citing a dream in which both his dead second wife and his sight returned temporarily. Milton married for a third time, in 1662—to Elizabeth Minshull, a woman 30 years his junior—by all accounts, happily.

Starting in the late 1650s, Milton devoted himself to writing his blank verse epic *Paradise Lost*, a vast cosmological vision spanning from Satan's revolt against God to the fall of Adam and Eve. Published in 1667, it consisted of more than 10,000 lines of verse in an elaborate, Latin-influenced style, and later established Milton as one of the greatest English poets. In his final years, Milton wrote *Paradise Regained*, a riposte to his earlier epic, and a tragic drama, *Samson Agonistes* (both 1671), a powerful evocation of both blindness and enslavement.

OLIVER CROMWELL

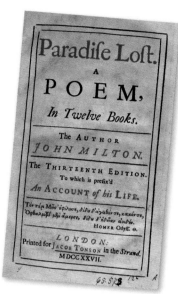

△ **FIRST EDITION**
*Paradise Lost* had a limited readership when first published, in part because of Milton's political and religious views. It dealt with weighty themes—the fall of man, good and evil, and the relationship between free will and authority.

▷ **MILTON'S STUDY**
Milton's study in his cottage in the village of Chalfont St. Giles, Buckinghamshire, is where he completed his masterpiece *Paradise Lost*.

# Molière

## 1622–1673, FRENCH

Molière was France's greatest comic playwright. More than this, he excelled in every aspect of stagecraft. He managed his own company; he wrote, produced, and directed his own plays; and he acted in them.

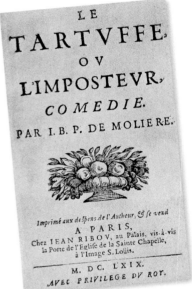

Jean-Baptiste Poquelin was born in Paris, the son of a court official. He was educated at the Collège de Clermont, a famous Jesuit school, and then began to study law. His father obtained a post for him as a royal upholsterer at court, but his plans came to nothing: in 1643, the young man announced that he was giving up both his job and his legal studies in order to become an actor.

It is not clear what fueled his desire for the stage. Poquelin may have been inspired by the Latin comedies and tragedies that were performed at his school, or he may have been tempted into the theater by his love for Madeleine Béjart, an actress four years his senior who became his mistress. The pair worked for the same company, *Illustre Théâtre*, which began performing in a converted tennis court in Paris. Within a year, Poquelin had established himself as the leader of the group and adopted the stage name of Molière.

The troupe's early efforts were not a success: within months, they were in financial difficulties, and Molière was almost imprisoned for debt. Cutting their losses, they left Paris and spent the next 13 years touring the provinces. This may have been a blessing in disguise since it enabled the budding playwright, Molière, to learn his craft away from the scrutiny of critics. The company performed a mixed repertoire of popular comedies and tragedies, as well as Molière's own plays. Some of these were elaborations of the comic scenarios devised by the commedia dell'arte (see box, below) while others focused specifically on the social satire that was to become his trademark.

### Court success

Molière's breakthrough came with a performance of one of his comedies (now lost) at the Louvre in October 1658, in front of the court. This won the favor of the king's brother, who secured him a base in the capital, which he shared with Tiberio Fiorillo's Italian players. Molière produced his greatest plays during the following decade. These included farcical, Italian elements, but also new developments. He perfected a comedy of manners, satirizing groups such as affected society women (*The Affected Young Ladies*) and would-be gentlemen (*The Bourgeois Gentleman*), and created complex character studies that blended boisterous comedy with penetrating insights. Some of his most popular comic creations are eccentric obsessives, such as a miser (*The Miser*) and a hopeless hypochondriac (*The Imaginary Invalid*).

### Scandalous liaisons

Molière's plays were immensely popular, but his career was not without controversy. His marriage to Armande Béjart caused a scandal (she was rumored to be the daughter of his former mistress) and his study of religious hypocrisy (*Tartuffe*) was banned for several years. Nevertheless, he continued acting until the very end. Ironically, he died after appearing in a performance of *The Imaginary Invalid*.

△ **TARTUFFE**

Molière's *Tartuffe* was first performed in 1664 and the manuscript was published five years later. The whole play is written in rhyming couplets in which each line has 12 syllables.

▷ **MOLIERE AS CAESAR**

Molière usually took the leading role in his company's stage productions. This portrait by Nicolas Mignard shows him as Julius Caesar in the play *The Death of Pompey* by Pierre Corneille.

## IN CONTEXT
### The commedia dell'arte

Molière always acknowledged the huge debt he owed to the commedia dell'arte. This form of theater originated in Italy in the 16th century, but became popular in France and other parts of Europe. The masked and costumed players did not work from a set script, but improvised their performances from loosely constructed scenarios, interspersing these with a variety of *lazzi* (comedy routines). Molière was able to observe the Italians at close quarters when they shared a theater in Paris. He drew inspiration from their stock characters—the greedy old man, the jealous husband, the wily servant, for example—and borrowed many of their comic turns.

STYLIZED COSTUMES OF THE COMMEDIA DELL'ARTE

# Aphra Behn

## 1640–1689, ENGLISH

Behn is hailed as one of the first women in Britain to earn her living by the pen. She produced fiction, plays, and poems, and had a huge influence on the development of the novel. She was also a government spy.

As empire and exploration expanded rapidly in the 17th century, so too did the British appetite for reading about distant lands—narratives that formed part of "the energizing myth of empire." It is perhaps unsurprising, then, that the novel *Oroonoko*—a transatlantic slave story set in Suriname, and with a vision of the "noble savage" at its core—should have been a resounding success on publication in 1688. What is more remarkable is that it was written by Aphra Behn at a time when women's voices were largely absent from the public sphere. Despite her feigned protestation early in *Oroonoko* that hers is "only a female pen," at the end of the text she makes a more strident appeal about her authorial status: "I hope the reputation of my pen is considerable enough to make his glorious name to survive all ages."

### Uncertain beginnings

The details of Behn's life are sketchy and disputed. It likely that she was born Aphra Johnson, into a humble background in Canterbury. In 1663, she spent some time in Suriname (then an English colony), which later formed the setting of *Oroonoko*, her most famous work. Soon after returning to England in 1664, she married Johan Behn, a merchant of German or Dutch extraction, but the marriage was short-lived. Two years later, she was recruited as a government spy and sent to the Netherlands (see box, below).

### Versatile output

Behn wrote in all genres on a wide range of themes, from love, marriage, prostitution, and sexuality, to class, politics, and the brutal world of slavery and colonialism. Particularly striking for the age is her discussion of female desire in a song from her third play, *The Dutch Lover* (1673), and the examination of gender roles in her famous poem "The Disappointment" (1680). Between 1670 and 1688, 19 of her plays (both comedies and tragicomedies) were performed.

Although acknowledged as a major writer in her lifetime, Behn's popularity waned for two centuries after her death because her work was considered too bawdy. For many years, the fact that she was a female writer hindered serious discussion of her texts. But aside from the wit and brilliance of many of her plays, poems, and short stories, *Oroonoko* can undoubtedly be considered one of the earliest novels and one that greatly influenced the development of the genre. It also preceded Defoe's *Robinson Crusoe* (1719), which is often credited as the first English novel. In recent years, Behn's work has attracted renewed interest and acclaim, particularly from feminists and literary and cultural theorists.

Behn died in 1689 and was buried in Westminster Abbey. Two and a half centuries later, leading feminist writer Virginia Woolf famously paid tribute to her in *A Room of One's Own* (1929): "All women together ought to let flowers fall upon the tomb of Aphra Behn ... for it was she who earned them the right to speak their minds."

△ **DORSET GARDEN THEATRE**
Many of Behn's plays premiered at East London's Dorset Garden Theatre (also called the Duke's Theatre), which was built in 1671. Behn lived nearby, close to her friend and fellow playwright and poet John Dryden.

◁ **APHRA BEHN, c.1670**
Behn became well known in her life, principally for her "scandalous" plays and her homoerotic verse. Her portrait here was painted by Sir Peter Lely, a Dutch-born artist who became painter to the English court.

### IN CONTEXT
### The secret agent

From 1665 to 1667, the English were at war with the Dutch over trade routes. Behn, a Tory and resolute monarchist, was recruited as a spy for the government of Charles II and was sent to Antwerp with a brief to unearth any plots to attack England or destabilize the government. Using the code names "160" and "Astrea," she sent back reports to the Home Office, including one alerting them to a Dutch plan to send a fleet up the Thames. Returning to London in 1667, Behn was unable to pay expenses she had incurred in the service of the Crown, and was sent to debtors' prison. After her release, penniless, she turned to writing plays to earn money.

*THE EENDRACHT AND A FLEET OF DUTCH MEN-OF-WAR, LUDOLF BAKHUIZEN, c.1665*

# Matsuo Bashō

## 1644–1694, JAPANESE

Japan's most famous poet, Bashō elevated the haiku to a sublime art form. He moved from urban literary circles to rural wandering in search of spiritual experience in which to root his transcendent poetry.

Bashō was born Matsuo Munefusa in Ueno, near Kyoto, the second son of a minor samurai. His father died when he was 12, and 6 years later Bashō entered the service of a local samurai general as a page to his son, Tōdō Yoshitada. The two young men were united by a love of verse, and Bashō published his first known poem in 1662, under the pen name Sōbō. After the early death of Yoshitada in 1666, Bashō left the service of his noble master, and lived for a while in Kyoto.

By the 1670s, he was building his reputation as a writer, compiling anthologies of poetry such as *The Seashell Game* (1671). At the age of 28, he moved to Edo (now Tokyo), where he took a job in the department of waterworks while continuing to write under the pen name Tōsei. The predominant poetic style of the time was the playfully satirical *haikai no renga* (see box, right), which was produced collaboratively—poets gathered together to write short verses that would form part of a much longer poem, with a traditional structure. In Edo, Bashō joined the Danrin school of poetry under the renowned poet Nishiyama Sōin.

### Spiritual journeys

By 1680, Bashō had become a respected teacher of writing, but he was restless and had started to study Zen Buddhism. In 1680, he moved out of bustling Edo into a small hut on the edge of the city. It was at this time that he began to write under the name Bashō (meaning "banana tree") and his poetry became more innovative and darker in tone. In late 1682, Bashō's life was turned upside down. His hut was destroyed by fire, and he learned that his mother had died. He stayed with friends in Kai province, intensified his Zen studies, and by 1684 began to wander through the country in search of inspiration. The result of the first of his walking trips was the travel journal *Records of a Weather-Beaten Skeleton*, written in the form of *haibun*—a combination of prose and poetry.

In 1689, Bashō set off on a 1,200 mile (2,000km) trek that would become the subject of his masterpiece, *Narrow Road to the Deep North*. With a companion, Sora, he explored the remote, rugged northern interior of the country in a journey that was as much spiritual as physical. Beside an ancient battlefield, he wrote: "Summer grasses / all that remains / of warriors' dreams." During a stormy interlude, he showed his wry, earthy sense of humor with: "Fleas, lice / now a horse pisses / by my pillow."

On his return to Edo in 1691, Bashō was thrown once more into the busy life of a famous poet, which conflicted with his desire for solitude. It was at this time that he formulated the concept of "lightness" that would inform the remainder of his poetry.

In 1694 he set out on what would be his final journey. He died of a stomach ailment in Osaka at 50, surrounded by his disciples. His last poem was: "On a journey, ailing—/ my dreams roam about / over a withered moor."

▽ **WILD INSPIRATION**
Bashō traveled the wilderness of northern Japan. His poetry was inspired by his direct experience of nature—such as the stillness of stone or the movement of water.

## ON FORM
### Haiku

At the beginning of the long, linked-verse haikai at which Bashō so excelled was a three-line stanza of 17 syllables (5–7–5) called the hokku. Under Bashō's influence, the hokku took on an importance in its own right, later becoming known as a haiku. Haiku attempts to convey the essence of nature, containing a seasonal reference and two linked but often paradoxical images or ideas. Bashō drew on Zen Buddhism and on the more introspective Chinese poetic tradition to elevate the haiku to an intensely resonant poetic form, hugely expressive despite its brevity. His most famous haiku (1686) is: "Old pond / a frog jumps in / water-sound."

**A HAIKU BY BASHŌ INSCRIBED IN STONE**

▷ **CONTEMPLATIVE WALKS**
This 19th-century woodcut by Tsukioka Yoshitoshi shows Bashō on one of his many journeys, speaking with two men at the side of the road.

# Daniel Defoe

## 1660–1731, ENGLISH

A devout Presbyterian, merchant, writer, journalist, government spy, pamphleteer, and propagandist, Defoe was a man of diverse talents whose fictional works had an immense and far-reaching cultural impact.

◁ **PLOT AND TREASON**

This etching depicts the execution of the Duke of Monmouth after his unsuccessful plot to displace James II. The duke was defeated by the king's forces at the Battle of Sedgemoor.

**IN PROFILE**
**William of Orange**

Born in The Hague in the Dutch Republic, William (1650–1702) was destined to become the Dutch head of state. He was seen as a Protestant hero when he drove French Catholic forces out of the Dutch Republic in 1673. In 1677, he married his cousin, Mary, who was the daughter of James, Duke of York—the heir to the English throne. When James became king in 1685, many English Protestants were suspicious of his Catholic faith, and they feared a Catholic succession when James produced an heir in 1688. The king's opponents secretly urged William to invade England; after his forces landed in 1688, James capitulated, and William ruled the country jointly with his wife, Mary.

Daniel Defoe is perhaps best known for his satirical pamphleteering and as a literary pioneer, but his personal life was also remarkable. Born into a merchant family in St. Giles, London, six years before the Great Fire of 1666, he was originally named simply Daniel Foe, and added the "De" later—by all accounts, to give himself an air of dignity and aristocracy. His family were Presbyterians of Flemish descent and so were considered Dissenters—outside the Anglican mainstream of English (especially court) society—which barred Defoe's entry to the great English universities. Instead, he was educated at the London academy for Dissenters run by Charles Morton, a minister who became vice president of Harvard College in Massachusetts.

### A career in business

Defoe seemed destined for a career as a minister, but instead he chose to go into commerce. At around the time of his marriage in 1684 (he went on to have six children with his wife, Mary), he started a business selling gentlemen's garments and, by the 1690s, had built up a thriving trade in tobacco, wine, and property. He then branched out into more speculative ventures, including an ill-fated foray into insurance that brought about his bankruptcy in 1692; it took him the next decade to pay off his debts.

While running his businesses, Defoe remained actively involved in politics, writing pamphlets in support of his Dissenter beliefs. When the pro-Catholic James II ascended to the throne in 1685, Defoe joined the Monmouth Rebellion, narrowly avoiding execution for his part in this attempt to overthrow the king.

◁ **DANIEL DEFOE**

Defoe liked to exaggerate his wealth and flaunt his foppishness through his dress, as shown in this early-18th century engraving. He favored a long wig, lace ruffles, and often carried a sword.

> "**Justice** is always **violence** to the **party offending**, for every man is **innocent** in his own eyes."

DANIEL DEFOE, *THE SHORTEST WAY WITH THE DISSENTERS*

**GLAZED DELFTWARE BUST OF WILLIAM OF ORANGE (WILLIAM III)**

## IN CONTEXT
### Whigs and Tories

The Glorious Revolution of 1688, which brought William of Orange to the English throne, permanently established parliament as the ruling power in the country. "Whig" and "Tory" refer to opposing factions in the British parliament during the 18th century. Both words originated from terms of abuse—Whig referring to a horse thief and Tory to a papist outlaw. In Defoe's time, the Tories were country gentry who until recently had believed in the Divine Right of Kings, and objected to religious tolerance. Whigs meanwhile represented the landowners who sought to keep the monarchy in check, and the newly wealthy middle classes.

ENGRAVING PRESENTING CARICATURES OF TORIES (LEFT) AND WHIGS (RIGHT), THOMAS SANDERS, 18TH CENTURY

### Satire and sedition

Defoe was a passionate supporter of William of Orange, who became monarch in 1689. William's Glorious Revolution of 1688 marked the transition to parliamentary rule in Britain and affirmed the supremacy of the Protestant faith, creating a benign climate of freedom for Dissenters. However, after William's death in 1702, the devoutly Anglican Queen Anne—who despised all Dissenters and sympathized with the Tories (see box, above)—succeeded to the English throne and immediately set about curtailing the activities of the Dissenters. In response, Defoe produced a pamphlet titled "The Shortest Way with the Dissenters." In a sharp parody of Tory thinking, he argued that Dissenters should be done away with: "Now let us Crutcifie the Thieves."

When the pamphlet's satirical intent was revealed, the establishment was outraged. Defoe was charged with seditious libel, sent to the pillories three times, and cast into Newgate

Prison, where he met Moll King, the inspiration for his novel *Moll Flanders*. The secretary of state, Robert Harley (a leading Tory), saw advantages in putting Defoe's skillful rhetoric, guile, and ingenuity to good use. He secured Defoe's release and sent him across the country to establish a network of spies; in Scotland, Defoe even sowed discord and uncertainty in advance of the vote for the 1707 Act of Union, which joined the two countries together. He often went incognito on these trips, traveling under a number of assumed identities.

### The question of truth

Defoe came to fiction late in life, writing *The Life and Strange Surprizing Adventures of Robinson Crusoe*—the work for which he is most famous—at the age of 57. His novels were written and published as though they were "true" autobiographical accounts: readers were led to believe that Robinson Crusoe and Moll Flanders were the authors of those respective works. Defoe's name does not appear on either publication: *Robinson Crusoe*, written in the direct style of a journal, is credited to Crusoe "Himself," the work's fictional protagonist (see title page opposite); and the novel *Moll Flanders* claims to be "written from her own Memorandums."

Similarly, Defoe's 1722 novel *A Journal of the Plague Year*, which chronicles a man's experiences during the outbreak of bubonic plague in London in 1665, was doubtless thought by his readers to be a work of straightforward journalism, with Defoe acting as the book's editor rather than its writer. The text includes painstakingly accurate references to dates and places, and replicates tables of plague victims; in it, Defoe displays meticulous journalistic reconstruction.

◁ **STOKE NEWINGTON HOME**
As a Dissenter, Defoe could not be part of the English establishment. He therefore made his home some distance from the City of London, in Stoke Newington.

" **Nature** has left this **tincture** in the **blood**, That **all men** would be **tyrants** if they could. "

DANIEL DEFOE, *THE HISTORY OF THE KENTISH PETITION*

## KEY WORKS

**1702**
Defoe's satirical pamphlet "The Shortest Way With The Dissenters" is published, earning him a stint in prison.

**1704**
Writes *The Storm*, an account of a storm that hit England in 1703. It is considered to be one of the first works of modern journalism.

**1719**
Achieves success with his novel *Robinson Crusoe*, following it up with *The Further Adventures of Robinson Crusoe* the same year.

**1722**
Publishes *A Journal of the Plague Year* under the name H. F. (the initials of his uncle Henry Foe, who lived through the plague).

**1722**
Writes *Moll Flanders*, a picaresque novel about the changes in fortune of a beautiful woman born in Newgate Prison.

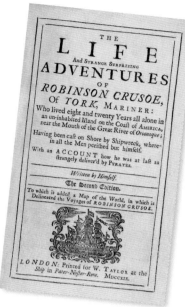

△ **ROBINSON CRUSOE, 1719 EDITION**
Defoe's tale of conquest and survival is one of the most successful books of all time. It is second only to the Bible as the most translated work in the world.

In fact, his intentions seem to have been altruistic, since at the time there were rumors of a fresh bout of plague spreading from France. By depicting events accurately, Defoe hoped to give readers a better chance of survival.

### The modern novel
Published in 1719, *Robinson Crusoe* is widely credited—along with Cervantes' *Don Quixote* (1705)—as one of the early examples of what is now called a novel. These works shared certain features. For example, they were fictional prose narratives, intended to be read alone rather than out loud, unlike the poetry and prose epics of former ages, which were designed to be performed. They were also written for a new and burgeoning, literate middle class. And quite unlike Milton's poems and Shakespeare's plays, they did not feature emperors, kings, and gods as their main protagonists, but ordinary people whose stories took place in situations to which readers could relate.

### Island narratives
*Robinson Crusoe* struck a mighty chord with its audience (four editions were printed in its first year of publication), partly because it is such a compelling human story—the tale of a man set adrift on a desert island, battling the elements and "ill fate" to survive. Some critics have read the text as a metaphor for the struggle of every person's life. For others, the book's importance lies in the fact that it is a product of its time and uncritically displays the ideology that led to Europe's colonization of large parts of the globe. The relationship between colonizer and colonized is played out in the novel's interaction between Friday, the island's local inhabitant, and Crusoe, the bearer of "civilization." With the help of a gun, Crusoe teaches the "savage" Friday to recognize the ways of the Western world—including, crucially, submission to authority.

There were numerous shipwrecks and maroonings in Defoe's day, and multiple stories circulated about these real-life experiences. Defoe would have used many of these accounts as inspiration for his island tale, including those of Alexander Selkirk, who spent years on a Pacific island, and Henry Pitman, a castaway who escaped from a Caribbean penal colony.

Daniel Defoe's last years were spent in failing health, in debt, and hiding from creditors. He died in 1731, probably from a stroke, seven years after the publication of his final novel, *Roxana*. A monument to him stands in Bunhill Fields, North London.

▽ **ROBINSON CRUSOE ISLAND**
This Pacific island, about 400 miles (650 km) west of Chile's central coast, was the temporary home of Scottish castaway Alexander Selkirk, who is thought to have been one of many sources of inspiration for Defoe's famous island story.

▷ **SWIFT, DEAN OF ST. PATRICK'S**
This 1718 portrait of Swift by Charles Jervas shows the writer dressed in his clerical robes and collar. On the table are copies of Aesop, Horace, and Lucian.

# Jonathan Swift

**1667–1745, IRISH**

Swift was an outstanding prose satirist who raged with indignation against war and imperialism. He parodied the cruelty and absurdity of humankind in his fantasy work *Gulliver's Travels*.

# "Satire is a sort of glass wherein beholders do generally discover everybody's face but their own ... "

JONATHAN SWIFT, *THE BATTLE OF THE BOOKS*

Jonathan Swift was born just seven months after the sudden death of his father, a legal officer at the King's Inns in Dublin. Facing penury, his mother, the daughter of an English cleric, returned to England, leaving Jonathan in the care of his uncle. Swift was sent to Kilkenny School, the best school in Ireland, and later graduated from Trinity College, Dublin, in spite of running afoul of its regulations.

Between 1689 and 1694, Swift read voraciously in the library of Moor Park, Surrey, where he worked as secretary to the diplomat Sir William Temple. He met Esther Johnson, the frail young daughter of the housekeeper, who became his friend and pupil. After a clerical job in Ireland, and then studies at Oxford, Swift returned to Moor Park to find that his protégée had become "one of the most beautiful, graceful, and agreeable young women in London, only a little too fat."

## A change of direction

In his 30s, Swift published a series of satirical works either anonymously or under a pseudonym. In *A Tale of a Tub* (1704) he satirized the ethics and morals of the age, and in the "Bickerstaff" pamphlets (1708–1709) he demolished the career of the popular astrologer John Partridge by prophesying his death. In London, he founded the Scriblerus Club with the poet Alexander Pope and the dramatists William Congreve and John Gay. He also edited the newspaper *The Examiner* and became a propagandist for the Tory government. Swift had hoped for a high clerical position in England, but instead was made dean of St. Patrick's Cathedral in Dublin in 1713.

There were romantic dalliances, in particular with Esther Vanhomrigh (nicknamed Vanessa) who featured in Swift's poem "Cadenus and Vanessa," but all the while Swift wrote to Esther Johnson (nicknamed Stella); his candid, tender letters about his life in London were later collated and published posthumously as *Journal to Stella*. Whether Swift married Esther remains unclear to this day.

With the fall of the Tory government, Swift was exiled to Ireland where, in 1724, he published *Drapier's Letters*, a fierce attack on English subjugation of Irish life, and just two years later *Gulliver's Travels*, which was written "to vex the world, not to divert it." This was followed by "A Modest Proposal" (1729), which suggested that Irish babies might be sold as a delicacy, being the only item of commerce unrestricted by the English.

Around 1742, a stroke left Swift paralyzed and unable to speak. He died in 1745, at 77, and was buried alongside Esther Johnson in St. Patrick's Cathedral. His self-penned epitaph says that he lies "where savage indignation can no longer tear his heart."

△ **FIRST EDITION, 1726**
*Gulliver's Travels* chronicles castaway Lemuel Gulliver's adventures among the tiny Lilliputians, among giants, and in a land where civilized horses called Houyhnhnms control vile human Yahoos. It is a corrosive satire on all aspects of humanity.

### IN CONTEXT
#### Politics and religion

As an Anglican, Swift was opposed to James II's attempts to restore a Catholic monarchy and supported the Whig principles of civil and religious freedom and a monarchy under parliamentary control. He switched allegiance to the Tory government under Queen Anne, but the Tory collapse after her death ended his hopes of advancement in the Anglican church. Ironically, he became a national hero among the (mostly Catholic) people of Ireland thanks to his writings that highlighted England's unjust colonial rule.

*QUEEN ANNE, MICHAEL DAHL, c.1714*

▷ **MOOR PARK, SURREY**
This drawing by Charles Herbert Woodbury shows the house where Swift lived and worked from 1689 to 1699. It was here that he began work on *A Tale of a Tub*.

# Voltaire

## 1694–1778, FRENCH

Voltaire was the epitome of the Age of Enlightenment. His copious works satirize the superstitions of the Catholic Church and the arbitrary exercise of state power, advocating freedom of speech and religious tolerance.

François-Marie Arouet, who became known by the pseudonym Voltaire, was born in Paris in 1694. The son of a minor court official, he was educated at the prestigious Collège Louis-le-Grand, where the strict Jesuit religious instruction induced in him deep scepticism rather than the intended devotion. As a young man, he turned away from the legal career that he had been expected to follow and immersed himself in the study of literature.

Voltaire began to move in elite social circles frequented by free-thinking libertines, and his audaciously witty sniping at religious and political authority won him many admirers. However, in 1717, he crossed a line by slandering the French regent and was jailed for 11 months. Voltaire boasted that his imprisonment in the Bastille gave him time to think and to write the first of his tragedies, *Oedipus*, which was staged in Paris in 1718, earning him both praise and money. It was followed by an epic poem, *The Henriade* (1723), which used the story of the French king, Henri IV, to denounce religious fanaticism and intolerance.

◁ **VOLTAIRE WITH LA HENRIADE**
In this portrait from 1728, Voltaire holds an open copy of *The Henriade*, a poem that uses an account of the siege of Paris to probe the political state of France.

### English experiences

Voltaire moved to Britain following a personal dispute with the Chevalier de Rohan, a member of a powerful noble family. The two years that he spent in London crystallized his thinking on religious tolerance, political freedom, and the value of evidence-based science. On returning to France, he published *Letters on the English* (1733), in which he criticized his country's government, church, and society by comparison with practices on the other side of the Channel. These essays were denounced as anti-Catholic, and Voltaire took refuge in Switzerland, before discreetly settling at Cirey, the rural home of his mistress, Madame du Châtelet (see box, right).

### Satirical writing

Voltaire admired Frederick II of Prussia as an "enlightened despot" and in the early 1750s spent three years at Frederick's court in Berlin, before fleeing, caught up in scandal once more. He settled at Ferney in southeast France, with his young niece, Madame Denis, as his mistress. From there, he mounted a series of campaigns against religious-inspired injustices in France, such as the barbarous torture and execution of the Chevalier de la Barre for blasphemy in 1766.

Voltaire's most widely read works today are his *contes*—short fictions that satirize contemporary society and philosophical ideas, the most famous of which is *Candide* (1759). In this, Voltaire savagely attacks the view—attributed to Leibniz—that "all is for the best in the best of all possible worlds." The book concludes that the only sensible response to a world out of order is withdrawal "to cultivate one's garden."

Voltaire died in 1778, after a triumphant return to Paris for the performance of his last tragedy, *Irène*.

▽ **CANDIDE, 1759 EDITION**
Although written in a light, witty style, Voltaire's *contes* present a bleak view of the state of the world, with irrationality and cruelty on the rise everywhere.

> " If **this** is **the best** of **possible worlds**, what are **the others**? "

VOLTAIRE, *CANDIDE*

# Directory

## François Villon

### 1431– UNKNOWN, FRENCH

The best-known French poet of the late Middle Ages, François Villon graduated from the University of Paris in 1452. He associated with a bad crowd and, four years later, killed a priest in a street brawl. From then on his life became a hopeless tale of lawlessness and punishment.

Villon was forced to flee Paris after a theft of gold coins; he was imprisoned in 1461 and arrested again in Paris in 1462; he was then condemned to be hanged, but his sentence was commuted to exile. Beyond 1463, no trace of his life survives. Sardonic, bitter, funny, compassionate, and self-pitying, Villon's poetry speaks eloquently of poverty, crime, squalor, the passage of time, and death. He occasionally uses obscure thieves' slang, but his major work, *The Testament*, has a charming lucidity. Sometimes he addresses his own experience with directness, especially in the "Ballad of the Hanged Men."

**KEY WORKS:** *The Legacy* (or *Le Petit Testament*), c.1457; *The Testament*, c.1461; *Ballad of the Hanged Men*, c.1463

## Luís Vaz de Camões

### 1524–1580, PORTUGUESE

Portugal's most celebrated poet, Camões led an adventurous life. As a young man he lost an eye while fighting Muslims in Morocco and most of his adult years were spent in outposts of the Portuguese empire, such as Goa in India and Macau in China. After many vicissitudes, he arrived back in Portugal in 1570 carrying the manuscript of a vast historical epic, *The Lusiads*.

A fictionalized account of the voyage to India by the Portuguese explorer Vasco da Gama, the poem draws on the author's experience of perilous ocean voyages and exotic lands; reality is intertwined with myth, the gods of Olympus presiding over men's fate. Although *The Lusiads* earned Camões a royal pension, his final years were spent in poverty and he was buried in a communal grave. His lyric poems—including his emotionally and intellectually complex sonnets—were not published until after his death.

**KEY WORKS:** *The Lusiads*, 1572; *Rhythmas*, 1595; *Rimas*, 1598

## ▽ Torquato Tasso

### 1544–1595, ITALIAN

The son of a poet and courtier, Tasso was a child prodigy and had written his first epic poem, *Rinaldo*, by the age of 18. He became a favorite at the Renaissance court of the D'Este family in Ferrara, addressing hundreds of love poems to ladies of the court and creating the pastoral drama *Aminta* for performance there. Written in the 1570s, his masterpiece was the historical epic *Jerusalem Delivered*. Based on the events of the First Crusade, it combines accounts of notable battles and sieges with

△ *TORQUATO TASSO*, ARTIST UNKNOWN

melancholic love stories. Sadly, Tasso began to lose his mental stability. Criticism that *Jerusalem Delivered* was unorthodox in religious and literary terms helped plunge him into persecution mania and he was locked in an asylum for seven years. Released in 1586, he died in Rome, where he had come to be crowned with laurel leaves by the pope for being the foremost poet of his time.

**KEY WORKS:** *Aminta*, 1573; *Jerusalem Delivered*, 1581; *Re Torrismondo*, 1587

## Lope de Vega

### 1562–1635, SPANISH

One of the most prolific authors of Spain's Golden Age, Lope de Vega was of humble birth. He ran away from Jesuit college and a training in the priesthood to pursue a woman, setting the pattern for a life of tempestuous liaisons, as well as two marriages. He had begun writing plays before he served as a soldier in the armada, the fleet sent to invade England in 1588.

Becoming a priest in 1614 did not noticeably affect Vega's lifestyle. His dramas, including "cloak-and-sword" comedies and history plays, broke the classical rules to appeal to an audience of common people, using "the language of fools since it is they who pay us." His poetry included *La Dragontea* (1598), an epic poem about Sir Francis Drake, and *La Gatomaquia* (1634), a mock epic about cats.

**KEY WORKS:** *El Acero de Madrid*, 1608; *Peribáñez y el comendador de Ocaña*, c.1609; *Fuente Ovejuna*, c.1613

## Christopher Marlowe

### 1564–1593, ENGLISH

The first great Elizabethan playwright, Marlowe established tragedy as the supreme form in English drama. His short life was full of mystery. Son of a Canterbury shoemaker and a graduate of Cambridge University, he may have

△ *JEAN DE LA FONTAINE*, HYACINTHE RIGAUD, 1675–1685

been a government spy, and his death, after he was stabbed in a tavern, may not have been simply the result of a drunken fight over money.

Writing for the theater company The Admiral's Men, Marlowe created some of the most popular works in English drama. He showed equal facility in blank verse and rhyme. His tragedies, such as *Tamburlaine the Great* and *Doctor Faustus*, paved the way for William Shakespeare—and indeed, it is thought that Marlowe may have collaborated on the Bard's early plays. Aside from his tragedies, he is noted for the lyric "The Passionate Shepherd to His Love," as well as the sensuous long poem *Hero and Leander*.

**KEY WORKS:** *Tamburlaine the Great*, c.1586–1587; *The Jew of Malta*, c.1590; *Doctor Faustus*, c.1592; *Edward the Second*, 1593

## △ Jean de La Fontaine

1621–1695 , FRENCH

La Fontaine is known for his *Fables*, the sly, witty retelling of old stories in memorable verse. He spent most of his life in Paris, where he associated with the dramatists Racine and Molière and the literary critic Boileau. Although careless with money, he always found patrons and benefactors to support him. He rarely saw his wife and child: on meeting his grown-up son, he failed to recognize him.

La Fontaine began publication quite late in life with his irreverent and lecherous verse *Tales*. His *Fables*, based on Aesop and other classical authors, were an immediate success. Including such favorites as *The Ant and the Grasshopper*, *The Fox and the Grapes*, and *The Hare and the*

*Tortoise*, they often carried a social or political message beneath their amusing surface. Charming and not pompous, yet rich in moral and psychological insights, they still delight children and adults alike.

**KEY WORKS:** *Tales and Novels in Verse*, 1664, 1666, 1671; *The Love of Cupid and Psyche*, 1669; *Selected Fables in Verse*, 1668, 1678, 1694

## Madame de La Fayette

1643–1693, FRENCH

La Fayette founded the tradition of the French psychological novel with her story of frustrated love *La Princesse de Clèves*. Born Marie-Madeleine Pioche de la Vergne, when 21 she married the Comte de La Fayette, an army officer 18 years her senior. She had two children, but left home to join a circle of Paris intellectuals, which included the Duc de La Rochefoucauld, renowned for his perceptive *Maxims*.

Publishing anonymously, La Fayette found her subject matter with the novella *La Princesse de Montpensier*, a tale of adultery. *La Princesse de Clèves*, a more mature exploration of the same theme, tells of a dutiful wife whose life is devastated by falling in love. The refined lucidity of La Fayette's prose and her precise analysis of emotion made the novel an instant success.

**KEY WORKS:** *La Princesse de Montpensier*, 1662; *Zaïde*, 1670; *La Princesse de Clèves*, 1678

## Henry Fielding

1707–1754, ENGLISH

Best known as the author of the comic novel *Tom Jones*, Fielding first won fame writing satirical plays for the London stage. A tightening of theater censorship in 1737 ended his career as a playwright, but the success of Samuel Richardson's novel *Pamela* in 1740 provoked him to write a parodic

response, *Shamela*. This led to his first full-length novel, *Joseph Andrews*, a bawdy burlesque, which he described as "a comic epic poem in prose."

*Tom Jones* continued in the picaresque genre. Its rags-to-riches tale benefits from an attractive hero, an ingeniously worked plot, and strongly drawn characters. Fielding was also a magistrate, founding the Bow Street Runners, London's first police force. After the death of his first wife, he caused a scandal by marrying her maid. He died in Portugal, where he had gone in an effort to salvage his failing health.

**KEY WORKS:** *The History of the Adventures of Joseph Andrews*, 1742; *The Life and Death of Jonathan Wild, the Great*, 1743; *The History of Tom Jones, a Foundling*, 1749

## Jean-Jacques Rousseau

1712–1778, SWISS

Known for his egalitarian philosophy, Rousseau was also a forerunner of literary Romanticism. The son of a Geneva watchmaker, he lived much of his life in France. He came to prominence with his *Discourse on the Arts and Sciences* (1750), arguing that culture corrupted the natural goodness of humankind. His belief that equality and freedom were the natural human condition culminated in *The Social Contract*, with its ringing opening sentence: "Man is born free, and everywhere he is in chains."

Rousseau's only novel, *La Nouvelle Héloïse*, was a best seller, its sensitive descriptions of nature and elevated emotions encapsulating a new pre-Romantic sensibility. The candor of his autobiographical works, *Reveries of the Solitary Walker* and *Confessions*, exemplified his radical belief in personal authenticity and truth to one's self.

**KEY WORKS:** *Julie, ou La Nouvelle Héloïse*, 1761; *The Social Contract*, 1762; *Reveries of the Solitary Walker*, 1782; *Confessions*, 1782, 1789

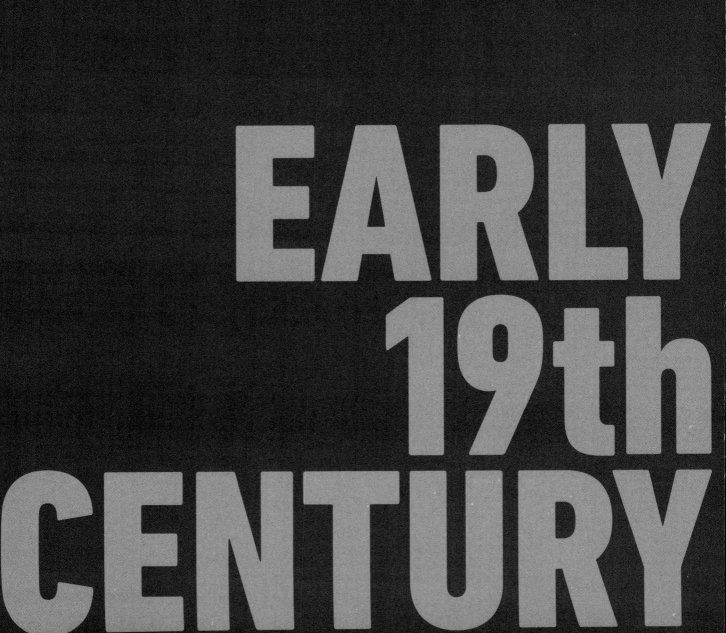

EARLY
19th
CENTURY

**CHAPTER 2**

# J. W. von Goethe

## 1749–1832, GERMAN

A master of German literature, Goethe had written a best seller by the age of 25. In his prolific works, which included poetry, drama, and fiction, he grappled with the contradictions and complexities of human experience.

In August 1831, Johann Wolfgang von Goethe sealed the manuscript of the second part of *Faust*, with instructions for it to be published after his death. It was the final work in a writing career that lasted more than 60 years, and the pinnacle of an extraordinary body of writing that ran to 40 volumes of astonishing variety and complexity. Goethe's life spanned

◁ **GOETHE, 1828**
This portrait of the author at the age of 70 was made by Joseph Karl Stieler, who was the royal court painter of the Bavarian kings.

a time of revolution and war that reshaped Europe, a period of great cultural change when artists and writers negotiated their way through the Enlightenment, Romanticism, and neoclassicism. This rich diversity of influences can be seen in the evolution of the author's work.

### Family and education

Born in Frankfurt on August 28, 1749, Goethe was the eldest child of Johann, a cultured man who lived well on his inherited fortune, and Catharina, the daughter of a powerful Frankfurt family, who was more than 20 years

younger than her husband. Goethe's sister, Cornelia, was the only one of his siblings to reach adulthood and the two remained very close until her death in 1777.

Goethe was educated at home by his father until the age of 16, when he went to study law in the city of Leipzig. There, his romantic life—notably his passionate love for unobtainable women—fed his early work. His rejection by an innkeeper's daughter, Kätchen Shönkopf, was reflected in his play *Partners in Guilt*, but the theme found famous expression in *The Sorrows of Young Werther*, Goethe's story of a young man who commits suicide after being caught in a painful friendship with both the woman he loves and her fiancé. The story was based on the suicide of a lovesick friend, but it reflected elements of Goethe's relationship with his sister Cornelia and her husband. Published in 1774, *Werther* was an immediate sensation. Young men across Europe, including Goethe himself, were soon donning Werther's famous blue coat

◁ **GOETHE'S GARDEN HOUSE**
Goethe bought this former vineyard cottage when he arrived in Weimar in 1776. He returned there in his old age, when the house provided a sanctuary where he could work undisturbed.

GOETHE–SCHILLER MONUMENT, WEIMAR, ERNST RIETSCHEL, 1857

" **Behavior** is a **mirror** in which everyone shows his **image**. "
J. W. VON GOETHE, *MAXIMS AND REFLECTIONS*

## The bildungsroman

In *Wilhelm Meister's Apprenticeship*, which was first published in 1796, Goethe established the template for what was to become known as the bildungsroman, a novel that deals with a young person's moral development. In Goethe's tale, suffering and loss drive the young Wilhelm on a quest for self-fulfillment and wisdom. The bildungsroman became a major narrative form, as evident in works such as Charles Dickens's *David Copperfield* and Hermann Hesse's *Siddhartha*.

**YOUNG WILHELM DEPICTED IN AN ETCHING IN GOETHE'S NOVEL**

and buff vest and pants, and a spate of copycat suicides sparked outrage. The book was a classic of the proto-Romantic *Sturm und Drang* (Storm and Stress) movement, which had taken root in Germany. Its authors rejected the rationalism of the Enlightenment to write novels and plays that were characterized by extreme emotion, immense energy, and artistic creativity.

### The Weimar court

Goethe's fame brought him to the attention of Charles Augustus, the 18-year-old Duke of Saxe-Weimar, and in 1776 he was summoned to court to work as privy councillor. The two men were closely bound together by the Enlightenment ideals of tolerance, equality, and intellectual endeavor, and for 10 years Goethe worked extremely diligently at the court, becoming an expert on taxation, the highways, farming, and mining, as he restored order to the state's affairs.

In 1782, now essentially acting as Weimar's prime minister, Goethe was ennobled, becoming von Goethe, and moved into a large house on Frauenplan in Weimar. His platonic affair with an older, married woman, Charlotte von Stein, brought him comfort, and his writing moved away from the intense drama of *Sturm und Drang* as he sought calm and began to

explore humanism in more depth, as in his neoclassical prose drama *Iphigenia in Taurus*. However, by 1780 he was in desperate need of inspiration. His poetry had all but dried up and he had to force himself to keep writing *The Theatrical Mission of Wilhelm Meister*. As he would always do in times of creative drought, he dabbled in biology and other forms of science, but it was becoming increasingly evident to Goethe that his work at court was incompatible with his vocation as an author.

In 1786, Goethe left Weimar to make a long-planned trip to Italy. For two years he immersed himself in classical art and architecture, and he returned to Weimar a changed man—utterly convinced of the merits of classical

culture and finally ready for a fulfilling relationship with a woman. He took a young lover, Christiane Vulpius, and wrote a series of erotic poems in classical meter, found in *Roman Elegies*.

Christiane provided a stable home and children for Goethe, although only one son would survive to adulthood. With a secure relationship, and freed from his administrative duties at court, Goethe was able to concentrate on being a poet. While in Rome, he had labored on an edition of his collected works; completed a novel, *Egmont*; and found the inspiration for *Torquato Tasso*, a tragedy about an Italian poet of the late Renaissance. By 1789, the collected works were nearly finished and the following year he published the first fragment of *Faust*.

▷ ***GOETHE AND VON STEIN*, c.1790**
This unattributed watercolor shows Goethe in conversation with his friend and confidante Charlotte von Stein, lady in waiting to Anna Amalia, a German princess. Charlotte was Goethe's muse, his ideal of feminine beauty. He wrote her at least 1,500 letters.

## KEY WORKS

**1774**
Goethe's epistolary novel *The Sorrows of Young Werther* brings him European fame.

**1795**
Schiller convinces Goethe to publish *Roman Elegies*, an erotically charged tribute to the Latin love poets.

**1810**
Goethe publishes *Theory of Colors*, an exploration of the nature of colors and their links with the emotions.

**1832**
Goethe completes *Faust*, the tale of an aristocratic scholar who signs a pact with the devil.

◁ **ITALIAN JOURNEY**
Goethe was almost 40 years old—and already famous as a writer—when he visited Italy in 1786. His stay in Rome, where he lodged with the painter Johann Heinrich Tischbein, signaled a creative rebirth. A visit to the Colosseum is recorded here by the German landscape painter Jakob Philipp Hackert.

▽ *FAUST*
Goethe's greatest work, *Faust*, is a version of a 16th-century German legend. It tells the story of a man who, in his search for supreme knowledge, makes a bargain with the demon Mephistopheles. Goethe's play has inspired many interpretations in music, movies, and opera. The opera of the same name by the French composer Charles Gounod was first staged in Paris in 1859.

## Military campaign

Goethe's writing was interrupted in 1792–1793 when he was summoned to join the Duke of Saxe-Weimar on his campaigns against revolutionary France. The experience confirmed Goethe's dislike of militarism and of large centralized states whose authorities cared little for the people they governed. He had previously explored such themes in his drama *Götz von Berlichingen* (1773), which was based on the life of the maverick hero Gottfried von Berlichingen.

In 1794, Goethe met the man who would influence one of his most productive periods—Friedrich Schiller. Their correspondence ran more than 1,000 letters and Schiller's friendship was to provide the impetus for some of Goethe's most successful work, including his epic poem *Hermann and Dorothea* for *Wilhelm Meister's Apprenticeship*—the novel he had started years before—and for Part One of his play *Faust*.

When Schiller died in 1805, Goethe was bereft. A year later, Weimar was sacked by Napoleonic troops following the Battle of Jena (October 1806) and only Christiane's courage and quick thinking saved Goethe's house. Soon afterward, the two were married, but the commitment, it seems, proved too much for Goethe, who fell in love with a young woman called Wilhelmina Harzlieb. Once again, he channeled his complicated attitude to love into his writing—*Elective Affinities* (1809) explores the conflict between social conventions and passion, and offers the bleak conclusion that being moral is difficult and brings little consolation. However, Goethe emerged from these gloomy reflections clearly resolved not to give up on love. He began to exchange love poems with a woman who was half his age in 1815 and, following the death of his wife in 1816, proposed marriage to a 19-year-old girl when he was 73.

## Final years

Goethe spent his final years preparing one last collection of his works and several volumes of the autobiography that he had begun with *Italian Journey* in 1813. Finally, he finished *Faust*, his tragic two-part drama, which is the story of a man who—much like Goethe himself—spends a lifetime searching for the essence of life. With his work complete, Goethe died at home in his armchair in 1832.

> " **Art** is long, **life** is short, **judgment** difficult, **opportunity** fleeting. **Action** is easy, **thinking** is **hard**: **acting** after thinking, **uncomfortable**. "
>
> J. W. VON GOETHE, *WILHELM MEISTER'S APPRENTICESHIP*

# William Wordsworth

**1770–1850, ENGLISH**

A key figure in the English Romantic movement, Wordsworth combined mystical nature worship with concern for the lives of the rural poor. His use of "the real language of men" had a lasting influence on English verse.

◁ **ESTHWAITE WATER**
Wordsworth spent long hours walking around this lake, which had "miles of pleasant wandering." It is the location for "Lines Left Upon A Seat In A Yew-Tree," which features in his *Lyrical Ballads*.

Born at Cockermouth in Cumberland, northwest England, in 1770, William Wordsworth was the son of a lawyer who worked as a legal agent for the Earl of Lonsdale, a local landowner. He was one of five children. Both Wordsworth's parents had died by the time he was 13, and he was due a substantial inheritance, which was delayed for 20 years by legal disputes. The children were all high achievers: William's oldest brother became a prosperous London lawyer; another brother rose to be master of Trinity College, Cambridge.

### Childhood and study

The episodes from an idyllic rural childhood that form a memorable part of Wordsworth's autobiographical poem *The Prelude* (1805)—skating on a frozen lake, climbing rocky crags in search of bird's eggs—took place while he was boarding at Hawkshead Grammar School, in a small village on Esthwaite Water in the Lake District.

He grew up as, in his own words, "a wild unworldly-minded youth, given up / To Nature and to books." Three years at St. John's College, Cambridge, starting in 1787, lent him a veneer of sophistication, although he was an indifferent student of any subject but English poetry.

### Revolutionary adventures

Electing not to follow a traditional clerical or legal career, Wordsworth entered an experimental phase of his life. The outbreak of the French Revolution in 1789 had fired up British radicals, and in 1791–1792 Wordsworth made an extended visit to France, where he was converted to revolutionary republicanism. He would later celebrate his emotions of that period with the famous lines: "Bliss was it in that dawn to be alive / But to be young was very heaven!" His preoccupations were not entirely political, however. A French royalist woman, Annette de Vallon, became his mistress and pregnant with his child. Their relationship was interrupted by the outbreak of war between Britain and France and the degeneration of the revolution into mass slaughter. Returning to England, Wordsworth lost contact with Annette and his daughter.

> **" Bliss** was it in that dawn **to be alive,** But **to be young** was very **heaven! "**

WILLIAM WORDSWORTH, *THE PRELUDE*

▷ **WILLIAM WORDSWORTH, 1842**
This portrait of Wordsworth at the age of 72 is by Benjamin Haydon. Wordsworth approved of the image, describing it as "a likeness of me, not a mere matter-of-fact portrait, but one of a poetical character."

△ **FALL OF THE BASTILLE, 1789**
Wordsworth was profoundly affected by the fervor unleashed by the French Revolution. As a young man, he visited Paris soon after the Storming of the Bastille, an event depicted in this painting by François Léonard.

In 1793, Wordsworth published his first poems, *An Evening Walk* and *Descriptive Sketches*. Around this time, he revived his relationship with his sister Dorothy, which had waned over the previous years, and they became inseparable. In the mid-1790s, he experienced a breakdown, an intense depression possibly caused by his disillusionment with the course of the French Revolution, in which he had invested such hopes. He was also frustrated as an author, finding no one prepared to stage his historical play *The Borderers*, written in 1795–1796.

In 1797, Wordsworth found a path forward through his alliance with another poet, Samuel Taylor Coleridge. Living as neighbors in the Quantock Hills in Somerset, they shared a taste for long country walks, folk ballads, and debate about the limitations of Enlightenment Rationalism.

The fruit of their collaboration was the publication of *Lyrical Ballads* in 1798. Here, Wordsworth's identity as a poet took shape as he used unclichéd language to express the elevated emotions inspired by nature and to tell stories of the rural poor, whose unspoiled hearts he believed revealed the essence of human nature.

## The Lake Poets

Entering a period of intense creativity, Wordsworth began working on an autobiographical blank-verse poem, *The Prelude*, which was intended to be the first part of a longer philosophical epic, *The Recluse*, which was never written. During this period, he also wrote *Tintern Abbey* (1798), with its evocation of a sublime spirit "interfused" with nature, and the lyrical *Lucy* poems (1798–1781), whose subject has never been identified as any real woman in Wordsworth's life.

At the end of 1799, Dorothy and William returned to the Lake District, settling at Dove Cottage on Grasmere. There, Wordsworth was joined by Coleridge, and, with the poet Robert Southey who lived nearby, they became known as the Lake Poets.

The poems continued to flow, including masterpieces such as "Resolution and Independence," inspired by an encounter with a poor leech gatherer, and "Ode: Intimations of Immortality," praising the superiority of a child's vision over that of adults. Wordsworth also began writing sonnets, finding solace in the strict verse form from "the weight of too much liberty." His finest sonnets, such as "The world is too much with us," an attack on contemporary materialism, and "Upon Westminster Bridge," were written at this time.

△ **WORDSWORTH'S DESK**
Wordsworth's writing desk and some of his papers are shown here at his home in Cockermouth, Cumberland, northwest England. The Georgian townhouse was the poet's birthplace and childhood home.

▷ **DOVE COTTAGE**
Wordsworth lived in this small limewashed cottage on the outskirts of the village of Grasmere from 1799 to 1808 and wrote many of his best-loved works there. The cottage is now preserved as a museum.

### Declining powers

In 1802, Wordsworth finally received his inheritance and felt able to take a wife. He married Mary Hutchinson, whom he had known since childhood; they went on to have five children. Wordsworth continued living at Dove Cottage with his sister, wife, and family until 1808. Some of his best-known poems, including "The Solitary Reaper" and "Daffodils," date from this period, but his powers were waning: "The Excursion" (another part of his planned epic *The Recluse*) showed a marked decline from the standard of *The Prelude*.

Various misfortunes preyed upon Wordsworth's spirits. The death of his brother John in a maritime disaster in 1805 was followed by the end of his friendship with Coleridge, who was descending into opium addiction. The hostile response to the publication of *Poems in Two Volumes* in 1807 (Lord Byron described his language as "not simple, but puerile") hurt him deeply, and the death of two of his children in 1812 was a great personal tragedy.

From 1813, Wordsworth lived at Rydal Mount near Ambleside. He obtained an official sinecure as the Distributor of Stamps for Westmoreland, which kept him financially secure. By now, his political attitudes had reversed. Once spied on by government agents as a potential subversive, he had instead become a trenchant supporter of the monarchy and the established church, writing patriotic poems in praise of British military victories and opposing all popular protests and political reforms. He became an establishment figure, ridiculed by a younger generation of Romantic poets such as Percy Bysshe Shelley, but he continued to champion the cause of the poor and outcast, vigorously opposing the 1830s Poor Law, which condemned the unemployed to the workhouse. Wordsworth's inspiration dried up as his official recognition grew; he was appointed poet laureate in 1843. In his later years, as Dorothy declined into premature senility, Wordsworth's daughter Dora became another of the women who ministered to his needs, before she escaped into marriage against her father's wishes at the age of 39. Her death in 1847 was the final grief of Wordsworth's life. He died, at 80, on April 23, 1850.

## KEY WORKS

**1798**
*Lyrical Ballads*, containing poems by Wordsworth and Coleridge, is published anonymously.

**1800**
*Preface to the Lyrical Ballads* sets out Wordsworth's manifesto, giving his views on poetry.

**1802–04**
"Ode: Intimations of Immortality," a meditation on childhood and the loss of innocence, is published.

**1804**
"Daffodils" is published and becomes Wordsworth's most famous lyric poem.

**1805**
*The Prelude*, the first version of Wordsworth's blank-verse autobiography, is published.

**1814**
*The Excursion*, intended as part of a longer philosophical poem, *The Recluse*, is published.

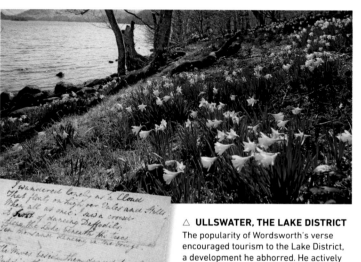

△ **ULLSWATER, THE LAKE DISTRICT**
The popularity of Wordsworth's verse encouraged tourism to the Lake District, a development he abhorred. He actively opposed the building of a railroad that would give people access to the Lakes.

◁ **DAFFODILS**
This copy of the poem "Daffodils" is in Wordsworth's own hand. The poem begins with the famous line "I wandered lonely as a cloud ...," which was inspired by an entry in his sister Dorothy's diary.

### ON FORM
### *Lyrical Ballads*

The poetry collection *Lyrical Ballads* (1798), which contained works by Wordsworth and Coleridge, was a reaction against 18th-century poetic convention—Wordsworth stated that the poems should be "considered as experiments." Their radicalism lay in their simple directness of style and, in the case of Wordsworth's verse, in the choice of everyday subjects. Some poems, such as Wordsworth's "The Idiot Boy," imitated folk ballads, traditional narrative poems in short stanzas. The original critical response to the book was muted, but it is now regarded as a seminal work of English Romanticism.

**SAMUEL TAYLOR COLERIDGE**, PIETER VAN DYKE, 1795

> " ... **poetry** is the **spontaneous overflow** of powerful **feelings**; it takes its origin from **emotion recollected** in **tranquillity** ..."

WILLIAM WORDSWORTH, *PREFACE TO THE LYRICAL BALLADS*

# Jane Austen

## 1775–1817, ENGLISH

Austen was one of Britain's greatest novelists. Coming from a modest, rural background, she painted a vivid picture of the society of her time with deft irony and a penetrating eye for character.

Jane Austen was born in the village of Steventon, Hampshire, the seventh of eight children. Her father, George, was rector of the local church, and though he came from a good family and had been educated at Oxford, he lived a life of genteel poverty. George had no land, no tenants, and no private income, so to make ends meet he had to give lessons to the sons of some of the local gentry.

Some critics dismiss Austen's novels for their preoccupation with money, rich relatives, and the making of advantageous marriages, but these themes are entirely understandable. At a very early age, Jane would have been exceedingly aware of her limited prospects. She would have realized that, without a dowry, her chances of finding a suitable husband were severely diminished. At the same time, she could also see that there were ways of escaping one's destiny. In around 1783, her brother Edward was adopted by distant relatives, the wealthy but childless Knight family—adoptions of this kind were not unusual at the time. In this single act, Edward's fortunes changed, as he gained a new lifestyle and status. To the young Jane, this transformation must have seemed almost magical, so it is not surprising that she later tried to give the heroines of her books similar, Cinderella-like experiences.

### Home life

Jane had a happy childhood. She was particularly close to her older sister Cassandra and was educated with her, first at Mrs. Cawley's boarding school in Oxford and later at the Abbey School in Reading. The girls were content there, but the fees proved to be too steep for George Austen, so at the end of 1786 they returned home. The two sisters remained very close and their correspondence has provided invaluable insights into Jane's views and interests. Unfortunately, though, Cassandra destroyed many of Jane's letters after her death, leaving tantalizing gaps in the narrative.

△ **LETTERS TO CASSANDRA**
Austen's life was interwoven with that of her beloved elder sister, Cassandra, and she wrote often to her whenever they were apart.

◁ **STEVENTON, HAMPSHIRE**
Austen's father was the rector of St. Nicholas Church in Steventon. He was a calm, scholarly man who championed his daughter's writing.

*FANNY BURNEY*, EDWARD FRANCIS BURNEY, 1784–1785

> "The person, be it **gentleman** or **lady**, who has **not pleasure** in a **good novel**, must be **intolerably stupid.**"

JANE AUSTEN, NORTHANGER ABBEY

▷ *JANE AUSTEN*, c.1788
This unsigned, undated portrait, attributed to Ozias Humphry, is believed by many to show Jane Austen at the age of 13, although recent scholarship has raised questions about its origins.

△ **FIRST EDITION**
Austen's *Pride and Prejudice* has been in print since the first edition of 1813. It is one of the most popular works in the English language, with more than 20 million copies sold worldwide.

After 1786, Jane remained at home with her family, delving into her father's library to round out her literary education. Beyond this, life was rarely dull. Her eldest brother, James, loved organizing theatrical entertainments, there were frequent visits from relatives and friends, and she played the piano well, rising an hour before the rest of the family in the mornings to practice. More importantly, she started to write: at about the age of 12, she began filling up three bound notebooks, given to her by her father, with stories, poems, and historical sketches. These volumes, now known collectively as the *Juvenilia*, give evidence of Jane's extensive reading, particularly of authors like Samuel Richardson and Henry Fielding.

### The epistolary form
The final date in the notebooks is 1793. From this point on, Austen seems to have begun working on her novels, although it would be years before any of them were published. Initially, she favored an epistolary format—that is, conveying her story entirely through exchanges of letters between the principal characters. She also used other documentary forms, such as journals or diaries. Jane certainly wrote *Elinor and Marianne* (an early version of *Sense and Sensibility*) in this format, and there are strong hints that her first version of *Pride and Prejudice* was also developed in this manner.

Epistolary novels were widely read throughout the 18th century. In England, they were popularized by Samuel Richardson, one of Jane's favorite authors. He had used the technique to great effect in his most famous books, *Pamela* (1740) and *Clarissa* (1749).

By the end of the century, however, the epistolary novel was going out of fashion and this is undoubtedly why Austen decided to abandon the format. In its place, she introduced an entirely new form of narration, which modern critics have dubbed "free indirect style" (or "free indirect discourse"). This was a variant of third-person narration, but it incorporated the essence of first-person speech. In other words, the narrator could convey the thoughts or speech of the character without the need for such terms as "she said" or "she thought."

### Novel technique
Austen used her newly developed technique of merging narrator and character with immense subtlety. In *Emma*, for example, where the heroine persistently misreads the intentions and affections of her friends, Austen teases the reader by using the narrator to report Emma's delusions as if they were facts. The reader cannot be sure of the reality of the situation until Emma herself realizes that she is in love with Mr. Knightley. Austen also employed free indirect style in a physical sense, as if the narrator were inside the character's body. Thus, in *Persuasion*, when one of the female characters lowers her eyes and curtsies in front of a gentleman, the narrator only records things that can be heard, excluding anything that the character cannot see.

### Reluctant publishers
As a woman, Austen found it difficult to get her work published. In 1797, her father was so enthusiastic about *First Impressions* (Austen's initial version of *Pride and Prejudice*) that he wrote to the publisher Thomas Cadell, asking if he would read the manuscript. Cadell declined. Austen herself fared no

## IN CONTEXT
### Bath

The Austen family lived in Bath for five years (1801–1806). Jane was not particularly fond of the city, which had passed its fashionable heyday, but it provided invaluable material for her novels, frequently serving as a catalyst in her plots. In the strictly regulated society of the time, meeting suitable people was often difficult, but encounters were easier in Bath. In the mornings, the upper echelons of society gathered in the Pump Room to take the waters, and in the evenings there were concerts and subscription balls in the Assembly Rooms. All the social events were overseen by a Master of Ceremonies.

*THE ROYAL CRESCENT, BATH (ENGRAVING), JOHN HILL, 1804*

"It is **a truth** universally acknowledged, that a **single man** in **possession** of a **good fortune**, must be in **want of a wife**. "

JANE AUSTEN, *PRIDE AND PREJUDICE*

better. In 1803, she sold *Susan* (later renamed *Northanger Abbey*) to the publisher Crosby & Co. for £10 ($45). This was her first major novel, a gentle satire on the contemporary vogue for Gothic horror stories. The publisher did nothing with the manuscript and eventually, in 1816, Austen's brother Henry bought back the copyright. The book was not published in her lifetime.

### Bath years

In 1801, Austen's father retired as rector and the family moved to Bath. Here, Austen experienced an episode that could have come straight out of one of her novels. In December 1802, Harris Bigg Wither, the brother of one of Austen's friends, proposed to her. She accepted immediately but, after sleeping on it, she changed her mind. There has been much

speculation about her reasons for doing so, but there is no definitive answer. Perhaps she valued her independence too highly to exchange it for financial security.

Austen's father died in 1805 and the family had to leave Bath. They were short of money, but were rescued by Edward Austen Knight, who offered to let them live in one of his properties—a cottage in the Hampshire village of Chawton. It was here that Jane's writing career finally took off. In 1811, *Sense and Sensibility* became her first published novel, winning favorable reviews and selling well. It appeared anonymously (the credit being "By a Lady"), which was a common practice for female authors at the time, although Austen's identity was certainly an open secret in literary circles. Austen soon gained many admirers, including the writer

Sir Walter Scott and the Prince Regent (the future George IV), who requested that she dedicate *Emma* to him. She reluctantly did so; and in 1815, she received an invitation to inspect his remarkable library at Carlton House.

Sadly, Austen did not have long to enjoy her successes and accolades. In 1816, she began to suffer from a mystery illness—now usually identified as Addison's disease—and she died the following year. She was buried in the nave of Winchester Cathedral.

△ **CHAWTON COTTAGE**
Austen lived in this house in Hampshire with her mother, her sister Cassandra, and their friend Martha Lloyd. The cottage was close to the grand home of Jane's wealthy brother Edward Austen Knight, and she was a frequent visitor there.

▷ **WRITING BOX**
Austen's portable writing box was a gift from her father when she was 20. It is now on display in the British Library in London.

## KEY WORKS

**1803**
Austen sells *Northanger Abbey*, her first major novel (originally titled *Susan*) to a publisher. It is printed in 1817.

**1811**
Reshaped from its original epistolary (letter) form, *Sense and Sensibility* appears in print.

**1813**
*Pride and Prejudice* is published. The novel was begun in 1796, rejected for publication, then revised by Austen in 1811–1812.

**1814**
*Mansfield Park* appears in print. Critical opinions are divided, but the book is popular with the public and sells very well.

**1815**
Austen's *Emma* is published. The author describes Emma as a "heroine whom no one but myself will much like."

**1817**
*Persuasion*, Austen's somber final novel, written when her health was failing, is published posthumously.

# Mary Shelley

## 1797–1851, ENGLISH

One of the leading exponents of the Gothic novel, Shelley was famed above all for her iconic horror story, *Frankenstein*. She was also a talented short-story writer, essayist, and travel writer.

Mary Shelley's introduction to the 1831 edition of *Frankenstein* provides a dramatic account of the genesis of the author's masterpiece. In June 1816, she and her future husband, Percy Shelley, had been staying with Lord Byron and his physician friend, John Polidori, at the Villa Diodati near the shores of Lake Geneva. It was a wild night, with flashes of lightning from an electrical storm raging overhead, and the friends stayed up until dawn reading German horror stories by the flickering candlelight. The group then decided to have a competition to see which of them could write the best ghost story. Two hugely influential works emerged from this contest—Polidori's *The Vampyre* and Shelley's *Frankenstein*.

◁ **MARY SHELLEY, 1840**
Mary Shelley, painted here by Richard Rothwell, never repeated the success of her debut novel, but she continued to write and her literary reputation grew.

Shelley was the child of William Godwin, a radical philosopher and novelist, and Mary Wollstonecraft, the champion of women's rights who wrote *A Vindication of the Rights of Woman*, a landmark text of the feminist movement. She began writing at an early age and enjoyed mixing with her father's literary friends, among whom was the poet Percy Bysshe Shelley. They met in 1812 and fell in love. Their favorite rendezvous was by the grave of Mary's mother, who died 11 days after Mary was born.

### Subverting nature

At the age of 16, Mary eloped to France with Percy, causing a scandal. They married in 1816; by then, she had given birth to two illegitimate children.

It was against this background that she wrote *Frankenstein*. The novel capitalized on the vogue for Gothic horror, rejecting order and reason and focusing on terror and the macabre. However, Shelley's tale—especially her radical reworking of the theme of monstrosity—transcended the genre, drawing on scientific, social, and political debates of the day, such as the origins of life; religion versus science; the question of evil; and the role of environment and upbringing in shaping character. The creation of the monster was inspired by late 18th-century experiments with galvanism: that is, using electricity to make the muscles of a dissected animal twitch. In recent decades, Shelley's text has generated important feminist debate on, for example, the consequences for women when men assume total control; the issue of motherlessness; the manipulation and violation of nature; and the male quest to remove the female from the act of creation.

*Frankenstein* was an instant success. It went through several editions and spawned popular stage productions. But Shelley's triumph was tainted by tragedy. By 1824, she was the only survivor from that stormy night in Geneva. Polidori committed suicide in 1821, Byron perished in the Greek War of Independence (1824), and Percy died in a boating accident in 1824. Nevertheless, Shelley continued to write: *The Last Man* (1826) is the most highly regarded of her later novels, while "Transformation" (1831) is one of her finest short stories.

**POSTER FOR *FRANKENSTEIN* WITH BORIS KARLOFF, 1931**

◁ **VILLA DIODATI, 1833**
This engraving, from a drawing by William Purser, shows the villa where Lord Byron and John Polidori stayed in 1816. The fierce storms that inspired the story of Frankenstein were believed to be the result of climate abnormalities caused by the eruption of Mt. Tambora in 1815.

# Lord Byron

## 1788–1824, BRITISH

**Flamboyant, freethinking, and fashionable, Byron came to embody 19th-century Romanticism. His clever rhymes, wittily ironic style, and beautiful use of language set him apart as one of the greatest poets of his age.**

George Gordon Byron was born in 1788 to Captain John Byron and his second wife, Catherine Gordon. The family settled in Aberdeen, in part to distance themselves from John's numerous creditors. The captain's death in 1791 was followed by that of Byron's great uncle, whereupon the boy became the sixth Baron Byron, inheriting Newstead Abbey, a romantic Gothic house in Nottinghamshire.

Byron was sent to Harrow School, where he formed close friendships with the other boys—and also with Mary Chaworth, a distant cousin and an early love. He then entered Trinity College, Cambridge, where he became better known for his adventurous love life and indulgence in frivolous diversions, such as gambling and boxing, than for his academic prowess.

At the age of 17, Byron produced his first volume of poems, *Fugitive Pieces*, but withdrew it from publication when he was told that it contained work that was considered indecent. His first properly published collection, *Hours of Idleness* (1807), was panned in the Scottish magazine *The Edinburgh Review*, prompting a riposte from Byron in the form of a satirical poem, *English Bards and Scotch Reviewers*.

### Travels and troubles

In 1809, Byron's travels in Portugal, Spain, Malta, Greece, and Turkey—places far off the usual grand-tour itinerary—inspired his first long poem, *Childe Harold's Pilgrimage*, which chronicles the journeys of a disillusioned young man—the original "Byronic hero" (see box, right). When the first two cantos of the poem were published in 1812, they made Byron's name and opened doors into London's literary society. He had an affair with the glamorous (married) Lady Caroline Lamb, and published a series of heroic verse tales with exotic settings, which became popular and profitable; these included *The Giaour* (1813) and *The Corsair* (1814).

In 1815, Byron married Annabella Milbanke. The couple had a child, but Annabella left him after rumors of his relationship with his half-sister Augusta, whose daughter, born in 1814, was said to be his. Byron found himself a social outcast, and left England in 1816, never to return.

### Italian and Greek adventures

Byron stayed in Geneva with Claire Clairmont and Percy and Mary Shelley and worked on *Childe Harold* and another poem with a Byronic hero, *Manfred*. He later moved to Italy. In Ravenna, he started a long-term relationship with Teresa Guiccioli, a young, married Italian countess, and in Venice he wrote *Beppo*, set during the city's famous carnival. This was the poem in which he adopted the ironic, digressive, witty style that marks his later work and that features in his last masterpiece, *Don Juan*, a long poem in 16 cantos that was unfinished when he died. Don Juan, with his many loves, made a scandalous subject, but the poem won admiration from the public and fellow writers, including Goethe.

Byron adopted the cause of Greek independence from the Ottomans and traveled to Greece, prepared to fight to "save a country." Before he could take part in the action, he became ill with a fever and died in April 1824.

IN CONTEXT
### The Byronic hero

The phrase "Byronic hero" has come to mean a temperamental outcast who exhibits romantic melancholy and comments in a sardonic way on society. The character is to some extent a self-portrait: Byron was a man of extremes in thought and deed, writing: "I am such a strange mélange of good and evil, that it would be difficult to describe me." The heroes of several of his works, including Childe Harold, Conrad in *The Corsair*, and Manfred, conform to Byronic type. Don Juan, a later character, is a variation on the theme, more detached and ironic, and described in a way that is often very humorous.

**FRONTISPIECE OF *CHILDE HAROLD'S PILGRIMAGE* (1825)**

◁ ***THE RECEPTION OF LORD BYRON AT MISSOLONGHI*, 1861**
This painting by Theodore Vryzakis shows Byron beginning his Greek adventure in Missolonghi. His death in Greece made him a national hero there and promoted the Greek cause in Europe.

▷ ***GEORGE GORDON BYRON*, 1813**
Byron was a brilliant writer with a reckless character. In this portrait by Richard Westall, Byron—at 25—cuts a handsome Romantic figure.

▷ **BALZAC**, 1836
This portrait of the author at the age of 37 by Louis Candide Boulanger was commissioned by Balzac's mistress, Ewelina Hanaska. It shows Balzac dressed in the somewhat monastic robe that he liked to wear at home when writing.

# Honoré de **Balzac**

## 1799–1850, FRENCH

Balzac painted a vast picture of 19th-century French society in the interconnected novels and novellas of *The Human Comedy*. He is considered one of the founding fathers of literary realism.

# "The **secret** of **great fortunes** ... is a **crime forgotten**, because it was **properly** done."

HONORE DE BALZAC, *OLD GORIOT*

Honoré Balzac was born in Tours in central France in 1799. He later added "de" to his name in a spurious claim to aristocratic status. Balzac's father, originally an artisan, was an energetic social climber who made a loveless marriage to a woman of higher status. As a child, Balzac received very little parental attention, and at the age of eight he was sent as a boarder to the Oratory School in Vendôme, not even returning home for holidays. His 1832 novel *Louis Lambert* draws upon this harsh experience of schooling.

## Early struggles

Moving to Paris, where he would spend the rest of his life, Balzac worked as an associate in a law firm, an experience that gave him valuable insight into the petty chicaneries and greed of the propertied classes.

In the 1820s, after rejecting a career in law, he struggled to establish himself as a writer. He wrote for the theater first, without success, and then turned to fiction, churning out anonymous potboilers. Attempts at business ventures in publishing and printing were costly failures. While living on the edge of poverty, he gained entry to the fashionable world through liaisons with various aristocratic women. His struggle to maintain an elegant appearance on a small income provided material for novels such as *The Wild Ass's Skin* (1831) and *Old Goriot* (1835).

## A portrait of society

Balzac's first success as a writer came in 1829 with the historical novel *The Chouans*, which was set in the time of royalist insurrection against the French Republic. In 1832, the year of his celebrated novella *The Vicar of Tours*, he conceived the project of portraying the entirety of French society in a succession of novels. He later named this work *The Human Comedy*, by analogy with Dante's *Divine Comedy*. *Eugénie Grandet* (1833), a powerful study of the corrosive influence of miserliness on human relationships, was his first best seller. A string of other successes followed, from *Old Goriot* and *César Birotteau* (1837) through the three volumes of *Lost Illusions* (1837, 1839, 1843) to *Cousin Bette* (1846) and *Cousin Pons* (1847).

## An eye for detail

The novels of *The Human Comedy* are grouped into categories such as Scenes of Provincial Life, Scenes of Parisian Life, and Scenes of Private Life. They depict a society open to ruthless ambition, in which the strong can make fortunes and the weak go bankrupt. Although Balzac's plots often veer toward melodrama, his work shows an impressive grasp of life at all levels of society, reflected in exhaustive descriptions of clothes and furniture and precise details about wealth and income. The larger-than-life characters are powerfully drawn, and greed, social ambition, and sexual obsession are depicted with clear-eyed cynicism.

Balzac was driven by a constant need for money that persisted even after he had become famous. He often wrote for 15 hours a day, and his output was astonishing; *The Human Comedy* eventually comprised some 90 novels, novellas, and short stories. Always in poor health, he died in 1850 at the age of 51, five months after marrying Polish aristocrat Ewelina Hanaska, his long-term mistress.

△ **BALZAC'S WATCH**
Balzac was an acute observer of class and society. Details such as the shape and style of a pocket watch, for example, could affect his judgment of a character.

## ON STYLE
### Recurring characters

An innovative feature of Balzac's *Human Comedy* was his use of the same characters in different novels. Rastignac, for example, the ambitious young man who is a major character in *Old Goriot*, also appears, or is mentioned, in 17 other novels. Among the other recurring figures are the poet and journalist Lucien de Rubempré, the usurer Gobseck, the underworld villain Vautrin, and the banker Nucingen. A technique now much used in movies and television series, the use of recurring characters creates a sense of an extensive and closely interwoven society.

**THE VILLAIN VAUTRIN, ILLUSTRATED IN AN EDITION OF *OLD GORIOT***

◁ **COUNTRY RETREAT**
Balzac lived in Paris, but often visited the Château de Saché near Tours, which was owned by his friend Jean de Margonne. He wrote at the desk in his bedroom. The house is now preserved as a museum.

# Victor Hugo

## 1802–1883, FRENCH

Hugo was a towering figure in 19th-century French literature. Immensely prodigious, he produced poetry, drama, and novels; he was an active campaigner for the rights of the poor and oppressed.

Born in 1802, Victor Hugo was the third son of a French army officer. His father had joined the army to fight for the cause of the French Revolution and had met Hugo's mother, Sophie Trébuchet, in Brittany, where he had been sent to put down a counterrevolutionary revolt by French Catholic royalists. The stark contrast between his father's firm commitment to the Revolution and his mother's religious monarchism did not make for a happy or stable family, and his parents were soon leading largely separate lives.

Some of Victor's most stimulating early experiences were of journeys with his mother for brief stays with his father on service in Spain and Italy. The exoticism of Spain made an especially strong impression on the growing boy, who later drew on it in adulthood for dramatic works such as *Hernani* (1830) and *Ruy Blas* (1838).

### Early talent
Hugo and his brothers were mostly raised in Paris by their mother. To break their mother's influence on them, their father insisted that they go to boarding school. But it was in vain—the boys grew up Catholic and royalist.

Hugo was astonishingly precocious in his literary talents. By the age of 14, he had already written thousands of lines of verse and at 17 he joined

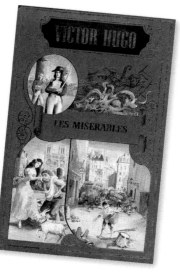

his brothers in founding a literary magazine. Hugo's mother gave her full support to this pursuit of literature, fending off pressure from the boys' father to direct them into more lucrative professions.

By the time his mother died in 1821, Hugo was already in love with his future wife, Adèle Fouchet. It was in order to establish himself as a worthy candidate for her hand that he published his first book of poems, *Odes and Other Poems*, at the age of 20. The couple married in 1822. Thereafter, Hugo was reconciled with his father, and this had a

◁ **LES MISERABLES**
Hugo's most famous work is a story of injustice, heroism, and love. It combines an exciting narrative with an account of France's turbulent revolutionary history.

profound influence on his political views: abandoning monarchism, Hugo became a great admirer of Napoleon Bonaparte, under whom his father had served.

### A Romantic revolution
In the 1820s, Hugo established himself as the leader of the French Romantic movement, expressing a thirst for freedom, in literature and politics. The preface to his epic verse drama *Cromwell*, written in 1827, was a manifesto of French Romanticism, while his 1829 poetry collection *Les Orientales* celebrated the Greek struggle for national liberation from Turkish rule (as well as satisfying contemporary taste for the exotic sensuality of an imaginary East). In the same year, he published the novella *The Last Day of a Condemned Man*, an impassioned protest against the death penalty, and just one year later, he delivered a blow against the restrictions of the classical tradition of French theater in *Hernani*, which brought a Shakespearian freedom to the French stage.

◁ **VICTOR HUGO, 1879**
An aging, dignified Hugo is depicted here by Léon Joseph Bonnat. If Hugo had not established his towering reputation as a writer, he would have been celebrated as a politician and social reformer.

" In the **twentieth century** war will be **dead...** **royalty** will be **dead**, and **dogmas** will be **dead**; but **man will live**. "
VICTOR HUGO

> " It is **man's consolation** that the **future** is to be a **sunrise** rather than a **sunset**. "
>
> VICTOR HUGO, "WILLIAM SHAKESPEARE"

△ *LEOPOLDINE HUGO,* c.1835
This painting of Hugo's daughter is by the French poet and artist Auguste de Châtillon. Léopoldine's death by drowning haunted Hugo for the rest of his life and found expression in elegiac poems such as the famous "At Villequier" (1847).

## IN CONTEXT
### Coups and revolutions

The French Revolution of 1789 initiated a turbulent century in France. Napoleon Bonaparte took power in a military coup in 1799, crowning himself emperor in 1804. Ten years later, a monarchy was restored. In 1830, the July Revolution brought the Orléanist Louis-Philippe to the throne, but in 1848 another revolution created the Second Republic. Three years later, a coup by Napoleon Bonaparte's nephew, Louis-Napoleon, established the Second Empire. This regime, hated by Hugo, lasted until France's defeat in war with Prussia in 1870. The Third Republic was founded and survived after suppressing the Commune uprising in Paris in 1871.

**LOUIS-NAPOLEON,** FRANZ WINTERHALTER, c.1850

▷ **HAUTEVILLE HOUSE**
Hauteville House in St. Peter Port, Guernsey, was Victor Hugo's home for 14 years, when he was in exile from France. He had the house decorated in his own style, and wrote many of his best-known works there.

Hugo sustained his phenomenal literary output in the 1830s. In addition to the successful Gothic novel *The Hunchback of Notre-Dame* (1831), verse collections such as *Autumn Leaves* (1831) and *Songs of the Half-Light* (1835) upheld his claim to be France's leading lyric poet, and the 1838 verse drama *Ruy Blas* proved to be the best of his plays.

### Personal turmoil
Hugo's private life was energetic and turbulent. He had four children with Adèle but their marriage was not a success. She fell in love with the critic Charles-Augustin Sainte-Beuve, a less forceful and more refined man than her husband; and Hugo gave his own ebullient desires free range. A long-term liaison with the actress Juliette Drouet, who devoted her life to him, did not preclude multiple other affairs, including an adulterous relationship with Léonie Biard that resulted in a criminal prosecution instigated by her husband; Hugo escaped prison, Mme. Biard did not. There was also tragedy when his favorite daughter, Léopoldine, and her husband were drowned in a boating accident in 1843.

### Political activity
Hugo sought official recognition under Louis-Philippe's "bourgeois monarchy." He was elected as a member of the Académie Française in 1841 and granted a peerage. However, the revolution of 1848 halted his integration into the establishment (see box, left). Hugo's involvement in politics had, until now, been only theoretical, but with the monarchy again overthrown and the Second Republic established, he put himself forward as a spokesman for freedom and the rights of the "small people," while also rejecting disorder and anarchy. When Louis-Napoleon carried out a coup in December 1851 that turned the Republic into the Second Empire, Hugo was among those who protested on the streets. On the defeated side, he fled into exile in the Channel Islands—initially in Jersey and then in Guernsey.

### Return from exile
In exile, Hugo delivered a scathing attack on Louis-Napoleon's Second Empire in the poetry collection *The Empire in the Pillory* and, less directly, in *Les Misérables*, which he began in the 1840s and completed in 1862.

A vast, 650,000-word novel full of authorial digressions, *Les Misérables* made plain Hugo's identification with the poor in their revolt against wealth and power.

During this time, Hugo became fascinated by spiritualism and séances. His obsession with his dead daughter haunted the poems of *Les Contemplations*, published to acclaim in 1856. His idiosyncratic vision of religion and history played an ever larger part in his poetry, which took on an epic quality in works such as *The Legend of the Ages*, the first collection of which appeared in 1859. The 1866 melodramatic novel *Toilers of the Sea*, set in Guernsey, showed a diminution of his powers.

The fall of the Second Empire after the disasters of the Franco-Prussian War in 1870 brought Hugo back from exile to Paris in time to share the privations of the city under German siege. His attempts to play a political

role in the events that followed—the foundation of the Third Republic and the Commune uprising in Paris—were largely unsuccessful. His life was also darkened by personal loss, his wife dying in 1868 and his sons in 1871 and 1873. But his boundless energy remained, as shown in the completion

of his last novel, *Ninety-Three* (1874); in his continuing sexual conquests; and, from 1876, in his political activity as a senator. Aided by the popular success of his warm and simple treatise *The Art of Being a Grandfather* in 1877, Hugo achieved a kind of apotheosis in his final years as an icon of French

patriotism, republicanism, and the optimistic cult of human progress. His 80th birthday was declared a national holiday—an occasion for celebration. When he died in 1883, he was given a lavish state funeral, and a vast crowd watched as his body was borne to the Pantheon.

△ **LIBERTY LEADING THE PEOPLE**
Hugo took inspiration for his writing from the work of the great Romantic painter Eugène Delacroix. The character of Gavroche in his masterpiece *Les Misérables* is thought to have been influenced by the figure of the pistol-wielding boy in Delacroix's *Liberty Leading the People* (1830), shown here.

## KEY WORKS

### 1822
*Odes and Other Poems*, Hugo's first book, attracts favorable attention from Louis XVIII.

### 1830
*Hernani* receives a delirious reception on its first night, announcing the triumph of Romanticism in France.

### 1831
*The Hunchback of Notre-Dame*, a melodramatic novel set in medieval Paris, confirms Hugo's popular reputation.

### 1856
*Les Contemplations*, a collection of Hugo's lyrical poems on memory, love, and death is published during his exile.

### 1862
*Les Misérables*, is published— an epic story of love and a denunciation of poverty and exploitation.

### 1883
*The Legend of the Ages*, the last volume of Hugo's humanist poetic epic, is published 24 years after the first volume.

# Hans Christian Andersen

## 1805–1875, DANISH

Andersen's life story reads much like one of his fairy tales. He rose from rags to riches to become one of the most widely published authors in literary history—but his personal life was blighted by unrequited love.

Hans Christian Andersen was born in Odense, near Copenhagen. His father died in 1816 and his mother, a washerwoman, struggled to make ends meet and to pay for her son's education. Andersen's exceptional soprano voice brought him to the attention of the Danish Royal Theater in Copenhagen, and even though his hopes of a life on stage were dashed when his voice broke, he made the acquaintance of Jonas Collin, one of the theater's directors. Collin became a benefactor and—with additional financial support from the Danish king, Frederick VI—helped to send Andersen to a secondary school, southwest of Copenhagen.

◁ **CHILDHOOD PERSPECTIVE**
Andersen, pictured here in 1860, was a true innovator in children's literature. His often bittersweet stories reflect the trials of his own childhood.

Although Andersen was unhappy and depressed at the school, it enabled him to gain entrance to the University of Copenhagen in 1828.

A year later, he wrote his first significant work, *A Walk from Holmen's Canal to the East Point of the Island of Amager in the Years 1828 and 1829*, in which the narrator encounters a series of fantastical creatures and characters while journeying along a path in Copenhagen. It was a great success in Denmark. Encouraged, Andersen continued writing novels, poetry, and plays, which received a mixed reception. He developed a love of travel, visiting Scandinavia, Southern Europe, Asia Minor, and Africa—trips that informed his works.

Andersen drew heavily on his own childhood experience in the fairy tales for which he became best known. He imbued these stories with complex and often conflicting emotions, and populated them with archetypal characters from folk stories that resonated across the generations and across cultures. Tales including "The Little Mermaid," "The Emperor's New Clothes," and "Thumbelina" were published as a collection called *Fairy Tales* (1837), but despite their quality and accessibility they barely sold at first in his native Denmark.

### Unfulfilled desires

Andersen never married, but was prone to infatuation. His open passion for Swedish opera singer Jenny Lind is considered the basis for his tale "The Nightingale," and her rejection of him may have led to his writing "The Snow Queen." He also expressed strong feelings for men, including the Grand Duke of Weimar and the famous dancer Harald Scharff, but he declared in a letter that such sentiments "must remain a mystery."

Andersen's stories were translated into English and appeared in the literary magazine *Bentley's Miscellany*, which featured the work of such giants as Charles Dickens. Andersen continued publishing his tales in installments and his worldwide fame grew. His stories are still popular and have influenced generations of children's writers.

△ **THE SNOW QUEEN**
Andersen's stories have fueled a huge industry, from illustrated books and ballet productions to animated films. Disney's box office hit *Frozen* (2013) was inspired by Andersen's "The Snow Queen."

### IN CONTEXT
### Friendship with Dickens

Andersen corresponded with the acclaimed British novelist Charles Dickens, whom he first visited in England in 1847, and then again a decade later. They were both published in the magazine *Bentley's Miscellany* (which Dickens edited for a time) and both wrote about the adversities faced by the poor. But in 1857, Andersen outstayed his welcome at Dickens's Kent home, Gad's Hill Place. He extended his two-week stay to five, and Kate Dickens recalled that her father subsequently described Andersen as "a bony bore." Sensing disapproval, Andersen was contrite and sought to revive the friendship but Dickens wrote a terse letter that brought it to an end.

CHARLES DICKENS AT HIS HOME AT GADSHILL WITH HIS DAUGHTERS

▷ **THE LITTLE MERMAID**
Edvard Eriksen's bronze statue of Andersen's fairy-tale character has been a major tourist attraction in the city of Copenhagen since 1913.

▷ **EDGAR ALLAN POE**, 1848
Poe presented this portrait of himself
to Sarah Helen Whitman—a widowed poet
and essayist whom he met in 1848 and
pursued romantically. The two writers
were briefly engaged but their relationship
proved to be far too stormy to survive.

# Edgar Allan Poe

## 1809–1849, AMERICAN

Creator of the detective story and tales of Gothic terror and suspense,
Poe is a giant of literary history. His life—dogged by alcohol abuse,
poverty, instability, and depression—was as bizarre as his death.

# "I became insane, with long intervals of horrible sanity."

EDGAR ALLAN POE

Writer, poet, editor, and critic, Edgar Allan Poe is best known for his short stories and as the founder of the detective thriller and "dark Romanticism." His parents were both impoverished actors in Boston, Massachusetts, and after the death of his mother when he was two he was fostered by the Allan family from Virginia (he later added "Allan" to his name). In 1815, the family moved to Britain. They stayed there for five years, during which time Poe boarded at Manor House School in London—a miserable experience, which he drew upon in his story "The Fall of the House of Usher."

In 1826, Poe went to the University of Virginia to study languages, but soon ran up large debts from gambling and drinking. By the end of the year, his funds had run dry and he abandoned his studies, enlisting in the US Army where he quickly was promoted to sergeant major. Poe enrolled at West Point Military Academy but soon wanted to leave; he orchestrated his own expulsion in January 1831 by

◁ **VIRGINIA ELIZA CLEMM**
Poe's bride—his first cousin—was half his age when they married in 1835. Her death seven years later sent Poe into the depths of depression.

contravening academy rules. Poe's *Tamerlane and Other Poems*—a slim volume of romantic poetry, inspired by Byron—received little attention when it was published in 1827. It was not until 1833 that the young writer achieved some success, winning a literary prize for "MS. Found In a Bottle," a horror story set on board a ship.

## Serial successes

Poe moved back to Virginia in 1834, where he married his cousin, Virginia Clemm. Unable to make a living from writing fiction, he worked as an editor and critic for various periodicals. It was in these journals that many of his stories first appeared, including "The Fall of the House of Usher" (1839), in which the protagonist's descent into madness is mirrored by the collapse of his decaying house.

This was followed by works such as "The Murders in the Rue Morgue" (1841), considered to be the very first detective story, and "The Black Cat" (1843), a tale of mental deterioration. A breakthrough came in 1845 with the publication of the poem "The Raven," which brought fame, but not wealth.

Poe's stories were published in serial form, which suited his writing style. The installments were often short, and he usually established a powerful atmosphere early on, in order to draw his readers into his tales of Gothic horror and suspense. Many consider that Poe's greatest skill was this ability to create a mood, often of claustrophobia and mounting tension—magnificently accomplished in, for example, "The Fall of the House of Usher" and his final, multilayered tale, "The Cask of Amontillado" (1846).

## A mysterious end

Poe's life came to an end in October 1849, two days after he was found "in great distress" on a Boston street in clothes that were not his. The cause of death is unknown, but speculation has ranged wildly—from drug and alcohol abuse to heart disease, syphilis, and infection from a rabid vampire bat. Only seven people attended his funeral. What is certain is that Poe was well placed to convey the dark, internal anguish of a deranged mind. His fiction frequently hints at the tormented psyche of a writer who precariously straddled the border between insanity and genius.

**BELA LUGOSI IN THE 1935 MOVIE ADAPTATION OF "THE RAVEN"**

### IN CONTEXT
#### Poe's legacy

In a career that lasted a mere decade, Poe transformed the literary landscape. Countless major British and American writers, from Hawthorne, Dickens, Melville, and Stevenson to Wilkie Collins and Agatha Christie, were inspired by Poe's strange genius. His ultrarational French detective C. Auguste Dupin—who first appeared in the "The Murders in the Rue Morgue"—was the forerunner of Conan Doyle's famous supersleuth, Sherlock Holmes.

Prominent late-19th-century French authors, such as Baudelaire, Rimbaud, and Mallarmé, are indebted to Poe's work, as are the symbolist and surrealist movements. His writing has also influenced popular culture—music, television, and cinema (notably the successful movie adaptations of the 1960s)—and it continues to inspire the genres of science fiction and fantasy fiction. In the last 50 years or so, his work has had particular resonance for literary theorists (including structuralists and post-structuralists), as well as for those interested in the relationship between literature and psychoanalytic theory.

◁ **THE POE COTTAGE**
In 1846, Poe, his wife, and her mother moved into this modest cottage in the village of Fordham (now part of the Bronx), New York. The house was preserved and relocated to a nearby park after the author's death.

# Charles Dickens

## 1812–1870, ENGLISH

The quintessential Victorian author, Dickens overcame adversity to achieve great success with his serialized novels. His works are known for their epic scope, taut plots, and richly drawn characters.

Charles Dickens enjoyed a happy, unhampered childhood. The second of eight children of John and Elizabeth Dickens, Charles John Huffam was born in Portsmouth, England, where his father worked in the Navy Pay Office. Three years later, the family briefly relocated to Fitzrovia in London before moving to Kent.

### Early influences

While his father was gainfully employed, the family could afford to educate Charles, first at a dame school (a type of elementary school that was usually run from the homes of older, female teachers), then at William Giles's school in Chatham. The young Dickens was a voracious reader, raiding his father's library for the books of Tobias Smollet and Henry Fielding, whose episodic adventure novels featured witty or tragic heroes, such as the foundling Tom Jones. Dickens was entranced by their meticulously planned plots and the clear moral distinctions that they drew. He was also hugely influenced by *Arabian Nights*, a collection of tales from the Middle East that had been translated into English early in the 18th century. He read and reread the tales, returning to the scenes of love and derring-do described in a range of genres, from tragedy to comedy.

Like many of his characters, Dickens suffered a dramatic change of fortune in his youth. Having amassed a huge burden of debt, Dickens's father was sent to the Marshalsea debtors' prison in Southwark in 1824, where he was jailed for money owed to a baker. The family joined their father in prison, as was customary at the time, but the impressionable Charles, just 12 years old, and his older sister Fanny were excluded. Charles had to lodge in Camden Town with an aging family friend, Elizabeth Roylance, who later became the inspiration behind Mrs. Pipchin in *Dombey and Son* (1846–

△ **WRITING INSTRUMENTS**
Dickens was very particular about his writing supplies, and in his letters often referred to the quality of the ink and quills at his disposal. The image above shows part of his manuscript of *The Pickwick Papers*.

## IN CONTEXT
### Victorian London

Dickens is the quintessential Victorian author and produced almost all of his work during the queen's long reign (1837–1901). City life in his time was cruel and often short: about a quarter of Londoners suffered from typhus in the 1840s, and the average life expectancy was just 27. The word "Dickensian" is now often used to describe the unsanitary, smog-filled streets inhabited by London's poor. Dickens "walked about the black streets of London fifteen or twenty miles many a night" so that he could observe London society up close. His work provided a running commentary on slum conditions, the maltreatment of children, and the disparity between the English classes. Throughout his career, he effected social change through storytelling, raising awareness among those who could provide charity.

*STREETS OF VICTORIAN LONDON, GUSTAVE DORE, 1782*

> "Whether **I** shall turn out to be **the hero** of **my own life** ... these **pages must show**."
>
> CHARLES DICKENS, *DAVID COPPERFIELD*

▷ **CHARLES DICKENS, 1859**
This portrait by William Powell Frith shows Dickens at the height of his fame. The writer is in his study at his house in Bloomsbury, with part of *A Tale of Two Cities* on the desk in front of him.

## ON STYLE
### Characterization

Dickens had a lifelong passion for the theater, and many of his novels have been adapted for both stage and screen. Theater provided him with inspiration for his characterizations and dialogue. The names that he gave his characters were so distinctive that they sometimes became incorporated into vernacular language—a Scrooge (from *A Christmas Carol*), for example, is a miser, while a Pecksniff (from *Martin Chuzzlewit*) is a hypocrite. Dickens imbued his characters with depth and intrigue. From the cockney twang of his pickpocket Artful Dodger in *Oliver Twist* to the Kentish drawl of kindly blacksmith Joe Gargery in *Great Expectations*, Dickens's use of dialect was masterly, conveying a powerful sense of place and also adding great characterization to his compelling fictional portraits.

HELENA BONHAM CARTER AS MISS HAVISHAM IN *GREAT EXPECTATIONS*

1848). This was followed by a stint living in the attic room in the household of Archibald Russell, a jolly, fat man, later immortalized as Mr. Garland in *The Old Curiosity Shop* (1840–1841). Fanny and Charles were allowed access to Marshalsea, and Dickens wove the setting into his later novel *Little Dorrit* (1855–1857).

### Poverty and redemption

With no means of support, Dickens had no choice but to abandon his studies. In order to pay for his lodgings, he worked in a bootblacking warehouse in Charing Cross, then on Chandos Street, where workers were put on display to passersby. This bitter experience had a profound effect on Dickens, sowing the seeds of his later passion for social reform. He later addressed many of the issues about which he felt strongly—such as the appalling conditions endured by prisoners, the misery of the poor and homeless, and the plight of London's prostitutes—in his most closely autobiographical novel, *David Copperfield* (1850).

By a stroke of good luck, Dickens's father inherited the sum of £450 and was able to pay off his creditors. The family returned home, but to Charles's lasting anguish, his mother did not immediately call for him to return. He wrote: "I never afterwards forgot, I never shall forget, I never can forget, that my mother was warm for my being sent back [to work]."

### Career path

With the family now clear of financial trouble, Dickens was able to resume his studies for three years, joining the Wellington House Academy until 1827. He left there to become a junior clerk in a Gray's Inn law office, and it was there that he built up his knowledge

◁ **OLIVER TWIST**
In 1846, Dickens published *The Adventures of Oliver Twist*, a single-volume version of his story. It explored childhood poverty and slavelike apprenticeships. The book was illustrated with 24 steel-engraved plates by George Cruikshank.

of the legal system—a system that shamelessly punished the poor and protected the rich. He famously satirized its cruelty in no less than three novels—*Nicholas Nickleby* (1839), *Dombey and Son* (1848), and *Bleak House* (1853).

Disillusioned by the law, Dickens sought a new direction in life. He was already known as a talented mimic by his friends and colleagues and had acted in some of London's minor theaters, so he was initially drawn to the stage. However, he postponed a scheduled audition with a professional actor-manager, and continued to write. After his story "A Dinner at Poplar Walk" was accepted for publication in the *Monthly Magazine*, Dickens's career as a writer began.

Changes in Victorian society, notably higher levels of literacy and growing mechanization in the printing industry, drove demand for

newspapers and journals, and in turn for good writers. Dickens, helped by his uncle William Barrow, found work on *The Mirror of Parliament*, where he reported on parliamentary debates; at around this time, he also began to cover election campaigns for *The Morning Chronicle*.

Invigorated and inspired by his new job, he began to write a series of his own stories, observations, and character sketches, which were published in various periodicals under the title "Sketches by Boz" (Dickens's nickname). In 1836, he began working with the respected London publishers Chapman and Hall on a series of illustrated stories, but after the death of the original illustrator, Dickens suggested that the stories be focused more on the text than on the images. The first installment of the resulting serial publication—*The Pickwick Papers*—sold 500 copies when published in March 1836; the last episode sold 40,000 in the following year.

### Social circles

Dickens's career in journalism connected him with influential people in London, and the editor of the *Chronicle*, George Hogarth, took the young writer under his wing. Dickens was delighted to visit the Hogarth family in their Fulham home, and it was here

▷ **PICKWICK MERCHANDISE**
*The Pickwick Papers* was a commercial sensation, spawning a wide range of merchandise, from Pickwick cigars to china figures of the book's central characters.

△ **BLOOMSBURY HOME**
1836 was a significant year for Dickens: he married Catherine Hogarth and they moved into their first family home, at 48 Doughty Street in Bloomsbury, London. It was here that Charley, the first of their 10 children, was born.

that he met his future wife, Catherine Hogarth, and her sisters. Gaining in status and popularity, he also joined the bachelor set that met regularly at the home of the novelist William Harrison Ainsworth. Other members of the group included Benjamin Disraeli and John Macrone, who became Dickens's first publisher.

In November 1836, Dickens took on the editorship of *Bentley's Miscellany*, a monthly magazine in which he published his story *Oliver Twist* in serial form over a period of two years.

Each installment was illustrated by George Cruikshank—one of several talented artists with whom Dickens worked throughout his career.

### Foreign adventures

Dickens became a prolific author, producing around one novel a year, and his commercial success was boosted by his business acumen—evident when he took control of his work, buying back the publishing rights from John Macrone and Richard Bentley. However, while his fame

increased, his personal life seemed to falter. Dickens became critical of his wife, Catherine, complaining of her lethargy and dull intellect. He started to make inappropriate passes at young women in public, and began to spend more time away from home on reading tours and other expeditions.

Dickens embarked upon a series of foreign excursions, including trips to the US and Canada. Part of his mission there was to influence the reform of copyright law, because his own work had been widely pirated, but

" A man in **public life** expects to be sneered at—it is the **fault of his elevated situation**, and not of himself. "

CHARLES DICKENS, *NICHOLAS NICKLEBY*

> "It is strange with **how little notice**, good, bad, or indifferent, a **man may live** and die **in London**."

CHARLES DICKENS, *SKETCHES BY BOZ*

△ **ELLEN (NELLY) TERNAN**
Ternan became Dickens's mistress in 1857; some historians believe that the couple had at least one child together.

◁ **HOUSEHOLD EDITION**
Dickens's works became so popular that they were issued in well-priced multiple-volume "household editions" that made them affordable for almost all readers.

his US journeys also exposed him firsthand to the iniquities of slavery and poverty, and so helped to crystallize his views on social justice and the urgent need for reform. On his return to England, and after a visit to the Field Lane Ragged School—an institution that was set up to help London's starved, illiterate street children—he resolved to address the issue of poverty and inequality in his writing. His next novel, *A Christmas Carol*, did just that, and became enormously popular—the first edition sold out within just five days of its publication in December 1843.

As Dickens entered middle age, his work took on a more serious tone; in 1853, he produced *Bleak House*, a satire of the iniquitous legal system, and he followed this a year later with *Hard Times*, in which he lambasted the harsh philosophy of utilitarianism, the idea that the moral value of an action is measured by its utility, which was responsible for the poor conditions endured by people in their workplaces across the country. At the end of the decade, he published his most somber novel, *A Tale of Two Cities* (1859), a work of historical fiction set in London and Paris during the years of the French Revolution.

## Later works
In 1956, Dickens realized a long-held ambition when he bought Gad's Hill Place, a large country home in Kent, which he had coveted from childhood. Around this time, he confided to his friend (and later biographer) John

Forster that he had long struggled in his relationship with his wife, Catherine. His marital difficulties were not helped by his ardent interest in the actress Ellen Ternan, whom he had first seen perform at The Haymarket Theatre. When Dickens helped to stage the play *The Frozen Deep* (written by his friend Wilkie Collins), he recruited Ternan—along with her mother and sister—to the cast. Despite a 27-year

## IN PROFILE
### Hablot Knight Browne

Dickens worked with a number of artists whose work illustrated his stories: indeed only two of his major novels—*Hard Times* and *Great Expectations*—were not illustrated. Dickens chose the talented engraver and watercolorist Hablot Knight Browne (known as "Phiz" to Dickens's "Boz") to illustrate *The Pickwick Papers*, and the two worked together closely for the following 23 years. In total, Brown contributed more than 700 designs for Dickens's books, adapting his work to match changes in the writer's style and outlook, in one of the most fruitful collaborations in publishing history.

*LITTLE DORRIT* (ILLUSTRATION), HABLOT KNIGHT BROWNE

age difference, the two began an affair and Charles formally separated from Catherine in 1858.

Dickens stayed with Ternan until his death, setting up households for her under pseudonyms and living with her in France, although he balked at taking her on a second tour of the US due to the negative publicity that such a flouting of convention would attract.

In the final decade of his life, Dickens produced *Great Expectations*, *Our Mutual Friend*, and *The Mystery of* *Edwin Drood*, which was unfinished at the time of his death. In 1865, he was involved in a train crash while traveling with Ternan and her mother to Folkestone. There were 10 fatalities and Dickens's health was severely affected by the accident. He lost his voice for more than two weeks, and by 1868 he was beginning to experience episodes of dizziness and even paralysis. He had a stroke that year and collapsed while on a reading tour in Preston in 1869.

Dickens died on June 8, 1870 at Gad's Hill Place following another stroke. In his will, he left generous amounts of money to his family and to his close colleague, John Forster, and even bequeathed a sum of nearly £20 to each of his servants. He had requested burial at Rochester Cathedral but the nation demanded that "England's most popular author" be interred at Poet's Corner, Westminster Abbey. A group of 12 family members and friends attended his intimate funeral.

△ **DICKENS'S DREAM, 1875**
This unfinished painting by Robert William Buss shows the writer relaxing in his study at Gad's Hill Place, surrounded by many of the characters from his novels. The artist was a great admirer of Dickens, despite having been passed over for the commission to illustrate *The Pickwick Papers*.

# KEY WORKS

**1836–37**
The first of Dickens's full-length works, *The Pickwick Papers*, is published in 20 installments.

**1837–39**
The *Adventures of Oliver Twist* appears as a monthly serial in the magazine *Bentley's Miscellany*.

**1849–50**
Dickens's most autobiographical work, *David Copperfield*, is published.

**1852–53**
*Bleak House*, Dickens's ninth novel, is considered by many, including respected critic G. K. Chesterton, to be his best work.

**1860–61**
Dickens's *Great Expectations*, is published. It explores social tensions between the haves and the have-nots.

**1870**
Dickens dies, leaving *The Mystery of Edwin Drood* incomplete. Its conclusion has perplexed readers ever since.

# Charlotte and Emily Brontë

**1816–1855 (CHARLOTTE), 1818–1848 (EMILY), ENGLISH**

Charlotte and Emily Brontë transformed English literature with their radical novels that often focused on the complex interior life of women. The sisters both lived harsh lives that were cut tragically short by illness.

The Brontë family arrived in the picturesque Pennine village of Haworth, West Yorkshire, England, in 1820. Reverend Patrick Brontë was originally from Ireland and his wife—formerly Maria Branwell—was of Cornish descent. Patrick had left his homeland to improve his career prospects, and in 1806 he graduated in theology from St. John's College, Cambridge. There, he changed the spelling of his Irish last name, Brunty (or Prunty), to Brontë, which translates from Greek as "thunder."

Patrick and Maria met in Yorkshire. Maria had moved there to support her aunt in the management of a new Methodist training school. Patrick, now a curate in Shropshire, was also invited to work at the school, as an external examiner. They fell in love at first sight and married soon after, moving to Hartshead, where their first daughter, Maria, was born. Elizabeth, Charlotte, Branwell (their only son), Emily, and Anne were born in Thornton, before the family took up residence at Haworth Parsonage.

## IN CONTEXT
### The literary world

The well-stocked library at Haworth Parsonage meant that the Brontës had access to a number of key texts: not only religious works, but books by authors such as Bunyan, Byron, Homer, Milton, Scott, and Virgil. Living in the countryside in the north of England, however, the sisters were cut off from London literary society.

Emily died soon after she had made a name with *Wuthering Heights* (but had not revealed her true identity). Charlotte lived to enjoy fame and met with various writers, including Thackeray. But after meeting Dickens, she said that she did not like him and refused to see him socially.

**HAWORTH PARSONAGE, HOME TO THE BRONTË FAMILY**

◁ **THE BRONTË SISTERS, c.1834**
This portrait of the Brontës shows Anne (left), Emily (center), and Charlotte (right). It was painted by their brother, Branwell, who originally included his own image in the work (center), but later painted over it.

## Tragedy strikes

The Brontës' life at Haworth took a tragic turn in 1821, when their mother, Maria, died from ovarian or uterine cancer, leaving six children under the age of eight. The sisters later fictionalized this early trauma by depicting many of their female characters as motherless or orphaned. Their aunt, Elizabeth Branwell, moved to the parsonage to help her brother-in-law with the children and the overall running of the household. In 1824, the four oldest girls were sent to boarding school in Cowan Bridge, Lancashire, with the purpose of later becoming governesses. Their father, despite his limited financial resources, wanted them to receive a good education. But the

▷ **REVEREND PATRICK BRONTË**
The father of one of Britain's most famous literary families outlived his wife and his children. This portrait was taken in 1860, the year before he died, at 84.

" ... we were wholly **dependent** on **each other**, on **books** and **study**, for the **enjoyment** and **occupations** of life. "

CHARLOTTE BRONTË

Eng. by O JEWITT. DUSFIELD OF DERBY

△ **COWAN BRIDGE SCHOOL**
A 19th-century wood engraving shows the school in Tunstall that was made famous by Charlotte Brontë's depiction of it as "Lowood School" in *Jane Eyre*.

▽ **MINIATURE BOOKS**
These dainty "Little Books," created by the Brontës—shown alongside one of their quills—are hand sewn, and written in miniature script.

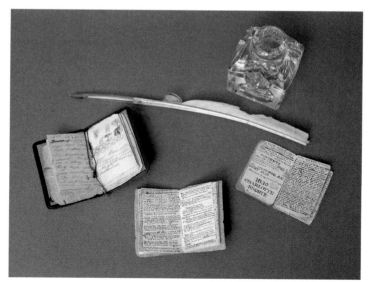

experience, reworked in Charlotte's depiction of Lowood School in *Jane Eyre*, was far from empowering. The dismal conditions, including poor food hygiene, had tragic consequences: Maria and Elizabeth contracted consumption (tuberculosis) and were sent home, but died in May and June of 1825.

From that point on, Charlotte and Emily were educated at Haworth with Branwell and Anne. In addition to being enlightened, their father was kind, buying toys and books for them on request. He stocked the parsonage with a respectable library, and their aunt—who had a personal income from her wealthy family—subscribed to magazines, which Charlotte later admitted to reading secretly and with immense pleasure.

## Imaginative play

Led by Charlotte and Branwell, the children devised elaborate imaginative kingdoms (Glass Town, Angria, and Gondal), ripe with intrigue. These three kingdoms were the inspiration for various articles and poems that were published in their own miniature "magazine," *Branwell's Blackwood Magazine* (which Charlotte renamed *The Young Men's Magazine*). Charlotte wrote six of the nine editions and took the editorial name "Captain Tree," but

also signed her work as "the genius, C. B." The magazines measured just $1\frac{2}{5}$ in by $2\frac{2}{5}$ in (35 mm by 61 mm), as if produced by—and for—Branwell's 12 toy soldiers, which had been given to him by his father.

Emily was far more focused on writing stories and poetry for the fantasy island Gondal, which were created and shared with her younger sister, Anne. But of these, only a few poems by Emily have survived.

The children also spent time on the moors that rose behind Haworth's back door. It is this wild and rugged landscape that dominates Emily's only novel, *Wuthering Heights*, which was to become a classic of English fiction. Brimming with Gothic elements (supernatural events, ominous settings, and foreboding signs), it is an intense tale of desire, passion, and revenge. Wuthering Heights, the

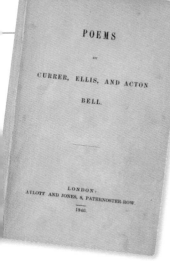

◁ **POEMS, FIRST EDITION**
The Brontës' first published work and their only public collaboration, *Poems* (1846), includes 19 of Emily's poems and 21 each by Charlotte and Anne.

At the age of 20, Emily secured a job as a teacher, but could not deal with the 17-hour workday. She returned to Haworth and took on domestic duties there until 1842, when Aunt Branwell stepped in to provide an income that enabled Emily and Charlotte to travel to Brussels together to improve their French and German, under the instruction of Constantin Héger, so that they could eventually set up their own boarding school at Haworth. Both Emily and Charlotte were diligent students, although Emily did not take to life in Belgium and felt somewhat out of place. Their stay there came to an abrupt end, however, when their aunt died, and they returned home to England.

Charlotte had nevertheless forged a link in Brussels and she went back to teach there the following year. Her letters reveal that she had developed a passion for Constantin Héger, which seems largely unrequited. Although the experience did not end positively, it inspired her novel *The Professor* (which was written in 1847 but published posthumously in 1857), some of the material from which she used in her final novel, *Villette* (1853).

## A secret passion

The sisters were reunited at Haworth from 1844. Their attempt to set up a school, however, failed, and so Emily secretly turned to her poetry, writing in two notebooks, which she was careful to hide from her siblings.

To Emily's great dismay, Charlotte found the books and argued insistently that the verses be published. Around this time, their younger sister, Anne, revealed that she, too, had been

### IN PROFILE
### Anne Brontë

Anne was the youngest, least famous and, according to some, woefully overlooked member of the three literary Brontës. Born in 1820, she spent most of her short life in and around Haworth. In addition to her poetry, Anne wrote two novels: *Agnes Grey* (1847), a tale of endurance and suffering that fictionalizes her experiences working as a governess for a wealthy family; and *The Tenant of Wildfell Hall* (1848), her more famous novel, credited to Acton Bell, which is a powerful account of a woman's courageous bid to gain independence from an abusive husband. Anne Brontë died of tuberculosis in 1849, at the age of 30.

▽ **TOP WITHENS, NEAR HAWORTH**
This remote and ruined farmhouse on the windswept Yorkshire moors is believed to have inspired the Earnshaws' house in Emily Brontë's *Wuthering Heights*.

gloom-laden house on the moors, is a site of claustrophobia and abuse, and a symbol of the psychological turmoil of the book's protagonists.

### Early careers
The highly charged creative atmosphere of Haworth Parsonage was dispelled by Patrick Brontë's concern that his daughters should earn a living. So from 1831 to 1832, Charlotte trained as a governess at Roe Head school in Mirfield. She returned to the school in 1835 to teach. In 1836, Emily attended the school as her pupil but became homesick; Anne then took her place.

In 1833, at the age of 17, Charlotte wrote her first novella, *The Green Dwarf*, using the pen name Wellesley, and she continued writing poetry while teaching at Roe Head. Her writing was a source of great comfort at that time—she felt despondent and isolated at the school, describing her students as "fat-headed oafs." After three years, she became a private governess in various Yorkshire homes, and wrote to Emily of even more misery and indignation: "a private governess has no existence, is not considered as a living and rational being except as connected with the wearisome duties she has to fulfill."

" This then is the **authoress**, the **unknown power** whose **books** have set **all London** talking, reading, speculating ... "

ANNE ISABELLE THACKERAY RITCHIE (ON CHARLOTTE BRONTË)

△ **HAWORTH VILLAGE**
The haunting, rugged moors above the village of Haworth, West Yorkshire, formed the ever-present backdrop to the Brontës' life and work.

writing verse in private; the three sisters eventually resolved to publish their work jointly.

They compiled a slim collection of poetry, which was self-published through Aylott & Jones under the pen names Currer, Ellis, and Acton Bell. Charlotte later explained that they had made the decision to use pen names because they had "the vague impression that authoresses are liable to be looked on with prejudice." In later years, the poems—particularly those by Emily (as Ellis)—earned considerable admiration and, in 1941, nearly a century after Emily's death, her complete poems—almost 200 in all—were published in recognition of their literary merit. After publication of the book in 1846, however, just two copies were sold. The reaction of the sisters to such a poor debut is not recorded, but Emily certainly turned from writing poetry to focus on prose. But now that they had unveiled their passion for writing, their search for a publisher became central.

△ **EMILY'S ART AND GEOMETRY BOX**
All the Brontë children studied painting and drawing: the girls mostly created watercolor landscapes and botanical illustrations, while Branwell produced portraits in oil.

" *Wuthering Heights* was hewn in a **wild workshop,** with **simple tools,** out of **homely materials**. "

CHARLOTTE BRONTË

## KEY WORKS

**1846**
Poems is published. Funded and written by Anne, Charlotte, and Emily, it uses male pseudonyms.

**1847**
Charlotte's novel Jane Eyre is credited to the pen name Currer Bell and becomes an instant success on publication.

**1847**
Wuthering Heights, Emily's first and only novel, is published just months after her sister's book, Jane Eyre.

**1849**
Charlotte publishes Shirley soon after the tragic deaths of her siblings Branwell, Emily, and Anne.

**1853**
Charlotte's Villette, seen as her most mature work, revisits themes of her earlier texts, such as female identity.

**1857**
The Professor is published posthumously and draws on Charlotte's experience of life in Brussels.

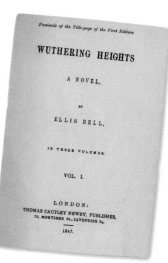

△ **WUTHERING HEIGHTS**
Emily Brontë's only novel, credited to Ellis Bell, was initially published in three volumes. The title page of the first volume of the first edition (1847) is shown here.

### Going public

On April 6, 1846, Charlotte wrote to Aylott & Jones that "C., E., and A. Bell are now preparing for the press a work of fiction, consisting of three distinct and unconnected tales": these were Charlotte's The Professor, Emily's Wuthering Heights, and Anne's Agnes Grey. But it was the publisher Thomas Newby who eventually consented to publish the latter two novels. The Professor, although declined by several publishers, won encouragement from Smith, Elder & Co., who asked to see longer works by Currer Bell. In August 1847, Charlotte sent them Jane Eyre: An Autobiography—it was published six weeks later. The meticulously plotted bildungsroman (coming-of-age novel), underpinned by issues of identity, gender, race, and class, follows the heroine's progress from youth to adulthood.

The anonymous authors created shock waves in literary circles. The visceral scenes of cruelty and raw emotional content in Wuthering Heights met with shock, outrage, and unabashed admiration in equal measure. Jane Eyre similarly baffled but impressed readers. George Henry Lewes, the partner of George Eliot, noted, in his review for Fraser's Magazine, that the characters were "drawn with unusual mastery," but that

the style was "peculiar." He suggested that the author might be a woman— much to Charlotte's disappointment, as she felt that this was a distraction and invited unwanted speculation.

### Dark years

Emily was not to complete another novel. The sisters' domestic life was plagued with ill health—their father had cataracts and their brother had squandered his talents, becoming an alcoholic and possibly also a laudanum (opium) addict. He died in September 1848. Emily became consumptive and died in December of the same year, at just 30; she was so thin that her coffin was only 16 in (40 cm) wide. The youngest sister, Anne, followed Emily in May 1849.

In the wake of so much loss, Charlotte's second novel, Shirley (a bleak tale of technological change

and social discord and hardship), which she had begun in 1848, was arguably less powerful than Jane Eyre. But again, writing was a comfort for Charlotte, this time in bereavement. Villette, depicting adventure and romance in a French-speaking school, was published four years later and met with critical and public approval, although Lucy's character was seen by some as unfeminine. Before the publication of Villette, which was to be her final novel, Charlotte agreed to marry her father's curate, Arthur Bell Nichols. After some hesitation, and encouragement from fellow author Elizabeth Gaskell (who wrote the first biography of Charlotte), she went ahead with the wedding in 1854. Tragically, however, she died while pregnant with her first child, just months after her marriage, at the age of 38.

### IN CONTEXT
### Representing gender

Female characters in 19th-century fiction were generally represented in terms of their physical appearance and beauty (or lack of it), and as either submissive and angelic or oversexed and rebellious. The Brontës upturned such vapid stereotypes—both Jane Eyre and Wuthering Heights focus on the complex inner worlds of their female protagonists: Cathy Earnshaw, wild and melancholic; Jane Eyre, stoic and resourceful; Bertha Mason, the condemned, broken rebel. The 19th-century critic Elizabeth Eastlake condemned Jane Eyre as "the personification of an unregenerate and undisciplined spirit."

FLIRTATION, ARTIST UNKNOWN, c.1882

# Directory

## William Blake

1757–1827, ENGLISH

A poet, artist, and mystic, Blake was the son of a London shopkeeper. He claimed to have seen his first vision, of angels in a tree, at the age of 10. Trained as an artist, he became an outstanding, innovative printmaker. From the *Songs of Innocence* onward, Blake's poetry was published with his own illustrations. Many of his best-known verses appeared in *Songs of Experience*, including "The Tyger," "The Sick Rose," and "London." Far exceeding these short poems in quantity were his long prophetic books, such as *The Book of Thel* and *The Marriage of Heaven and Hell*, in which he expounded his social and religious views in terms of a complex private mythology. Much of his poetry attacks the corruption of contemporary society and protests at its frustration of physical desire. His most famous poem, "Jerusalem," is a vivid expression of social idealism rooted in religious faith.

**KEY WORKS:** *Songs of Innocence*, 1789; *The Marriage of Heaven and Hell*, 1790–1793; *Songs of Experience*, 1794; *Milton*, 1804–1808

△ *MADAME DE STAEL*, AFTER FRANÇOIS GÉRARD, c.1849

## Friedrich Schiller

1759–1805, GERMAN

Germany's most important Romantic dramatist, Schiller was training to be an army doctor when he wrote his first play, *The Robbers*. A violent melodrama, the work epitomized the rebellious emotional extremism of the *Sturm und Drang* (Storm and Stress) period of German Romanticism and caused a sensation when it was first performed, applauded by the public and condemned by the authorities.

Later, Schiller became associated with Goethe in the movement known as Weimar Classicism, developing a complex theory of aesthetics and a more subtle view of human freedom. A historian as well as a playwright, Schiller wrote a stream of fact-based historical verse dramas on themes of oppression, injustice, and resistance. His poetry ranged from the elevated sentiments of the "Ode to Joy"—later set to music by Beethoven—to lively ballads such as the "Cranes of Ibycus" (1797). He died of tuberculosis at the age of 45.

**KEY WORKS:** *The Robbers*, 1781; *Don Carlos*, 1787; *The Wallenstein Trilogy*, 1796–1799; *William Tell*, 1804

## ◁ Madame de Staël

1766–1817, FRENCH

A novelist and intellectual, Mme. de Staël is recognized as one of the founders of French Romanticism. She was born Anne-Louise Germaine Necker, the daughter of a Swiss banker who became France's finance minister under Louis XVI. As a child, she met stars of the Enlightenment at her mother's Parisian salon. Despite an arranged marriage to the Swedish ambassador, Baron de Staël-Holstein, she lived an independent life. The French Revolution of 1789 and the subsequent seizure of power by Napoleon Bonaparte forced her into long periods of exile. In the 1800s, her salon at Coppet in Switzerland was a center of resistance to Napoleon's rule. Her two novels, *Delphine* and *Corinne*, focus on the emotions of strong female characters embroiled in a conflict between love and duty in a patriarchal society. Her 1800 essay "On Literature" was a groundbreaking examination of the influence of social conditions on writing.

**KEY WORKS:** *Delphine*, 1802; *Corinne, or Italy*, 1807; *Ten Years' Exile*, 1821

## Samuel Taylor Coleridge

1772–1834, ENGLISH

One of the leading poets of the Romantic movement, Coleridge was a radical in his early years and once planned to found a commune in the US. Starting in 1797 he wrote in collaboration with Wordsworth, producing the conversation poems "Frost at Midnight" and "This Lime Tree Bower My Prison," as well as the famous "Rime of the Ancient Mariner," a tale of sin and redemption narrated with hallucinatory vividness in a ballad style. "The Ancient Mariner" was published alongside Wordsworth's work in *Lyrical Ballads* (1798).

Another poem of this fertile period, the exotic "Kubla Khan" (which was allegedly the product of an interrupted dream), did not appear in print until 1816. Coleridge suffered for several years from anxiety and depression, ill health, and opium addiction. In an unhappy and failing marriage, and infatuated with another woman, his distress is evident in the moving ode "Dejection." Coleridge's last years were given to philosophical musings on the nature of the creative imagination.

**KEY WORKS:** "The Rime of the Ancient Mariner," 1798; "Dejection: An Ode," 1802; "Kubla Khan," 1816; *Biographia Literaria*, 1817

△ *STENDHAL*, OLOF JOHAN SÖDERMARK, 1840

## △ Stendhal

### 1783–1842, FRENCH

Marie-Henri Beyle, who wrote under the pseudonym Stendhal, was a novelist who brought the analytical rationalism of the Enlightenment to bear upon the emotional subject matter of the Romantic era. The son of a provincial lawyer, Stendhal experienced the excitement of travel and action while working for Napoleon's military services stationed in Italy. His writing career began after the fall of Napoleon in 1815.

A serial womanizer, he used his own experiences as the basis for a clinical analysis of romantic passion in the theoretical work *On Love* (1822). His most famous novels, *Le Rouge et le Noir* and *La Chartreuse de Parme*, recount the adventures of energetic young heroes driven by love or cynical ambition to challenge the social order. The books are written with exceptional verve and spontaneity—especially *La Chartreuse*, allegedly completed in seven weeks. The autobiographical *The Life of Henri Brulard*, published posthumously, contains penetrating psychological insights.

**KEY WORKS:** *Armance*, 1827; *Le Rouge et le Noir*, 1830; *La Chartreuse de Parme*, 1839; *The Life of Henri Brulard*, 1895

## Alessandro Manzoni

### 1785–1873, ITALIAN

Manzoni is remembered chiefly for his masterpiece, the novel *The Betrothed*, which made a vital contribution to the growth of an Italian sense of national identity. Born into a distinguished Milanese family, he began his career as a poet and dramatist. His verse drama, *Il Conte di Carmagnola*, was praised by Goethe, and his poem "The Fifth of May," written on the death of Napoleon, became one of the most popular lyrics in the Italian language.

*The Betrothed* is a love story set in the 17th century, when Milan was a plague-ridden city under Spanish rule. Its radicalism lay in the choice of peasants as its hero and heroine, and in its evocation of the intense hardships of foreign rule at a time when northern Italy was dominated by Austria. Manzoni produced no more significant creative work after that, spending the remainder of his life quietly on his estate outside Milan.

**KEY WORKS:** *Il Conte di Carmagnola*, 1820; "The Fifth of May," 1821; *The Betrothed*, 1825–1827

## Percy Bysshe Shelley

### 1792–1822, ENGLISH

The most rebellious of the English Romantic poets, Shelley was expelled from his university for professing atheism and eloped with 16-year-old schoolgirl Harriet Westbrook. The marriage soon broke down and Harriet killed herself. Shelley then married his lover, Mary Godwin (who later wrote the novel *Frankenstein*). From 1818, he lived in Italy, where most of his best-known verse was written. At the age of 30, he drowned in a boating accident at sea and was cremated on the beach at Viareggio.

Deploying virtuoso technique, his poetry expresses an idealistic view of life tempered by personal depression. Some works, such as "The Masque of Anarchy" (1819), were explicit attacks on British government and society. Others, such as "Ozymandias," voice a generalized contempt for power. Shelley's belief in poetry as an agent of political and moral change, evident in his essay "A Defence of Poetry," found its finest lyrical expression in his "Ode to the West Wind."

**KEY WORKS:** "Ozymandias," 1818; *Prometheus Unbound*, 1820; "Ode to the West Wind," 1820; "Adonais," 1821

## John Keats

### 1795–1821, ENGLISH

The quintessential Romantic poet, Keats was the son of a London stable keeper. He abandoned his study of medicine to concentrate on poetry, but his first collection was largely ignored and the long poem *Endymion* received scathing reviews. However, he never lost confidence in his own genius, and in six years' writing he produced odes, sonnets, medieval romances, and epic blank verse, as well as copious letters containing statements of his poetic philosophy that was based on "the holiness of the heart's affections and the truth of the imagination." Contracting tuberculosis, Keats traveled to Rome in search of a cure but died there at the age of 25.

**KEY WORKS:** *Poems*, 1817; *Endymion*, 1818; *Lamia, Isabella, The Eve of St. Agnes and other Poems*, 1820

## Heinrich Heine

### 1797–1856, GERMAN

Heine brought Romanticism down to earth with political commitment, satirical wit, and everyday language. Born into a German Jewish family, he studied law but found progress in this career blocked by anti-Semitism. His early poems were collected in *The Book of Songs*, published in 1827. Love lyrics with a dash of malice, many were later set to music.

In 1831, Heine moved to Paris; from this self-imposed exile he was able to attack German authoritarianism and complacency in political journalism and satirical verse, most notably the epic "Germany: A Winter's Tale." His late poems are haunted by sickness and death. His books were banned in Germany during his lifetime and then again by the Nazi regime, 80 years after his death.

**KEY WORKS:** *The Book of Songs*, 1827; "Germany: A Winter's Tale," 1844; *Romanzero*, 1851

## ▷ Alexandre Dumas

1802–1870, FRENCH

Dumas's historical novels were best sellers in their day and have made an enduring contribution to popular culture. The son of a general, Dumas achieved his first success with the history play *Henry III and his Court*, staged when the Parisian craze for Romantic drama was taking off in 1829. He wrote other successful plays before his first novel, *Captain Paul*, appeared in serial form in 1838.

Feeding a public demand for swashbuckling adventure stories, Dumas set up a virtual production line, with assistants such as Auguste Maquet supplying ideas and text for novels that were published under Dumas's name. His total output is estimated at more than 100,000 pages of printed text. Creations, such as the musketeer D'Artagnan, the Count of Monte Cristo, and the Man in the Iron Mask achieved legendary status. Dumas rapidly earned a fortune but his lavish spending on women and good living led him into debt. Pursued by his many creditors, he lived abroad for many years, and never stopped writing. Dumas's later works included a book on pets and a 1,000-page dictionary of cuisine.

KEY WORKS: *The Three Musketeers*, 1844; *The Count of Monte Cristo*, 1845–1846; *The Queen's Necklace*, 1849; *The Black Tulip*, 1850

△ *ALEXANDRE DUMAS*, ETIENNE CARJAT, c.1862

## Nathaniel Hawthorne

1804–1864, AMERICAN

The author of the renowned Gothic novel *The Scarlet Letter*, Hawthorne was born in Salem, Massachusetts, the descendant of a judge in the town's infamous witch trials. An early novel and the short story collection *Twice-Told Tales* made little impact, but *The Scarlet Letter* proved an instant best seller. Described by the author as a "romance," because it abandoned realism in pursuit of moral truth, the novel uses the story of the outcast adulterer Hester Prynne to challenge the Puritan tradition of guilt and the suppression of sexuality.

Hawthorne's next novel, *The House of the Seven Gables*, exploited similar themes with a larger element of the supernatural. *The Blithedale Romance*, a lighter novel, reflected his rejection of Transcendentalism (a philosophical movement of the 1820s–1830s that championed human intuition over scientific empiricism). In 1853, he was appointed a US consul and spent seven years in Europe, without noticeable benefit to his creativity. He died leaving three novels unfinished.

KEY WORKS: *Twice-Told Tales*, 1837; *The Scarlet Letter*, 1850; *The House of the Seven Gables*, 1851; *The Blithedale Romance*, 1852

## George Sand

1804–1876, FRENCH

George Sand was a female novelist who challenged the restrictions imposed on women's search for fulfillment. Born Aurore Dupin, she was brought up by her grandmother on an estate at Nohant, south of Paris, which she later inherited. In 1831, she fled an unhappy marriage to live a bohemian life in Paris, becoming a journalist and successful novelist under the pseudonym George Sand. She flouted convention, adopting men's clothing, and conducted highly publicized love affairs, most notably with Frédéric Chopin.

All her books are romantic novels with realistic settings; many depict women in emotional revolt against unsatisfactory lives. They also reflect the author's sense of social injustice— Sand played an active role in France's 1848 Revolution—and her love of the countryside. Living in rural seclusion with her grandchildren at Nohant, she was visited by most of the great writers of her time.

KEY WORKS: *Indiana*, 1832; *Consuelo*, 1842–1843; *La Mare au Diable*, 1846; *La Petite Fadette*, 1849

## Elizabeth Barrett Browning

1806–1861, ENGLISH

The Victorian poet Elizabeth Barrett Browning was more famous in her lifetime than her poet husband Robert

Browning. The fortune of her family, the Moulton-Barretts, depended on slavery in the West Indies, which as an adult she vigorously denounced. Her poetic talent was precocious—her epic *The Battle of Marathon* was published privately when she was 14.

Partially disabled, Barrett was dependent on the opiate laudanum; she led a confined life of Victorian respectability while building her literary reputation with *Prometheus Bound* (1833) and *The Seraphim*. Her 1844 volume *Poems*, both a critical and popular success, made her a serious candidate for the post of poet laureate.

In 1845, Barrett married Robert Browning clandestinely, against her father's will, and the couple ran off to live in Florence, Italy. Her passionate love for her husband is celebrated in her *Sonnets from the Portuguese*, which includes the verse "Number 43" that begins with the famous line, "How do I love thee? Let me count the ways." The autobiographical "verse-novel" *Aurora Leigh* was the culminating achievement of her later years.

**KEY WORKS:** *The Seraphim and Other Poems*, 1838; *Poems*, 1844; *Sonnets from the Portuguese*, 1850; *Aurora Leigh*, 1856

## Nikolai Gogol

1809–1852, RUSSIAN

A master of satire and grotesque caricature, Gogol wrote novels, plays, and short stories depicting the absurdity of life in czarist Russia. The son of a Ukrainian landowner, he went to St. Petersburg intending to be a poet. He supported himself through minor administrative jobs, an experience that gave him keen insight into the workings of state bureaucracy. With encouragement from Aleksandr Pushkin, he finally became a full-time writer.

Gogol's absurdist, satirical vein surfaced in 1836 with the brilliant theatrical farce *The Government Inspector* and the surreal short story "The Nose." Fearing persecution by the government, for the following 12 years he lived abroad, mostly in Rome, where he wrote his masterpiece *Dead Souls*, which pokes fun at the Russian middle classes and the greed and corruption of landowners. This novel, along with the short story "The Overcoat," established Gogol as Russia's leading prose writer.

In his final years, Gogol descended into religious mania and failed to realize grandiose literary projects.

**KEY WORKS:** "The Nose," 1836; *The Government Inspector*, 1836; *Dead Souls*, 1842; "The Overcoat," 1842

## ▷ Alfred, Lord Tennyson

1809–1892, ENGLISH

Queen Victoria's longest-serving poet laureate, Tennyson at his best wrote poems of exceptional musicality and technical virtuosity. Born in Lincolnshire, the son of a vicar, he published his first books of verse in the 1830s but they were not well received, despite including such later anthology favorites as "Mariana" and "The Lady of Shalott." His breakthrough came with the *Poems* of 1842, which included "Locksley Hall," "Ulysses," and "Break, Break, Break." This was followed by the powerful sequence *In Memoriam A. H. H.*, a melancholy meditation on the death of his friend, the poet Arthur Hallam, who had died young from a brain hemorrhage.

As poet laureate, beginning in 1850, Tennyson's output ranged from the jingoistic Crimean War poem "The Charge of the Light Brigade" (1854) to the complex and impassioned love lyrics of *Maud*. His 12-part Arthurian cycle *Idylls of the King*, beloved by the Victorian public, appeals less to modern taste. Tennyson was granted a peerage in 1883.

**KEY WORKS:** *Poems*, 1842; *In Memoriam A. H. H.*, 1850; *Maud: A Monodrama*, 1855; *The Idylls of the King*, 1859–1885

## Elizabeth Gaskell

1810–1865, ENGLISH

Novelist Elizabeth Gaskell was a perceptive observer of the social effects of the Industrial Revolution. Born Elizabeth Stevenson, she was brought up by an aunt in a country town in Cheshire, the model for her fictional Cranford. Making a contented marriage to a Unitarian minister, she settled in the booming industrial city of Manchester, where she undertook charitable work for the poor.

The death of an infant son prompted her to write a novel as a distraction. A sympathetic description of poverty among the Manchester working class, *Mary Barton* was an immediate success with the Victorian public. The small-town novel *Cranford* confirmed her popular reputation, but *Ruth* (1853), a portrayal of a "fallen woman," and *North and South*, which deals with the conflict between workers and their employers, were controversial. Gaskell's late novel *Wives and Daughters* is considered by some critics to be her best. She also wrote a notable biography of her friend Charlotte Brontë.

**KEY WORKS:** *Mary Barton: A Tale of Manchester Life*, 1848; *Cranford*, 1851–1853; *North and South*, 1854–1855; *Wives and Daughters: An Everyday Story*, 1864–1866

△ *ALFRED, LORD TENNYSON, c.1865*

LATE
19th
CENTURY

CHAPTER 3

# George Eliot

**1819–1880, ENGLISH**

As a best-selling author and a favorite of Queen Victoria, Eliot gained huge wealth and popularity, but her unconventional personal life precluded her from being fully accepted by the British establishment.

George Eliot gave herself different names in distinctive phases of her life. For the purposes of her literary career she chose a male nom-de-plume, and agreed with her publishers to remain anonymous. Although forced to reveal her identity when a pretender tried to claim authorship of her works, the pen name George Eliot persisted.

Eliot was born Mary Anne Evans in Nuneaton, Warwickshire. Her early life was shaped by her father's decision to send her to school (a privilege that was usually reserved for sons). She possessed a voracious appetite for books, mining the library at Arbury Hall, where her father worked as a land agent. But her formal education came to an end at 16, when the death of her mother meant that she had to return home as housekeeper.

Five years later, she moved with her father to a house near Coventry. Here, her circle of friends included the rich philanthropist Charles Bray and his wife Cara, who encouraged her writing and a freedom of thought that her father did not approve of.

The inheritance that Eliot received upon her father's death in 1849 set her free. She spent time in Switzerland before moving to London, determined to pursue a career in journalism. In the capital, she joined the household of political publisher John Chapman,

whom she had met through the Brays. He employed her as assistant editor of the *Westminster Review*, a position rarely bestowed on Victorian women.

## London life and loves

In London, Eliot became infatuated with one man after another, but in 1851 she finally found love with George Henry Lewes. The relationship was complicated because Lewes was already married. Unable to divorce his wife Agnes (since he had given his name to her illegitimate children), he and Eliot chose to cohabit outside marriage. At this time, Eliot called herself Evans Lewes.

She had already resolved to write novels but it wasn't until she found contentment with Lewes that she embarked on this career as George Eliot. She used a male name partly to distance herself from what she considered to be the "mind-and-

millinery" pulp written by "silly women novelists," thereby giving her work greater authority. She admired the realism of contemporary European novels and resolved to write similarly authentic works. Her *Scenes of Clerical Life* was published in installments in 1857 and her first full-length novel, *Adam Bede*, appeared in 1859. She wrote five more novels, including *Middlemarch*—rated as one of the finest works of Victorian literature—and many volumes of poetry, essays, and articles.

Although bereft at Lewes's death in 1878, and no longer writing fiction, she chose to marry, becoming Mary Anne Cross. But controversy surrounded the marriage because her husband was some 20 years her junior. The relationship was short-lived, since George Eliot died of kidney disease at her luxury home in Chelsea in 1880. She was buried next to Lewes in Highgate Cemetery.

△ **DANIEL DERONDA**
Eliot's works explored the psychological complexity of English life with a didactic realism unknown at the time. Her last novel, *Daniel Deronda* (1876), depicted repression in the upper classes and confronted the controversial topic of the status of Jews in British society.

◁ **GEORGE ELIOT**
After her father's death, Eliot stayed for a while in Geneva at the home of the Swiss painter François D'Albert Durade. He painted this portrait of the 30-year-old writer in 1849.

**IN CONTEXT**
### Sunday radicals

Eliot's relationship with the author, philosopher, and scientist George Henry Lewes brought her into contact with the literary and intellectual elite of London. They were leading members of a circle of writers that included William Thackeray, Thomas Carlyle, and John Stuart Mill. In their meetings on a Sunday afternoon at the Priory—Eliot and Lewes's home—these thinkers initiated a movement in literature that embraced groundbreaking philosophical, psychological, and sociological theories.

**THE PRIORY, ELIOT'S HOME IN ST. JOHN'S WOOD, LONDON**

# Herman Melville

## 1819–1891, AMERICAN

Melville was a skilled storyteller and a master of realism, whose true greatness was revealed in the rich symbolic and thematic depths of his complex and strange masterpiece, *Moby-Dick*.

◁ **HOME AT ARROWHEAD**
Melville wrote *Moby-Dick* at this desk at his home, Arrowhead, in Pittsfield, Massachusetts. The house, built in the 1780s, featured in several of his stories and was the author's home for 13 years.

### Experiences at sea

After several years crewing whaling ships, Melville returned to Boston in 1844 with exotic tales of adventure, mutiny, and cannibalism in the South Seas that formed the basis of his first novels, *Typee* (1846) and *Omoo* (1847). These romantic, sensationalist stories were popular and sold well, enabling the author to marry Elizabeth Shaw in 1847. Two years later, the couple had the first of four children.

Melville's next book, *Mardi* (1849), was less successful. His readers, expecting another adventure, were disappointed by a story that quickly abandoned its realism and romantic plot in favor of philosophizing and allegory. Its publication, however, marked a change in Melville's literary ambitions, which he revealed in a message to his good friend Nathaniel Hawthorne: "What I feel most moved to write ... will not pay. Yet, altogether, write the other way I cannot."

Melville poured his experience of the sea, along with all that he had learned from his voracious reading, into his next project, *Moby-Dick*. He gave the novel a powerful plot, based on the true story of the sinking of the ship *Essex* by a whale, and an extraordinary, flawed hero in the vengeful, fanatical Captain Ahab. But amid Melville's evocative descriptions of life at sea were explorations of class and status, good and evil, madness, duty, defiance, friendship, and death, bound together by rich symbolism and a wealth of styles and literary devices, including prose, poetry, catalogues, stage directions, soliloquies, and asides. *Moby-Dick* was in many ways, as Melville predicted, "a botched job." It was also a commercial failure.

### Late recognition

Melville's later novels also failed to find an audience, and his attempts to earn a living by giving public lectures went nowhere, so in 1866 he accepted a position as a customs inspector in New York City. He turned to poetry, publishing two collections, neither of which excited much attention. Yet the siren song of the sea was strong, and before his death in 1891, Melville was once more working on a seafaring tale, published posthumously as *Billy Budd, Sailor* in 1924. By then, his reputation was on the rise and *Moby-Dick* was finally recognized as a masterpiece of American literature.

Herman Melville was one of eight children of a once-prominent New York clan. The family's fortunes declined in the boy's youth and he was denied the comforts of inherited wealth. Melville drifted from job to job, working as a clerk and a teacher before studying surveying in the hope of finding secure employment. When this failed to materialize, he turned to a life at sea, starting as a cabin boy on board the merchant ship *St. Lawrence*.

## IN CONTEXT
### Literary influences

Melville's influences ranged from Milton, Pope, and Rabelais to the Bible and Shakespeare. A simple "Terrific!" written in the margin of his copy of *King Lear* shows the delight he found in the Bard's works. Shakespeare's influence is apparent in *Moby-Dick*'s soliloquies and stage directions, and in the extracts from his plays. Melville also cast the book's main character, tyrannical Captain Ahab, in the mold of a Shakespearean tragic hero.

**POSTER FOR THE 1956 MOVIE OF *MOBY DICK*, WITH GREGORY PECK AS AHAB**

> " Familiarity with **danger** makes a **brave man** braver, but **less daring**. "
> HERMAN MELVILLE, *WHITE JACKET*

▷ **MELVILLE IN LATER LIFE**
This portrait shows Melville at the age of 66, just six years before his death from a heart attack, at a time when his writing career was languishing. His masterpiece, *Moby-Dick*, was acclaimed after his death.

# Walt Whitman

## 1819–1892, AMERICAN

In *Leaves of Grass*, Whitman created an epic in which a host of themes—from love to war, slavery to democracy—were explored. He used free verse to render the voice not of a great hero but of an ordinary American.

Walt Whitman—named Walter but known as Walt to distinguish him from his father—was born in West Hills, Long Island, in 1819, the second of nine children. Walter hoped to improve the family's fortunes by building houses, living in them for a while, and then selling them for a profit, but his speculations were unsuccessful; Walt left school at the of age 11, going to work to augment the family's income.

### Editorial training

The young Whitman was initiated into the newspaper business at his local paper, *The Long Island Patriot*, and then worked as a printer in Brooklyn, where he developed his interest in literature and published his first works of poetry. A downturn in the economy forced him to return to his family on Long Island and work as a teacher—a job he detested. In 1838, Whitman founded his own weekly newspaper, *The Long-Islander*, doing much of the work—editing, printing, and distribution—himself.

◁ **WHITMAN, c.1890**
Whitman did not gain much of a popular following in his own country during his lifetime but is now considered America's preeminent 19th-century poet. His celebration of freedom, nature, body, and soul continues to inspire.

△ **WHITMAN'S BIRTHPLACE**
Whitman was born and spent his first four years in this simple Long Island farmhouse before his family moved to Brooklyn in search of opportunity.

He sold the venture and left for New York City, taking on various journalistic posts before becoming editor of the *Brooklyn Eagle* in 1846. He was known there for his strong, often unpopular opinions, and was eventually fired for supporting the antislavery branch of the New York Democratic Party when the paper's owner belonged to the pro-slavery faction.

### Early publications

The 1850s was a pivotal decade for Whitman. He published prose, including a serialized novel, *The Life and Adventures of Jack Engle*, and a curious self-help manual called *Manly Health and Training*, as well as poetry.

In July 1855, he published *Leaves of Grass*, a collection of 12 poems that he would continue revising and adding to throughout his life. Whitman paid to have the first edition printed. The slim volume would have seemed unusual to the contemporary reader: the author's name did not appear on the title page, and the poems were unnamed. All are now accepted as classics; they include "I Sing the Body Electric," "Song of Myself," and

**IN CONTEXT**
### The symbolism of grass

For Whitman, grass was a symbol with many meanings. Growing everywhere, it stood for universality and was a symbol of nature, renewal, eternity, and the cycle of life. A group of love poems in his epic *Leaves of Grass* is called *Calamus*, the name of a specific type of grass, *Acorus calamus*, or sweet flag. Kalamos was also the name of a youth in Greek mythology who fell in love with another, drowned in a river, and was given new life as a water reed. For many readers, therefore, *Calamus* represents the love between men that is celebrated in Whitman's poems.

**SWEET FLAG, *ACORUS CALAMUS***

" Born here **of parents** born here **from parents** the same, and **their parents** the same. "

WALT WHITMAN, "SONG OF MYSELF"

# "It is **you talking** just as much as **myself** ... I act as the **tongue of you**."

WALT WHITMAN, "SONG OF MYSELF"

AMERICAN ESSAYIST RALPH WALDO EMERSON, c.1870

"The Sleepers." *Leaves of Grass* was revolutionary. Its long, unrhymed, free verse lines were unlike anything most people had read. Many thought it unpoetic and found its descriptions of sensual pleasure obscene. The book received high praise in other quarters, including from Ralph Waldo Emerson, one of the most prominent American writers of the age, who wrote to Whitman, saying: "I greet you at the beginning of a great career."

## War poetry

When the Civil War began, Whitman, a Democrat and abolitionist, supported the Union. His brother, George, was wounded in battle, and Whitman traveled to a fever-ravaged Washington, D.C., to find him. Moved by the terrible suffering that he witnessed in the makeshift military hospitals, he stayed in the city to help wounded soldiers, supporting himself by working as a clerk. These events inspired Whitman's collection of war poems, which was published in 1865 as *Drum-Taps*. It encompasses his reactions to the conflict—from naive excitement to doubt, and then compassion for the victims of war.

The aftermath of war brought poems on the death of Abraham Lincoln, such as "O Captain! My Captain!," which was Whitman's most popular poem during his lifetime, and the moving "When Lilacs Last in the Dooryard Bloom'd."

## An evolving epic

All the while, Whitman continued to revise *Leaves of Grass* by reordering it, adding new poems, and incorporating those previously published in *Drum-Taps*. Multiple editions followed, so that the book, which had started as a collection of just 12 poems, eventually included 383.

Expanding the book in this way allowed Whitman to explore a variety of themes: education, democracy, slavery, social change, work, love, the American landscape, war—in short, the US itself. With its broad sweep, the book has been called an American epic, but it is an epic like no other before it, without a noble hero and centered on an ordinary US citizen—Whitman himself—whose experiences, values, and thoughts are thought to embody those of all citizens of the country.

If the book's breadth of reference was revolutionary, so was its style. Many of Whitman's lines have a very free rhythm, varied in length and meter, and unlike the regular patterns of traditional poetry. However, the poet took his inspiration from a very traditional source—the Bible—the syntax and rhythms of which he often adopted. Like the Bible, *Leaves of*

△ **WHITMAN AND DOYLE**
When in Washington, D.C., Whitman formed a close, and possibly romantic, relationship with Peter Doyle, a streetcar conductor.

*Grass* features catalogs and lists, often presented using repeating words. Whitman was especially fond of the rhetorical device called anaphora, in which a line or sentence begins with the same phrase (such as the lines beginning "Out of the ..." and "And every day ..." in "Out of the Cradle Endlessly Rocking"). These devices help to give his poetry a lofty, unrhymed style.

## KEY WORKS

**1842**
*Franklin Evans* is published—a tale of a young man in New York succumbing to the temptation of alcohol.

**1855**
*Leaves of Grass* appears in a run of just 800 copies.

**1860**
The third edition of *Leaves of Grass* attracts attention for its treatment of love and male relationships.

**1865**
*Drum-Taps* is inspired by Whitman's experience of nursing injured soldiers in the Civil War.

**1871**
In *Democratic Vistas*, Whitman comments on postwar politics and the rise of materialism in the US.

**1892**
*Leaves of Grass*, the final edition, is completed while Whitman is suffering from lung and kidney disease.

## Sex and censure

One aspect of *Leaves of Grass* caused particular controversy: the poet's handling of love and sex. Whitman wrote frankly about prostitution, for example, at a time when the subject was not discussed in polite circles. People also found the poet's writing about male relationships problematic. He dwells at length and with intensity on male "comradeship" and affection, and some readers have questioned whether these are thinly veiled references to romantic love between men. The same ambiguity surrounds the poet's personal life. He had a number of very close friendships with men, but it is not known whether these were sexual relationships. When asked about this particular aspect of his work, Whitman replied that he was horrified that it should be seen as that, but not all readers have accepted his denial. Publishers were also dubious, and the edition of *Leaves of Grass*

▷ **FIRST EDITION**
The first edition of *Leaves of Grass* did not name Whitman as the author, but instead featured a deliberately iconoclastic portrait of the poet.

that Whitman had hoped to bring out in 1866 had to wait until a willing publisher was found the following year.

## Final revisions

In the early 1870s, Whitman juggled writing, working in the Attorney General's office in Washington, and taking care of his aged mother, who suffered from arthritis. However, in 1873, the poet himself had a stroke and had to move in with his brother, George, in Camden, New Jersey. Their mother died later that year and Whitman remained with George, continuing to revise his great book and producing others, including *Memoranda During the War* and

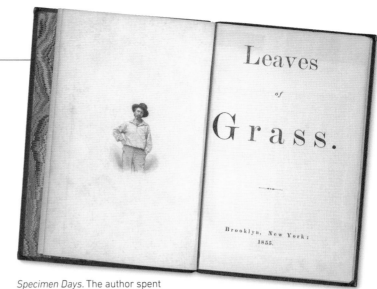

*Specimen Days.* The author spent his last years, from 1884 on, in his own house in Camden and in a summer residence in Laurel Springs, southern New Jersey. Here he found some tranquility, living with his housekeeper, former neighbor Mary Oakes Davis, and working on the final version of *Leaves of Grass*, now known as the Deathbed Edition, which he completed before he died of pleurisy and tuberculosis in 1892.

▽ **DOCUMENTS OF WAR**
This historical painting by Ole Peter Hansen Balling depicts General Ulysses S. Grant, who led the Union army to victory over the Confederacy. Although Whitman had worked as a journalist, he did not report on the Civil War as a regular newspaper correspondent. Instead, he documented the pomposity, brutality, and tragedy of war in his poems, which appeared together in *Drum-Taps.*

# Charles Baudelaire

**1821–1867, FRENCH**

Baudelaire was one of the greatest French poets of the 19th century. His most famous book, *Les Fleurs du mal*, caused outrage, but is now seen as a masterpiece, forming a bridge between Romanticism and symbolism.

The roots of many of Charles Baudelaire's most controversial poems can be found in his troubled upbringing. He was born in Paris, the only son of an elderly father and a younger mother. His father, François, was a cultivated man, a civil servant, but he died when the boy was just six.

Charles doted on his mother, who swiftly remarried in 1828. Her new husband, Lieutenant Colonel Jacques Aupick, had a distinguished career, eventually becoming France's ambassador in Spain and Turkey, but he had little time for his stepson. The boy was sent away to a succession of boarding schools and positioned for

a future law career. Charles bitterly resented the separation from his mother and often complained of his solitude and isolation.

### Family dispute

Baudelaire soon acquired a rebellious streak, and, in spite of his academic prowess, he was expelled from his school in Lyon. Then, following his parents' wishes, he enrolled as a law student in Paris, but was soon drawn into a bohemian lifestyle. He drank, he visited prostitutes—contracting the syphilis that was to affect him for the rest of his life—and he began to squander money at an alarming rate.

△ **PORT LOUIS, MAURITIUS**
During his stay on the Indian Ocean islands, Baudelaire met a prostitute working to buy her sister out of slavery. She was the inspiration for his prose poem "La Belle Dorothée."

In 1841, Aupick sent Baudelaire on a year-long trip to India, hoping that he would see sense. The move failed. Baudelaire jumped ship on the Indian Ocean island of Mauritius and was back in Paris within a few months.

The poet's brief stay on Mauritius and Réunion inspired the exotic maritime imagery in some of his verse, but the experience did nothing

*JEANNE DUVAL*, CHARLES BAUDELAIRE

> **"** *Les Fleurs du mal* ... is **clothed** in a **sinister** and **cold beauty**: it was **composed in fury** and **patience**. **"**

CHARLES BAUDELAIRE

▷ **BAUDELAIRE, c.1866**
This tinted portrait by Etienne Carjat shows the poet near the end of his life. Baudelaire posed for it despite stating that photography was "the refuge of every would-be painter, every painter too ill-endowed or too lazy to complete his studies."

notorious Club des Hachichins held its meetings, later recounting his experiences in *On Wine and Hashish* (1851) and *Artificial Paradises* (1860). He also announced that he had no intention of practicing law, but was going to pursue a literary career.

His family took drastic action. At the age of 21, Baudelaire had inherited a sizable bequest from his father, but it was dwindling fast, so in 1884 Aupick placed the money in trust, allowing Charles only a modest allowance, which was administered by a lawyer. This transformed his lifestyle. For the remainder of his career, Baudelaire lived on the brink of poverty, partially estranged from his family. More than the money, he was appalled by the fact that his affairs were handled by strangers. His relationship with his mother suffered, improving only after Aupick's death in 1857.

## Scandalous works

The financial restraints did at least galvanize Baudelaire into action. He could not earn his living by poetry, so he began working as an art critic. His 1845 review of the Salon—the official art exhibition in Paris—built his reputation in this field, but he did not confine his interests to painting. He also wrote extensively on music, becoming one of the first critics to champion the work of Richard Wagner, and he developed a fascination for the writings of Edgar Allan Poe (1809–1849). Baudelaire felt a strong kinship with this American author, who had experienced similar financial issues and family struggles. He produced a biographical study on Poe in 1852, followed by translations of his stories, which began to appear in 1856.

△ **LES EPAVES, 1866**
The frontispiece of Baudelaire's collection *Les Epaves* (*Scraps*) is decorated with an engraving by Félicien Rops. The skeleton symbolizes the tree of good and evil; above it, a portrait of Baudelaire is borne away by a chimera. It was the final volume produced by the poet.

By this stage, Baudelaire had already finished a book of his own—a novella called *La Fanfarlo*—and was building a reputation as a poet. His initial instinct was to shock. He announced that his first collection was to be called *Les Lesbiennes*, though he later thought better of this. Even so, when the first official edition of *Les Fleurs du mal* (*The Flowers of Evil*) was published in 1857, shock was the prevailing public reaction. The text was confiscated by the authorities, and Baudelaire and his publisher were charged with indecency and immorality. As it turned out, both were fined and six poems were removed because of their sexual content. This scandal did the poet no harm at all: it earned him celebrity status and boosted sales of the book.

△ **HOTEL PIMODAN, PARIS**
The Club des Hachichins (the Hashish-Eaters' Club) met in this house on the Ile Saint-Louis, where Baudelaire had his apartment. Members of the club included Alexandre Dumas, Eugène Delacroix, and Dr. Jacques-Joseph Moreau; they met regularly in the late 1840s to share drug-induced experiences.

to alter his behavior. On his return, he embarked on an affair with Jeanne Duval—a relationship that he knew full well would never meet with the approval of his family—and he began experimenting with cannabis and opium. In 1843, he rented an apartment in the Hôtel Pimodan, where the

## KEY WORKS

**1847**
*La Fanfarlo* is published. The semiautobiographical novella examines a failed romance between a poet and an actress, La Fanfarlo.

**1857**
*Les Fleurs du mal* scandalizes the authorities and leads to the prosecution of the poet. An expanded edition is produced in 1861.

**1860**
In *Artificial Paradises*, Baudelaire describes the effects of wine and hashish that he experienced at the Club des Hachichins.

**1863**
*The Painter of Modern Life* is published, the most notable of Baudelaire's studies of art. It includes his analysis of beauty.

**1869**
*Le Spleen de Paris*, a collection of 50 short prose poems, is published. Its aim is to celebrate the beauty of modern city life.

# "Modernity is the transient, the fleeting, the contingent."

CHARLES BAUDELAIRE, *THE PAINTER OF MODERN LIFE*

The poems in *Les Fleurs du mal* were composed over a long period of time, since Baudelaire would often tinker with his verses for years. Some dated back to the 1840s, while an enlarged edition was released in 1861. The collection is remarkable for its tone, content, and imagery. Baudelaire looked for his "*fleurs*"—his sense of beauty—not in nature, but in the "*mal*"—the tawdry reality of the everyday world. It could be found in the grime of modern city life or in the sweaty reality of animal passion. Equally, it could be extracted from moments of reverie, boredom, or despondency.

## Poetry of the senses

Baudelaire has been hailed as one of the first truly modern poets. This stems from the highly personal and confessional tone of his writing, which sometimes reads like the pages of a diary. There is no attempt to conceal shameful thoughts or feelings. Thus, in "A celle qui est trop gaie" ("To she who is too gay"), the poet begins by likening his beloved's face to a beautiful vista and her laughter to a playful breeze before, within the space of a few lines, expressing a desire to creep into her room at night, to chastise her perfect flesh and infuse her with his venom.

Baudelaire's imagery is hugely rich and evocative. He explained the theory behind this in his poem "Correspondances," which was loosely based on the ideas of the philosopher Emanuel Swedenborg. In it, he writes that nature contains a "forest of symbols / Which look at [man] with understanding eyes / Like prolonged echoes mingling in the distance." For Baudelaire, "Perfumes, sounds, and colors correspond." His direct experience of synesthesia, where a heady perfume might conjure up the texture of hair, a striking color, or a beautiful song, gave his poetry its sensual power. The imaginative associations that could result from this inspired the symbolists. The younger generation of poets (Rimbaud, Mallarmé, and Verlaine) considered Baudelaire a genius.

## A mother's wishes

After the publication of the second edition of *Les Fleurs du mal*, Baudelaire concentrated increasingly on prose poems. His later years were dogged by poor health and money problems. In 1864, he embarked on a disastrous lecture tour in Belgium, where he suffered a stroke. Baudelaire never recovered from this and died in his mother's arms in August 1867. She regretted that he had not followed Aupick's plans. He would not have made his mark on the literary world, she admitted, "but all three of us would have been happier."

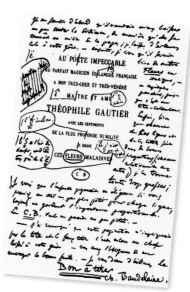

△ *LES FLEURS DU MAL*
This proof, corrected by Baudelaire, shows the dedication page of *Les Fleurs du mal*, dedicated to his fellow poet and friend Théophile Gautier.

## IN CONTEXT
### Art, art criticism, and poetry

Long before he established himself as a poet, Baudelaire had earned a reputation as a highly perceptive art critic. Beginning in 1845, he wrote several reviews of the Salon—the celebrated art exhibition held annually in Paris—and he also penned detailed studies of some of his favorite artists. In these writings on art, Baudelaire outlined the moral values and notions of beauty that were soon to be reflected in his verse. Initially, he idolized the Romantic painter Eugène Delacroix, but he reserved his greatest praise for artists such as Constantin Guys and Edouard Manet (who became a great friend), who captured "the heroism of modern city life."

*MUSIC IN THE TUILERIES GARDENS,*
*EDOUARD MANET, 1862*

# Gustave Flaubert

**1821–1880, FRENCH**

Flaubert was one of the greatest pioneers of the modern novel. Known for the rigorous perfectionism of his style, he scandalized the French public with the supposed immorality of his masterpiece, *Madame Bovary*.

◁ **CROISSET STUDY**
This 1870 drawing shows the study at Flaubert's home at Croisset. It was here that the author worked—mostly at night—searching for *le mot juste*.

Gustave Flaubert was born in Rouen, the son of an eminent surgeon and hospital director, Achille-Cléophas. His family's wealth was significant in shaping his career because it gave him the financial security to spend an inordinate length of time polishing and perfecting his writing style.

Flaubert attended a boarding school in Rouen. Although it was run with a strict, military discipline, it provided him with an excellent grounding in history and literature; while there, he contributed to the school newspaper and produced numerous pieces of fiction, mainly of a historical nature.

At the age of 19, Flaubert was sent to Paris to study law—a subject for which he had little enthusiasm. He was not too disappointed when illness—thought to have been a form of epilepsy—offered him an excuse to abandon the course. He suffered from seizures at various intervals throughout his life.

### Home in Croisset
After abandoning his studies, Flaubert returned to Rouen and settled there for the rest of his life. However, in 1846, a double tragedy struck: his father passed away, followed shortly afterward by his sister Caroline, who died in childbirth. Flaubert received a sizeable inheritance, and moved with his mother and his infant niece to a new home in Croisset, a hamlet on the outskirts of Rouen. Much of his writing was produced in the summerhouse there, overlooking the Seine. It was in the same year that he met the writer Louise Colet (see box, right), who became his mistress.

### Romanticism and realism
Flaubert had not yet published anything of note, but had firm ideas about the direction his writing should take. He had a dislike of bourgeois values and set himself against the Romanticism of the age. He sought to depict everyday life in precise, unadorned, "objective" prose—a style that finally led to his status as one of the pioneers of literary realism. Nevertheless, some of the themes in Flaubert's work reveal clear Romantic traits. He had, for example, a taste for the exotic, which emerged in *Salammbô*, set in ancient Carthage,

◁ **GUSTAVE FLAUBERT**
Flaubert was a private and famously cynical man. He gave no interviews and forbade the publication of photographic portraits. This portrait shows the author's trademark drooping moustache.

**LOUISE COLET**

> " I am the **obscure** and **patient pearl-fisher**, who **dives deep** and comes up **empty-handed** and blue in the face. "

GUSTAVE FLAUBERT

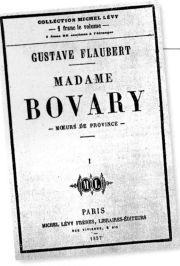

△ **MADAME BOVARY, FIRST EDITION**
With *Madame Bovary*, Flaubert was revealed as the finest prose stylist in 19th-century France. "A good sentence in prose," he wrote, "should be like a good line in poetry, unchangeable."

> "**Perfection** has everywhere **the same characteristic**: that's precision, **exactness.**"

GUSTAVE FLAUBERT

and in *Hérodias*, his interpretation of the biblical story of Salome. Flaubert was also drawn to fantasy, as is evident in *The Temptation of St. Anthony*, an extraordinary, hallucinatory account of the visions that bedeviled this early Christian saint. Flaubert completed his first version of this book in 1849 and read it aloud—over the course of four days—to his closest friends, Louis Bouilhet and Maxime Du Camp. They were instructed to listen without interrupting, but when Flaubert had finished, they both advised him to cast

the manuscript into the fire. Flaubert did not obey; instead, he reworked the text extensively over a number of years, doing meticulous research in pursuit of accuracy. His interest in St. Anthony—whose battle with temptation had been set in the Egyptian desert—was probably his motive for accompanying Maxime Du Camp on a photographic expedition to the Middle East. Similarly, when Flaubert was planning *Salammbô*, he made a point of visiting the site of Carthage, near Tunis.

### Madame Bovary

Flaubert began work on *Madame Bovary* in 1851. The germ of the idea came from a real-life tragedy, which had recently been reported, about a couple whose lives had been wrecked by a combination of adultery, debt, and suicide. The novel also gave Flaubert

▽ **THE PORT OF ROUEN, 1878**
This painting by Torello Ancillotti depicts a view of Flaubert's home city, Rouen. A sculpture of Salome over a cathedral doorway inspired Flaubert's *Hérodias*.

LE THÉÂTRE

◁ **HERODIADE, THE OPERA**
Flaubert's novella *Hérodias* was turned into an opera by Jules Massenet. The Paris production, starring Emma Calvé, featured in the magazine *Le Théâtre*.

ample opportunity to vent his spleen against the bourgeoisie—his generation came too late to see the overthrow of the Ancien Régime in France. In its place, he had to witness the rise of a wealthy middle class, along with its petty materialism and its desire for respectability. In *Madame Bovary*, he traced the decline of a woman who represented this class and who, blinded by romanticism, was destroyed by her deluded values.

Flaubert took five years to complete the novel. Taking in his friends' criticisms of *St. Anthony*, he determined to strip his writing of any Romantic excesses. He adopted a technique that has become known as "free indirect style" in which he remained detached from his characters and his text ("present everywhere and visible nowhere"). He set out to intimate his characters' impressions indirectly, with no moralizing, judgment, or commentary. He pared back his language, avoiding grand turns of phrase and high-flown metaphors. He weighed every sentence as carefully as a line of verse, and then would read his text out loud in his study, removing repeated syllables and any slack or unnecessary phrases. Inevitably, this process was slow and tortuous: the critic Walter Pater described Flaubert as a "martyr of literary style," while Henry James remarked that "he felt of his vocation nothing but the difficulty." Flaubert would spend hours searching for *le mot juste* (a term he is rumored to have coined), and in his letters he would complain of taking a whole afternoon to make just two corrections, or of the pain he felt when "eliminating a sentence that took several entire days to write."

### Critical responses

*Madame Bovary* was published in 1857 and soon ran into trouble with the authorities. By the standards of the time, the descriptions of Emma's infidelities were deemed too graphic and Flaubert was charged with corrupting public morals. Fortunately, he was acquitted and the scandal about the book brought him both fame and public success.

As a result of his exacting methods, Flaubert's literary output was relatively small, and he was often frustrated by the lukewarm critical response to his work. Reviewers were bored by the exhaustive historical detail in *Salammbô*; *Sentimental Education*—which centered on a young man's love for an older, married woman—was deemed a backward step, even though Flaubert regarded it as his masterpiece; and the final version of *The Temptation of St. Anthony* (which was eventually published in 1874) was all but ignored. His play *The Candidate* closed after four nights. Only *Three Tales*, published in 1877, was universally admired, but by this time Flaubert was beset by poor health and money troubles, which took the shine off his triumph.

Flaubert's reputation grew steadily following his death, particularly after his sparkling correspondence with Louise Colet was published. Both *Salammbô* and *Hérodias* were turned into operas, and writers such as Henry James, Franz Kafka, Guy de Maupassant, and Jean-Paul Sartre all acknowledged his influence. He is now regarded as a supreme master of style and one of the founders of the modern novel.

### IN PROFILE
### Maxime Du Camp

Du Camp (1822–1894) was one of Flaubert's closest friends and his favorite traveling companion. By far their most ambitious expedition was a 21-month tour around the Middle East in 1849–1851. Du Camp had gained official sponsorship to photograph the historic sites, and the results were published in *Egypt, Nubia, Palestine, and Syria*, (1852). This book became an instant best seller and won Du Camp the Légion d'Honneur medal. The young men recorded their experiences in their letters and journals. These included sexual adventures with local women, an episode when they were arrested as spies, and a hair-raising trip down the Nile.

MAXIME DU CAMP, NADAR, c.1857

## KEY WORKS

**1857**
Flaubert's *Madame Bovary* is published. It causes a sensation, not least because the author was taken to court for offending public morals.

**1862**
*Salammbô*—Flaubert's historical novel set in ancient Carthage—is published after painstaking and extensive research.

**1869**
*Sentimental Education* is published. It is set among the upheavals of the 1848 uprising that brought the Orleans monarchy to an end in France.

**1874**
*The Temptation of St. Anthony* is published. It is based on the visions of a third-century saint who lived as a hermit in the Egyptian desert.

**1877**
Three very different stories in *Three Tales* make the book one of Flaubert's most popular works ever, admired by critics and the public alike.

# Fyodor Dostoyevsky

## 1821–1881, RUSSIAN

Dostoyevsky probed the recesses of the human mind in works of great psychological and philosophical depth, examining religious and moral issues against the backdrop of a country undergoing rapid modernization.

△ **MIKHAIL DOSTOYEVSKY**
Dostoyevsky's father, Mikhail, was a disciplinarian with a quick temper. The mood of tension and intimidation that he created at home influenced his son's often turbulent writing.

▷ **DOSTOYEVSKY, 1872**
Vasily Perov's portrait shows the writer in declining health. At this time, he was suffering from shortness of breath and traveled to the spa town of Ems in Germany in search of a cure.

Dostoyevsky endured mock execution, exile to Siberia, epilepsy, and addiction to gambling—all of which left indelible marks on his life. They can be seen in his work in his empathy for troubled people, his religiosity, and his portrayal of suffering as a redemptive force.

Fyodor Mikhaylovich Dostoyevsky was born in Moscow on November 11, 1821, the second of eight children. His father was a doctor at the Mariinsky Hospital for the Poor, his mother the child of a merchant family. His early years were difficult: his parents were devout, his father strict and severe, and the large family lived in cramped conditions in a house on the hospital grounds.

### Education and early work
Dostoyevsky was educated at home until 1833 and was then sent to a boarding school in Moscow. In 1837, his mother died of tuberculosis, and that same year he was sent to St. Petersburg to attend the Academy of Military Engineering. He lacked enthusiasm for science, but loved literature, particularly Gothic and Romantic fiction, including the work of Sir Walter Scott, Ann Radcliffe, Friedrich Schiller, Nikolai Gogol, and Aleksandr Pushkin. The death of his father in 1839 coincided with the first signs of Dostoyevksy's epilepsy.

In 1843, Dostoyevsky passed his final exams and took a job as a lieutenant engineer in St. Petersburg. At first he supplemented his income by translating literary works, but just a year later, he resigned his commission to devote himself to writing full time. His first novel, *Poor Folk*, recounting the relationship between a poor clerk and a young seamstress in St. Petersburg's slums, was published in 1846 to great acclaim. It was singled out by the influential critic Vissarion Belinsky as Russia's first "social novel." However, Dostoyevsky's next work, *The Double*, received poor reviews. His brief stint in the literary limelight appeared to be over. More short stories followed, but these failed to revive his fortunes.

### Agitation and imprisonment
Dostoyevsky was opposed to the practice of serfdom (bonded labor) and began to associate with a group of radical social reformers known as the Petrashevsky Circle. In 1849, Czar Nicholas I (see box, below) had these "conspirators" arrested and sentenced to death; as they were lined up to face

### IN CONTEXT
### Politics in Russia

The mid-19th century was a turbulent time in Russia. The efforts of Czar Alexander I to both modernize and liberalize the immense, impoverished, backward Russian Empire were set back after the succession of his brother, Nicholas I, in 1825. Nicholas was an autocrat, ruling through a corrupt, repressive bureaucracy. The effects of the revolutions across Europe in 1848 rippled through to Russia, and when Alexander II became czar in 1855, Russians were ready for reform. In 1861, Alexander abolished serfdom, emancipating more than 23 million serfs and weakening the power of Russia's landowning aristocracy.

*ALEXANDER II PROCLAIMING THE EMANCIPATION OF THE SERFS, GUSTAV DITTENBERGER VON DITTENBERG, c.1861*

" It is **better** to be **unhappy** and know the **worst**, than to be **happy** in a **fool's paradise**. "

FYODOR DOSTOYEVSKY, *THE IDIOT*

a firing squad, a horseman raced up with a message that the executions had been stayed. The whole setup had in fact been a monstrous game designed to intimidate and punish the men. It succeeded: Dostoyevsky was profoundly scarred by the incident and in his later works several of his characters grapple with the experience of facing death.

### Imprisonment and freedom

Dostoyevsky spent four years in a Siberian labor camp for his part in the conspiracy. In order to survive mentally and emotionally, he took refuge in Russian Orthodoxy. It was in prison that he gained an understanding of the common people that would inform his later works. Although he was released in 1854, he had to remain in Siberia to

▷ **MOCK EXECUTION**
Here, an anonymous artist captures the mock execution of the Petrashevsky Circle in St. Petersburg's Semyonov Place in 1849.

serve another four years in the army. In 1857, he married a widow named Maria Dmitriyevna Isayeva, and two years later he was permitted to return to St. Petersburg.

Dostoyevsky threw himself back into the literary life, publishing his short stories and essays in journals and magazines such as *Vremya* (*Time*) and *Epokha* (*Epoch*), which he ran along with his brother Mikhail. In these essays and in *Notes from the Underground* (1864), he criticized the radicals of the Russian intelligentsia, changing the beliefs that he had held before his imprisonment. His work after his release from prison turned

△ *SENNAYA SQUARE*, 1841
St. Petersburg played a key role in Dostoyevsky's works. Here, the artist Ferdinand Perrot depicts the squalid location where Raskolnikov, the main protagonist of *Crime and Punishment*, has the initial idea for his crime.

to conservative values. Rejecting socialism, his ideas crystallized around the imperatives of personal freedom and responsibility, themes he explored in his later work.

In 1862 and 1863, Dostoyevsky traveled widely throughout Western Europe—whose culture he admired greatly but whose materialism he

> # "Accept suffering and achieve atonement through it—that is what you must do."
> FYODOR DOSTOYEVSKY, *CRIME AND PUNISHMENT*

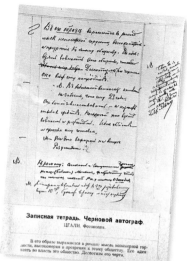

condemned. Around this time, he began to gamble heavily, suffering large losses, and had a tortured love affair with writer Polina Suslova, "a sick, selfish woman," who demanded that he divorce his wife (though she declined to marry him after Maria's death in 1864). His financial troubles were compounded by the death of his brother, Mikhail, whose family Dostoyevsky was obliged to support.

## Psychological realism

In 1866, Dostoyevsky's great novel *Crime and Punishment* was serialized in the journal *The Russian Messenger*. It tells the story of Raskolnikov, who commits murder for philosophical reasons, but is unable to overcome the torment of his own conscience. Its focus on psychological realism and mental drama (often at the expense of plot) departed from earlier Romantic fiction, in which virtue was typically rewarded and wrongdoing punished.

In the same year, Dostoyevsky published *The Gambler*—a short novel about what Ernest Hemingway called "the insanity of gambling." The work was completed, only just before the publisher's deadline, with the help of a young stenographer named Anna Grigoryevna Snitkina. He married Anna the following year, and the couple set off on a long trip around Europe, during which Dostoyevsky continued to gamble heavily. Despite his losses, the marriage was a happy one that produced four children, only two of whom survived to adulthood. In his novel *The Idiot* (1868–1869), Dostoyevsky attempted "to depict a completely beautiful human being"— a Christlike figure—in a world that sees him as an idiot. The book builds complex psychological portraits of its hero, Prince Myshkin, and other characters, and deals with themes of doubt, fear, and the proximity of death (Dostoyevsky's daughter died while he was working on it).

## Honors and hardships

In 1871, the family returned to Russia, where Dostoyevsky published *Demons*, a political allegory in which the author examines atheism and religious faith, suffering and redemption. In 1873, he began writing installments of *A Writer's Diary*, an experimental monthly journal made up of social and political commentary, sketches, essays, and literary criticism. By 1876, the diary had become so popular that Dostoyevsky was invited to present a copy of it to Czar Alexander II.

In the last few years of his life, Dostoyevsky received numerous honors and membership to many prestigious academies and committees. However, his professional success was paralleled by personal hardships. He suffered increasingly from epileptic seizures, and he was deeply affected by the death of his young son, Alyosha, from epilepsy in May 1878. But in spite of his grief, Dostoyevsky continued to write, and published his last, longest, and perhaps greatest novel in 1879–1880. With an act of patricide at its heart, *The Brothers Karamazov* dramatizes the moral struggles concerning faith, reason, and doubt, and probes the questions of free will and moral responsibility. Along with his other great works, it had a profound influence on numerous writers and philosophers over the years, including Aleksander Solzhenitsyn, Anton Chekhov, Sigmund Freud, Ludwig Wittgenstein, Franz Kafka, and the existentialists Jean-Paul Sartre and Albert Camus. Just a year after publishing *The Brothers Karamazov*, Dostoyevsky died of a pulmonary hemorrhage.

△ **CRIME AND PUNISHMENT**
Analysis of Dostoyevsky's manuscripts has shown that he changed *Crime and Punishment* from a first-person to a third-person narrative.

▽ **DOSTOYEVSKY'S STUDY**
Dostoyevsky's St. Petersburg apartment, where he lived in the last years of his life and wrote *The Brothers Karamazov*, is now a museum.

## KEY WORKS

**1846**
*Poor Folk*, the first novel by Dostoyevsky, is in letter form and deals with social themes.

**1862**
*The House of the Dead* initiates the tradition of novels about Russian prison labor camps.

**1864**
*Notes from Underground* is published; it is later considered to be one of the first existentialist novels.

**1867**
In *Crime and Punishment*, Dostoyevsky considers whether honorable ends can justify brutal means.

**1869**
In *The Idiot*, Dostoyevsky presents Prince Myshkin, a protagonist whose epilepsy informs his character.

**1872**
*Demons* is published, conceived as a reaction against the characteristic political and moral nihilism of the era.

**1880**
*The Brothers Karamazov* is published; it goes on to be one of the world's most highly regarded novels.

▷ **IBSEN AT HIS DESK, 1906**
Ibsen—photographed here in the year of
his death—was born and died in Norway,
but escaped the artistic constraints of his
home country to live and write in Italy and
Germany for 27 years. Most of his
dramas, however, are set in Norway.

# Henrik Ibsen

## 1828–1906, NORWEGIAN

Ibsen's dramatic works melded realistic settings and dialogue with
symbolism and psychological insight to lay bare the shortcomings
of contemporary society and reveal his characters' inner worlds.

# " I'm **inclined** to think **we are all ghosts**, Mr. Manders. "

HENRIK IBSEN, *GHOSTS*

Born on March 20, 1828, Henrik Ibsen spent his early years around Skien, a port in southern Norway. At the age of 15, he left the family home to apprentice as an apothecary in Grimstad. There, he fathered an illegitimate son with a servant girl, and published his first play, *Catiline* (1850), under the pen name Brynjolf Bjarme. It was not a success; nor were the verse dramas that followed his move to Christiana (Oslo), where the young Ibsen had hoped to attend university.

Fortunately, his theatrical talent was spotted by the famous violinist and cultural entrepreneur Ole Bull, who appointed Ibsen, now 23, as the director and in-house playwright of a new theater in the city of Bergen. During his six-year tenure there, and another five years at the Norwegian Theatre in Christiana, Ibsen was contracted to produce numerous historical plays for an aesthetically conservative public and press. His work during this long and rather unhappy apprenticeship at least gave him the opportunity to develop practical stagecraft skills and exposed him to exciting new developments in European theater.

In 1864, the Norwegian Theatre went bankrupt, and Ibsen—helped by friends and a small grant from the state—left Norway for Italy. Now free to write what he pleased, his work improved dramatically and he produced two great poetic dramas: *Brand* (1866), which focuses on the life of a priest to explore religious fanaticism and ruthless idealism;

and *Peer Gynt* (1867), which draws on Norwegian folklore to unravel a doomed existentialist quest. These two works secured Ibsen's reputation, both in his home country and abroad.

## Problem plays

A move to Germany coincided with a crucial change in direction in Ibsen's work. Turning away from historical subjects and verse, he dedicated himself to writing prose and dramas of contemporary life. There followed a series of plays characterized by biting social realism, in which the writer focused on moral, economic, and social problems. These plays explored the restrictions on individual freedom that had been created by the social and institutional forces of the day. Plays such as *A Doll's House* (1879) and *Ghosts* (1881), for example, caused outrage when they were first staged for their brutal critique of the institution of marriage and their candid portrayal of female subordination and inequality.

Ibsen's later work focused more closely on the complexities of the individual psyche—on the unconscious mind and the various hidden tensions that are at play in human relationships. He made increasing use of complex, layered symbolism in his work: in *A Doll's House*, for example, a Christmas tree initially represents joy and family happiness; but when it is stripped of its decoration, it transforms into a poignant symbol of lost innocence.

Of the six plays written in this vein, the most famous were *Hedda Gabler* (1890) and *The Master Builder* (1892); translations and multiple European editions appeared soon after their release. In 1891, after years as a recluse, Ibsen returned to Norway a national hero, ready to enjoy the attention lavished on him. *When We Dead Awaken* (1899) was his last play.

In 1900, Ibsen was incapacitated by a stroke. He died six years later and was given a public funeral.

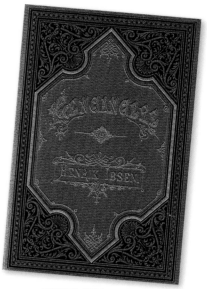

△ *GHOSTS*, 1881
Like many of Ibsen's works, *Ghosts* is an attack on the moral values of society, and tackles controversial themes, such as death, incest, venereal disease, and euthanasia. The "Ghosts" of the title refers not to spirits but to the corrosive, repeated patterns of behavior in which Ibsen's characters are trapped.

## ON STYLE
### Insight through realism

**Ibsen transformed modern drama with his use of realistic dialogue. He was determined that his characters should reproduce human conversation as faithfully as possible: actors were often scripted to speak very little and to participate in both the verbal and nonverbal conventions of language—including, for example, facial expression, hesitation, and interruption. Ibsen's genius lay in his ability to convey in these exchanges an unspoken "reality" beneath the surface. Through the nuances of his style and the use of symbolism, Ibsen's dialogue often has a dual meaning that expresses his characters' inner lives.**

SCENE FROM *A DOLL'S HOUSE* AT THE THEATRE ROYAL IN BATH, ENGLAND

# Leo Tolstoy

**1828–1910, RUSSIAN**

In his 82 years, Tolstoy moved from sinner to saint, and from soldier to social reformer. His work reached the heights of literary invention and style and explored the complexities and depths of philosophy.

Lev Nikolayevich Tolstoy was born into a long line of Russian nobles at his family's country estate, Yasnaya Polyana, on August 28, 1828. By the time of his birth, the family's fortunes had declined but his life was still very comfortable. He grew up surrounded by the love of his easygoing father, Count Tolstoy; his siblings; and "Aunt

△ **SOLDIER AND WRITER**
This photograph of Tolstoy shows him in his officer's uniform during the Crimean War. His understanding of the psychology of war came from his own experiences.

◁ **TOLSTOY**
Tolstoy radically changed his appearance after he left military service. He grew his trademark long beard and changed his wardrobe from the aristocratic attire of a count to simple peasant clothes.

Tatyana," a cousin who helped raise the children after their mother's death. He spent his childhood walking in the countryside, swimming in the pond in summer, tobogganing in winter, and listening to tales told by the family's blind storyteller (storytelling was then a common profession in Russia).

Everything changed in 1836, when the family moved to Moscow. Within two years, Count Tolstoy was dead and the family split apart: two of the boys stayed with their guardian, Aunt Aline, in Moscow, while Leo, his sister Mariya, and their brother Dmitry returned to Yasnaya Polyana.

## A dissolute scholar

Aunt Aline died in 1841, and Tolstoy and his brother traveled to a new guardian in Kazan, southwest Russia, where, three years later, he entered university to study Turco-Arabian literature. But Tolstoy was no scholar. He dropped out in his second year and fell into a dissolute life of drinking, gambling, and fornication. He returned to Yasnaya Polyana but, unsure what to do with his life, he soon reverted to bad habits, carousing and racking up large gambling debts.

## Military service

A way out of this self-destructive lifestyle was offered by his older brother, Nikolai, who persuaded Tolstoy to join him in the Russian army. He became a junker (junior officer) and found that the simplicity of army life suited him. More than that, the beauty of the landscape and hardiness of the people in the villages and mountains of the Caucasus region inspired him, and he began working on the first of three autobiographical stories, *Childhood* (1852).

◁ **YASNAYA POLYANA**
Tolstoy inherited his father's estate in 1847, and returned to live there a decade later. It was in this house that he wrote *War and Peace* and *Anna Karenina*.

### ON STYLE
#### The interior monologue

Tolstoy pioneered the use of the interior monologue in narrative fiction. Writing the stream of a character's thoughts and feelings (as in *War and Peace* and *Anna Karenina*) was a radical departure from the authorial summaries of motivations and emotions that had gone before. These interior monologues brought psychology to prominence in Tolstoy's fiction, drawing readers closer to the experiences of his characters.

***ANNA KARENINA*, ALEKSEI MIKHAILOVICH KOLESOV, 1885**

> "**Seize** the **moments of happiness, love** and be **loved**! That is the **only reality** in the world, all else is **folly**."
>
> LEO TOLSTOY, *WAR AND PEACE*

Tolstoy saw active service in the Crimean War and his experiences at the siege of Sevastopol provided him with material for *Sevastopol Sketches* (1855), in which he experimented with stream-of-consciousness writing. Much of this work would later be recast in scenes in his masterpiece, *War and Peace*. In this huge work, he would attempt to convey the panoramic scope of history by exploring the experiences of a vast range of characters—around 580 in total—during a period of eight years beginning in 1805. Some of the characters were based on members of his own family; others, including Napoleon and Czar Alexander were based on real historical figures.

## Marriage, work, and spirit

Tolstoy returned from the war to find himself in great demand in the literary scene in St. Petersburg, but he still vacillated hopelessly between sobriety and debauchery, struggling to balance his passions with a realistic plan for the future.

His attempt to live a simple life and to educate the peasants in his fields ended in failure, and he began gambling once more; later he would publish *The Cossacks* (1863) only to pay a debt of 1,000 rubles that he had incurred playing billiards with a publisher. In 1857, declaring himself an anarchist, he headed for Paris but was forced to return to Russia again when his debts caught up with him.

△ **SIEGE OF SEVASTOPOL, 1854–55 (DETAIL)**
This enormous panoramic image was painted between 1901 and 1904 by Franz Alekseyevich Roubaud. Tolstoy's experiences in the Crimean War gave rise to his insight, articulated in *War and Peace*, that history is created by many small, everyday actions rather than by the heroic deeds of individual leaders.

Tolstoy began to settle down in 1862, when he married a friend's sister, Sofia "Sonya" Andreyevna Behrs. Their partnership was tense—Sonya despaired of his inability to settle into the life of a respectable nobleman— but it was hugely productive. They had 13 children, and Sonya's notable organizational skills freed Tolstoy to focus on his writing. He published *War and Peace* in six volumes between 1863 and 1869, and in 1873 began writing *Anna Karenina*, in which Levin and Kitty's romance reflected elements of his own courtship of Sonya.

◁ **TOLSTOY'S STUDY**
The writer's house at Yasnaya Polyana is preserved as a museum. It contains Tolstoy's eclectic library of more than 20,000 books, ranging from the Greek philosophers to Montaigne, Dickens, and Thoreau.

## KEY WORKS

**1852**
*Childhood* is published: it is the first part of Tolstoy's trilogy of autobiographical stories that also included *Boyhood* and *Youth*.

**1863–69**
*War and Peace*, a vast work, charts the effects of war on several aristocratic families, and touches on the search for meaning in life.

**1879**
Tolstoy's *A Confession* is banned by the Orthodox Church and is not published in Russia until 1906.

**1898**
*What Is Art?* argues that beauty is not part of the definition of art; instead, Tolstoy claims, art is anything that communicates a feeling.

**1899**
*Resurrection*, a controversially scathing attack on hypocrisy, injustice, and corruption, is Tolstoy's last novel.

Despite the success of these books, by 1878 Tolstoy was suicidal and gripped by a spiritual crisis—explored in *A Confession*—which prompted him to reexamine his life, particularly his attachment to wealth and material possessions, and to change his outlook. Searching for meaning, he turned to the Orthodox Church, but he could not accept its teachings and instead developed his own ideology, Christian anarchism, which rejected organized religion, the state, and even the divinity of Christ in favor of a philosophy that was based on the teachings of the New Testament.

In both his fiction and nonfiction, Tolstoy began to criticize the church and the government, attracting the attention of the secret police, and was excommunicated from the Orthodox Church. In *The Kingdom of God is Within You* (1894), he expounded upon his pacifist doctrine of nonresistance and his belief that answers to moral questions could be found within oneself, winning many fervent followers. His determination to give away his money, however, put him at odds with his family.

Tolstoy continued along a path of extreme asceticism, giving up meat, tobacco, and alcohol and preaching chastity. His radical rejection of his earlier life further alienated his wife, as did the arrival at the family estate of Tolstoy's many disciples.

### Final days
By 1910, Tolstoy could stand no more conflict with his own family. At the age of 82, he renounced his claim to his estate and on October 10, 1910, he left a letter for Sonja, expressing his regret that his departure would distress her and saying that he was "leaving the worldly life to spend the last days of my life in peace and solitude." He boarded a train heading south, hoping to reach a commune set up by his followers on the shores of the Black Sea. However, he became ill with pneumonia and was forced to leave the train at Astapovo. He was taken to the stationmaster's house, which was soon surrounded by journalists. Sonya, who had unsuccessfully tried to drown herself, arrived at the scene but was not admitted to his room until Tolstoy had slipped into unconsciousness after

▷ **THE PHONOGRAPH**
In 1908, the American inventor Thomas Edison sent Tolstoy one of his early phonographs, and the writer made several recordings of his voice on wax cylinders. The surviving recordings cover a broad range of topics, from law and art to his philosophy of nonviolence.

uttering his final words: "Truth—I have much love ...." He died shortly before dawn on November 20th. Thousands of peasants attended his funeral, and he was buried at Yasnaya Polyana, at a favorite spot where he and his brother Nikolai had played as children.

### IN CONTEXT
### Mahatma Gandhi

Tolstoy rejected the creeds and doctrines of the church in favor of a Christian theory of life based on the Sermon on the Mount's call to love your enemies and to "resist not the evil person." Tolstoy's belief in both the power and rightness of nonviolence had a profound effect on Mahatma Gandhi, with whom he corresponded. Tolstoy's writing provided the basis for Gandhi's philosophy of determined but nonviolent resistance to evil— an idea that he called Satyagraha.

**GANDHI IN 1941**

"All **happy families** resemble one another, but **each unhappy family** is **unhappy** in its **own way.**"

LEO TOLSTOY, *ANNA KARENINA*

▷ **INTERNATIONAL RECOGNITION**
Machado de Assis wrote more than 200 short stories and 9 novels. His diverse output has only recently been appreciated by readers in the West—due perhaps to the difficulty of translating his nuanced work—but he is often compared with Franz Kafka and Samuel Beckett.

# Machado de Assis

## 1839–1908, BRAZILIAN

Widely considered to be the greatest Brazilian novelist, Machado de Assis rose from humble origins to a dominant position in Brazil's literary life. His innovative novels express a pessimistic world view in ironic style.

Joaquim Maria Machado de Assis was born in 1839. His father, a poor house painter, was the black son of freed slaves; his mother was a Portuguese washerwoman. As a person of mixed race in a racially stratified society, the young Machado had low status. He also struggled with epilepsy. After his mother's death, when he was 10 years old, his father remarried and Machado's stepmother arranged for him to be taught at a school where she worked as a maid.

## Rise from adversity

Despite his unpromising background, Machado's exceptional gifts and literary ambition became evident at an early age. His first poem was published in a newspaper when he was just 15. He found work as a typographer and proofreader, joining the circle around editor Francisco de Paula Brito, which brought him into contact with many of Brazil's leading political and cultural personalities. Machado proved to be a prolific writer, turning out articles and essays, poems, plays, and stories.

In 1867, his talents attracted official attention and he was awarded a lucrative position in the government bureaucracy, which enabled him to marry a woman of respectable status and enjoy a comfortable lifestyle. The marriage was a happy one despite the fact the couple had no children. From then on, Machado lived a quiet, fairly uneventful existence and never traveled more than a hundred miles from his native Rio de Janeiro.

## An original voice

When Machado began his writing career, the influence of the Romantic movement on Brazilian literature was evident. The writer's early novels, including *Helena* (1876) and *Iaiá Garcia* (1878), reflect this literary trend; they are emotionally expressive works in which the individual is pitted against a narrow-minded society. The novels were an undoubted success but they did not really reflect the author's temperament.

Instead, he found his own voice through reading the English 18th-century author Laurence Sterne, who makes use of digression to create comic effect. Machado adopted similar digressive techniques, but as a vehicle for his detached, ironic pessimism.

Machado's first novel in this style was *The Posthumous Memoirs of Bras Cubas* (1881). Told in the first person by a narrator who is dead, it paints a sardonic picture of a privileged life of absolute futility. Subverting traditional narrative, the text is broken up into short chapters that often diverge into fantasies or offbeat philosophical meditations. Although the narrator maintains a tone of disillusioned superiority, there is an unsettling undercurrent of bitterness throughout.

The novels that followed included *Quincas Borba* (1891), which ruthlessly satirizes humanist philosophy, and *Dom Casmurro* (1899), which tells a tragic tale of love and betrayal, but in a tone that is so offhand and digressive that the real horror of the story is undermined.

In his later years, Machado was revered as a cultural hero, founder and head of the Brazilian Academy of Letters. In addition to nine novels, he wrote several hundred short stories, to considerable acclaim. He died in 1908, four years after his beloved wife.

### IN CONTEXT
### The Empire of Brazil

Machado de Assis was born at the beginning of Brazil's Second Empire (1840 to 1889). Under Emperor Dom Pedro II, Brazil began to modernize and develop. Its growing international status attracted a wave of immigration from Europe that helped to nourish art, theater, and literature. Machado's work signaled the coming of age of writing in Brazil, superseding romantic tropes such as *Indianista* novels that idealized the simple lives of South American Indians. Machado supported monarchical rule in Brazil, remaining loyal to the emperor even after he was overthrown in a military coup in 1889 that founded the First Brazilian Republic. He described Dom Pedro as a humble, honest man "who had made of the throne a simple chair."

**EMPEROR DOM PEDRO II**

▽ **RIO DE JANEIRO**
Born in the poor outskirts of Rio de Janeiro, Machado maintained an outsider's view of the city's bourgeoisie, even when he moved in its circles. The hot, steamy, bustling city, complete with all its iniquities, is the setting for most of his works.

> " I am not exactly a **writer who is dead** but a **dead man who is a writer**. "

MACHADO DE ASSIS, *THE POSTHUMOUS MEMOIRS OF BRAS CUBAS*

# Emily Dickinson

## 1830–1886, AMERICAN

New England poet Dickinson wrote about 1,800 poems, most of which were not published until after her death. Seen as an eccentric at the time, she is now considered one of America's greatest poets.

Emily Dickinson was born in 1830 into a prominent family in the college town of Amherst, Massachusetts. Her ancestors had arrived as part of the Puritan migration to New England in the 1630s, and her grandfather had been instrumental in the founding of Amherst College, which, when Dickinson was born, was among the largest colleges in the US.

Along with her sister Lavinia, she attended Amherst Academy, where she was an excellent student. Pious Puritanism was the norm in Amherst, and Emily attended church regularly until—in about 1852—she abruptly stopped, writing in a poem: "Some keep the Sabbath going to Church— / I keep it staying at Home."

Dickinson studied science at Mount Holyoke Female Seminary, and when a religious revival swept through Massachusetts she refused to be "saved," demonstrating her scepticism in one of her poems: "'Faith' is a fine invention / When Gentlemen can see— / But Microscopes are prudent / In an Emergency." She left the seminary after one year to return home; aside from a visit to Philadelphia and Washington in 1855, she never left Amherst or "my father's house" again. Biographers have theorized about her reasons for this decision, citing illness or homesickness, or interpreting her actions as a way of controlling her destiny at a time when women had little say in their own lives. As the years passed, Dickinson became reclusive, withdrawing into her inner world, but still maintaining friendships and debates through her prolific correspondence.

### Civil War poems

The period 1860–1865 was Dickinson's most productive. This was the time of the Civil War, in which her friend Thomas Wentworth Higginson, a prominent literary critic and abolitionist, led the first black regiment in the Union army, and in which she lost loved ones. The battlefields were distant, but the war influenced poems such as "The name—of it—is 'Autumn'," which makes reference to the shedding of blood, and "My Portion is Defeat—today—."

Dickinson wrote in private, organizing her poems in bundles that she sewed together. She sent some to friends but most of them never saw the public light of day. Dickinson may have considered publishing her works, and in 1862 sought advice from Thomas Higginson, asking "Are you too deeply occupied to say if my Verse is alive?" Their correspondence lasted for 23 years, but her verse did not find a wide audience until after her death, when her sister Lavinia discovered around 40 bundles of poems. A first edition of heavily edited works was published in 1890, but it was not until 1955 that her letters and poems appeared in their original form.

MANUSCRIPT OF THE POEM "TWO — WERE IMMORTAL TWICE"

▷ **EMILY DICKINSON, c.1847**
This portrait shows Dickinson as a young woman. Later in life, she turned her back on society and, choosing to dress mainly in white, she kept to her room until her death, at the age of 55.

◁ **THE DICKINSON RESIDENCE**
Dickinson lived in this house in Amherst for most of her life, rarely leaving its grounds. When her correspondent Thomas Higginson suggested that they meet in Boston, she replied: "I do not cross my Father's ground to any House or town."

# Mark Twain

## 1835–1910, AMERICAN

Celebrated as one of the first authentic voices in American literature, writer and humorist Twain held a mirror up to the many faces of his rapidly evolving nation.

Samuel Langhorne Clemens, who later wrote under the name of Mark Twain, was born on November 30, 1835, the sixth in a family of seven children living in poverty in Hannibal, Missouri, close to the Mississippi River. He chronicled extraordinary times in American history, and his early years in a slave-owning state had a major impact on his later storytelling.

### On the river

After the death of his father, Clemens, at the age of 12, went to work as a typesetter and occasional writer for newspapers locally, and then farther afield in New York and Philadelphia. He returned home 9 years later, at the age of 21, to become an apprentice steamboat pilot on the Mississippi. Plying the great river between St. Louis and New Orleans was a high-status career that immersed Twain in the savage exuberance of life along its banks. However, in 1861 the Civil War ended river trade. Lured by the gold and silver rush in Nevada, the young Clemens journeyed west by stagecoach, encountering American Indian tribes, wild frontiersmen, and innumerable setbacks, which became the fodder for books such as *Roughing It* (1872).

Returning to work on newspapers in Virginia City and then San Francisco, he adopted the pen name Mark Twain—a steamboat man's term for safe water: two fathoms deep. His short story "The Celebrated Jumping Frog of Calaveras County" was his first success in 1865. Reinvented as a travel writer and lecturer, Twain toured Europe and the Holy Land aboard the ship *Quaker City*. In his hilarious account of travel with naive Americans, *The Innocents Abroad* (1869), he observes that the reader will "never know what a consummate ass he can become until he goes abroad." During the trip, he fell in love with a picture of Olivia Langdon, the sister of a travel companion. By 1870, he had married her and moved to Hartford, Connecticut.

### Later years

Twain wrote his most famous books while living in Hartford. *The Adventures of Tom Sawyer* (1876) was set in a fictional town based on his boyhood home of Hannibal. In 1882, Twain returned to the river to research *Life on the Mississippi* (1883), a memoir of his piloting days, but found his surroundings changed beyond recognition. A year later he wrote *Adventures of Huckleberry Finn*. Set 40 years earlier, amid slavery in the South and land grabbing in the West, Huck's journey down river on a raft with an escaped slave is a "boy's own" story with a radical heart: a scathing satire on racism.

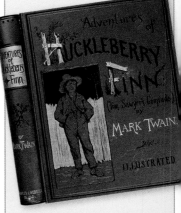

AN EARLY US EDITION OF *ADVENTURES OF HUCKLEBERRY FINN*, 1884

▷ **TWAIN IN HARTFORD**
Twain is pictured here in his later years at his home in Hartford, Connecticut. Over his lifetime he wrote 28 books and many short stories, letters, and sketches. He was awarded honorary doctorates by Yale and Oxford universities.

◁ **STEAMBOAT YEARS**
This bird's-eye view shows Twain's hometown of Hannibal, Missouri, in 1869. His writings draw heavily on his experiences as a steamboat pilot on the Mississippi River and the eccentricities of the people he met there.

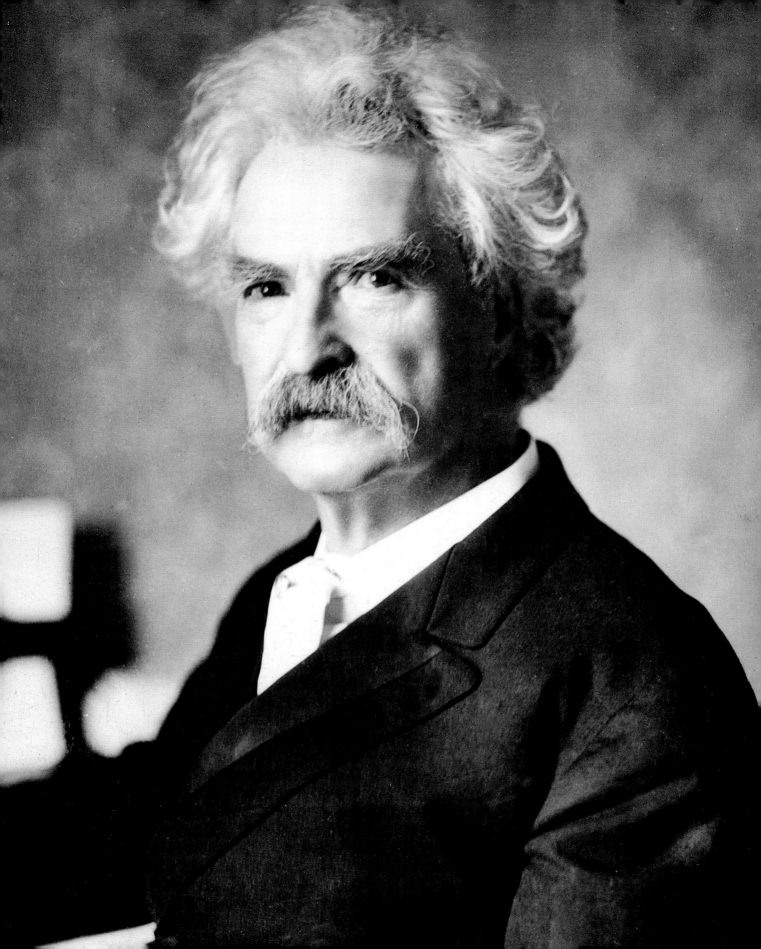

# Thomas Hardy

## 1840–1928, ENGLISH

One of England's best-loved novelists and poets of the 19th century, Hardy came from humble rustic origins and immortalized his native region in a series of sweeping, romantic tales.

△ **DORSET HOME**
Hardy was born in this cob and thatch cottage in Higher Bockhampton and lived there until he was 34. It was here that he wrote *Far from the Madding Crowd.*

Thomas Hardy's family background was highly significant in determining the themes that he would later explore in his novels. He was born in the cottage that his great-grandfather had built in the tiny hamlet of Higher Bockhampton, just outside Dorchester, the county town of Dorset in southern England. His father had done well as a master stonemason, but the family had its secrets. Hardy's parents had been obliged to marry hurriedly after his mother became pregnant, and his grandmother—the daughter of an affluent farmer—was disinherited after marrying a servant. She endured a terrible marriage, dying in poverty, since her husband turned out to be a violent drunk. Hardy did not reveal these events directly in his writing, but issues such as marriage between different classes, the shame of illegitimacy, and sudden reversals in financial fortunes were to figure prominently in his works.

Hardy was a sickly boy—he had nearly died at birth—but he was precociously gifted. He learned to read "almost before he could walk" and was an outstanding pupil at school. He dreamed of studying at one of the great universities, just like the main character in his novel *Jude the Obscure,* but his social status hindered this. Instead, he became apprenticed to a local architect, John Hicks. There, he met Horace Moule, a brilliant but erratic scholar, who had a profound influence on the youthful Hardy. Moule acted as his mentor, guiding his studies and encouraging his early efforts at writing poetry. The two men remained firm friends until Moule's tragic suicide in 1873.

### Stored experience

Hardy was a sensitive, impressionable character. This made him vulnerable to criticism, but also heightened his awareness of the suffering of others, and he would store his sometimes traumatic memories for later use. At the age of 16, for example, he witnessed the hanging of Martha Brown, who had been convicted of murdering her philandering husband. This was the last public execution of a woman in Dorchester and the gruesome spectacle remained in Hardy's mind for the rest of his life. It undoubtedly influenced both the plot and the character of the tragic heroine in *Tess of the d'Urbervilles.*

**A MAP OF THE ANGLO-SAXON KINGDOMS OF ENGLAND**

> " ... That which, **socially**, is a **great tragedy**, may be **in Nature** no **alarming circumstance**. "

THOMAS HARDY

▷ *THOMAS HARDY, 1923*
The English portraitist Reginald Grenville painted several images of Hardy when he stayed with the author at his home, Max Gate, in Dorchester.

EMMA GIFFORD

In 1862, Hardy moved to London to further his career, joining the architectural practice of Arthur Blomfield. He was fascinated by the capital, sampling the cultural delights of its theaters and galleries. Of his architectural work at this time, one curiosity survives. This is "Hardy's Tree," a circular arrangement of tombstones near St. Pancras, which he designed when he was clearing a graveyard in order to make way for a new section of the Midland Railway.

Hardy met his first wife through his architectural work. He was in Cornwall, determining the costs of repairs to the church of St. Juliot, when he made the acquaintance of Emma Gifford. Her father was a lawyer—a man of much higher social standing than Hardy's family—but he was a drinker and was bankrupt. Despite this, Hardy took pains to conceal his own background, ensuring that their respective families did not meet for several years. Their wedding in 1874 was witnessed only by Emma's brother and the daughter of Hardy's landlady. These were the kinds of social tensions that Hardy was to describe so well in his novels.

### Early writing
By this time, Hardy had committed himself firmly to a writing career. *Desperate Remedies* had appeared in 1871, though he had been obliged to subsidize its publication with his own money. It was followed by *Under the Greenwood Tree* (1872), a brief but charming novel that drew heavily on his childhood memories of the musicians (including his own father) who had played at his local church in Stinsford. The next book, *A Pair of Blue Eyes* (1873), featured a heroine who was modeled closely on Emma Gifford. However, it was Hardy's fourth novel— *Far from the Madding Crowd*—that brought him fame and recognition.

*Far from the Madding Crowd* was serialized in the prestigious *Cornhill Magazine* from January to December 1874, and then published in a two-volume edition. In the Victorian era, serialization was the sign that an author had arrived. It allowed them to earn a decent income, since they could reach a broad audience (magazines were much cheaper than books). However, it did impose restrictions on the style and structure of a novel: the action had to be spread evenly across the installments; the length of each episode was predetermined and had to be produced on a deadline; and the content had to be appropriate for family reading. Hardy struggled increasingly with this final condition (although adjustments could be made between the serial version and the eventual published book).

### Rural realities
*Far from the Madding Crowd* was pioneering in its portrait of rural life. While depicting the beauty of Hardy's native Dorset—its landscapes, and its traditions—it reflected the tough realities of living on the land, showing, for example, how easy it was for the shepherd Gabriel Oak to face ruin and humiliation, and for Fanny Robin to die in misery in the workhouse. The book provided the blueprint for Hardy's collection of stories *Wessex Tales* (1888), in which he continued to depict the countryside in a realistic and unsentimental way.

Hardy also documented the major changes that were taking place in the countryside. The growth of the railroad gave farm laborers the opportunity to

## KEY WORKS

**1874**
*Far from the Madding Crowd*, one of Hardy's best Wessex novels, is published. It takes its title from Thomas Gray's *Elegy in a Country Churchyard*.

**1878**
*The Return of the Native* is published. It is a tale of awakening passions suffused with the brooding atmosphere of Egdon Heath.

**1886**
*The Mayor of Casterbridge*, subtitled *The Story of a Man of Character*, is a tragic tale about the rise and fall of a lowly worker baling hay.

**1891**
Hardy writes *Tess of the d'Urbervilles*, his heartbreaking tale of seduction, betrayal, and murder.

**1895**
*Jude the Obscure* is Hardy's final novel. It is a bleak and controversial parable about the "deadly war ... between flesh and spirit."

move farther afield in their search for work, but the repeal of the Corn Laws caused a decline in British agriculture. Unemployment rose, as farmers' livelihoods were squeezed by cheap imports, and there was an increasing reliance on machines. In *Tess*, for example, the heroine's decline is mirrored by her move from a pleasant dairy to a grim, "starve-acre" farm,

◁ *FAR FROM THE MADDING CROWD*
Hardy's novel follows the life and loves of farmer Bathsheba Everdene. Despite its outwardly happy ending, it is an unsettling and often dark novel.

Flintcomb-Ash, where the workers are forced to do hard physical labor and where Tess struggles to cope with the "monstrous" threshing machine.

Hardy's rural homeland provided a rich backdrop for his heady cocktail of dramas, which included seductions, desertions, broken marriages, and unwanted children. These became increasingly pessimistic, often with an overriding sense of fatalism.

In his last two novels (*Tess of the d'Urbervilles* and *Jude the Obscure*), it almost seemed as if the main characters were being punished for trying to rise above their station and better their lives.

Hardy gave up writing novels after *Jude the Obscure*. It had been heavily attacked for its apparent criticism of organized religion and the institution

of marriage, and dubbed "Jude the Obscene" by one critic. Hardy devoted the rest of his career to verse. Many of his poems were about age and the passage of time, but he also produced war poems and verses about Emma (despite having remarried two years after she died). After his death, he was honored with a place in Poets' Corner, Westminster Abbey, while his heart was buried in Dorset.

△ **HARDY COUNTRY**
The Blackmore Vale near the town of Blandford in north Dorset features in *Tess of the d'Urbervilles*, where Hardy calls it the Vale of the Little Dairies.

▽ **THE LIBRARY AT MAX GATE**
Hardy designed Max Gate—his grand house in Dorchester—in 1885 and lived there until his death. It was here that he wrote *Tess of the d'Urbervilles* and *Jude the Obscure*.

" Let me **repeat** that **a novel** is an **impression**, not an **argument**. "

THOMAS HARDY, PREFACE TO *TESS OF THE D'URBERVILLES*

# Emile Zola

**1840–1902, FRENCH**

The foremost French fiction writer of the late 19th century, Zola extended the range of the novel with his cynically "naturalist" account of life at all levels of society and his depictions of sex.

Emile Zola was born in Paris in 1840, the son of an Italian engineer and a French mother. Initially prosperous, the family moved to Aix-en-Provence in southern France in 1843. The father's death four years later reduced them to genteel poverty. In 1858, Zola returned to Paris, where he eked out a living from clerical jobs, and met a working-class Parisian woman, Alexandrine Meley, whom he later married. His experience of life at the lower levels of Parisian society was later put to good use in his novels.

During the 1860s, while working in the sales department of the publisher Hachette, Zola began to establish himself as a journalist and fiction writer. With his childhood friend, the painter Paul Cézanne (see box, right), he frequented the circle of artists later called the Impressionists. His first significant novel was the sensational melodrama *Thérèse Raquin*, published in 1867, a lurid tale of lust, murder, and guilt; in the following year, he planned a series of novels to rival Balzac's *Human Comedy*. Written

according to the scientific principles of "naturalism," these works would show how heredity and environment shaped the lives of members of a single family, the Rougon-Macquarts. Executing this plan was to occupy Zola for more than two decades.

## Naturalism

The first of the 20 Rougon-Macquart novels, *The Fortune of the Rougons*, appeared in 1871, but it was the seventh, *L'Assommoir* (1877) that established Zola's reputation. Making extensive use of Parisian slang, the novel was a vivid portrayal of working-class lives destroyed by poverty and alcohol. A series of scandalous successes followed, including the story of a prostitute, *Nana* (1880); *Germinal* (1885), set in the mines of northeast France; and *The Debacle* (1892), depicting the war and revolution that engulfed France at the end of the Second Empire. Despite the scientific pretensions of Zola's naturalism and the research that he conducted before writing, these were epic visionary dramas painted with a broad brush and heavily loaded with symbolism.

Exploiting the freedom of expression allowed by the French Third Republic, Zola was able to write about topics that had previously been taboo, such as masturbation, referenced

in his rural novel *The Earth* (1887). He also rejected conventional morality in his private life, maintaining a relationship with a young mistress, Jeanne Rozerot, starting in 1888, with whom he had two children.

In 1898, Zola became involved in France's greatest political scandal, the Dreyfus affair (see page 175) denouncing the French authorities for anti-Semitism and the perversion of justice. He became a hero of the political left and a villain for the right. Prosecuted for libel, he fled to Britain. After returning to France, he died in 1902, poisoned by carbon monoxide from a blocked chimney.

△ *L'ASSOMMOIR* **POSTER**
Zola's novel was adapted into a play in Europe and the US, where its grim depictions of alcoholism and poverty were co-opted by the temperance movement.

◁ *ZOLA*, **1868**
Zola was a champion of Impressionist art, and in 1867 wrote a stern defense of the painter Edouard Manet against his conservative critics. In return, Manet painted this portrait of Zola.

## IN PROFILE
### Paul Cézanne

Zola and Cézanne went to the same school in Aix-en-Provence, and it was Zola who encouraged his friend to leave Aix for Paris. The novelist depicted Cézanne as the artist Claude Lantier in his 1873 novel *The Belly of Paris*. The two stayed friends until Zola's *The Masterpiece* (*L'Oeuvre*), 1886, a novel in which the painter Lantier is driven to suicide by his search for an artistic ideal. Cézanne returned the copy of *The Masterpiece* that Zola sent him and the two men never spoke again.

*SELF-PORTRAIT*, **PAUL CEZANNE, 1879**

" I want to **portray** ... the **fatal convulsions** that accompany the **birth** of a **new world**. "

EMILE ZOLA

# Henry James

## 1843–1916, AMERICAN

Known later in life as "the Master," James wrote novels, novellas, and short stories. His intense, finely worked psychological dramas raised the art of fiction to new levels of subtlety and complexity.

Born into a wealthy, intellectually distinguished family in New York, Henry James was brought up on French and English novels, and visited Europe with his family for five years when he was an adolescent. After making the decision to pursue a career as a novelist, the conflict between the culture and manners of US and European society presented itself as a natural subject.

The ironies of American innocence and European corruption provided the focus for early novels, such as *The Europeans* (1878), before James established his fame by inventing the bold, modern "American girl" in his novella *Daisy Miller* (1879) and the novel *The Portrait of a Lady* (1880–1881). From this time on, he lived exclusively in England and France.

The intimate side of James's life is obscure. If he was gay he concealed it, living an outwardly chaste life, but in his later years he experienced love—not necessarily sexual—with

two younger men. He also formed strong emotional bonds with women; the early death of his beloved cousin Minny Temple in 1870 haunted his fiction, and she was the model for the doomed Milly Theale in *The Wings of the Dove* (1902).

### Hidden desires

James typically smuggled forbidden subjects into his fiction. Lesbianism featured in *The Bostonians* (1886), pedophilia in *The Turn of the Screw* (1898), and incest in *The Golden Bowl* (1904)—all under cover of an elaborate style. Anything could be said as long as it was said obscurely. *What Masie Knew* (1897) portrayed affairs and adult power struggles seen through

the candid eyes of a supposedly innocent child. *The Ambassadors* (1903) told the tragic story—which may have been James's own—of a visitor to Paris from the puritan US whose moral conscience would never allow him to fully live life.

Later in life, James employed more indirect plots to explore the complexity of the human mind; he would refract events through the eyes of his characters, with their subtle self-deceptions and evasions.

His later works were dictated, since James found it increasingly hard to write by hand. After 1904, he wrote no major fiction. He became a British subject in 1915, and died in Chelsea, London, the following year.

**WILLIAM JAMES, PHILOSOPHER AND PSYCHOLOGIST**

◁ **HENRY JAMES**, 1913

James was acquainted with many of the leading cultural figures of his day, including the writers Gustave Flaubert; Alfred, Lord Tennyson; Emile Zola; and the painter John Singer Sargent, a fellow American expat. Sargent painted this portrait of the writer to mark his 70th birthday.

◁ **LAMB HOUSE, RYE**

For many years, James was a compulsive socialite, mixing with the London elite. From 1897 on, however, he withdrew to a comparatively reclusive existence at Lamb House on England's south coast.

" **Experience** is **never limited**, and it is **never complete**; it is an **immense sensibility**, a kind of huge **spider-web** ... "

HENRY JAMES, "THE ART OF FICTION"

⊳ *AUGUST STRINDBERG*, 1892
Strindberg knew many of his artistic
contemporaries, and formed a close
friendship with the Norwegian painter
Edvard Munch. The two shared ideas,
such as allowing the hand of chance into
artistic works. Munch painted Strindberg
and, similarly, Strindberg based some of
his characters on Munch's attributes.

# August Strindberg

## 1849–1912, SWEDISH

Often referred to as the father of modern Swedish literature, Strindberg
is best known as a playwright whose work was influential in the
transition from 19th-century naturalism to 20th-century modernism.

> "The **world**, **life** and **human beings** are only an **illusion**, a **phantom**, a **dream image**."

AUGUST STRINDBERG, *A DREAM PLAY*

◁ **INTIMATE THEATER POSTER**
In cofounding this theater in 1907 Strindberg "envisioned a theater where the harmony of the performance unfolded from the tones, rhythms, motifs, and movements of the script as if in a polyphonic musical composition."

Johan August Strindberg was born in Stockholm. His father was a shipping agent and his mother, who died when he was a boy, was a former maid. In his autobiography, *The Son of a Servant* (1913), he describes his childhood as unsettled and insecure.

His education was also unsatisfactory. He first studied theology and then medicine at the University of Uppsala, but attended only intermittently, taking short-term jobs—including freelance journalism and working as an extra at the theater—rather than devoting himself to his studies. He failed to graduate.

During this time, however, Strindberg developed a talent for writing, and even had two plays performed at the Royal Theater. Despite this success, he was uncomfortable with the stilted verse style of his early dramas, and set to work on *Master Olof*, a historical play written in colloquial prose. To his dismay, it was rejected by the Royal Theater, and was not performed until 1881. Disillusioned, Strindberg turned to journalism, and during the 1870s built a reputation as an angry critic of the Stockholm bourgeoisie. He fell in love with an aspiring actress, the baroness Siri von Essen, whom he married in 1877, but their life was

blighted by the death of their first child soon after birth and by Strindberg's bankruptcy in 1879. Nevertheless, he continued writing, and later that year published his first novel, *The Red Room*, a sparkling satire of the hypocrisy of Swedish society. Buoyed by its success, he went on to write a number of short stories, novels, and plays attacking the establishment.

### Symbolism and the occult

After traveling in France in the 1880s, Strindberg fell under the influence of naturalism, as advocated by Emile Zola. He put it into practice in his next plays, *The Father* (1887) and *Miss Julie* (1888), in which Siri played the lead. Just as the relationship depicted in *Miss Julie* (between an aristocratic

woman and a valet) was doomed to failure, Strindberg's own marriage also came to an end in 1891, marking another period of personal upheaval: a short-lived marriage to the Austrian journalist and translator Frida Uhl and a series of breakdowns put a temporary stop to his creativity. He became obsessed by religion, alchemy, and the occult, and was involved with the symbolist movement.

He chronicled this "inferno crisis" in the autobiographical novel *Inferno*, and applied his new ideas to his plays: his fantastical *To Damascus* starred the 20-year-old Harriet Bosse, who became Strindberg's third wife. After the turn of the century, he continued to stretch the bounds of symbolist writing with *The Dance of Death* (1900), *A Dream Play* (1901–1902), and *The Ghost Sonata* (1908), written for the Intimate Theater that he founded in Stockholm.

Strindberg's health declined following the collapse of the Intimate Theater and he died in his home in Stockholm on May 14, 1912.

△ **WONDERLAND, 1894**
Strindberg was an accomplished artist and painted as a form of therapy when suffering from writer's block. His inner turmoil is visible in many works; others, such as *Wonderland*, exude serenity. His refined visual sense is also evident in the theatrical directions in his plays.

## ON STYLE
### Beyond naturalism

Strindberg's first major plays were in the naturalist style, chronicling events in the lives of ordinary people, and highlighting the social and political situation of the time. However, his later fascination with the occult led to an interest in symbolism, shifting the emphasis in his work from the realistic and mundane to the imaginative and spiritual, expressed in dreamlike images with symbolic meaning. Instead of examining the psychology of domestic life, he focused on the universal and the unconscious, anticipating some of the elements of expressionism and surrealism.

SCENE FROM *A DREAM PLAY* AT THE NATIONAL THEATRE, LONDON, 2005

# Guy de Maupassant

## 1850–1893, FRENCH

Maupassant is noted for his candid and realistic portrayal of the lives of his contemporaries and, with his economy of style and exquisite control of pace, as one of France's greatest short-story writers.

Guy de Maupassant was born near Dieppe in Normandy into the kind of prosperous bourgeois family that would so often feature in his work. However, his comfortable early life was disrupted when his parents separated: Guy and his brother, Hervé, then moved with their mother to Etretat, some 45 miles (70 km) away.

### From war to Paris

The young Maupassant enjoyed an outdoor lifestyle, and his mother encouraged his love of literature. After receiving his baccalaureate in 1869, he was almost immediately drafted into the army. Clearly not cut out for combat, he served as a clerk in Rouen during the Franco-Prussian War (1870–1871), and in spite of reports that he served bravely, he later told his mother that he fled as the Prussians approached the town and "ran very well."

Maupassant's father bought him out of the army, and the young man became a civil servant in Paris. While his mother inspired a passion for

◁ **BEL-AMI, 1895**
Maupassant's novel charts the history of Duroy, a scoundrel who wins the affections of women to gain social advantage in fin-de-siècle Paris.

reading, his father seems to have passed on to him a taste for rampant promiscuity: the budding writer often indulged in the city's numerous brothels and took prostitutes on his many boating trips on the Seine. In Paris, he not only gained a reputation as a formidable oarsman but also found that he was suffering from syphilis. Undeterred by what must have been a frightening, although not uncommon, diagnosis, Maupassant began to write in earnest, pouring his experiences of the war, the provincial bourgeoisie, urban workers, and the civil service into a prolific body of work that would eventually comprise hundreds of short stories, six novels, three travel books, several plays, and poetry.

In 1880, he published one of his most famous stories, "Boule de suif" (loosely translated as "Ball of Fat"), and soon gained a following: his uninhibited approach to sexual matters, domestic violence, adultery, promiscuity, and prostitution certainly fascinated his readers. His volume of short stories reached its twelfth edition in two years and his novel, *Bel-Ami*, was reprinted a staggering 37 times in four months.

### Mental decline

With his growing wealth, the author bought a large apartment with an annex in which he could discreetly entertain Paris demimondaines. However, he did not relish the fame that came with his success and became increasingly isolated, often traveling alone around Algeria and Europe aboard his yacht *Bel-Ami*.

Over time, the mental instability that characterized those with syphilis turned Maupassant into an obsessive person who saw persecution everywhere. By 1892, it was clear that he was following closely in the footsteps of his brother, who died in an insane asylum. After trying to cut his own throat, Maupassant was committed to the asylum at Passy, where he died on July 6, 1893, at just 42.

**GUSTAVE FLAUBERT, c.1870**

▽ **CHATEAU DE MIROMESNIL**
Guy de Maupassant was a member of a prosperous bourgeois family and, according to his mother, was born in the grand Château de Miromesnil—a claim that has recently been disputed.

◁ **MAUPASSANT, 1888**
This portrait of Guy de Maupassant by Auguste Feyen-Perrin, reveals little of the complex character of a man who was described by Emile Zola as "the happiest and unhappiest of men."

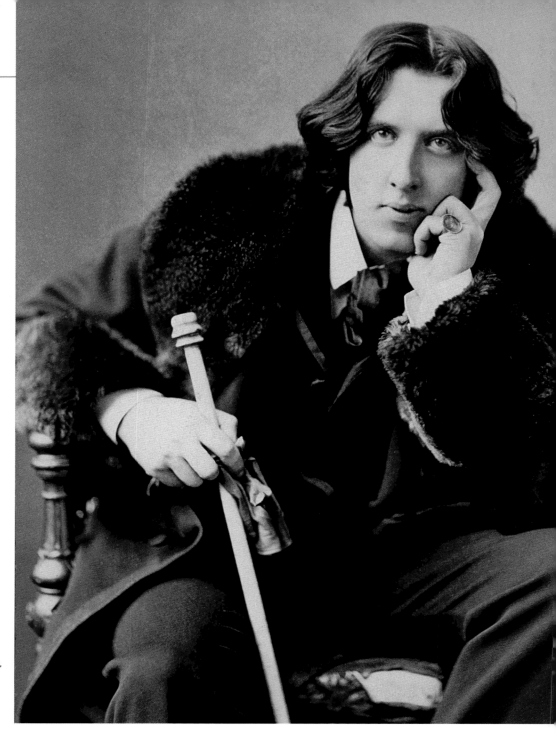

▷ **WILDE IN 1882**
Wilde displayed his commitment to the Aesthetic movement through his own appearance, donning ostentatious clothes, such as velvet jackets and knickers, for his lecture tours in the US. He wrote, "Beauty is the wonder of wonders. It is only shallow people who do not judge by appearances."

# Oscar Wilde

**1854–1900, IRISH**

Famed as much for his epigrams and commitment to Aestheticism as for the scandal of his private life, Wilde remains one of the wittiest and most imaginative authors of the late 19th century.

# "Vice and virtue are to the artist materials for an art."

OSCAR WILDE, *THE PICTURE OF DORIAN GRAY*

Oscar Wilde was born on October 16, 1854 into a well-respected, cultured Dublin family. His father was a doctor and an expert in Irish folklore, his mother a prominent nationalist poet. But despite this seemingly upright family background, Wilde's father had three illegitimate children and was accused of raping a former patient. No wonder that the potential for scandal and secret lives would come to feature so heavily in his son's work.

Wilde himself was able to remain relatively free of scandal until his mid-20s, in spite of a growing reputation as a dandy whose witty epigrams had gained him national fame—caricatures from the 1880s depict him in stockings and knickers, walking down the street clutching a sunflower. He was, however, a serious scholar who achieved a first-class honors degree in two subjects at Oxford and won the Newdigate Prize for Poetry. Nor was there any sign his sexuality that so defined his later life. Instead, for a time, Wilde seems to have been in love with Florence Balcombe, future wife of the Irish author Bram Stoker.

After Oxford, Wilde moved to London, where he carved out a modest living writing poetry, drama, essays, and reviews. A lecture tour of the US in 1882 earned him enough to spend five months in Paris, but he returned to London short of funds and nearing 30. He married a wealthy heiress, Constance Lloyd, and contributed to various periodicals before becoming editor of *Woman's World*. By that time, Wilde had been "seduced" by a young Canadian man, Robbie Ross, a meeting that set Wilde on the path to his own downfall but also fired his imagination. He poured his experiences into *The Picture of Dorian Gray* (1890), which was condemned for its immoral portrayal of male passions. Yet Wilde emerged with his literary reputation intact, and his subsequent plays—including *The Importance of Being Earnest* (1895)—were hits.

## Prison and downfall

In 1892, Wilde fell in love with Lord Alfred "Bosie" Douglas and was soon caught in the cross fire between Bosie and his father, the Ninth Marquess of Queensberry. When Queensberry left a calling card at Wilde's club addressed to "Oscar Wilde: Posing Somdomite" [sic], Wilde sued him for libel. It was a disaster. Queensberry's lawyers used Wilde's writings as evidence of homosexuality and Wilde was arrested on charges of gross indecency. In May 1895, he was sentenced to two years of hard labor. Suffering from hunger and dysentery, he was strapped to a treadmill for the first month and forced to walk six hours a day. In Reading Jail, he wrote a long letter of apology to Bosie, which was later published as *De Profundis*. The two tried living together in France after Wilde's release, but their relationship crumbled. By then, Constance had fled to Switzerland taking Wilde's sons with her. Broken by his various traumas, Wilde succumbed to meningitis and died in Paris on 30 November 1900.

△ *THE PICTURE OF DORIAN GRAY*
Wilde's only novel was published in 1890 in *Lippincott's Monthly Magazine* after heavy editing to avoid accusations of indecency. It is a Gothic tale of a beautiful young man who sells his soul in exchange for eternal youth; its homoerotic undertones caused outrage.

▽ LORD ALFRED DOUGLAS, 1902
Wilde's beloved "Bosie" was himself a writer, poet, and translator. During Wilde's imprisonment, Douglas petitioned Queen Victoria for the release of his lover.

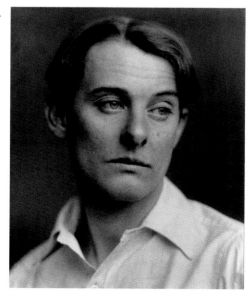

## IN CONTEXT
### Aestheticism

Wilde was a key figure in Aestheticism, a movement that promoted aesthetic value over social, political, or moral values. Rejecting the conservative Victorian tradition in which art and morality were inextricably linked, aesthetes created instead a cult of beauty at the heart of which was a desire to create "art for art's sake." Other notable aesthetes of the time included the painters James Abbott McNeill Whistler and Dante Gabriel Rossetti, whose work is notable for its sensuality and symbolism.

*PROSERPINE*, DANTE GABRIEL ROSSETTI, 1874

# Joseph Conrad

## 1857–1924, POLISH-BORN BRITISH

Polish by birth, Conrad became a major novelist writing in English. Drawing upon his experiences as a seafarer, he explored the dehumanizing effects of colonialism on people.

Josef Teofor Konrad Korzeniowski, later known as Joseph Conrad, was born in 1857 in Berdyczow, now in Ukraine. His parents belonged to the Polish landowning nobility. Since the 18th century, Poland had ceased to exist as an independent state and most Poles lived under the rule of the Russian Empire, a situation resented by the Polish aristocracy.

Conrad's father, Apollo Korzeniowski, a writer and idealistic patriot, moved to Warsaw in 1861 and attempted to organize resistance to Russian rule. Arrested by the authorities as a political subversive, he was exiled with his family to the cold and bleak marshlands of Vologda in northern Russia. Conrad's mother died in exile in 1865, her health destroyed by the harsh conditions. Apollo was allowed to return to Poland in 1867 but he was a broken man. He died in Kracow in 1869, after burning all his manuscripts.

### A life at sea

Whatever might have been expected of a Polish aristocrat orphaned under such tragic circumstances, it was certainly not that he should hear the call of the sea. But the young Conrad was an avid reader and books inspired a thirst for travel and adventure.

The efforts of his maternal uncle and guardian Thaddeus Bobrowski to direct him toward a more sensible path in life proved to be in vain, and by the age of 17, Conrad had decided to become a seaman. Bobrowski could not reasonably oppose the young man leaving Poland because, as the son of a subversive, he would always be a marked man to the Russian authorities, so he gave Conrad permission to leave for France and enroll in the merchant marine.

Established in the port of Marseille, Conrad led a feckless and disorderly existence. He was involved in gunrunning and smuggling; he was shot, either in a duel or suicide attempt; and he constantly pestered his guardian for money.

In 1878, under increasing pressure from Bobrowski to reform, Conrad moved to England and joined the merchant navy. He was to serve as a British sailor for the next 14 years. He had learned French as a child, but knew hardly a word of English. He taught himself the language while developing his naval career, progressing from coastal shipping to long-distance voyages and slowly rising through the ranks. He became a British citizen in 1886.

### Influential journeys

During these seafaring years, Conrad accumulated the experiences that would eventually provide inspiration for much of his later fiction. In 1881, he took a disastrous voyage aboard an unseaworthy sailing ship bound for Bangkok with a cargo of coal from Newcastle; the journey ended with the ship sinking and the cargo in flames.

◁ **APOLLO KORZENIOWSKI**
Conrad's introduction to the English language was through his father, a translator of Shakespeare. An ardent patriot, Apollo was given a hero's burial in Kracow after his death in 1869.

**POSTER FOR THE 1965 MOVIE ADAPTATION OF CONRAD'S** *LORD JIM*

▷ **LATE BLOSSOMING**
Conrad began to write in earnest relatively late in life, at the age of 36. He chose to write in English rather than his native Polish or adopted French.

> " **Every age** is fed on **illusions**, lest men should **renounce life early** and the **human race** come to an **end**. "

JOSEPH CONRAD, *VICTORY*

△ **TYPHOON, 1902**
Conrad's novella *Typhoon*, in which Captain McWhirr sails the SS *Nan-Shan* into the eye of a great storm, is a story of human will confronting an indomitable force of nature.

This episode later provided the material for his short story "Youth" (1898). A voyage from Bombay to London onboard the sailing ship *Narcissus* in 1884 would form the basis for the novel *The Children of the Sea* (1897)—the story of a dying black sailor on a stricken ship, which is an allegory of comradeship in the face of adversity.

In 1887–1888, Conrad stayed in Southeast Asia, meeting characters such as the laconic Captain John McWhirr, immortalized as the hero of the novella *Typhoon* (1902), and the trader Charles Olmeijer, who became Kaspar Almayer in his first novel, *Almayer's Folly* (1895).

### Adventures in the colonies
By 1888, Conrad had been given command of his own ship, but he remained restless and unsatisfied. In 1889, driven by a thirst for new experiences, he applied to serve the Belgians in Congo. Appointed captain

◁ **MARSEILLE, 1870s**
The young Conrad lived an adventurous life in the French port of Marseille. He was involved in political conspiracy and in smuggling arms to Spain, events that he later fictionalized in his novel *The Arrow of Gold* (1919).

### IN CONTEXT
#### Conrad's Congo

When Conrad traveled to Congo in 1890, it was effectively under the personal and undisputed rule of Leopold II of Belgium, who widely advertised his lofty humanitarian goals. In fact, Congo was exposed to ruthless economic exploitation and its people were subjected to forced labor and barbaric punishment. In 1904, a report by the British consul, whom Conrad had met during his time in Congo, exposed the full horror of conditions there. Leopold was forced to initiate reforms and Congo became a formal Belgian colony in 1908.

**PUNISHMENTS FOR CONGO'S FORCED LABORERS INCLUDED AMPUTATION**

of a riverboat whose previous commander had been murdered, he traveled overland to Kinshasa before sailing a "tin-pot steamer" up the Congo River to the Boyoma Falls. He almost died of dysentery and malaria, but worse than this suffering was the spectacle of moral degradation, as the European colonialists engaged in what Conrad described as "the vilest scramble for loot that ever disfigured the history of human conscience." The whole experience was memorably fictionalized in his celebrated novella *Heart of Darkness* (1899).

Conrad returned to England and the seafaring life, but he was increasingly dissatisfied with his existence. In 1894, after the abrupt cancellation of a voyage that he had

signed up for, he felt suddenly inspired to complete a piece of fiction he had been engaged in for some years— *Almayer's Folly*. It was accepted for publication and, together with *The Outcast of the Islands* (1896), established Conrad as a significant writer. To complete the transformation of his life, in 1896 he married Jessie George, a working-class woman 16 years his junior who earned her living as a typist. Her placid nature proved to be a fortunate complement to Conrad's unsettled temperament. They had two children.

### A settled life
Conrad devoted the remainder of his life to writing, living mostly in rural parts of southern England. His early works were based overwhelmingly upon his personal experiences of life at sea and in the European colonies. They reflected the author's ironic fatalism and his preoccupation with personal responsibility and codes of honor, notably in the novel *Lord Jim* (1900), which explores a man's efforts

" He **cried out twice,** a cry that was no more than a breath—**'The horror! The horror!'** "

JOSEPH CONRAD, *HEART OF DARKNESS*

to redeem himself after a shameful dereliction of duty. Conrad's portrayal of colonialism, and of what Europe saw as its "civilizing mission" in the outside world, was laced with sardonic skepticism. For Conrad, there was no moral distinction between the Europeans and the local populations that they ruled.

## Late works

Conrad's Polish background gave him a sharp awareness of political issues, which became increasingly prominent in his work. In 1904, he published *Nostromo*, a novel that moved away from his personal experience to portray the political and moral conflicts generated by the arrival of global capitalism in a corrupt and violent South American state. In *The Secret Agent* (1907), he made London the setting for a dark tale about the menace and futility of anarchist terrorism, and in *Under Western Eyes* (1911), he launched an attack on the moral nihilism of Russia's would-be revolutionaries.

Conrad had unexpected popular success with the novel *Chance* in 1913; and in his major late work, *Victory* (1915), he returned to the islands of Southeast Asia to make another powerful statement about his essentially bleak view of life. Some scholars suggest that the novel also engages with one of the author's own failings—an inability to handle sexual relationships.

Having become a grand old man of English letters, Conrad died in 1924, soon after refusing a knighthood. His works have continued to be influential, and have been referenced by T. S. Eliot and Bob Dylan, among others. *Heart of Darkness* inspired Francis Ford Coppola's Oscar-winning movie *Apocalypse Now* (1980).

△ **APOCALYPSE NOW**
Director Francis Ford Coppola relocated Conrad's *Heart of Darkness* to the jungles of Vietnam, taking a hard and critical look at US military action in the Vietnam War and examining the darkness present in the recesses of the human soul.

## KEY WORKS

# Rudyard Kipling

## 1865–1936, ENGLISH

Kipling was a prolific poet, short-story writer, and novelist. The range of his work, coupled with his popular style, brought him international fame. He was the first British writer to be awarded the Nobel Prize in Literature.

Rudyard Kipling was born into an artistic family in Bombay (now Mumbai), India. His father was a professor of sculpture at the local art school; his mother was the sister-in-law of the Pre-Raphaelite artist Edward Burne-Jones. His name came from Rudyard Lake in Staffordshire, where his parents did their courting.

Kipling lived in India until he was six, before being sent to England. Initially, he boarded with a family in Southsea—a miserable experience, described in his story "Baa Baa Black Sheep"—before moving to Westward Ho! in Devon. Here, he developed his interest in literature, becoming editor of his school magazine.

### Tales of India

In 1882, Kipling returned to India, taking a job as a journalist on the *Civil and Military Gazette* in Lahore. The paper gave him considerable latitude. Alongside the usual reports and gossip, he was able to include his own short stories and poems. These covered a huge variety of themes, reflecting Kipling's insatiable curiosity about every aspect of Indian life, and were later published in several collections. *Departmental Ditties* (1886) satirized English bureaucrats; *Plain Tales from the Hills* (1888) was inspired by high society at the hill station of Simla (now Shimla); while *Soldiers Three* (1888) dealt with one of his favorite subjects—the daily life of the British "Tommy" (common solider).

These books proved to be popular, not only in India but also in Britain and the US, and by the time he arrived in London in 1889, Kipling was already well known to readers. He consolidated his reputation with the *Barrack-Room Ballads*, which first began to appear in 1890. These deceptively simple verses were written in the vernacular of a common soldier's speech, echoing the rhythms of contemporary music-hall songs. Kipling used traditional forms, such as Victorian monologues, street songs, and ballads, to convey powerful, emotional messages in the simplest possible manner.

Kipling continued to draw on his Indian experiences in his writing, producing *Kim*—the finest of his novels—in 1901. By now, though, his life had taken a different turn. In 1892, he married an American woman, Caroline ("Carrie") Balestier, and went to live in Vermont. He began writing children's stories, notably the two volumes of *The Jungle Book* (1894 and 1895). The family later returned to England, settling in Sussex, but continued to visit the US until 1899, when his daughter Josephine died there. This inspired Kipling's most moving story, "They," about a father mourning his dead child.

This was not the only domestic tragedy that he suffered. In 1915, his only son was killed at the Battle of Loos after Kipling had apparently pulled strings to enable him to enlist. In later years, Kipling's patriotic attitude to war and to colonial rule (which some prefer to describe as jingoism) somewhat tarnished his reputation, though he was expressing views that were very widely held at the time. He was, in that sense, a perfect spokesman for his age.

### Children's books

Kipling's reputation has fluctuated over the years, but his books for children have always remained popular. They originated as bedtime stories for his own children, relying on the charm of giving animals anthropomorphic qualities. The *Just So Stories* (so called because Kipling's daughter insisted on them being recited just as she liked), published in 1902, focused on the origins of various animal traits ("How the Camel got his Hump," "How the Leopard got his Spots"). The witty illustrations, drawn by Kipling himself, are a particular delight. The two *Jungle Books*, describing how a boy was raised by a pack of wolves, have also never lost their appeal. Among other things, they inspired the famous Tarzan tales of Edgar Rice Burroughs and prompted Baden-Powell to found the Wolf Cub division of the Boy Scouts (now the Cubs).

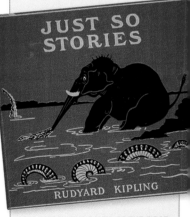

**DETAIL FROM THE COVER OF THE FIRST UK EDITION OF *JUST SO STORIES*, 1902**

▷ ***RUDYARD KIPLING*, 1899**
Kipling is shown deep in thought at his writing desk in this portrait by his cousin, Philip Burne-Jones. The painter's most famous work, *The Vampire*, inspired Kipling's poem of the same name.

◁ **BATEMAN'S, SUSSEX**
Kipling, his American wife, and their children lived at Bateman's, a grand house in East Sussex, from 1902 until the writer's death in 1936.

# Anton Chekhov

**1860–1904, RUSSIAN**

In his youth, Chekhov was a prolific short-story writer, producing snappy, humorous tales bursting with fresh ideas. Later, he switched to drama, creating subtle, mood-filled plays that revolutionized the theater.

△ **ALARM CLOCK MAGAZINE**
Chekhov contributed hundreds of stories to weekly satirical magazines such as *Alarm Clock*, principally to earn money. He later threw out these early works, calling them "literary excrements."

Anton Chekhov's career coincided with a golden age of Russian literature. Whereas many of the leading writers of the period came from noble stock (Tolstoy was a count and Gogol and Turgenev were of aristocratic descent), Chekhov grew up in extreme poverty. He was born in Taganrog, a port in southern Russia, into a family with six children. His grandfather had been a serf and his father was a grocer.

Although Taganrog was undeniably provincial, it had an opera house, a theater, and a good school, where Chekhov was educated. His world, however, was turned upside down when he was just 16. His father went bankrupt and fled to Moscow with his family, but left Chekhov behind to fend for himself. Showing the strength of character that was to bring him success later, Chekhov finished his schooling and, three years later, joined his family in Moscow, where he was accepted to medical school.

Alongside his studies, Chekhov began writing humorous pieces and short stories for small weekly magazines, to help support his family. The magazines had very strict word limits, and Chekhov soon developed a suitably economical style. He wrote impressionistically, capturing the essence of a character in a brief description or a few of lines of dialogue. He also learned the art of subtext, teasing readers with hidden layers of meaning.

Over the next few years, Chekhov wrote hundreds of short stories and vignettes for publication—a process that honed his skills and made him the family's main breadwinner: they were able to move out of their grim lodgings in the red-light district.

## Doctor and author

In 1884, Chekhov became a doctor, excelling at psychiatry and diagnosis—analytical skills that he also exploited in his writing. He continued producing short stories while practicing his new profession

◁ **ANTON PAVLOVICH CHEKHOV, 1898**
This portrait by Osip Braz shows Chekhov as a melancholy consumptive. The writer disliked the image, and refused to sign printed copies.

## IN CONTEXT
### Russian serfdom

Serfdom was a form of feudalism prevalent in Russia beginning in the 16th century. By the 19th century, about half of the 40 million Russian peasants were serfs—effectively, the property of landowning nobles, the czar, or religious foundations. In 1861, Czar Alexander II took the momentous step of abolishing serfdom in order to modernize the country. This reform had major long-term consequences, leading to the decline of the landed gentry—whose labor costs rose dramatically—and to the rise of a wealthy bourgeoisie. These changes were reflected in Chekhov's plays, particularly *The Cherry Orchard*, which was, in many ways, an elegy to a dying class.

*LANDLORD AND HIS SERFS*, KONSTANTIN ALEKSANDROVICH TRUTOVSKY, 1853.

> " Most **important of all**: keep watch, **observe**, **work** strenuously, **rewrite everything** five times, **condensing** and so on. "

ANTON CHEKHOV, LETTER TO HIS BROTHER ALEXANDER

△ **CHEKHOV'S DESK AT MELIKHOVO**
Chekhov lived at his estate in Melikhovo for over six years, sharing it with his parents and his sister, who acted as housekeeper. His writing at this time included stories about peasant life.

▽ **THE MOSCOW ART THEATRE, 1899**
Here, Chekhov is shown reading his play *The Seagull* to actors of the Moscow Art Theatre. The writer is shown in the center of the group, book in hand; to his left is the director and actor Konstantin Stanislavsky; and standing beside Stanislavsky is Olga Knipper, Chekhov's future wife.

and had no trouble combining the two disciplines: he referred to medicine as his "lawful wife" and literature as his "mistress." His medical knowledge even gave him the inspiration for several of his tales, which were structured around the progress of a disease. "Ward No. 6" and "A Dreary Story" are two of the most famous—and bleak—examples.

## Deeper stories

By this time, Chekhov had graduated from writing for cheap, disposable weekly magazines to more substantial monthly journals aimed at a more sophisticated readership. They paid better and, crucially, gave the writer the space to produce more complex and expansive pieces. A key figure in Chekhov's development was Aleksey

Suvorin, a St. Petersburg newspaper magnate, who paid three times as much as the Moscow editors, enabling Chekhov to live a more comfortable life and write at a less furious pace.

In his longer stories, Chekhov gave his characters more psychological depth and also began to subvert the traditional expectations of the genre: plots were not resolved neatly, lovers were not paired off in happy endings. Instead, relationships were muddied by confusion and poor communication. This atmosphere of uncertainty was to resurface later in the author's plays.

Chekhov published two collections of stories, *Motley Tales* (1886) and *In the Twilight* (1887), which were very well received, the latter winning him the prestigious Pushkin Prize for literature in 1888. Unfortunately, Chekhov's pleasure at this achievement was marred by events in his private life. After suffering cruelly for several months, his brother Nikolay died of

tuberculosis in June 1889, painfully reminding Chekhov—who suffered from the same disease—that his own health was worsening.

## Travels to the east

While in low spirits, Chekhov made one of the strangest decisions of his life: he embarked on a journey of around 4,000 miles (6,500 km) across Russia to study conditions in the penal colony on Sakhalin, an island between Siberia and Japan. The journey could easily have killed him, but he returned safely to write an extraordinary account of his experiences, *Sakhalin Island* (1893).

The change of routine seemed to galvanize Chekhov into action. In 1892, he purchased a small country estate at Melikhovo, just south of Moscow. There he built a lodge in the orchard, where he wrote some of his finest stories, along with the first draft of *The Seagull*. Chekhov had written plays

before, but early examples such as *Ivanov* (1887) and *The Wood Demon* (1889) were flops. He persisted because the theater was potentially profitable—authors could receive as much as 10 percent of the box office takings. Chekhov knew that even a modest hit in the theater would earn him far more than any of his stories.

Initially, though, it looked as if *The Seagull* would fare no better than his earlier efforts. The first production, which was staged in 1896, was an underrehearsed fiasco to which the unsympathetic audience responded with jeers and catcalls. Chekhov left before the end, vowing never to write another play. To compound his misery, his health was deteriorating. Under orders from his doctors, he was obliged to move from his beloved Melikhovo to the more temperate climate of Yalta, in the Crimea.

In his absence, *The Seagull* was revived by a brand-new company, the Moscow Art Theatre, with its director Konstantin Stanislavsky (see box, right) playing the part of Trigorin. This time, the play was a triumph, winning instant recognition for Chekhov's skill as a dramatist. He, in turn, forged a partnership with the Moscow Art Theatre, which created the defining productions of his quartet of masterpieces—*The Seagull*, *Uncle Vanya*, *Three Sisters*, and *The Cherry Orchard*. He even married the company's leading lady, Olga Knipper.

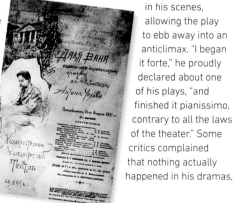

▷ *UNCLE VANYA PROGRAM*
Chekhov's play—a reworking of his earlier *The Wood Demon*—was first produced in 1899 by the Moscow Art Theatre.

## KEY WORKS

**1895**
Chekhov writes *The Seagull*, his first major play, in his lodge at Melikhovo. Its opening performance is a disaster.

**1898**
Paring down his earlier play *The Wood Demon* and reworking its ending, Chekhov produces *Uncle Vanya*.

**1899**
The short story "The Lady with the Dog" is published. It describes an affair between two people trapped in loveless marriages.

**1901**
The Moscow Art Theatre company first performs Chekhov's *Three Sisters*. Chekhov wrote the part of Masha for his future wife, Olga Knipper.

**1904**
Chekhov's final play, *The Cherry Orchard*, premieres in January, just a few months before the writer's death. It is judged a great success.

### A revolution in theater
Stanislavsky was skilled at presenting Chekhov's innovative dramas to the public. In them, Chekhov abandoned the theatricality of Russian drama, placing the emphasis on mood rather than action. His plays did not revolve around star performers, but were more about ensemble acting. They did not build to a climax—Chekhov often preferred to deflate tension in his scenes, allowing the play to ebb away into an anticlimax. "I began it forte," he proudly declared about one of his plays, "and finished it pianissimo, contrary to all the laws of the theater." Some critics complained that nothing actually happened in his dramas,

△ **LABOR CAMP, SAKHALIN**
In his account of the lives of prisoners on Sakhalin Island, Chekhov described the minutiae of existence in terrible conditions. The work remains an insightful and moving piece of investigative journalism.

but, instead of dramatic action, Chekhov preferred to portray the interior lives of his characters. They reminisce about the past; they muse about their failings in the present; and they dream about a better future.

Stanislavsky and Chekhov did not always see eye to eye. In particular, they clashed about the production of *The Cherry Orchard*. The author insisted that it was a comedy, but in Stanislavsky's staging its blend of humor and pathos came closer to tragedy. Sadly, it was to be Chekhov's last play. In the year that it opened, he finally succumbed to tuberculosis.

### IN PROFILE
#### Konstantin Stanislavsky

Stanislavsky revolutionized modern acting techniques with his celebrated "Method." This entailed training actors to learn the art of "experiencing" a part, rather than simply representing it. They were encouraged to examine their character's motivation, in order to convey their emotional and psychological state, as well as their subconscious behavior. Stanislavsky, who was an actor himself, put his ideas into practice in his own theatrical company, the Moscow Art Theatre. It achieved its first real breakthrough with a landmark production of *The Seagull* in 1898. This was a huge success, bringing out all the subtleties in Chekhov's text.

*STANISLAVSKY*, NIKOLAI ANDREEV, 1921

> **"Write** as much as you can! **Write, write, write** till your **fingers break!"**

ANTON CHEKHOV, LETTER TO MARIA KISELYOVA

▷ **TAGORE, 1925**
A man of distinctive appearance, Tagore was a true polymath. He was an accomplished musician and artist, an eclectic philosopher, and a passionate political activist. Above all, he advocated universalism and cultural freedom.

# Rabindranath Tagore

## 1861–1941, INDIAN

Tagore reshaped Bengali literature, introducing Western lyricism and naturalism into his explorations of India's people, spirituality, and nature. His pacifism and humanism gained him many admirers.

# "Let your **life** lightly **dance** on the **edges** of Time like **dew** on the **tip of a leaf**."

RABINDRANATH TAGORE, "THE GARDENER"

On August 7, 1941, Rabindranath Tagore's body was carried through Kolkata (formerly Calcutta), to the Ganges. As it went, people plucked hair from his head and before the body had been completely cremated, the crowd began picking through the remains in search of bones and other relics. It was a ghoulish end for a man revered as the poetic "soul" of India, but it was also a testament to the power of his reputation.

Tagore had been born some 80 years earlier into one of Kolkata's wealthiest families. The household was at the forefront of the Bengali cultural renaissance. Tagore wrote his first poetry at the age of 8, and at 16, he produced a collection of poems that was accepted as the lost works of a 17th-century Hindu poet.

## English influence

In 1878, Tagore was sent to school in England and then briefly studied law at University College London. While there, he deepened his knowledge of European literature and also heard the music hall and folk songs whose style he would later incorporate into the 2,000 songs of his own musical genre, *Rabindra Sangeet*.

Tagore returned to India, resolved to fuse European literature and Indian culture. Having married a 10-year-old girl, 12 years his junior, he moved to East Bengal in 1891 to manage his family's estates. There he came to know the local villagers, whose humble lives he poignantly—and with gentle irony—captured in Western-style short stories. He also started a school that sought to blend Indian and Western educational traditions.

## East to West

When his wife and two of his children died in 1902, Tagore poured his grief into a collection of poems, *Gitanjali (Song Offerings)*, which appeared in Bengali in 1910. Hoping to secure an English publisher, Tagore brought the manuscript to England, but promptly left it on the London Underground. Luckily it was found, and was published in 1912 in the author's own loose, interpretative translation. Conveying the peace of the soul in harmony with nature, the work struck a chord with readers in Europe—a continent on the brink of a bloody war. It garnered Tagore the Nobel Prize in Literature and brought him international fame. Mystical, sagelike, and exotic, Tagore seemed to embody what the West wanted the East to be, and in 1915, he was awarded a knighthood. His decision to return the honor in protest at the Amritsar massacre of 1919, however, showed that, despite his admiration for British culture, his loyalties lay with India.

Beginning the 1920s, Tagore focused on challenging conditions in India, not only campaigning against the caste system and untouchability, but also writing about the poverty of Kolkata. He dabbled in the nationalist movement and was close friends with Gandhi, but remained first and foremost Bengali. In 1937, Tagore fell into a coma. Although he recovered, it was the beginning of the end and he died four years later.

## ON FORM
### Tagore songs

Although best known for his verse, in his writing Tagore embraced novels, dramas, short stories, and thousands of songs in which he set his literature to music influenced by classical devotional songs as well as traditional folk forms. Tagore created a unique and innovative musical canon, which soon became deeply embedded in popular culture, so much so that his songs were adopted as the national anthems of Bangladesh and India.

STUDENTS PERFORM A DANCE DRAMA BASED ON A TAGORE SCRIPT

◁ **JORASANKO THAKUR BARI**
This grand house in Kolkata is the ancestral home of the Tagore family. It is the place where Rabindranath Tagore was born, grew up, and died. It is now a museum dedicated to the family's accomplishments.

# Directory

## Harriet Beecher Stowe

### 1811–1896, AMERICAN

Harriet Beecher Stowe was born in Connecticut, the daughter of Lyman, a Calvinist minister. At the age of 21, she followed her father to Cincinnati, Ohio, where she married the Biblical scholar Calvin Ellis Stowe. The pair became very active in the abolitionist movement, aiding fugitive slaves escaping from the South.

The couple was living in Brunswick, Maine, when Harriet wrote the novel *Uncle Tom's Cabin*. Skillfully crafted to engage the emotions of a white readership, the book sold 300,000 copies in under a year and is credited with shifting opinion in favor of the abolitionist cause. *Uncle Tom's Cabin* faced harsh criticism for depicting African Americans as passive victims, but her next novel, *Dred*, represented black resistance to slavery. Stowe, an international celebrity, went on to campaign for women's rights and write novels on New England society.

**KEY WORKS:** *Uncle Tom's Cabin*, 1851–1852; *Dred: A Tale of the Great Dismal Swamp*, 1856; *The Minister's Wooing*, 1859; *Oldtown Folks*, 1869

## Henry David Thoreau

### 1817–1862, AMERICAN

An essayist and poet, Thoreau is regarded as a forerunner of modern environmentalism and anarchism. Born in Concord, Massachusetts, he was encouraged to start writing by his neighbor, Ralph Waldo Emerson, and had his work published in the Transcendentalist magazine *The Dial*. In 1845, Thoreau embarked on a two-year experiment in simple living, occupying a cabin by Walden Pond near Concord. *Walden*, his most celebrated work, is an expression, in aphoristic prose, of his love of nature and radical individualism.

In protest of US government policies, Thoreau refused to pay his taxes and was briefly imprisoned, an experience that inspired his influential essay "Civil Disobedience." His reputation was enhanced by the posthumous publication of his copious journals and notes on nature. The popularity of his writings has steadily increased.

**KEY WORKS:** *A Week on the Concord and Merrimack Rivers*, 1849; "Civil Disobedience," 1849; *Walden; or, Life in the Woods*, 1854

## Ivan Turgenev

### 1818–1883, RUSSIAN

A novelist, short-story writer, and dramatist, Turgenev was born into the Russian landowning class. Rebelling against the czarist social system and the brutality of his domineering mother, he became an advocate of liberal reform. His first book of short stories, *A Sportsman's Sketches* (1852), earned him a sentence of house arrest for its critique of serfdom.

The 1862 novel *Fathers and Sons*, with its memorable portrait of the young nihilist Bazarov, expressed the author's despair at Russia's inability to change. Disappointed by the reception this book received, and pursuing a frustrated but faithful love for the French singer Pauline Viardot, he left Russia for good, eventually settling in France. Turgenev's dark psychological fictions, including the novella *First Love* and the novel *Torrents of Spring*, gained him a wide readership. He died in Paris.

**KEY WORKS:** *First Love*, 1860; *Fathers and Sons*, 1862; *Smoke*, 1867; *Torrents of Spring*, 1872

△ *THEODOR FONTANE*, CARL BREITBACH, 1883

## △ Theodor Fontane

### 1819–1898, GERMAN

The foremost German realist novelist of the 19th century, Fontane did not publish his first novel until the age of 58. Born in Neuruppin, Brandenburg, the son of an apothecary, he followed his father's profession before deciding to escape into journalism.

A foreign correspondent (he spent several years in London) and war correspondent, Fontane published travel books and military volumes but no fiction—with the exception of a disregarded novella—until *Before the Storm* appeared in 1878.

This historical novel, set in the Napoleonic era, was followed by a succession of novels that drew on Fontane's extensive experience of contemporary German society, dissecting its obsession with status and respectability in cool, ironic prose. He was especially sensitive to the situation of women, whose desires and aspirations so easily brought them into conflict with social convention. The culminating work of his career, *Effi Briest*, relates the tragic fate of an unremarkable woman (whose life is loosely based on that of Fontane's own grandmother), who is destroyed by the discovery of her adulterous past.

**KEY WORKS:** *Before the Storm*, 1878; *The Woman Taken in Adultery*, 1882; *Jenny Treibel*, 1893; *Effi Briest*, 1895

## Jules Verne

### 1828–1905, FRENCH

The inventor of what he termed "the novel of science," Jules Verne was a prolific writer with an enduring cultural influence. Born in Nantes, the son of a lawyer, he studied law in Paris and worked as a stockbroker, but never doubted that writing was his vocation. His breakthrough came with the publication of *Five Weeks in a Balloon* by Pierre-Jules Hetzel in 1863. Hetzel became the publisher of all Verne's books, which were branded "Extraordinary Voyages." They sought to present current geographic and scientific knowledge in the form of adventure stories, thus combining the seemingly incompatible realms of science and fantasy. It turned out to be a winning formula: some 54 novels appeared in the series.

Verne's works were scrupulously researched: his "inventions" such as the space rocket and submarine were logical projections from the cutting edge of 19th-century technology. The immense popularity of his novels has sometimes meant that their literary merit is underrated, but they currently stand high in critical esteem.

**KEY WORKS:** *Journey to the Center of the Earth*, 1864; *From the Earth to the Moon*, 1865; *20,000 Leagues Under the Sea*, 1870; *Around the World in Eighty Days*, 1873

## Christina Rossetti

1830–1894, ENGLISH

Victorian poet Christina Rossetti was the daughter of an Italian political exile living in London. Her talented siblings included the Pre-Raphaelite painter and poet Dante Gabriel Rossetti. Lively in her youth, her spirits were dampened by persistent illness and the influence of Anglo-Catholicism, which taught the sinfulness of pleasure and the duty of renunciation.

The publication of *Goblin Market and Other Poems* in 1862 earned Rossetti recognition as a major poet. The title poem, a fantasy tale of sisterly love and forbidden fruit, is among her most celebrated works. She received three proposals of marriage but remained single. Her limpid lyrics of pain, loss, and resignation express a conviction of the superiority of divine over earthly love. The sonnet sequence *Monna Innominata* (1881), with its biblical references, is a hymn to unfulfilled desire. Rossetti also

dealt with controversial issues such as the fate of "fallen women"; many of her later works were devotional.

**KEY WORKS:** *Goblin Market and Other Poems*, 1862; *The Prince's Progress and Other Poems*, 1866; *A Pageant and Other Poems*, 1881; *Verses*, 1893

## Lewis Carroll

1832–1898, ENGLISH

Under the pen name Lewis Carroll, Charles Lutwidge Dodgson produced some of the most imaginative writing in the English language. The son of a clergyman, Carroll was a brilliant mathematician who wrote poems and stories for amusement. He spent most of his life as an academic at Christ Church College, Oxford University. His most famous work, *Alice in Wonderland*, was invented to entertain Alice Liddell, the young daughter of the dean of the college.

Published in 1865, with illustrations by Sir John Tenniel, *Alice* was an instant success. The sequel, *Through the Looking Glass*, never achieved the same popularity, perhaps because it made Dodgson's concern with puzzles and mathematical conundrums too evident. Both books include nonsense verse and parodies of well-known authors; some, notably *The Hunting of the Snark*, are deliberately obscure in meaning. Carroll was also an accomplished photographer, but his extensive and sometimes controversial images of young girls has led to speculation about his repressed obsessions.

**KEY WORKS:** *Alice's Adventures in Wonderland*, 1865; *Through the Looking Glass*, 1871; *The Hunting of the Snark*, 1876

## ▷ Stéphane Mallarmé

1842–1898, FRENCH

Symbolist poet Stéphane Mallarmé was born into the Parisian middle class, married at the age of 21,

and worked as a schoolteacher for 30 years. While leading this conventional life, he pursued a radical artistic agenda, convinced that only a poet could save the world from futility and that "everything in the world exists to end in a book."

Initially influenced by Baudelaire and Poe, Mallarmé developed an enigmatic, compressed, syntactically complex poetic style, and harnessed obscure imagery to express the failed pursuit of an ever-elusive ideal. He brought rigor to fin-de-siècle decadence and his Tuesday salons became the hub of Parisian

intellectual life. Although published later, much of his most famous verse was written in the 1860s, including "The Afternoon of a Faun," a dreamlike monologue that relates the sensual experiences of a faun. A late burst of creativity culminated in the seminal prose poem "A Throw of the Dice ...," which used typography and the juxtaposition of words to explore the links between form and content.

**KEY WORKS:** "The Afternoon of a Faun," 1876; *Poems*, 1887; "Hérodiade," 1896; "A Throw of the Dice Will Never Abolish Chance," 1897

△ STEPHANE MALLARME, PHOTOGRAPHED BY NADAR, 1896

## Benito Pérez Galdós

1843–1920, SPANISH

Spain's most celebrated realist novelist, Pérez Galdós grew up in the Canary Islands and became a journalist in Madrid. The success of his first novel, *The Fountain of Gold*, in 1870 initiated an astoundingly prolific career as a fiction writer. From 1873 to 1912, Galdós wrote a series of 46 historical novels known as the *National Episodes*, dramatizing the history of Spain during the 19th century. This effort overlapped with a series of 22 novels focusing on contemporary Spanish life that were inspired by Honoré de Balzac's *The Human Comedy*. The series included *Fortunata and Jacinta*, which is often considered his defining masterpiece.

Galdós also wrote for the theater, his anticlerical play *Electra* (1901) provoking bitter controversy. He entered the Spanish parliament in 1907, but his political career was brief and ineffectual.

KEY WORKS: *The Fountain of Gold*, 1870; *Fortunata and Jacinta*, 1886–1887; *Tristana*, 1892; *Nazarin*, 1895

## Paul Verlaine

1844–1896, FRENCH

As famous for his dissolute life as for his lyrical verse, Verlaine published his first collection, *Poèmes saturniens*, in 1866, but found his true voice with the sad, sweet *Fêtes galantes* and *Romance sans paroles*. Using a short line (often with an odd number of syllables), he introduced a new note into French verse—evocative, musical, and plaintive. The cool orderliness of his poetry was not reflected in his life.

After marrying 16-year-old Mathilde Mauté, Verlaine left her and their newborn baby to live with the hell-raising young poet Arthur Rimbaud. In 1873, the stormy affair between the two poets culminated in Verlaine shooting Rimbaud in the wrist, for which he served two years in prison.

Subsequent efforts to regain stability, reflected in the poems of *Sagesse*, failed after the death of his lover Lucien Létinois in 1883. Verlaine's decline into absinthe addiction was paralleled by a rise in his reputation.

KEY WORKS: *Fêtes galantes*, 1869; *Romances sans paroles*, 1873–1874; *Sagesse*, 1880; *Jadis et Naguère*, 1884

## José Maria de Eça de Queirós

1845–1900, PORTUGUESE

Novelist José Maria de Eça de Queirós was the illegitimate son of a magistrate. As a young man angered by the backwardness and injustices of Portuguese society, he campaigned for political reform. In 1872, Queirós joined the consular service and from then on lived abroad, mostly in England and France.

His novels, heavily influenced by the French "Naturalist" Emile Zola, present a savagely satirical portrait of the vices and hypocrisies of Portugal's ruling classes. *The Sin of Father Amaro*, his most enduringly popular work, relates the torrid affair between a priest and one of his parishioners in a provincial town. *Cousin Bazilio* tells of an adulterous wife exploited by her lover and blackmailed by her maid. *The Maias*, a Lisbon-based family saga, uses incest as a symbol of the decline of the Portuguese aristocracy. Eça de Queirós died in Paris, having long abandoned aspirations to reform his native land.

KEY WORKS: *The Sin of Father Amaro*, 1875; *The Maias*, 1888; *The Noble House of Ramires*, 1900

## ▷ Henryk Sienkiewicz

1846–1916, POLISH

A prize-winning historical novelist, Henryk Sienkiewicz was born in Lublin province in the east of Poland to an impoverished landowning family. At the time of his birth, Poland was little more than a puppet state of the Russian Empire, by which it was formally swallowed in 1867. Sienkiewicz published his first novels and short stories in the 1870s and was also productive as a journalist and travel writer.

His series of historical novels known as *The Trilogy*—comprising *With Fire and Sword*, *The Deluge*, and *Fire in the Steppe*—was a huge success in Poland. Set in the 17th century, the novels flattered Polish patriotism without too greatly offending the Russian censors. Sienkiewicz's international reputation was made by the epic *Quo Vadis?* Set in the time of the emperor Nero, it affirms the triumph of Christian spirituality over Roman materialism.

Awarded the Nobel Prize in Literature in 1905, Sienkiewicz used his prestige to call for greater autonomy for Poland, but he was a moderate who rejected outright rebellion. He died in Switzerland during World War I.

KEY WORKS: *The Trilogy*, 1884, 1886, 1888; *Quo Vadis?*, 1895; *Without Dogma*, 1899; *Teutonic Knights*, 1900

△ *HENRYK SIENKIEWICZ*, KAZIMIERZ POCHWALSKI, 1890

## Joris-Karl Huysmans

1848–1907, FRENCH

The writer whose work defined French Decadence, Huysmans had a Dutch father, but was born and died in Paris. Supporting himself through a sinecure in the civil service, he embarked on a literary career under the influence of Emile Zola's "Naturalism," which shaped his early novels, such as *The Vatard Sisters*. He never married, and his novel *Downstream*, published in 1882, amusingly details the petty frustrations of a Parisian bachelor's life. It was with the publication of *Against Nature* in 1884 that Huysmans staked out his idiosyncratic territory. In Des Esseintes—the book's antihero—he created a prototype of the decadent fin-de-siècle aesthete.

Huysmans' style, packed with neologisms and archaisms, was as original as his subject matter. In subsequent novels, featuring his alter ego Durtal, he charted his own spiritual progress from a perverse curiosity about Satanism (in the luridly brilliant *The Damned*) to a guarded late conversion to Catholicism.

**KEY WORKS:** *The Vatard Sisters*, 1879; *Against Nature*, 1884; *The Damned*, 1891; *En route*, 1895

## Robert Louis Stevenson

1850–1894, SCOTTISH

A writer of adventure stories, Stevenson is perhaps best known for his psychological mystery tale *The Strange Case of Dr. Jekyll and Mr. Hyde*. Stevenson was the black sheep of a prominent family of lighthouse-builders, defying his father to become a writer rather than a civil engineer.

He was a bold traveler, and his first published works were accounts of his journeys, such as *Travels with a Donkey in the Cévennes* (1879). In 1880, he married US divorcee Fanny Vandegrift Osbourne, who accompanied him on his wanderings. The novels *Treasure Island* and *Kidnapped*, written for boys

△ **SELMA LAGERLÖF, c.1939**

but widely read by adults, along with *The Strange Case of Dr. Jekyll and Mr. Hyde*, made him famous. He also published poems for children that became Victorian classics. Stevenson was always in poor health and it was partly for the benefit of his lungs that he settled in Samoa in 1890. It was there that he died at the age of 44.

**KEY WORKS:** *Treasure Island*, 1883; *The Strange Case of Dr. Jekyll and Mr. Hyde*, 1886; *Kidnapped*, 1886; *The Master of Ballantrae*, 1889

## Arthur Rimbaud

1854–1891, FRENCH

As a rebellious teenager, French poet Rimbaud repeatedly ran away from his home in eastern France. Starting at the age of 15, he wrote poems that were visionary, tender, scatological, and blasphemous, declaring the poet's need for a "disordering of all the senses" to make himself "a seer." In 1871, he began a relationship with the

poet Verlaine. They were living in London when Rimbaud wrote most of his obscure, vivid prose poems *Illuminations*. Disillusion soon set in and there was a violent breakup with Verlaine. In *A Season in Hell*, Rimbaud recognized the failure of his project to transform life through the alchemy of words. At the age of 21, he stopped writing. When his poetry belatedly attracted attention in the 1880s, Rimbaud remained indifferent. After a wandering life, including a spell as an arms dealer in East Africa, he died in a Marseille hospital at 37.

**KEY WORKS:** "The Drunken Boat," 1871; *A Season in Hell*, 1873; *Illuminations*, 1886

## △ Selma Lagerlöf

1858–1940, SWEDISH

The first woman to win the Nobel Prize in Literature, Lagerlöf was a novelist and children's writer. Raised on an estate in Värmland in western

Sweden, she would often listen to the legends and fairy tales told by her grandmother. After her family's fortunes declined and their estate was sold, Lagerlöf worked as a teacher. Her first novel, *Gösta Berling's Saga*, which blends observation of Swedish rural life with fantasy, was published after she entered it in a competition. The success of this book allowed her to devote herself to writing full time. She is best loved for her children's book, *The Wonderful Adventures of Nils*, about a cruel boy who is transformed into a *tomte* (gnome) and travels on the back of a wild goose, learning lessons about life on the way.

An ardent campaigner for women's suffrage, Lagerlöf was emotionally involved with the writer Sophie Elkan and the suffragist Valborg Olander. When she won the 1909 Nobel Prize, she used the money to buy back her childhood home in Värmland.

**KEY WORKS:** *Gösta Berling's Saga*, 1891; *Jerusalem*, 1901–1902; *The Wonderful Adventures of Nils*, 1906; *The Ring of the Löwenskölds*, 1925

EARLY
20th
CENTURY

CHAPTER 4

# W. B. Yeats

## 1865–1939, IRISH

Known for his lyrical poetry celebrating Irish culture, Yeats also wrote plays and published work on mysticism. In his own words he became an "old lecher with a love on every wind"—troubled in love and afraid of aging.

Soon after William Butler Yeats's birth in Dublin in 1865, his family moved to Sligo, northwestern Ireland, the home of his mother, Susan Mary Pollexfen, who was from a merchant family. Just two years later, they relocated to London where Yeats's father, John, hoped to build his career as a portrait painter. Yeats went to school in the city, but spent his summers with his grandparents in Sligo, developing a close bond with the "country of the heart." The family returned to Ireland in 1880, and Yeats attended high school and then art college in Dublin.

Yeats found some early success in 1885, when his poetry was published in the *Dublin University Review*. In the same year, he had a meeting with the highly respected Irish nationalist John O'Leary, who encouraged the young poet to infuse his Romanticism with Irish history, folklore, and landscape.

Having moved back to London with his family in 1886, Yeats pursued an interest in the occult that had begun at college, becoming active in the Hermetic Order of the Golden Dawn, a society that advocated the practice of magic to attain enlightenment. His fascination with mysticism would be carried into his plays and poems, including "The Second Coming" (1919) and "Sailing to Byzantium" (1928), an allegory of a spiritual journey.

### Rejection and loves

In London, Yeats cofounded the Rhymers Club for poets, and met Maud Gonne, a strident and beautiful Irish patriot with whom he fell deeply in love. His unrequited passion for Gonne would cast a long shadow over his life and work. His proposal to her in 1899 was rejected, and she married Major John MacBride,

an Irish soldier. MacBride was later executed by the British for his part in the nationalist rebellion, and inspired Yeats's poem "Easter, 1916"—a work shot through with conflicted feelings at the major's death.

Yeats took years to recover from his painful attachment to Maud, but in 1917 he married Georgiana Hyde-Lees. He lived with her in Ireland, where they had two children. His wife shared his interest in the occult and together they practiced automatic writing (a process that involves letting go of conscious thought while writing), producing over 4,000 words in this way.

Yeats remained a patriot, and in 1922 he become senator to the Irish Free State. The following year, he won the Nobel Prize in Literature, mostly in recognition of his dramatic works. Unusually, much of the work for which he is best remembered was completed after winning the prize. His volumes *The Tower* (1928) and *The Winding Stair and Other Poems* (1933) are poignant explorations of life, art, and the cyclical nature of existence.

At the age of 69, Yeats had an operation to improve his libido (it was in fact a vasectomy). He claimed that the procedure was a success, enhancing his creative as well as his sexual energy: a "ferment," he said, "has come upon my imagination."

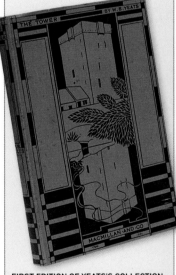

FIRST EDITION OF YEATS'S COLLECTION *THE TOWER*, PUBLISHED IN 1938

◁ **BEN BULBEN, SLIGO**
Yeats's love for his Irish heritage and his home in Sligo is evident in much of his poetry, such as "Under Ben Bulben" (1933). The last three lines of this poem make up the epitaph on his grave in Sligo: "Cast a cold eye / On life, on death. / Horseman, pass by!"

▷ **W. B. YEATS**, JOHN YEATS, 1900
This image of W. B. Yeats was painted by his father, who was an accomplished portraitist, though lacking in business acumen. Yeats's siblings Jack, Elizabeth, and Susan Mary also became artists.

▷ **PIRANDELLO, 1935**
Pirandello's revolutionary dramas changed the language of theater and made the writer an international celebrity. He is shown here in a picture taken for *Vanity Fair*, the magazine that focuses on fashion and culture.

# Luigi Pirandello

### 1867–1936, ITALIAN

Pirandello was awarded a Nobel Prize in Literature in 1934 for his strikingly original plays, described as "tragic farces." He was a prolific writer, producing more than 50 plays, as well as novels and short stories.

**MUSSOLINI ON A FASCIST POSTER**

> "**Life** is full of **strange absurdities**, which, strangely enough, do not even need to **appear plausible**, since they are **true**. "

LUIGI PIRANDELLO, *SIX CHARACTERS IN SEARCH OF AN AUTHOR*

Luigi Pirandello was born near the Sicilian city of Girgenti (now Agrigento), where his father ran a sulfur mining and trading company. Pirandello was expected to join the family business and was sent to a technical school, but he showed little interest in commerce and switched to study humanities when the family moved to Palermo, the capital of Sicily, in 1880. He worked for a while with his father, with whom he had an increasingly uneasy relationship, before enrolling at the University of Palermo. In 1887, he went to study in Rome, and then Bonn, where he received a doctorate in philology in 1891. Pirandello had already published collections of verse, and after settling in Rome in 1893, he finished his first novel, *Marta Ajala*, which was serialized in a popular Roman newspaper, and then published a collection of novellas in the *verismo* (Italian realist) style that was popular at the time.

In 1894, at his family's suggestion, he married Antonietta Portulano, the daughter of his father's business associate, and by the end of the century the couple had three children. Pirandello had established his reputation as a writer, held a teaching post, and had cofounded a weekly literary magazine, *Ariel*. The family's comfortable life was cut short in 1903, when a flood destroyed the Pirandello sulfur mines and thus their fortune. Antonietta suffered a severe mental breakdown from which she never recovered, and her increasingly violent paranoia led to her being put into an asylum in 1919.

A despairing Pirandello immersed himself in work, and there followed a period in which he wrote many of the most important essays, novels, and novellas of his career, including the quasi-autobiographical and psychologically probing *The Late Mattia Pascal*, which earned him international recognition.

### Dramas of the absurd

Pirandello is best known for his plays, which he published from 1918 to 1935 under the collective title *Naked Masks*. These tragicomic works explore the absurdity and irony of life's many contradictions. His first great success was *As Before, Better than Before* (1920); and in an intense five-week period in 1921, he finished his two great masterpieces, *Henry IV* and *Six Characters in Search of an Author*. The latter uses an innovative "play within a play" structure, in which the characters rebel against the writer, causing the play to break down into tragic and comic fragments.

For a while, Pirandello supported the fascists in Italy, and Mussolini appointed him director of the Teatro d'Arte di Roma, with which he toured in the mid-1920s. However, shocked by Mussolini's philistinism and his policies, he tore up his Fascist Party card in 1927. Financial problems at the Teatro d'Arte forced it to close in 1928, after which Pirandello spent most of his life traveling until his death at home in Via Bosio, Rome, on December 10th, 1936.

△ **SULFUR MINES, SICILY**
Pirandello's life was shaped by his Sicilian roots—events and gossip from the island provided him with material for much of his work. The bankruptcy of his family's mining business precipitated his wife's mental breakdown, which informed the themes of madness and illusion evident in much of his writing.

▷ **METATHEATER**
This scene is from a French production of Pirandello's *Six Characters in Search of an Author*. The avant-garde play was first staged in 1921 at Rome's Teatro Valle, where it was greeted with cries of "madhouse!" from the audience.

# Natsume Sōseki

## 1867–1916, JAPANESE

Sōseki was the first great Japanese novelist of the modern period. His lifetime spanned Japan's transition from a traditional to an industrial society, and his work reflects the implications of this rapid change.

Natsume Kinnosuke (who assumed the pen name Sōseki in 1889) was born in Edo (soon to be named Tokyo), at the beginning of the Meiji era (see box, right). Although this was an invigorating time for the country, Sōseki's family suffered financially under the new order and sent him to live with foster parents.

At school, Sōseki became interested in classical Chinese literature, but in line with the westernization of Japan, he studied English literature at Tokyo Imperial University, after which he taught at various schools over the next few years. The turning point in his career came in 1900, when the Japanese government chose him to receive one of the first scholarships to study English in England.

### ▽ THE HOUSE OF THE CAT
From 1903 to 1905, Sōseki rented this building in Tokyo—a town house typical of the period (built c.1887). It was here that he wrote his masterpiece, I Am a Cat.

Sōseki took classes at University College London and some private lessons with a prominent scholar of Shakespeare, but soon gave up both, feeling dispirited and alienated by life in England. He spent much of his two-year stay studying alone in his room in Clapham, south London.

### Times of change
Sōseki returned to Japan earlier than intended due to his poor physical and mental health. He took a teaching post at Tokyo Imperial University in 1903, a time of growing nationalism and modernization, and began to explore ways in which this profound social change could be reflected in literature—how to integrate Western ideas without simply copying them, and at the same time maintain continuity with the Japanese tradition.

He began writing short stories in a rather experimental style, while also composing more conventional haiku. The literary magazine Hototogisu

published one of these stories, "I Am a Cat," which, using the device of a cat as narrator, gives an outsider's wry look at the strange world of humans in modern society. More stories in the same vein followed, and were published together as a novel in 1905. Sōseki devoted more of his time to writing, publishing several novels and short stories before eventually giving up his teaching post in 1907, once he had finished his treatise on English literature, "Theory of Literature."

He was then offered a permanent contract with the Asahi Shimbun newspaper to write serialized stories, later published as novels. While his early works were full of humor, he later focused on exploring human psychology and more weighty themes, such as isolation, identity, and egoism. The trilogy Sanshirō (1908), And Then (1909), and The Gate (1910) helped establish him as a serious novelist.

More than any other of his works, his 1915 novel, Grass on the Wayside, was openly autobiographical and frankly portrayed his profound disillusionment with life in the modern world. His health, which had never been robust, deteriorated badly around this time, and he left an unfinished novel, Light and Darkness, when he died in 1916.

MUTSUHITO.
EMPEROR OF JAPAN.

**MEIJI, EMPEROR OF JAPAN**

### ▷ INNOVATION AND EXPERIMENT
This portrait of Sōseki was taken in 1912, four years before his death. Throughout his life, the writer experimented with styles and techniques learned from his study of English literature.

# Marcel Proust

**1871–1922, FRENCH**

Proust is renowned for a single novel, his seven-volume masterpiece *In Search of Lost Time*, a profound meditation on memory, art, love, and loss, and a satirical portrayal of snobbery and sexual hypocrisy.

Marcel Proust was born on July 10, 1871 in the Parisian suburb of Auteuil, where his family had taken refuge from the revolutionary Commune uprising that had rocked Paris the previous spring. His father was a distinguished professor of medicine, and his mother came from a cultured Jewish family. Elements in Proust's writing would display an analytic, diagnostic quality drawn from his paternal inheritance, but the dominant influence on his upbringing was his mother's warm humanism and her unquestioning respect for the value of art and literature.

At the age of nine, Proust almost died from an asthma attack. For the rest of his life he would be defined as a semi-invalid. Aside from fulfilling a year's military service, he never left his Parisian family home except for vacations. While his younger brother followed in his father's footsteps, becoming a distinguished surgeon, Marcel indulged in the frivolous life of a socialite, cultured dilettante, and amateur litterateur. A sensuous Parisian environment—cafés and brothels, Impressionist art, and the Ballets Russes—formed Proust's refined aesthetic sensibility. His intelligence and taste earned him a place among the cultured elite, but aside from a number of essays and translations, he published nothing until the age of 42. Supported by his parents, he never worked for money.

## Early writing

The apparent frivolity and idleness of Proust's life were an illusion. We now know that he wrote with single-minded seriousness of purpose at least from the 1890s. Although they were not published until 30 years after his death, his abandoned novel *Jean Santeuil* and unfinished critical work *Contre Sainte-Beuve* reveal that Proust was trying to write his masterpiece for at least 13 years before the key elements of the novel began at last to come together beginning around 1909. By this time, both of his parents

△ **RARE EDITION**
This extremely rare original edition of the novel *Swann's Way*, published by Grasset, was dedicated and signed by the author in 1916.

## IN CONTEXT
### The Dreyfus affair

In 1894, Jewish French army officer Alfred Dreyfus was wrongly convicted of treason. The case ignited anti-Semitism on one side and anticlericalism on the other, tearing the French Third Republic apart. Jewish on his mother's side, Proust became engaged in the storm of protest that arose over Dreyfus's fate. In *In Search of Lost Time*, the author satirizes the anti-Semitic response of Parisian society, while also remaining critical of some of the attitudes struck by Dreyfus's supporters. Dreyfus was pardoned and released in 1899.

**ALFRED DREYFUS ON DEVIL'S ISLAND, FRENCH GUIANA**

◁ **PROUST'S PARIS**
Toulouse-Lautrec captures Proust's Paris in his painting *At the Moulin Rouge* (1894–1895). Under the Third Republic, Paris flourished as a city of pleasure, high fashion, and cultural modernism.

◁ **THE YOUNG PROUST, 1892**
This portrait by French artist Jacques-Emile Blanche shows Proust as a young man. The author was influenced by the writings of Montaigne, Flaubert, Tolstoy, and Dostoyevsky, among others. He developed his ideas of the place of the artist in society through readings of Thomas Carlyle and John Ruskin.

" **Love** is **space** and **time** made **sensitive** to the **heart.** "
MARCEL PROUST, *THE PRISONER*

△ **CELESTE ALBARET**
Albaret, shown here, served as Proust's companion, cook, and secretary for nine years during the writing of *In Search of Lost Time*. She arranged her life around his odd routines, which included waking at 4pm and writing through the night.

had died and Proust's health was deteriorating. Living as a recluse in his cork-lined Parisian apartment, the author devoted the last decade of his life to finishing the enormous book that would justify his entire existence and cement his reputation.

### The work of a life
When Proust offered the first volume, *Swann's Way*, to publishers in 1913 they were unimpressed; the book appeared only because the author agreed to pay all of the costs. The outbreak of World War I interrupted further publication, although Proust continued work on the novel in Paris. The second volume, *In the Shadow of Young Girls in Flower*, appeared in 1919 and won the prestigious literary prize the Prix Goncourt. Now famous, Proust worked feverishly at preparing the remaining volumes, but on November 18, 1922, persistent poor health at last defeated him. The last volumes were published posthumously in an imperfect state without final revisions.

*In Search of Lost Time* has been described as a creative autobiography, a fictional recreation of the author's own life. The first-person narrator

△ **MADELEINES**
In *Swann's Way*, the narrator tastes a madeleine, a small cake, shown here. He dunks it in his tea, and in an instant, the whole world of his childhood vacations with his Aunt Léonie is restored from oblivion and vividly brought back to life by "involuntary memory."

of the novel is not the author, but resembles him very closely. Virtually every incident, location, and character in the book is based, at least in part, on a real-life original. The family servant, Françoise, one of the most complex characters in the novel, is recognizably related to Céleste Albaret, who served the author in his final years; Combray, the rural site of many of the narrator's childhood experiences, is the village of Illiers in northern France; Balbec, where the narrator spends seaside vacations, is the fashionable resort of Cabourg in Normandy; and so on.

### Author or narrator
The novel's narrator differs from Proust in two major respects. The narrator is not Jewish, that aspect of Proust's life being projected upon the attractive, cultured figure of Charles Swann, hero of the novel's only third-person narrative section, *Swann in Love*; nor is the narrator gay.

◁ **ILLIERS-COMBRAY**
Proust spent his childhood vacations with his aunt and uncle in Illiers, shown here. He immortalized their home and the town (in the guise of Combray) in his great novel. In 1971, the town was renamed Illiers-Combray in homage to the writer.

" If **day-dreaming** is dangerous, the cure for it is not to dream less, but to **dream more**, to **dream all the time**. "

MARCEL PROUST, *SWANN'S WAY*

## KEY WORKS

**1913**
*Swann's Way*, the first volume of *In Search of Lost Time*, includes childhood scenes as well as a self-contained story of jealous passion.

**1919**
*In the Shadow of Young Girls in Flower*, the second volume, explores themes of love, friendship, and the illusions of youth.

**1920–21**
*The Guermantes Way* are volumes that contrast the frivolous life of the rich with the death of the narrator's grandmother.

**1921–22**
*Sodom and Gomorrah* is the volume in which Proust brings gay themes to the fore.

**1923**
*The Prisoner* addresses the narrator's attempt to possess the elusive Albertine—a volume that reveals the futility of love.

**1925**
*The Fugitive* is an extensive meditation on loss and the unknowable nature of other people.

**1927**
*Time Regained*, the concluding volume, is set in World War I. It pits the redeeming power of memory and writing against aging and death.

The great love of Proust's life was his chauffeur, and later secretary, Alfred Agostinelli, whom he met at Cabourg in 1907. Their relationship, which was unrequited, ended in tragedy in 1914 when Agostinelli, who was training to become a pilot, plunged to his death in the Mediterranean. The chauffeur appears in Proust's novel as a woman, Albertine.

Though predominating in the *Sodom and Gomorrah* section, sexuality is a theme throughout the book, from the narrator's childhood discovery of lesbian sex in a voyeuristic episode in Combray to the climactic gay brothel scene in Paris in *Time Regained*. The Baron de Charlus, an outrageously arrogant closeted gay man with a gift for scatological invective, is one of Proust's finest creations.

### Memory and experience

The novel has no plot in a strictly conventional sense: instead, an elaborate development of recurring themes and characters is held together by the narrator's rich, metaphorical prose style. *In Search of Lost Time* opens with a seminal event, a child's anxiety at being deprived of his mother at bedtime and an unexpected reprieve from this deathlike separation. It is typical of Proust to endow such a minor event with heavy significance, yet carry it off with gentle charm and pathos.

The imaginative force of Proust's evocation of early experiences and his exploration of memories has often dominated perceptions of the novel at the expense of the comedy of manners in status-ridden Parisian society that makes up so much of the book. Keenly observant and often very funny, the social element of the novel focuses on the "little clan" of the Verdurins—pretentious, middle-class, bohemian social climbers—and the aristocratic Guermantes family—witty

and elegant but made spiritually sterile by their adherence to a narrow set of values. Along with scenes of social life, the later parts of the novel focus on the narrator's jealous love for Albertine. For Proust, sexual love is futile because the lover's emotions are fixated upon a person who does not exist, a figment created by their desire. There is no true relationship between the lover and the beloved. The only genuine pleasure lies in allaying the anxiety created by the beloved's absence. This bleak view of love is articulated in a long analysis that many readers regard as one of the novel's regrettable excesses.

### In search of purpose

The last volume returns to the theme of "involuntary memory" as a way of triumphing over the destructive effects of time. But for Proust it is clear that the ultimate victory over time comes less from memory than from the work of the creative artist. Some of the novel's finest passages evoke the experiences of reading, listening to music, or looking at paintings, teasing out the reasons why these experiences are of such transcendent value.

In the end, *In Search of Lost Time* is about how the author/narrator comes to write *In Search of Lost Time*, thereby achieving his spiritual purpose of redeeming life's futility.

**THE LAST HANDWRITTEN NOTEBOOK OF PROUST'S GREAT NOVEL**

◁ **SEASIDE RECOLLECTION**
The Normandy resort of Cabourg, with its seaside and Grand Hotel—shown in this postcard from 1908—is where Proust spent every summer from 1907 to 1914. The resort was the model for the fictional town of Balbec.

▷ **WILLA CATHER, c.1926**
Cather is photographed here at the height of her creativity. She became best known for her novels about frontier life, although she lived much of her life in New York City with her partner, the magazine editor Edith Lewis. Before finding success as a novelist, she was one of the most eminent female journalists in the US.

# Willa Cather

## 1873–1947, AMERICAN

Cather's evocatively nostalgic novels, written in a consciously conservative style, were inspired by her teenage experiences of life among the immigrant farming families of the Great Plains of America.

> # "There are only two or three **human stories**, and they go on **repeating themselves** as **fiercely** as if they had **never happened before**. "
>
> WILLA CATHER, *O PIONEERS!*

With her characteristic stubbornness, Willa Cather always insisted that she had been born in 1876, three years later than her actual date of birth in 1873. She was given the name Wilella, which she hated, preferring to be called Willie, or the tomboyish William, before she settled on Willa. Soon after her birth, the family moved into Willow Shade, a house built by Cather's grandfather near Winchester, Virginia.

## Virginia to Nebraska

In 1883, the Cathers left for Nebraska and made their home in Red Cloud, a small town on the frontier of the Great Plains. Although separated from familiar landscapes and surrounded by mainly German and Scandinavian settlers who farmed the prairie land, Cather adjusted quickly to her new life, and befriended many of the immigrant families. Starting at the age of 11, she attended Red Cloud High School and—unusually for a country girl— graduated and went on to study English at the University of Nebraska. There, she wrote short stories and reviews for local newspapers, soon gaining a reputation as a merciless theater critic. Outspoken and mannish in her clothes and appearance, she challenged gender roles of the time— never more so than in choosing the male-dominated field of journalism as her career. After graduating in 1895, she moved to Pittsburgh to work as the editor of *Home Monthly* magazine, and later became drama and music critic for the *Pittsburgh Leader*.

On a visit to New York in 1899, Cather met Isabelle McClung—also from Pittsburgh—with whom she began a close relationship. McClung encouraged Cather's creative writing, and provided her with a study in the McClung family home.

## Journalist and novelist

In 1902, Cather and McClung traveled to Europe together, and on their return, Cather published *April Twilights* (1903), a collection of poems, and *The Troll Garden* (1903), a volume of short stories. Still reluctant to give up her career in journalism, Cather moved to New York in 1906 to work for *McClure's Magazine*, becoming its managing editor a couple of years later. This was also the beginning of a new chapter in her personal life; in 1908 she moved into an apartment with Edith Lewis, who was to become her lifelong companion.

Disillusioned with the direction *McClure's* was taking, Cather resigned in 1912—the year in which her first novel, *Alexander's Bridge*, was published—and became a full-time writer. Drawing on memories of life on the Great Plains, she wrote several novels, including *O Pioneers!* and *My Antonia*, but it was not until 1920, when the publisher Alfred Knopf took over management of her books that she achieved popular success. Her World War I novel, *One of Ours*, won the Pulitzer Prize in 1923.

Cather and Lewis were now living in Greenwich Village, and spending their summers in a remote cottage in Whale Cove, New Brunswick. As Cather's reputation grew, she became more reclusive, and through the 1930s she suffered from various ailments that hindered her ability to write. She was also deeply affected by the death of her parents and by McClung's long battle against serious kidney disease. Cather wrote her final novel, *Sapphira and the Slave Girl*, in 1940. Her health continued to deteriorate and she died from a stroke in 1947. She is buried in Jaffrey, New Hampshire, where she had regularly visited McClung.

◁ **CATHER'S HOME IN RED CLOUD**
Cather's move from the mountainous state of Virginia to the wide-open plains of Nebraska had a profound effect upon her work. She drew on her experiences in Nebraska in seven of her novels.

## ON STYLE
### Writing the plains

Cather is sometimes criticized for the nostalgia of her work, but many of her themes were quite revolutionary at the time. Against literary convention, she often depicted strong young women and female immigrant laborers, and peppered her work with disguised sexual metaphors. Her novels also reflected her passion for the Nebraska plains, which were presented almost as a romantic character in her work. In *My Antonia*, for example, the boy Jim writes of the vast landscape: "At any rate, that is happiness; to be dissolved into something complete and great."

**WILLA CATHER'S** *MY ANTONIA*, 1918

# Thomas Mann

## 1875–1955, GERMAN

The most prominent German writer of the early 20th century, Mann was both a traditionalist and an innovator who cast an ironic light on the decadence of modern European culture and society.

Paul Thomas Mann was born in Lübeck, northern Germany, in 1875. His father was the head of a long-established trading company and prominent in the city government. Both Thomas and his brother Heinrich refused to enter the family business, preferring to pursue literary careers.

Living with his half-Brazilian mother in Munich after his father's death, Mann published a number of well-received short stories in the 1890s, and a novel, *Buddenbrooks*, which appeared in 1901. This was a four-generation family saga loosely based on the writer's own background. It hinged on the conflict between orderly bourgeois values and the attractions of art and sensuality, which eventually lead to the family's decline. Along with the novellas *Tristan* and *Tonio Kröger*, (both 1903), *Buddenbrooks* established Mann as a major literary figure.

### The politics of art

In pursuit of respectability and status, Mann married Katia Pringsheim, a woman from a sophisticated Munich family. The couple had six children and Mann enjoyed the role of conventional patriarch, but his own sexual tastes drew him to young men and boys. His famous novella *Death in Venice* (1912)—about a dying writer's total obsession with a beautiful Polish youth—is a meditation on art and life and a symbolic representation of a decaying civilization, but it is also a disguised confession of Mann's desires.

During World War I (1914–1918), he took on a public role as defender of German culture and Germany's monarchical government. His conservative stance was expressed in *Reflections of a Nonpolitical Man* (1918). The war influenced the development of his novel *The Magic Mountain* (1923). Set in a sanatorium in the Swiss Alps, this complex work employs sickness as a metaphor for the destructive state of modern civilization.

In 1929, having been awarded the Nobel Prize in Literature, Mann was Germany's most famous living writer. However, political events increasingly confronted him with what he called "the problem of being German," and he made his hostility to the Nazi Party plain in his 1930 novella *Mario and the Magician*. When Adolf Hitler took power in 1933, Mann went into exile, eventually moving to the US in 1939.

During this period, Mann turned away from society to write a biblical tetralogy, *Joseph and His Brothers* (1943). His next novel, *Doctor Faustus* (1947), the story of a composer who pays for genius with self-destruction, was an allegory of the Nazi period in Germany and an expression of Mann's lifelong ambivalence about art, viewed as both the supreme human achievement and a form of decadence.

He settled in Switzerland, where he died in 1955, leaving unfinished *The Confessions of Felix Krull*, a comedy about a con man which plays with the idea that all art is a confidence trick.

**HEINRICH MANN**

◁ **MANN IN 1934**
Pictured here for *Vanity Fair* magazine, Mann achieved professional success and immense fame. But his personal life was marred by tragedy: two of his sons and both his sisters committed suicide.

◁ **DEATH IN VENICE**
Mann's novella was adapted into a movie directed by Luchino Visconti. The role of its main protagonist, Gustav von Aschenbach (a veiled version of Mann), was played by British actor Dirk Bogarde.

▽ **BUDDENBROOKS**, FIRST EDITION
Published when Mann was just 26 years old, *Buddenbrooks* is constructed from accounts of bourgeois births and funerals, weddings and divorces, and family gossip, woven together with Mann's earthy wit.

▷ **WRITING A MODERN CHINA**
Lu Xun—pictured here in 1930 in Shanghai—is celebrated not just as a writer of stories, but as a highly accomplished critic and satirist. He translated numerous Western texts and became a champion of modern Chinese literature.

# Lu Xun

## 1881–1936, CHINESE

One of China's greatest writers, Lu Xun helped establish the short story in Chinese literature. Sardonic and pessimistic, his work reflected contemporary society as China moved from imperialism to communism.

# " **Hope** is like a road in the country; there was never a road, but when **many people** walk on it, the road **comes into existence**. "

LU XUN, *HOMETOWN*

At the beginning of the 20th century, a new generation of artists and intellectuals began to challenge traditions and conventions that bound China to its feudal past. Foremost among them was the writer Zhou Shuren, better known by his pen name, Lu Xun.

He was born in September 1881 in Zhejiang Province, into a wealthy and scholarly family. But in 1893, his grandfather became embroiled in a political scandal that left the family ostracized by their peers and provided Lu Xun with firsthand experience of the cruelty and corruption that marred Chinese society around that time.

## Travels to Japan

Lu Xun left in 1902 to study medicine in Japan, where he met other Chinese thinkers eager to transform their homeland. Abandoning his ambition to become a doctor, he turned to the work of saving the "soul" of the Chinese people by spreading new, socially aware forms of literature and art. It was this idea that drove his work after the fall of China's

◁ **SPROUTS**, 1930
Lu Xun was the editor of this journal, which showcased left-wing writers and Marxist literary theory.

last imperial dynasty, the Great Qing, and the founding of the Republic of China in 1911–1912. The author returned to his homeland in 1909 and settled in Beijing, where he lectured on literature and continued to seek a social purpose to his writing.

## Vernacular style

Finding a readership in a new crop of literary magazines, he had his first success with "The Diary of a Madman," an excoriating attack on traditional Confucian values that told the tale of a madman who believes he is the only sane one in a society of "man-eaters." It was the first Western-style short story to be written in vernacular rather than classical Chinese, and it was revolutionary since it was written for ordinary people rather than for an educated elite. The stories that followed were similarly sardonic and pessimistic: "The True Story of Ah Q" lampooned the Chinese tendency toward fatalism and self-abasement, and in "Kong Yiji" a group of drunkards revel in a local man's humiliation.

## Political philosophy

Lu Xun left Beijing to live in Shanghai with his lover and former student, Xu Guanping. The couple never married but they did have a son in 1929. By the 1930s, Lu Xun had abandoned fiction for critical essays, written as a form of political protest. He came to believe that communism could solve China's social and political problems, and his translations of Marxist works did much to promote the cause. Yet he never joined the Communist Party, remaining instead a "fellow traveler" who criticized both the left and the right of the political spectrum. He died in Shanghai in 1936.

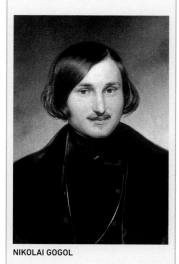

**NIKOLAI GOGOL**

◁ **ANCESTRAL HOME**
Lu Xun's home in Shaoxing is built in traditional style. The tablet above its entrance signifies a member of the Imperial Academy—a highly prestigious title. Lu Xun grew up here, and the house and its gardens provided many details that he incorporated into his later works.

# James Joyce

## 1882–1941, IRISH

Joyce was one of the most influential novelists of his era. He pioneered the "stream of consciousness" technique to convey his characters' thoughts and developed the use of multiple styles to suit his varied subject matter.

◁ **JESUIT SCHOOL**
Starting at the age of six, Joyce was educated at Jesuit schools, including Clongowes Wood College. His experiences there feature in his novel *A Portrait of the Artist as a Young Man*.

The couple settled in Trieste, where they had two children, George (or Giorgio) and Lucia. Joyce taught English and began to write the books that would make him famous, beginning with *Dubliners*, a collection of short stories, and the novel *A Portrait of the Artist as a Young Man*. The stories in *Dubliners* featured characters at different stages of life, from childhood to maturity, but their frankness and closeness to reality led publishers to fear prosecution for libel; completed in 1905, the book did not appear until 1914. Joyce also found it hard to publish his autobiographical novel *A Portrait of the Artist as a Young Man*, which appeared in several installments in the magazine *The Egoist* in 1914–1915. It is famous for its vivid writing about the hero,

James Joyce was born in West Rathgar, Dublin, in 1882. His family was middle class but poor because his alcoholic father mismanaged their finances. Joyce was educated at Jesuit schools, an experience that was a key part of his conflicted relationship with the Catholic faith, and then at University College, Dublin (which was then a Jesuit-run institution). He read widely and excelled at languages; by 1901, he had taught himself enough Norwegian to write a letter of appreciation to the playwright Henrik Ibsen.

Disliking the bigotry and narrow-mindedness he experienced in Ireland, he moved to Paris the following year, initially to study medicine. In 1903, when his mother died, he returned to Dublin; in 1904 he met Nora Barnacle, a young woman who was working as a chambermaid, and the two left for Europe together.

◁ **JAMES JOYCE, 1935**
This portrait of the writer was painted in Paris by the French artist Jacques-Emile Blanche. Joyce's head is turned to the side because he was sensitive about the thick glass of the left lens of his glasses.

### IN PROFILE
#### Harriet Shaw Weaver

Harriet Shaw Weaver (1876–1961) was born in Cheshire, England; her father was a doctor and her mother an heiress with a large fortune. As a young woman, she became a socialist and developed an interest in women's suffrage, which led her to bail out *The Freewoman*, a feminist review in financial trouble. Later, at the suggestion of the poet Ezra Pound, she renamed the journal *The Egoist*. Under the co-editorship of Weaver and her close friend Dora Marsden, *The Egoist* published material by numerous modernist writers, including T. S. Eliot, William Carlos Williams, and James Joyce. Although the magazine folded at the end of 1919, Weaver continued to give Joyce financial support and was his literary executor when he died.

**MASTHEAD OF *THE EGOIST* MAGAZINE, JULY 1914**

> " **History** is a **nightmare** from which I am **trying** to **awake**. "
>
> JAMES JOYCE, *ULYSSES*

# "I want to give a **picture of Dublin** so complete that if the city suddenly **disappeared** from the earth it could be **reconstructed** out of my **book.**"

JAMES JOYCE

Stephen Dedalus, particularly in a scene depicting a sermon that leads Stephen to religious doubt. The novel is also innovative for the way in which its style develops as its protagonist matures—it begins with baby talk and ends in sophisticated prose.

### Move to Paris
Joyce and Nora moved to Zurich in 1915 and spent the war years enjoying the city's cosmopolitan atmosphere. During this time, they struggled financially, although Joyce received some support from Harriet Shaw Weaver, the founder of *The Egoist*,

who sent money anonymously. He was also assisted by the poets W. B. Yeats (who was an old friend from Dublin) and Ezra Pound, who both reviewed his works favorably; with their backing, Joyce was awarded a Royal Literary Fund grant in 1915.

After the war, the couple moved back to Trieste, but following a visit to Paris in 1920, they decided to settle in the French capital. By this time, Joyce was putting the finishing touches on the book on which he had been working since the beginning of the war—his masterpiece, *Ulysses*. This long novel portrays one day in

the life of three characters—young Stephen Dedalus (hero of *A Portrait of the Artist as a Young Man*); an advertising canvasser, Leopold Bloom; and Bloom's wife, Molly.

The groundbreaking novel used a raft of literary techniques—including parody, internal monologue, and prose that ranged from explicit realism to fantasy—and was structured in 18 chapters that mirrored episodes of Homer's *Odyssey*. It was rooted in the geography of Dublin, Joyce's home city, a place that he described with great precision even though the book was written in exile.

▽ **NORA JOYCE**
James Joyce met his muse and future wife, Nora, in Dublin in 1904. Their first tryst—on June 16—was the date on which Joyce chose to place the events of *Ulysses*. It is now commemorated as "Bloomsday," after the novel's main character, Leopold Bloom.

▷ **JOYCE'S DUBLIN**
Joyce's experimental, allusive epic, *Ulysses*, charts the various appointments and meetings of Leopold Bloom over the course of a single day, using the city of Dublin as a microcosm of life.

◁ **PARISIAN MEETING**
Joyce meets with his publisher, Sylvia Beach, in an office in Paris. The writer wore an eye patch to rest the failing vision in his left eye, which some historians now attribute to syphilis.

## ON STYLE
### Stream of consciousness

The technique for which *Ulysses* is most famous is the stream of consciousness. This enables a character's unspoken thoughts, impressions, and memories to be represented as if they are overheard by the reader, without intervention or commentary by a narrator. In addition, these thoughts are expressed in a series of often ungrammatical and sometimes illogical phrases. Joyce said that he discovered this technique during his first trip to Paris in 1903, when reading a novel by the French writer Edouard Dujardin.

**1922 EDITION OF *ULYSSES*, ONE OF 750 COPIES MADE ON HANDMADE PAPER**

The frank language that Joyce used in *Ulysses*—particularly in descriptions of sexuality and bodily functions—once again caused problems. Parts of the work were serialized in the *Little Review* in 1918–1920, but the conviction of its editors on charges of obscenity meant that no British or US publishers would produce *Ulysses* in book form. In the end, it was first published in France in 1922 by Sylvia Beach, who ran the Paris bookstore Shakespeare and Company, a familiar meeting place for expatriate writers such as Pound, Joyce, and Hemingway. Despite being praised by reviewers such as T. S. Eliot for its inventiveness and power, it did not appear in an official edition in the US until 1934; a British edition followed in 1936.

### Experimental writing

Although he was recognized by his peers as a great writer, Joyce enjoyed little commercial success during the 1920s and '30s. He was dogged by both health and family problems. His work was hampered by glaucoma, which was causing his eyesight to deteriorate, and by the nine operations that he endured in the 1920s in order to address the problem. In addition, his daughter, Lucia, was diagnosed with schizophrenia in the mid-1930s and spent much of her later life in an asylum. Although the exact nature of her condition is a matter of controversy, her illness, her frequent arguments with Nora, and the impossibility of a cure affected the writer deeply.

### Late work

In spite of these troubles, Joyce spent much of the 1920s and '30s on his last large-scale work, the novel *Finnegans Wake*. Like several of his earlier books, it was first published in installments (under the title *Work in Progress*), this time in the experimental literary magazine *transition*. Maria and Eugene Jolas, the founders of *transition*, became friends and supporters of Joyce, but most readers of their journal could not understand Joyce's new work, which was met by almost universal bafflement, even after a group of friends, including Samuel Beckett, published a series of essays attempting to explain it.

*Finnegans Wake*, which was finally published in complete form in 1939, is packed with puns and invented words, and is full of foreign terms (from at least 40 different languages). It is a dream novel, depicting a stream of the unconscious—doing for sleep what *Ulysses* did for waking life. It is impenetrable, and most readers are still defeated by it, aside from a few passages, which can be alternately beautiful and hilarious.

*Finnegans Wake* was Joyce's last work. In January 1941, he had an operation for a perforated ulcer, and died soon afterward. He is buried in Zurich, since the Irish authorities refused Nora permission to take his remains to Dublin for burial.

## KEY WORKS

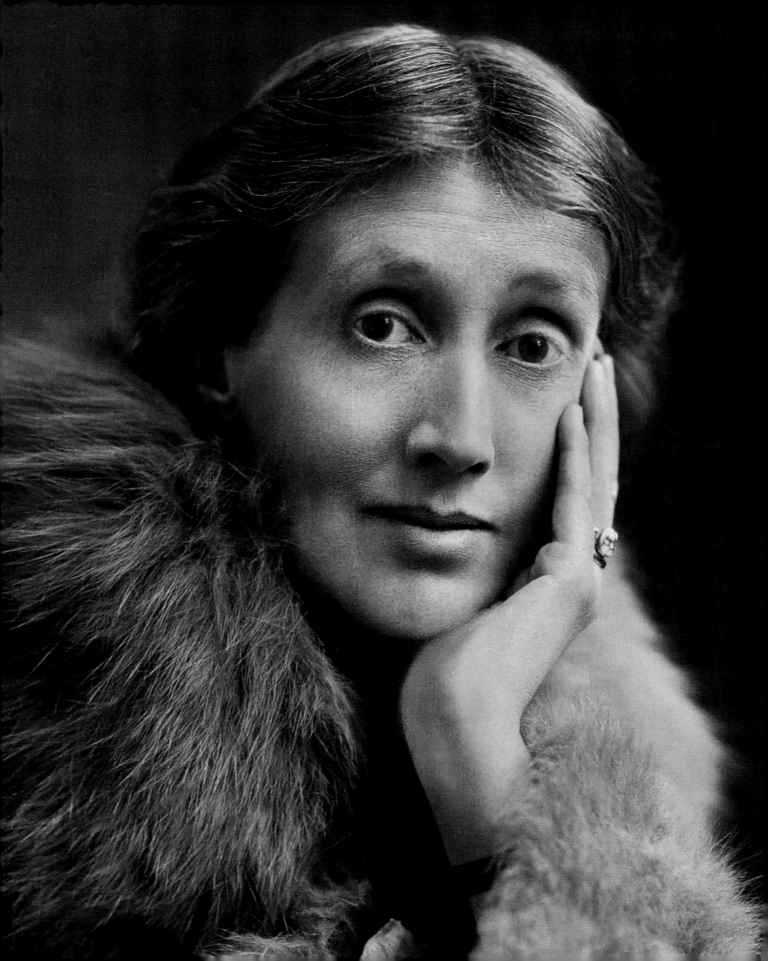

# Virginia Woolf

**1882–1941, ENGLISH**

Novelist, essayist, and feminist, Woolf was at the heart of the modernist movement, transforming fiction with her innovative style and carving out a place for women in literary history.

Adeline Virginia Stephen (later Woolf) was born in London into a privileged upper middle-class world. Her father, Sir Leslie Stephen, was a prominent philosopher, writer, and historian; her mother, Julia Jackson, a former muse of painters in the Pre-Raphaelite movement. Virginia had four half-siblings from her parents' previous marriages—George, Stella, and Gerald Duckworth, and Laura Stephen—while she, Vanessa, Thoby, and Adrian were children of the second marriage.

The family's connections put this grand and busy household at the heart of Victorian literary and intellectual society. The boys were treated very differently from the girls, however. While her brothers were sent to private schools and university, Virginia, an immensely intelligent child, was educated at home, albeit with the free run of her father's extensive library.

### Childhood recollections

The death of her mother when Virginia was 13 years old prompted the first of many mental collapses. The fleeting happiness of her childhood and the melancholy of time passing was captured 32 years later in *To the Lighthouse*. In this novel, she shifts her childhood vacations from Cornwall to Scotland, but renders her parents (as Mr. and Mrs. Ramsay) in full. Mr. Ramsay is pedantic, egotistical, and tyrannical. Mrs. Ramsay, meanwhile, is the perceptive, generous heart of the house in the first half of the book, and a deeply felt absence in the second.

Woolf's diaries suggest that both she and Vanessa were sexually molested by their half-brothers in the years after their mother's death, and her fragile mental state was compromised still further by the tragic death of her half-sister, Stella. Virginia sought solace in education, and between 1897 and 1901, studied ancient Greek, Latin, German, and history at the Ladies' Department of King's College London.

The deaths of Virginia's father in 1904 and her favorite brother, Thoby, in 1906 provoked another collapse, and were followed by a radical change in her lifestyle. Virginia had always considered herself a writer and began making regular contributions to *The Times Literary Supplement*. She moved with her

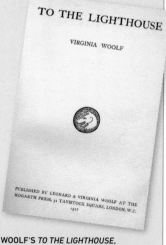

TO THE LIGHTHOUSE

VIRGINIA WOOLF

PUBLISHED BY LEONARD & VIRGINIA WOOLF AT THE HOGARTH PRESS, 52 TAVISTOCK SQUARE, LONDON. W.C. 1927

**WOOLF'S *TO THE LIGHTHOUSE*, PUBLISHED BY THE HOGARTH PRESS**

◁ **CORNISH SUMMERS**
Woolf's childhood summers were spent at Talland House in St. Ives, Cornwall. The distant views of Godrevy lighthouse, always out of reach across the bay, inspired her novel *To the Lighthouse*.

◁ **A FEMINIST LEGACY**
Virginia Woolf is pictured here in 1927, not long after the publication of her fourth novel, *Mrs. Dalloway*, had brought her fame and critical praise. Her work became less popular in the postwar years, but was championed by the feminist movement of the 1970s.

"Why is **life** so **tragic**; so like a little strip of pavement **over an abyss** ... I **wonder** how I am ever to **walk to the end**."

VIRGINIA WOOLF, *A WRITER'S DIARY*

△ **HOGARTH PRESS**
The books produced by the Woolfs' Hogarth Press were often hand stitched and bound; the cover of the first edition of *The Years* (1937) was designed by her sister, Vanessa Bell.

> "A woman must have **money** and a **room of her own** if she is to **write fiction**."

VIRGINIA WOOLF, *A ROOM OF ONE'S OWN*

remaining siblings to Bloomsbury in London, where a cluster of houses in Gordon Square became a hub of artistic activity, attracting philosophers, historians, artists, and writers (see box, below). This group, in words attributed to the US satirist Dorothy Parker, "painted in circles, lived in squares and loved in triangles," which offers a clue to their complex, unconventional love lives.

### Fear and frustration

A proposal of marriage from a Bloomsbury Group founder, Lytton Strachey, was withdrawn because Virginia was being pursued by Leonard Woolf, a publisher and civil servant. With the casual racism of the time, she referred to him as a "penniless Jew," and was not attracted to him. Nonetheless, they were married in 1912. Soon afterward, she wrote: "... it is enormous pleasure being wanted: a wife." However, she

confided to a female friend: "I find the climax immensely exaggerated." According to Leonard Woolf's own account, the wedding night was a disaster. It is likely that he remained celibate throughout their marriage for fear of his wife's nervous attacks, and for the same reason Virginia was advised not to have children.

Woolf's first novel, *The Voyage Out* (1915), simmers with an underlying fear of sexual intimacy. It was an arduous production that triggered another breakdown and a suicide attempt before its publication. Her doctors strongly urged her to avoid any intellectual pursuits, which they believed were triggering her attacks, in favor of physical activity.

Woolf's husband nevertheless continued to encourage her writing: he installed a printing press at the couple's home, Hogarth House in Richmond, London, in 1917 and began publishing her works.

### Exploring sexuality

Woolf's close friend Vita Sackville-West, an aristocratic writer and garden designer, also urged her to write and in the libidinous climate of the Bloomsbury set, the two women became lovers. Many years later, Woolf's most free and fanciful work, *Orlando*, about an androgynous poet, was an undisguised tribute. Sackville-West's son, Nigel Nicholson, described it as "the longest and most charming love letter in literature."

*Night and Day*, a novel that explores love and marriage, was published in 1919, the year the Woolfs bought Monk's House in Rodmell, East Sussex. This 17th-century cottage—along with Charleston, also in East

▽ **FATHER AND DAUGHTER, c.1900**
A youthful Virginia Woolf is pictured with her father, the critic and scholar Sir Leslie Stephen, who encouraged her scholarly pursuits and love of the outdoors.

## IN PROFILE
### The Bloomsbury Group

Virginia Woolf's writing was at the core of the Bloomsbury Group, which included in their number the writer Giles Lytton Strachey; the economist John Maynard Keynes; and artists Roger Fry, Duncan Grant, and Clive and Vanessa Bell. Their ideas on feminism, pacifism, and sexuality were a rejection of Victorian values, and their influence on literature, economics, and art was profound. They were champions of the Postimpressionist art of Gauguin, Matisse, and Van Gogh. The Hogarth Press not only published Woolf's novels but many other important books, including T. S. Eliot's *The Waste Land*, the novels of E. M. Forster, and the groundbreaking works of the psychoanalyst Sigmund Freud.

*VANESSA BELL*, ROGER FRY, 1916

▷ **WRITER'S LODGE, MONK'S HOUSE**
Virginia Woolf wrote at this desk in the lodge in the yard of Monk's House. She commuted to the lodge daily, and would even sleep there on occasion. Visitors to the lodge in Woolf's day reported that it was always strewn with books and papers.

Sussex, where Woolf's sister, Vanessa, lived with her husband, Clive Bell—became country retreats for members of the Bloomsbury set.

*Night and Day* was followed three years later by the experimental novel *Jacob's Room*, in which Woolf sketches her main character almost entirely from the perspective of the women in Jacob's life. T. S. Eliot declared that Woolf had freed herself of any compromise between the traditional novel and her original gift as a writer.

## A feminist manifesto

Woolf's 20 diaries reveal her intense emotional investment in her writing—an order for 50 copies of one of her books at Hogarth Press could lift her spirits as powerfully as any drug—and her obsession with the opinions of other writers and intellectuals. A meeting with E. M. Forster in Cambridge provokes the diary comment: "I always feel him shrinking sensitively from me, as a woman, a clever woman, an up-to-date woman."

Woolf read extremely widely, devouring the ancients, often in the original Greek, and the traditional novelists and poets such as Dickens, the Brontës, Byron, and Milton. She reveled in comparing these texts with those of experimental writers, such as Wyndham Lewis and Ezra Pound, who were engaged in the "shock of the new." After her first reading

of James Joyce's innovative novel *Ulysses*, she declared it "pretentious" and "underbred in a literary sense," revising her opinion only after *Ulysses* was celebrated in reviews.

The novels that Woolf produced in the mid- to late 1920s became her defining works. Her multisensory experiential books *Mrs. Dalloway* and *To the Lighthouse* were followed by the feminist polemic *A Room of One's Own* (1929), which explored the difficulties women faced in a society in which men held disproportionate power.

In a 1931 lecture to aspiring women professionals, Woolf called for the end of the "angel in the house," the charming, unselfish heart of the household who resorts to tender

flattery of the works of men. She said, "I did my best to kill her," and what remained was a young woman in a bedroom with an ink pot who "had only to be herself."

World War II brought the devastation of war to the Bloomsbury companions. Woolf retreated to the countryside to work, but her mania was an ever-present threat, made worse by visits to London, where she found Bloomsbury bombed into ruins. In 1941, at the age of 59, she wrote goodbye notes, filled her pockets with stones, and walked into the Ouse River near Rodmell to end her life, leaving a legacy of journals, letters, essays, and nine "modern" novels that still astonish readers today.

△ **VITA SACKVILLE-WEST, c.1925**
A decade-long relationship between Woolf and the younger Vita Sackville-West began in 1922. Sackville-West became Woolf's muse and lover and was the inspiration for her 1928 novel *Orlando*.

## KEY WORKS

**1915**
*The Voyage Out* reflects Woolf's own journey from a repressive household to the intellectual stimulation of the Bloomsbury Group.

**1925**
*Mrs. Dalloway* describes a day in the life of a society hostess in a stream of consciousness that draws in the lives of other characters.

**1927**
*To the Lighthouse* is Woolf's attempt to understand her past and also the nature of time and immortality.

**1928**
*Orlando* is a satirical romp through English literary history, based on fantasy meetings between writers. It came to be regarded as a feminist classic.

**1929**
*A Room of One's Own* is published—Woolf argues for a literal and figurative space for women writers in a patriarchal literary tradition.

# Franz Kafka

## 1883–1924, CZECH

Kafka died young and left much of his work unfinished. His haunting stories of alienation—sometimes including elements of the bizarre— make him one of the most compelling writers of the 20th century.

Franz Kafka was born into a middle-class Jewish family in Prague, capital of Bohemia, then part of the Austro-Hungarian Empire. His family was German-speaking and well-off; Kafka's father, Hermann, was the owner of a business selling women's clothes and fancy goods, and the writer's mother also worked at the company. Hermann was a strong character—loud, assured, and domineering—and his son found it hard to get along with him. Franz had three sisters and two brothers, but both brothers died young, leaving Franz the eldest of the family.

### Education and employment

Kafka was taught in the German language at elementary school and then at Prague's highly prestigious state Gymnasium, but he also spoke Czech, and studied Latin and Greek. He finished school with good grades and went on to study law in college in Prague. There, he met several writers, including Max Brod (see box, right), with whom he began a lasting friendship. Within his circle, Kafka was known as a convivial and amusing companion—traits that surprise many readers of his fiction, with its focus on struggle and alienation.

Graduating with a doctorate in law in 1906, Kafka went to work for Assicurazioni Generali, an insurance company in Prague. He disliked the long hours there, and after a year moved to another company, the Worker's Accident Insurance Institute, where he handled compensation claims from lone workers against powerful companies. In this environment, Kafka would have witnessed the legal and bureaucratic forces that limited an individual's freedoms—themes that would inform his later work. He was soon promoted, becoming responsible for writing the company's annual reports. More importantly, his working hours were shorter, which gave him time to write—although, living at home with his parents, he was also expected to lend a hand at the Kafkas' store.

### Letters and love

In 1912, Kafka met Felice Bauer, a distant relative of Max Brod's who worked in Berlin. The couple became close, but since they lived apart their relationship was mainly one of furious

△ **THE METAMORPHOSIS, 1915**
The first edition of Kafka's famous story, was published in 1915, though he had completed the work in 1912. Complex negotiations with publishers—typical of Kafka—delayed its appearance.

## IN PROFILE
### Max Brod

The writer Max Brod (1884–1968) became a lifelong friend of Franz Kafka when they met in 1902. They had much in common: both were German-speaking Jews from Prague who had studied law but held literary ambitions. Brod published a number of novels that blended fantasy, love, and mysticism, the most notable of which was *The Redemption of Tycho Brahe* (1916). He is best remembered as Kafka's literary executor—the person who brought the author's work to public recognition. In 1939, Brod escaped from Czechoslovakia to Palestine carrying a suitcase filled with Kafka's papers, just minutes before the Nazis sealed the border.

MAX BROD, c.1937

> " My **guiding principle** is this: **Guilt** is never to be **doubted**. "

FRANZ KAFKA, *THE METAMORPHOSIS*

▷ **FRANZ KAFKA, c.1910**
Handsome but deeply insecure, Kafka suffered from depression and anxiety throughout his life. He also reported a variety of other ailments, from migraines and insomnia to constipation and boils. His torment is fully revealed in his literary works.

## KEY WORKS

**1908**

*Contemplation*, a series of short stories, is Kafka's first publication. It appears in the Munich-based literary journal *Hyperion*.

**1915**

*The Metamorphosis*, a short story that approaches novella length, is Kafka's first major work to be published.

**1925**

*The Trial*, Kafka's most famous novel, is published posthumously. It tells the story of Josef K.'s struggles against officialdom.

**1926**

*The Castle*, abandoned by Kafka in 1922, is finally published two years after the author's death.

**1927**

*Amerika*, unfinished by Kafka, is published. It includes details of the experiences of Kafka's relatives who had immigrated to the US.

▽ **JEWISH QUARTER**
Kafka was born and lived in Prague's Jewish Quarter and was a prominent member of the city's Jewish-German intelligentsia. Although his parents paid lip service to Jewish tradition, Kafka himself was increasingly drawn to a Jewish cultural identity and—under the influence of Max Brod—to Zionism.

correspondence. Kafka wrote to her regularly (often daily) from 1912 to 1917, and his *Letters to Felice* were published in 1967. Their intense attention to minute details and their obsessive character (the writer ceaselessly worried if a letter from his fiancée did not turn up) reveal the deep tensions in Kafka's mind. The couple was engaged twice, but the author's inhibitions (some biographers suggest that he was racked with guilt

for his own sexual, possibly homoerotic, fantasies) and his eventual illness prevented them from marrying.

### A productive period

During this period, Kafka wrote and published some of the short stories for which he would later become famous. "The Judgment" was written in a single night in 1912 and dedicated to Felice; and his most famous story,

*The Metamorphosis*, came out in 1915. Kafka's tale of a man who wakes up to find that he has turned into an insect is typical of his blending of the realistic and the fantastic. It is memorable for the way in which bizarre events are described in the clear, simple, matter-of-fact prose that became typical of the author's style.

Further prose pieces followed, some of which were collected in *A Country Doctor*, but by the time that it was published in 1919, Kafka was sick with tuberculosis and was taking regular periods of sick leave from work.

In the same year, he received a letter from the journalist and writer Milena Jesenská, who wanted to translate one of Kafka's stories, "The Stoker," from German into Czech. The pair wrote to one another often, and with increasing passion, but they met on only two occasions. Kafka eventually broke off the relationship because it

became obvious that Jesenská would not leave her husband for him. Kafka's *Letters to Milena* were published in 1952.

## Illness

It is clear from Kafka's correspondence that he considered himself to be a martyr to his work: "My penchant for portraying my dreamlike inner life has rendered everything else inconsequential," he wrote in one diary entry—a feeling no doubt intensified by his imprisonment in his ailing body. Kafka was aware that his tuberculosis was incurable, and in 1922 he retired from work and moved to Berlin in order to focus on his writing. He lived briefly with his lover, Dora Diamant, a 25-year-old teacher, but returned to Prague when his illness worsened.

## Literary legacy

Kafka died of TB in June 1924 in a sanatorium near Vienna. Before his death, he asked his friend and executor Max Brod to burn his manuscripts and not to republish work that had already appeared. Brod, however, decided that his friend's work was too significant to

△ **KAFKA'S RELATIONSHIPS**
Kafka is photographed here in 1917 with his fiancée Felice Bauer. He struggled with relationships, harboring a distaste for the physical: intimacy was, for him, always associated with guilt.

destroy, and began to publish Kafka's major works beginning in the mid-1920s. Three novels—*The Trial*, *The Castle*, and *Amerika*—and the short-story collection *The Great Wall of China*, established Kafka's reputation.

*The Trial* is the story of Josef K., a bank employee who is accused of a crime, although neither he nor the reader knows what he is supposed to have done. Using the standard tools of a mystery novel (suspense and intrigue) it tells the story of K.'s attempts to obtain justice, involving battles with a tortuous bureaucracy. *The Castle*'s protagonist—also called K.—is a land surveyor who arrives in a village to do a job, but again has to struggle with impenetrable officialdom. The fragmentary novel *Amerika* (titled by Kafka *The Man Who Disappeared*) treats a similar theme, albeit with more humor.

## Fact and fantasy

The books' common subject—the pervasive struggle of the individual against an unknowable and all-powerful authority—has led to Kafka's name becoming a byword for labyrinthine administrative and political systems, and for the nervous, angst-ridden state of mind that such systems engender in people.

## Bureaucracy and dislocation

For many people reading his works after World War II, Kafka's novels seemed to prophesy how communist authorities—not just in Czechoslovakia but also in other countries of Central and Eastern Europe—trapped people, stifled their individuality, and crushed their spirit.

However, Kafka's model for the isolation that he explored in his books was life within the complex bureaucracy of the Austro-Hungarian Empire and, more specifically, the dislocation that he faced daily in his home city of Prague (see box, above). His works also echoed the treatment of similar themes by earlier psychological writers such as Dostoyevsky, and incorporated elements of the avant-garde Expressionist movement that had flourished in Germany at the beginning of the 20th century.

Despite his limited output, Kafka's ability to present uncanny events in a plain, direct prose style and his use of parable and fable in his short stories have left an indelible imprint on 20th-century literature.

▷ **THE CASTLE, 1926**
This novel is Kafka's most human, dealing with the search for companionship and respect in a seemingly hopeless world.

▽ **DORA DIAMANT**
Kafka met Dora, a Polish-born Jewish woman and his last companion, while taking a vacation on the Baltic coast in Muritz. After Kafka's death she tried acting in Berlin, but was forced to flee to England when the Nazis came to power.

'It is often **safer** to be **in chains** than to **be free**. ''

FRANZ KAFKA, *THE TRIAL*

▷ **EZRA POUND, c.1930**
At the time this photograph was
taken, Pound was living in Rapallo, Italy.
Behind him is an (unidentified) painting
in characteristic Vorticist style. Vorticism
was a movement in art with which
Pound was closely associated.

# Ezra Pound

## 1885–1972, AMERICAN

Pound made his name in London and Paris, where he became established
as an innovative Modernist poet, translator, and editor. His reputation
was, however, tarnished by his pro-fascist and anti-Semitic activities.

# "Great literature is simply language charged with meaning to the utmost possible degree."

EZRA POUND, *ABC OF READING*

Ezra Loomis Pound was born on October 30, 1885 in the mining town of Hailey, Idaho, where his father Hector worked for the federal land office. His mother, Isabel, was unhappy in the small town, and the family moved to Wyncote, just north of Philadelphia, where young Ezra attended a number of schools before being sent to the nearby Cheltenham Military Academy in 1897. After transferring to a local pubic high school, he was accepted to the University of Pennsylvania in 1901.

## Academic career

At college, Pound had his first serious romantic affair, with Hilda Doolittle, and met his lifelong friend, the poet William Carlos Williams. He moved to New York to complete his studies, graduating from Hamilton College in 1905, and then returned to the University of Pennsylvania to study for a doctorate on troubadour poetry. He grew restless and left college, but by this time he had a considerable knowledge of European literature, and was able to speak several languages. Pound's academic career finally ended after a disastrous few months teaching at the conservative Wabash Presbyterian College in Crawfordsville, Indiana, where his bohemian lifestyle was barely tolerated. The last straw broke when he allowed a chorus girl, stranded by a snowstorm, to stay in his room overnight. Despite his insistence that nothing improper had happened, he was dismissed in February 1908.

## Travels to Europe

Breaking his engagement with Hilda, he set off to Venice, where he self-published his first volume of poems, *A Lume Spento (With Tapers Quenched)*. Practically penniless, he made his way to London, taking copies of his book with him. He approached the bookseller and publisher Elkin Matthews, who agreed to help promote his work, and *A Lume Spento* soon gained him entry into London's literary circles. Among the people he met was the novelist Olivia Shakespear, who introduced him to other writers, including W. B. Yeats. Pound began a long courtship with Shakespear's daughter Dorothy, a young painter, which culminated in their marriage in 1914.

## Modernist experiments

At a time of exciting innovation in the arts, Pound was eager to develop a new "modern" style of poetry. He associated himself with the "school of images"—centered around the idea of the image as the organizing principle of poetry—pioneered by the poet and philosopher T. E. Hulme. Pound drew further inspiration from artist friends, including the painter Wyndham Lewis and the sculptor Henri Gaudier-Brzeska, who were developing a post-Cubist geometric style that Pound dubbed "Vorticism."

Hilda Doolittle arrived in London in 1911 and influenced a change in the direction of Pound's poetry. Despite having broken off their brief engagement before leaving the US, Pound and Doolittle remained close and, with the poet Richard Aldington (later Doolittle's husband), they founded a movement in poetry that they called Imagism, which emphasized great clarity of expression in short, free-verse poems.

Pound soon tired of the group, and thought it was not going far enough in its modernity. He became interested in Asian poetry, especially its concentrated use of language with no superfluous words and its striking use of imagery. He began working on a translation of Chinese poems in 1913, and realized that this was the style he wanted to adopt in his own poetry: concise, direct, and dynamic.

⊲ **HILDA DOOLITTLE**
Doolittle, who published as H. D., was a member of the avant-garde Imagist group. Pound was influential in Doolittle's development as a poet and writer.

*HIERATIC HEAD OF EZRA POUND,*
*HENRI GAUDIER-BRZESKA, 1914*

"**Good writers** are those who **keep** the **language efficient**. That is to say, **keep** it **accurate**, **keep** it **clear**."

EZRA POUND, *ABC OF READING*

▽ **RAPALLO, ITALY**
The seaside resort of Rapallo became a haven for Modernist writers and artists. In addition to Pound, it attracted W. B. Yeats and the younger poets Basil Bunting and Louis Zukofsky.

Pound achieved some commercial success with his collections *Personae* (1909) and *Ripostes* (1912), and around 1915, he embarked on a major new project—a challenging, complex epic poem that was later to become *The Cantos*. He also worked as the London correspondent of the magazine *Poetry*, in which he championed his own work and that of his friends, including H. D. and Richard Aldington and W. B. Yeats, and promoted the early work of James Joyce and T. S. Eliot.

### Postwar disillusion
With World War I raging around him, Pound became increasingly depressed and disillusioned. After the conflict, he was also angered by what he saw as a lack of social and political direction, which mirrored his own feelings of purposelessness. He devoted much of his time to studying economics and politics, and became heavily critical of British society. His long, satirical, two-part poem *Hugh Selwyn Mauberley* (1920) is a portrait of a disappointed poet out of tune with a sterile modern society that is addicted to materialism, blind to art, and desires only "an image of its accelerated grimace."

### From Paris to Italy
Tired of London, Pound and Dorothy moved to Paris in 1921. He continued work on *The Cantos*, and gained a reputation as an editor, contributing critical commentary on Eliot's *The Waste Land* and stories by his friend Ernest Hemingway. It was in Paris

that Pound began an affair with the violinist Olga Rudge that lasted for the rest of his life. Neither he nor Dorothy warmed to the city and in 1924 they moved to Rapallo, Italy, where Pound felt he could work in peace.

That peace was disrupted, however, when Olga, now pregnant with Pound's child, also moved to Italy. Dorothy, who had previously turned a blind eye to her husband's infidelities, separated from Pound when she heard about the birth of his daughter, Mary; but she was herself pregnant and the couple reunited before their son, Omar, was born in Paris in 1926. Despite these domestic upheavals, Pound continued to write, publishing the first volumes of *The Cantos*, and *Personae*, a collection of poems, while Mary was taken care of by a foster mother and Omar was sent to Dorothy's mother, Olivia, in London.

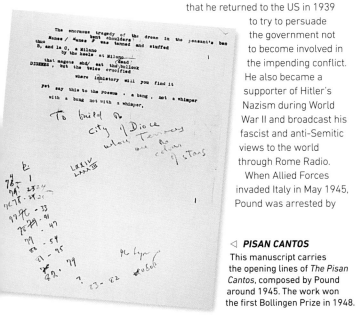

### Politics and arrest

The Pounds had moved to Italy not long after Benito Mussolini and his fascist party had come to power. Pound was a great admirer of "Il Duce" (whom he called "the boss"), and became increasingly politically active during the 1930s, so much so that he returned to the US in 1939 to try to persuade the government not to become involved in the impending conflict. He also became a supporter of Hitler's Nazism during World War II and broadcast his fascist and anti-Semitic views to the world through Rome Radio.

When Allied Forces invaded Italy in May 1945, Pound was arrested by

◁ **PISAN CANTOS**
This manuscript carries the opening lines of *The Pisan Cantos*, composed by Pound around 1945. The work won the first Bollingen Prize in 1948.

◁ **OLGA RUDGE**
For many years after World War II, Olga Rudge devoted herself to defending Pound against the charges held against him by the US government.

the US for treason and detained in a prison camp near Pisa. He was placed in solitary confinement, in primitive conditions, but still managed to write, producing what became known as *The Pisan Cantos*. In November, he was moved to the US to stand trial, but was eventually declared insane and committed to St. Elizabeth's Hospital in Washington, D.C. Despite his apparent instability, this was when he produced much of the finest work in *The Cantos*.

### An uneasy legacy

Pound's friends and fellow writers campaigned for his release, which was eventually granted in 1958. He immediately returned to Italy—apparently unrepentant, since he gave a fascist salute upon arriving in Naples. He and Dorothy lived with Mary for a while in the Tyrol, then returned to Rapallo, where they joined Olga in an uneasy ménage à trois, until Dorothy finally left to live with Omar in London.

Throughout the 1960s, Pound was a broken man, suffering from depression and self-doubt, and his declining health prevented him from writing much more than the *Drafts and Fragments: Cantos CX–CXVII*. His reputation, thanks to his outspoken fascist views, was also compromised, and opinion was (and still is) divided as to how much his achievement as a poet should be honored. He died the day after his 87th birthday, while in Venice with Olga.

### IN CONTEXT
#### Fascist beliefs

For Pound, Western society had lost its way culturally, economically, and politically after World War I. He believed that the solution lay in the principles of national community (unity in a struggle against the bourgeoisie) espoused by Mussolini in Italy. At first he was suspicious of Germany's brand of fascism, but as the outlook of Il Duce became more closely aligned with that of Hitler in the mid-1930s, Pound followed suit. He began to see Jewish "usury" as an existential threat and he publicly defended the right of Germany and Italy to rule over the "inferior" peoples of eastern Europe, Asia, and Africa. He later renounced his position, in public at least, admitting that "the worst mistake I made was that stupid, suburban prejudice of anti-Semitism."

**ADOLPH HITLER STANDS ALONGSIDE BENITO MUSSOLINI**

## KEY MOMENTS

| 1908 | 1915 | 1920 | 1925 | 1948 | 1969 |
|------|------|------|------|------|------|
| *A Lume Spento* (*With Tapers Quenched*), Pound's first book of poetry, is published at his own expense. | *Cathay* is published. It consists of free-verse versions of Ernest Fenollosa's translations of Chinese poems. | *Hugh Selwyn Mauberley* marks a turning point in Pound's career as he leaves England for mainland Europe. | The first collection of *The Cantos*, Pound's epic poem, is published as *A Draft of XVI Cantos*. | *The Cantos LXXIV–LXXXIV*, written while detained by US forces near Pisa, is published as *The Pisan Cantos*. | The unfinished final section of *The Cantos* is published as *Drafts and Fragments: Cantos CX–CXVII*. |

# D. H. Lawrence

## 1885–1930, ENGLISH

Lawrence's writing sparked allegations of obscenity and antimilitarism and was repeatedly suppressed by censors. His dramatic personal life was also widely regarded as scandalous.

◁ **JESSIE CHAMBERS**
Lawrence's friend and inspiration, Jessie, provided the basis for the character Miriam Leivers in *Sons and Lovers*. She later published an account of Lawrence's childhood and youth.

In his short life, David Herbert Lawrence produced 12 novels, numerous short stories, and about 800 poems, plays, and nonfiction texts. He is often hailed as one of the finest writers of modern English literature for his poignant evocation of the natural world and his candid depiction of social change, familial and sexual relationships, and the complexities of desire. His semiautobiographical novel *Sons and Lovers* (1913) paints a vivid picture of his early life in the poor mining community of Eastwood, and of his parents, Arthur and Lydia.

### Encouragement and adversity
Bullied at school for his physical frailty, Lawrence befriended Jessie Chambers, a girl who lived at Haggs

Farm, near Lawrence's home. In Jessie, he found a confidante, muse, and intellectual equal, and in Haggs Farm and its surroundings his "first incentive to write." In 1901, he was stunned by the sudden death of his brother and laid low by pneumonia, but that year he also started work as a student teacher and later began his first novel, *The White Peacock.*

In 1906, he left for Nottingham to study for a teaching certificate. A breakthrough came when Jessie sent some of his poetry to Ford Madox Hueffer, editor of *The English Review*, whose encouragement galvanized Lawrence's ambition. However, his progress was thwarted: pneumonia, the death of his beloved mother, and a string of ill-considered relationships led him to abandon his teaching post and return to Eastwood.

In 1912, Lawrence met Frieda Weekly, the wife of his former professor and the mother of three children. They fell passionately in love, and within months eloped to Europe. Their relationship, which endured until

Lawrence's death, was beleaguered by ill health and poverty, but with Frieda, Lawrence discovered a new appetite for writing. They traveled widely, and Lawrence published the first of his essays on life abroad, *Twilight in Italy* (1916). On their return, Britain was under the shadow of war and Frieda's German nationality aroused mistrust. Isolated in Cornwall, Lawrence completed *The Rainbow* (1915), which was banned. Defiant, he continued work on *Women in Love.*

In 1919, the couple left Britain for an itinerant life that lasted more than a decade—Lawrence described these travels as a "savage pilgrimage." Their restlessness took them far and wide, across Europe, to Sri Lanka, the Americas, and Australia. Aside from three brief visits home, Lawrence remained an expat. Nonetheless he was preoccupied with Britain, the class system, and its people, which found full expression in his last novel, *Lady Chatterley's Lover.*

**COAL MINERS FROM A NOTTINGHAM MINE ON THEIR WAY HOME FROM WORK**

> ## ON STYLE
> ### Writing in dialect
> Lawrence's novels introduce a cast of Nottinghamshire characters, whose colloquial speech and rhythmic idiom breathe life into the writer's portrait of life in the county's mining towns and villages. Lawrence had an intimate knowledge of the local dialect and used it very precisely in his writing. He also wrote poetry in dialect, which allowed him to leaven the hardships that he described in his verse with comedy: for example, the poem "The Drained Cup" begins, "Tha thought tha wanted ter be rid o' me./ 'Appen tha did, an' a.'"

◁ **LADY CHATTERLEY'S LOVER**
Centered on an affair between Lady Ottoline Morrell and a young stonemason, the story was heavily censored for its sexual scenes and language. In 1960, Penguin finally published an unexpurgated version.

▷ **D. H. LAWRENCE**
Despite persistent poor health, Lawrence was a prolific writer. His work was often heavily autobiographical and referenced his early years in Nottinghamshire. He died of complications from tuberculosis in Vence, France, at the age of 44.

> " **Money poisons** you when you've got it, and **starves** you when you haven't. "
> D. H. LAWRENCE, *LADY CHATTERLEY'S LOVER*

# Raymond Chandler

## 1888–1959, AMERICAN

Chandler was the finest crime writer of his or any other generation. His greatest creation was the hard-bitten private eye Philip Marlowe, who epitomized the cynicism and pessimism of the Depression.

Raymond Thornton Chandler was born in 1888 in Chicago, the son of an alcoholic railway engineer. His parents separated and he moved to Britain with his Irish-born mother. They settled in London, and Chandler was educated at Dulwich College. He was an excellent pupil, and after leaving school he passed the civil service exams and took a job in the Admiralty, but left after barely a year.

Unsure of his direction, Chandler worked briefly as a journalist at the *Daily Express*, before returning to the US in 1912. He settled in Los Angeles the following year and took various jobs, including stringing tennis-rackets and picking fruit. When war intervened, Chandler enlisted in the Canadian Expeditionary Force, serving in France; after the Armistice, he returned once more to Los Angeles.

### From commerce to pulp

Chandler found some stability when he met Pearl "Cissy" Pascal. They were an unlikely couple—she was twice divorced and 18 years older than him—but they married in 1924. By now, Chandler was working for an oil syndicate, rising from bookkeeper to become vice president of the company.

Things went well until 1930, when the marriage began to fail and the Depression hit Chandler's business. He began drinking and womanizing, and in 1932 he was fired. During this bleak period, he read a lot of pulp magazines, "because they were cheap enough to throw away." Calling on his journalistic experience, Chandler began to write pulp fiction, and his first story was published in *Black Mask* in 1933. It was well received. At the age of 45, he had found his vocation.

Chandler's writing fit perfectly with the new genre of detective fiction. This was the "hard-boiled" style—a terse, straight-shooting form that mirrored Prohibition and the organized crime that went with it. The style had been pioneered in the 1920s by Carroll John Daly and Dashiell Hammett, but Chandler raised it to a new level. The hero at the heart of these thrillers was invariably a private eye. With Daly it had been Race Williams, and with Hammett, Sam Spade, but Chandler's Philip Marlowe eclipsed them both. He was something of an antihero, a bruised romantic, who could be gentle with life's victims but tough and uncompromising with the violent thugs who confronted him.

### Novels and screenwriting

Chandler's first novel, *The Big Sleep*—cannibalized from two of his *Black Mask* stories—was published in 1939. It was an instant success and transferred easily to the big screen. Soon Chandler was also in demand as a screenwriter. His greatest achievement in this field was the noir classic *Double Indemnity*, which he co-wrote with Billy Wilder. Chandler produced only seven novels before succumbing to alcoholism in later life. All but one of them were filmed and all are essential reading.

> **CHANDLER WITH TAKI, 1940s**
Chandler is shown here with his beloved cat, Taki, whom he referred to as his "secretary." He fondly imagined Taki looking up as if to say: "'The stuff you're doing's a waste of my time, bud'."

◁ ***THE BIG SLEEP***
Humphrey Bogart starred as Philip Marlowe in Howard Hawks's adaptation of the *The Big Sleep* (1946). He was the perfect vehicle for Marlowe's sparkling dialogue, full of cynical wisecracks, as befitted a man who had seen the world at its worst and expected nothing better.

▷ **T. S. ELIOT, c.1959**
By the time this photograph was taken,
T. S. Eliot had become one of the most
honored poets in history, having been
awarded an OBE, the Nobel Prize in
Literature, the Dante Gold Medal,
and the Goethe Prize.

# T. S. Eliot

## 1888–1965, AMERICAN

Eliot's poetry helped shape the modernist movement and voiced
the disillusionment of an age. But the writer's personal life was often
clouded by unhappiness, and sometimes by anxiety and depression.

# "This is the way **the world ends** Not with **a bang** but **a whimper**. "

T. S. ELIOT, *THE HOLLOW MEN*

T. S. Eliot was born in St. Louis, Missouri, and defined, in his view, by his childhood there, but he later transformed himself into a London-based man of letters, a publisher, and a playwright. A polyglot with Harvard degrees in comparative literature and philosophy, he embraced disorder and fragmentation in his mature poetry, counterbalancing song and rhythms of speech with academic references.

## From the US to England

Thomas Stearns Eliot, named after his maternal grandfather, was the last of six surviving children born to successful businessman Henry and his wife Charlotte, who wrote poetry. Eliot revealed a bookish nature at a young age; biographers attribute this in part to a congenital hernia that prevented much physical activity and so focused him on literature. He began writing poetry at 14 but took years to develop his style; his astonishing debut "The Love Song of J. Alfred Prufrock" was not published for another 13 years.

After Harvard and the Sorbonne, Paris, Eliot accepted a scholarship to Merton College, Oxford, in 1914 as war broke out. He often escaped to London, complaining of the stifling life of academics: "I don't like to be dead." In the capital, he met his lifelong advocate and fellow US exile, Ezra Pound. The two authors collaborated extensively, matching each other's energy for writing and promoting Modernist poetry.

In 1915, Eliot was introduced to Cambridge governess Vivien Haigh-Wood and just three months later they were married. Their union, which was beset by argument and crisis—much of it fueled by Vivien's frail physical and (according to some) mental health—ended in separation in 1933. Their dysfunctional relationship, however, undoubtedly stimulated Eliot's creativity, most notably in his writing of *The Waste Land* (1922), which he began when recovering from a bout of depression. The poem is structured loosely around the legend of the Holy Grail, and references classic literature from diverse cultures. Deliberately obscure and difficult, it was a landmark in modernism as well as one of the most influential pieces of writing of the 20th century.

## Publishing success

When *The Waste Land* was published, Eliot founded *Criterion*, which was to become an important literary journal; two years later, he left his regular job in a bank to become a director of the publishing house Faber & Gwyer (later Faber & Faber). Here, he found his true forte and over the course of four decades promoted and published such writers as W. H. Auden, Ezra Pound, and Ted Hughes, as well as his own work. He also famously procrastinated over the publication of Joyce's *Ulysses* and rejected Orwell's allegorical novel *Animal Farm*.

## Late years

In 1927, Eliot became a British citizen. He later described his dual nationality as key to his success: "it wouldn't be what it is if I'd been born in England, and it wouldn't be what it is if I'd stayed in America." He had two more significant companions in his life, eventually marrying Esme Valerie Fletcher, who was 38 years younger than him. Eight years later, in 1965, he died of emphysema and had his ashes scattered in his ancestral village, East Coker, which features in *Four Quartets*.

## IN CONTEXT
### Faith and poetry

Eliot was raised in a Unitarian family, and he soon realized that the faith's puritan values could be a force for social good. At college, he was introduced to a wide range of Eastern as well as Western belief systems, but his conversion to Anglo-Catholicism, an orthodox branch of Anglicanism, in 1927 shocked many of his modernist contemporaries, for whom almost any religion was anathema. His beliefs influenced the themes of his later poetry, notably *Four Quartets*, which comprises four interlinked poems, published over six years, that focus on the individual's relationship with time, the universe, and the divine.

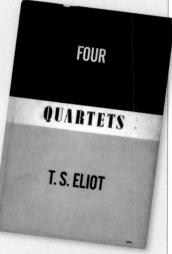

**FOUR QUARTETS**, FIRST EDITION, 1943

▽ **POET AND PUBLISHER**
T. S. Eliot (far left) attends a meeting of the board of directors at the publishing house Faber & Faber in London on March 25, 1944, to discuss how to best deploy their wartime paper ration.

▷ **JEAN RHYS, 1921**
The young Rhys is captured here by London-based photographer Pearl Freeman at the time that she was experimenting with her writing.

# Jean **Rhys**

1890–1979, DOMINICAN

Prostitution, alcoholism, displacement, and despair are the markers of Rhys's troubled life. Similar themes shaped her fiction, which railed against the plight of the marginalized and dispossessed.

Jean Rhys burst into the limelight in the mid-1960s with her masterpiece *Wide Sargasso Sea*, which tells the backstory of the imprisoned "white Creole" Bertha Mason in Charlotte Brontë's *Jane Eyre* (1847). Of her literary predecessor, Rhys (also a white Creole) wrote: "Brontë must have had something against the West Indies and I was angry about it. Otherwise, why did she take a West Indian for that horrible lunatic?" The details of Rhys's personal history set her decision to "vindicate the mad woman" (see box, right) in context.

## Colonial history

Ella Gwendolen Rees Williams, later Jean Rhys, was born on the island of Dominica in 1890. The daughter of a Creole mother and a Welsh father, and the great-granddaughter of a colonial landowner, she was dubbed "the white cockroach" at school. This colonial background, and rejection by her mother for being too fair, contributed to Rhys's sense of herself as an outsider—a theme that haunts her fictional works and her unfinished autobiography, *Smile Please* (1979).

In 1907, at 16—well versed in Shakespeare, Dickens, Milton, and Byron—she was shipped to England to live with her aunt, who was irritated by her niece's refusal to react to the country with "the grateful enthusiasm of a young colonial." In Dominica, the girl's pale skin had marked her as an

◁ **FORD MADOX FORD**
The English writer had a huge influence on literature in the 1920s through the literary magazines that he edited. His affair with Rhys lasted a year and a half.

outsider and she "prayed to be black." In England, she was not white enough: she was called a "coon" at school in Cambridge and taunted for her accent. Thereafter she spoke in a whisper.

After two terms at the Academy of Dramatic Art in London in 1908, and a brief stint as a chorus girl, her life descended into chaos in London and Paris. Homesick for the Caribbean, impoverished, rootless, and unstable, she had a string of damaging relationships and resorted to alcohol and, briefly, to prostitution. She began writing in earnest following rejection by one of her lovers, the author and editor Ford Madox Ford, producing anguished works, including *Postures* (1928), *After Leaving Mr. Mackenzie* (1931), *Voyage in the Dark* (1934), and *Good Morning, Midnight* (1939).

## Challenging power

Rhys stripped language to the bone, producing unadorned prose of great clarity, remarkable for its ability to create a sense of claustrophobic tension and high emotion. Rich in modernist and postmodernist devices, such as the use of multiple viewpoints, narrative shifts, and stream-of-consciousness techniques, her work embraces key issues, including gender, relationships, identity, and oppression. As one commentator noted, Rhys "unpicks ... [the] language by which the powerful keep control." Her writing has been at the forefront of feminist and postcolonial theory since the early 1980s. *Wide Sargasso Sea* in particular is a key text of postcolonial writing and is taught in literature classes throughout the world for—among many reasons—the brilliance and complexity of its response to one of the great English novels.

## From obscurity to fame

Rhys married three times; two of her husbands were imprisoned for shady financial dealings. Her son died three weeks after his birth; her daughter spent long periods away from her side. During and after World War II, Rhys's life continued to be turbulent, and included arrests for drunkenness, psychiatric assessment, and a brief stay in prison. She lived as a recluse for two decades or more—many believed her to be dead—but she resurfaced in 1966 with *Wide Sargasso Sea*, a book that had taken her about 20 years to write. Rhys was awarded the prestigious W. H. Smith Literary Award the following year, but said that recognition had "come too late." She died in an Exeter nursing home in 1979, alone and alcoholic.

## IN CONTEXT
### The other story: the madwoman in the attic

*Wide Sargasso Sea* tells the backstory of Bertha Mason, the Creole woman confined in an attic by her husband, Mr. Rochester, in Brontë's *Jane Eyre*. In Rhys's narrative, the Creole heiress marries Rochester, an impoverished Englishman, who inherits all her money and takes her from Jamaica to England, where she descends into despair and eventual madness.

Whereas in Brontë's text Bertha's madness is linked to her "uncivilized" place of birth, in Rhys's rewrite her insanity is triggered by her husband's betrayal and abuse of power, and her alienation in a hostile land. The text thus offers an alternative view of female derangement and colonial otherness. However, Rhys's use of different voices confuses any sense of a clear central truth in the text. The fragmented narrative underlines the woman's struggle to find her voice and to make sense of her fractured world—a far cry from the unfaltering progress from chaos to stability of Brontë's heroine, Jane Eyre.

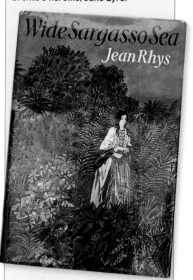

**WIDE SARGASSO SEA, FIRST EDITION**

◁ **ROSEAU, DOMINICA**
Rhys was born in the capital of Dominica, in the West Indies. It was a society divided along racial lines: slavery on the island was not abolished until 1834.

# Marina Tsvetaeva

**1892–1941, RUSSIAN**

The turbulent period of history from Czarist rule to Soviet totalitarianism formed the backdrop to Tsvetaeva's unsettled life. She found solace in her poetry, adopting a very personal, lyrical style.

◁ **THE TSAR-MAIDEN, A POEM FAIRY TALE, 1922**
Marina Tsvetaeva's verse is known for its swift shifts of pace, unusual syntax, and references to Russian folk songs.

Marina Tsvetaeva was born in Moscow in 1892 into a family of intellectuals. Her mother, Maria, a frustrated concert pianist, was the second wife of a professor of art history, and there was constant tension between Marina and her half-siblings. The family was always on the move, travelling around Europe; Marina was educated in Italy, Switzerland, and Germany.

In 1908, she studied literary history at the Sorbonne in Paris; and in 1910, she self-published her first collection of poems, *Evening Album*.

Having moved to Crimea, she joined a circle of writers based in the Black Sea resort of Koktebel. It was here that she met Sergei Efron, a poet and cadet in the Officers' Academy, whom she married in 1912. They had two daughters, Irina and Alya, and although the marriage was happy, it did not prevent Marina from having affairs, notably with the poets Osip Mandelstam and Sophia Parnok, while Sergei was away fighting in the Civil War.

## From Moscow to Paris

Tsvetaeva and her daughters moved to Moscow in 1917, hoping to join Sergei, but instead found themselves poor and alone in a city suffering from famine. Marina decided to put her daughters into a state orphanage for safety. Irina died of starvation in 1920, and a year later, Marina and Alya went to join Sergei, who was by now in Berlin. The family eventually settled in Paris in 1925, but life was far from easy. They were still living in poverty, and had an extra mouth to feed with the birth of a son, Georgy, in 1925. Unbeknown to Marina, Sergei began working for the Soviet secret police and in 1937 he was accused by the French police of murdering a Soviet defector. He fled to the USSR, joining Alya, who had moved there earlier that year. When Marina returned to the USSR in 1939 she found it impossible to find steady work, let alone a publisher. Then, both Sergei and Alya were arrested on espionage charges: Alya was sent to a labor camp and Sergei was executed. With the German invasion of the USSR in 1941, Marina was evacuated to Yelabuga. Displaced, and with no means of making a living, she hanged herself on August 31, 1941.

## Literary legacy

Tsvetaeva is best remembered for her volumes of lyric poetry, in which she explores her affairs, her unrequited loves, and her inner life with sincerity and passion. "I do not believe in poems which pour slowly; I believe they should rush from your heart," she wrote, and in her works she confronts with burning intensity a range of sometimes controversial topics ranging from female sexuality and infanticide to women's experiences during Russia's "terrible years."

**STATUE OF VOLOSHIN IN KOKTEBEL, CRIMEA**

"What is the **main thing in love**? To **know** and to **hide**. To **know** about **the one you love** and to **hide** that you **love**."

MARINA TSVETAEVA, *THE HOUSE AT OLD PIMEN*

▷ **MARINA TSVETAEVA, 1911**
This portrait of the poet was made by her friend and mentor, Maximilian Voloshin at his large house in Koktebel, Crimea.

# F. Scott Fitzgerald

## 1896–1940, AMERICAN

Fitzgerald is famous for his portrayals of the lives of wealthy Americans during the Jazz Age. His books, some partly autobiographical, describe vividly the glamour, but also the deep flaws, of his characters.

◁ **FIRST EDITION**
Despite its status today as one of the great works of American fiction, Fitzgerald's *The Great Gatsby* received mixed reviews when first published and its early sales were disappointing.

turned down by New York publishers Charles Scribner's Sons. He shined in Princeton's literary circles, and made lasting friendships with other young writers, such as Edmund Wilson, who became a prominent literary critic. He also fell in love with Chicago debutante Ginevra King, who was to become the model for several of the female characters in his novels, including Daisy in *The Great Gatsby*.

Francis Scott Key Fitzgerald was born in St. Paul, Minnesota, in 1896. His family was well off—his mother, Molly McQuillan Fitzgerald, was from an Irish-American family that had prospered as wholesale grocers. He was named after Francis Scott Key, the lyricist of "The Star-Spangled Banner," a relative on his father's side.

Fitzgerald went to various Catholic schools, and then Princeton University, where he became a member of the socially prominent Triangle Club (a dramatic society that staged musical comedies), and wrote a novel that was

### Scott and Zelda

Fitzgerald's literary activities and his unrequited love for King distracted him from his studies, and in 1917 he left Princeton without finishing to join the army. He expected to fight in World War I, but the conflict ended before he was sent to the front and he remained stationed in the US. At this time, he met Zelda Sayre, daughter of an Alabama Supreme Court judge, and the two became engaged.

Fitzgerald got a job in advertising in the hope of earning enough to marry Zelda, but she broke off the

engagement, partly because he was not wealthy enough. He returned to St. Paul, took a job repairing car roofs, and concentrated on writing a novel based on the one he had written at Princeton. Now titled *This Side of Paradise*, the book was published in 1920. It tells the story of a young man who attends Princeton, serves in the army, and is passed over by the woman he loves for a richer rival. Healthy sales of the book signaled the

▷ **F. SCOTT FITZGERALD, 1928**
Pictured here at the height of his fame, Fitzgerald was known to the public as a raffish playboy. Despite his reputation for drinking and partying, he was a meticulous writer who repeatedly revised and refined his text.

**IN PROFILE**
### Maxwell Perkins

The editor Maxwell Perkins (1884–1947) worked for the New York publisher Charles Scribner's Sons from 1910 until he died. When he started at the company, it mostly published established authors, but Perkins had a genius for spotting new talent, and was the first to publish books by F. Scott Fitzgerald, Ernest Hemingway, Thomas Wolfe, and many other notable US writers. This approach was new at the time—publishers did not usually hunt for promising writers. Perkins was also good at helping his authors improve their work, polish details, produce better narrative structures, and cut irrelevant material. He had a lasting impact on writing and publishing in America.

**PERKINS AT HIS DESK**

" So **we beat on**, boats **against the current**, borne back **ceaselessly** into the **past**. "

F. SCOTT FITZGERALD, *THE GREAT GATSBY*

△ **THE FITZGERALDS IN ITALY**
F. Scott Fitzgerald, his wife Zelda, and their daughter Scottie are pictured here in Italy. Like many of the "lost generation" of US writers, Fitzgerald traveled widely and lived abroad.

△ *SAVE ME THE WALTZ*
While she was recovering from a breakdown, Fitzgerald's wife Zelda wrote her own novel, which was published in 1932 as *Save Me the Waltz*. The semiautobiographical account of Zelda's life upset Fitzgerald, not because of the invasion of his privacy, but because he thought that she had used what he regarded to be his own artistic material.

beginning of Fitzgerald's literary career. He had shown Zelda that he could make good money from writing; the two were married soon afterward.

A second novel, *The Beautiful and Damned*, about a glamorous young couple who decline into alcoholism while waiting to inherit a fortune, appeared in 1922. The book was not as successful as its predecessor, but the fame brought by *This Side of Paradise* meant that Fitzgerald

could command high fees for short stories, many of which appeared in magazines such as *The Saturday Evening Post* and *Collier's Weekly*.

*The Beautiful and Damned* was in a way Fitzgerald's warning to himself. Both he and Zelda drank excessively, and to escape the pressures of life in the US they moved to France, becoming prominent members of expat society on the Riviera. Soon after settling in France, Fitzgerald completed his most famous book, *The Great Gatsby* (1925). The novel deals with a group of rich neighbors on Long Island, and centers on Jay Gatsby and his love for the beautiful Daisy Buchanan. It is a questioning account of the American Dream,

in which wealth, style, and glamour are eclipsed by drinking, adultery, and violent death. *The Great Gatsby* epitomizes Fitzgerald's mature style, with its vivid, sometimes lyrical descriptions, and its artful use of the narrator Nick Carraway as a fascinated and innocent observer.

### Drinking and decline

Fitzgerald's stories centered on promising heroes who came to grief through weakness, corruption, or alcohol; his own life was following a similar path. He drank increasingly, and the lavish life that he and Zelda led in France made them constantly short of money. Fitzgerald's editor, Maxwell Perkins, and his agent,

## KEY WORKS

**1920**
*This Side of Paradise* is published at the insistence of Maxwell Perkins. It sells nearly 50,000 copies and makes Fitzgerald famous.

**1922**
*The Beautiful and Damned* is published, but Fitzgerald realizes that the income from even highly successful novels will not make him rich.

**1922**
Fitzgerald's collection *Tales of the Jazz Age* includes the short story "The Diamond as Big as the Ritz," a parable of the perils of wealth.

**1925**
*The Great Gatsby* is published. It is later widely regarded as Fitzgerald's masterpiece.

**1941**
*The Last Tycoon* is Fitzgerald's last, unfinished, novel. The author's friend Edmund Wilson edits it for publication.

> "Whenever you feel like **criticizing** somebody, just **remember** that all the people in this world haven't **had the advantages** that you've had."
>
> F. SCOTT FITZGERALD, *THE GREAT GATSBY*

Harold Ober, regularly loaned him money, and when Ober finally refused to continue bailing him out, Fitzgerald cut his links with him.

By the late 1920s, it became clear that Zelda's mental health was fragile, and in 1930 she was diagnosed with schizophrenia. The stress, the need to take care of Zelda, and the mounting bills from doctors put increasing pressure on Fitzgerald—and meant that he had to publish yet more stories to meet the costs. The couple returned to the US, where Zelda was hospitalized in Maryland, and Fitzgerald started work on his next novel. But the need to write lucrative short stories meant that his progress was slow. *Tender is the Night*, about a psychiatrist who falls in love with one of his patients, finally came out in 1934.

## Hollywood years
Fitzgerald had previously done some writing for the movies, and in 1937 he signed a screenwriting contract with Metro-Goldwyn-Mayer. Meanwhile,

Zelda's condition had worsened—she had become increasingly violent—and she was permanently hospitalized. Fitzgerald moved to Hollywood, where he lived in a studio-owned bungalow and worked on numerous screenplays, including an unproduced version of *Gone With the Wind*. He disliked the work (the filmmaker Billy Wilder compared him to a great sculptor hired to do a plumbing job), but it gave him a good income. He began a relationship with the columnist Sheilah Graham, which brought him more contentment, but his heavy drinking still, on occasion, provoked outbursts of violence.

While living with Graham, Fitzgerald began his final novel, *The Last Tycoon*. Its story is set in Hollywood and its central character, Monroe Stahr, the tycoon of the title, is based on the movie producer Irving Thalberg. It seemed that his writing was reaching a new high, but in 1940, at the age of 44, Fitzgerald had a heart attack and died, and the novel remained unfinished.

## Fragile dreams
Each of Fitzgerald's novels portrays a different aspect of the American dream, exploring the inevitable fragility of that dream and the ways in which people's lives become derailed, leaving their hopes unfulfilled. Most of the works also have autobiographical elements: Fitzgerald's own life had been one of immense potential—with his wealthy background, elite education, and close relationship with Zelda, yet he was only able to achieve limited fulfilment.

Fitzgerald became a celebrity during his lifetime and gained a reputation as a playboy, but he is now regarded as one of the great American novelists. His dramatizations of the highs and lows of life in the US, his vivid portrayal of the "lost generation" of the country in the 1920s and '30s, and the lasting appeal of his characters have ensured that his works have remained in print, and his novels, especially *The Great Gatsby*, have inspired numerous adaptations and movies.

△ **SHEILAH GRAHAM, c.1945**
Fitzgerald's British-born lover, Sheilah Graham, was a highly influential gossip columnist who wrote about the lives and loves of Hollywood celebrities. She described life with Fitzgerald in her book *Beloved Infidel*, which was later adapted into a movie starring Gregory Peck and Deborah Kerr.

## IN CONTEXT
### The Gold Coast
In 1922, when Scott and Zelda Fitzgerald had just become parents, they rented a house in Great Neck, Long Island. The nearby North Shore of Long Island (the so-called Gold Coast) was a popular summer retreat for the super-rich—families such as the Vanderbilts, the Woolworths, and the Guggenheims. The Fitzgeralds attended lavish parties thrown by the wealthy at their vast estates, and it was in this decadent, elitist atmosphere that the idea for *The Great Gatsby* took shape. In the book, the nouveau riche inhabit the fictional area of West Egg; while families with old money are to be found in East Egg.

**FITZGERALD'S HOUSE IN GREAT NECK, LONG ISLAND**

# William Faulkner

**1897–1962, AMERICAN**

Nobel Prize–winning writer Faulkner set most of his works in his native Mississippi. A technically daring author of great imaginative power, he is often described as the leading American fiction writer of the 20th century.

William Cuthbert Faulkner was hostile to the idea of linking his work to his biography. He once wrote that he wanted the recorded history of his life to be no more than: "He made the books and he died." Yet his fiction is deeply rooted in his social background and is haunted by his private demons:

▽ **COLLEGE EDUCATION**
Faulkner briefly attended the University of Mississippi under a special provision for war veterans, even though he had never graduated from high school.

it could certainly have been written only by a white man from the Deep South.

Faulkner was born in New Albany, Mississippi, in 1897 and grew up in nearby Oxford, where he was to live for most of his adult life. He would imaginatively transform this area of northern Mississippi into the fictional Yoknapatawpha County, in which most of his novels are set. Although it was home to the University of Mississippi, in the early 20th century Oxford had a population

of only 2,000. Growing up in this small rural town, Faulkner mixed with all levels of society, despite his privileged background. An ability to capture the precise nuances of speech of poor people of varied racial backgrounds, picked up from childhood, became one of the strongest elements in his writing.

## Southern history

The Faulkners—or Falkners as their name was traditionally written—were local aristocracy. William Faulkner's great-grandfather had been a

### IN PROFILE
### Sherwood Anderson

Faulkner's literary mentor in the 1920s, Sherwood Anderson (1876–1941), came from a poor background in rural Ohio. He first made a career as a businessman before abandoning his job and his family to become a writer in Chicago. Anderson's reputation was established with *Winesburg, Ohio*, a collection of short stories published in 1919, which is still considered his finest work. His novels include *Many Marriages* (1923) and *Dark Laughter* (1925). John Steinbeck and Ernest Hemingway, among others, were influenced by Anderson's writing.

SHERWOOD ANDERSON IN CHICAGO, 1922

◁ **FAULKNER, 1955**
The writer is captured here, pipe in hand, in the year that his novel *A Fable* won the Pulitzer Prize for Fiction. He was awarded the prize a second time (posthumously) for his picaresque *The Reivers* (1962).

" I am **telling** the **same story over** and **over**, which is **myself** and the **world**. "
WILLIAM FAULKNER

Confederate colonel in the Civil War, a violent hero around whose name folk legends grew. Faulkner's father was a feeble inheritor of the family tradition. He struggled to make a good living despite the privileges of his background, and was despised by a wife who aspired to the status of a Southern lady.

Faulkner's books are shot through with a sense of this historical context, of a society conscious of failing to live up to its semi-mythical past and wedded to an antiquated code of honor out of step with modern circumstances. And Faulkner was, of course, also sharply aware of the dark flaw in the white South's view of its past—the failure to come to terms with the great crime of slavery. One of the strongest attachments of his childhood was to his black nanny, Callie Barr—the prototype of the strong, sympathetic character Dilsey

▷ **SANCTUARY, 1940 EDITION**
Faulkner wrote the crime drama *Sanctuary* as a "potboiler"—for the money. The publishers gave it a lurid cover to boost sales.

Gibson in his novel *The Sound and the Fury* (1929). At the same time, he was never able to see black people as the complete equal of whites.

## War years

Faulkner received only a sketchy formal education, failing to apply himself at school or during his brief college career. In adolescence, however, he began to read a lot of modern literature and to write poetry, by his own account chiefly to "further various philanderings."

He always felt pressure from his peers to prove himself a man of action, but when the US entered World War I in 1917, he

was rejected by the army as unfit for service because he was too short. Faulkner reacted to this humiliation by volunteering to join the British forces as a pilot. Although he trained as a pilot in Canada, he never flew before the war ended—but he gave people the impression that he

▽ **COTTON PLANTATION**
Faulkner's writings, including *Absalom, Absalom!*, offer insight into plantation culture and the brutal intensity of life for the slaves who worked in the fields. This lithograph shows a 19th-century cotton plantation on the Mississippi River, an area that Faulkner knew well.

had done so, or had even been wounded in combat. His first novel, *Soldier's Pay* (1926), uses the point of view of a character who is bitter that the war has ended too soon for him to see any action.

## A creative explosion

Faulkner thought of himself as a poet in the years just after the war. His first published book was a collection of verse, *The Marble Faun* (1924), but poetry was a genre for which he had little talent. In the mid-1920s, he lived for a time in New Orleans, moving in the city's vibrant bohemian artistic circles, and there he met established novelist Sherwood Anderson. It was under Anderson's influence that he turned to writing novels. *Soldier's Pay*, accepted by a New York publisher, was followed by *Mosquitoes* (1927), a satire on the New Orleans intelligentsia. Neither book caused any great stir. Faulkner was still searching for his voice.

The change in Faulkner that produced the astonishing burst of creativity leading to his great novels of the late 1920s and early 1930s will always remain obscure. However, it was certainly a time of emotional turbulence. Back in Oxford, Mississippi, he married the woman he had loved and lost in his youth, Estelle Oldham, now a divorcée, but his feelings about this union were gloomy and violent rather than warm and romantic. His literary career seemed a failure: his third novel, *Flags in the Dust*, the first to draw on his family history and set in the imaginary Yoknapatawpha County, was rejected by his publisher in 1927 (a revised version was later published as *Sartoris* in 1929).

Faulkner reacted to rejection by writing a novel just for himself, without any regard for potential

◁ **WILLIAM AND ESTELLE**
Faulkner poses with his wife, Estelle, in front of their home, Rowan Oak. Estelle already had two children from her first marriage. The couple's first child, Alabama, died in infancy in 1931; their second, Jill, survived to adulthood.

publishers or the public. The result was *The Sound and the Fury*, a novel whose first chapter, told through the time-shifting stream of consciousness of an adult with the mental age of a small child, seemed destined to deter readers. Yet Faulkner had discovered how to inhabit the minds of the characters through whom the novel is narrated and could express their experiences, sometimes funny but mostly distressing, in a style appropriate to each. He was also mining emotional material that

stretched back into his own childhood. The result was a masterpiece, though one that failed to achieve real success for several years.

## Fading finances

Desperate for cash to support an expensive lifestyle, Faulkner next wrote what he hoped would be a commercial novel in the popular hard-boiled crime genre. *Sanctuary* was a brutal tale of rape and abduction that expressed the author's bitter misogyny. With

### ON FORM
## Two stories, one novel

Faulkner's novel *The Wild Palms* (1939)—which was later republished under its intended title, *If I Forget Thee, Jerusalem*—consists of two apparently unconnected stories, "Wild Palms" and "Old Man," which are told in alternate chapters. "Wild Palms" is a tortured love story that ends in a woman's death during an abortion. "Old Man" tells of a convict who helps a pregnant woman to escape from a Mississippi flood and give birth, before returning to captivity. There are parallels between the two stories, each five chapters long, notably in the theme of pregnancy, but critical opinion is divided as to whether Faulkner succeeded in creating a significant whole by juxtaposing them.

**THE WILD PALMS, FIRST EDITION, 1939**

> " If I had **not existed**, someone else would have **written me**, Hemingway, Dostoevsky, **all of us ...** "
>
> WILLIAM FAULKNER

△ **MOVIE ADAPTATION**
A poster advertises the movie *Intruder in the Dust* (1949), adapted from Faulkner's novel of the same name and shot in the author's hometown of Oxford, Mississippi. The book tells the story of an African American farmer who is accused of murdering a white man; it demands that Southern whites come to terms with their traditional racism and overcome it.

its memorably terrifying villain, the gangster Popeye, and its shocking scenes of sexual violence, it proved to be Faulkner's first successful book when it was published in 1931. It also drew retrospective critical attention to *The Sound and the Fury*. Faulkner's financial difficulties,

however, persisted since most of his novels sold no more than a few thousand copies.

## Hollywood years

In late 1929, Faulkner wrote the novel *As I Lay Dying* during six weeks of working night shifts at the University of Mississippi power plant. Building on the technical achievement of *The Sound and the Fury*, with the number of different narrative voices expanded to 15, it was another work destined to be recognized as a literary classic. *Light in August* followed as the last book of this exceptional creative period: it was a morally complex novel about outcasts and misfits, addressing attitudes to race and the prejudices of a tight-knit community.

Although he never stopped writing novels and short stories, for over a decade, starting in 1932, Faulkner

found a solution to his need for money by signing up as a Hollywood scriptwriter. His heavy drinking and his general unreliability soon became legendary, but he was protected from the wrath of the movie moguls by his friendly relationship with the director Howard Hawks. His biggest contribution to movies was writing part of the script for *To Have and Have Not* (1944).

It was in Hollywood that Faulkner began a passionate affair with Meta Doherty, which complicated his life and his marriage for many years. It also contributed to the doomed affair that makes up one half of the two-story novel *The Wild Palms* (also known as *If I Forget Thee, Jerusalem*) that appeared in 1939.

By that time, Faulkner had become famous. In January 1939, his picture graced the cover of *Time* magazine, belatedly convincing the inhabitants

**IN CONTEXT**
**Civil rights**

In Faulkner's lifetime, African Americans in Mississippi experienced racial segregation and the denial of their basic rights. This situation was challenged by the rise of the Civil Rights Movement in the 1950s, which questioned the prejudices and assumptions of white Southerners. In the early 1960s, the whites-only University of Mississippi in Oxford, Faulkner's hometown, became a focus for federal-backed attempts to enforce integration, despite violent resistance from segregationists. Faulkner was torn between respect for black aspirations to equal rights and his own attachment to the history and traditions of the white South.

**US SOLDIERS ESCORT AN ARRESTED SEGREGATIONIST AFTER A RIOT AT THE UNIVERSITY OF MISSISSIPPI CAMPUS**

## KEY WORKS

**1929**
*The Sound and the Fury*, Faulkner's first masterpiece, recounts the decline of the once proud Compson family.

**1930**
*As I Lay Dying* tells of the death of Addie Bundren and the fate of her dysfunctional family as they attempt to bury her.

**1931**
The dark and brutal *Sanctuary* is the first novel to bring Faulkner widespread attention.

**1932**
*Light in August* centers on the fate of a man haunted by doubt about his racial identity.

**1936**
In *Absalom, Absalom!* a series of unreliable narrators tells the story of a sexually profligate plantation owner.

**1939**
*The Wild Palms* tells of a convict's escape and recapture and of an agonized, passionate affair.

**1951**
In *Requiem for a Nun*, which alternates between play script and narrative prose, Faulkner continues to experiment with form.

> " The **artist** is of **no importance**. Only **what he creates** is important, since there is **nothing new** to be said. "

WILLIAM FAULKNER

of Oxford, Mississippi, that this son of the Faulkners was not a complete wastrel. Yet wealth and popularity still evaded him, the quality of his work was declining, and by 1946 all of his novels were out of print. In 1948, however, he wrote *Intruder in the Dust*, a novel with a clear, although not simplistic, message. A tale of relations between races, it argued that the mistreatment of African Americans in the South had to be stopped by white Southerners facing their history of "injustice and outrage and dishonor and shame," rather than by intervention from Northerners or the federal government. Its powerful message contributed to Faulkner's being awarded the Nobel Prize in Literature the following year. It also earned him money, since the movie rights were sold.

### Late works

Honored and successful at last, Faulkner continued to write, pursuing his search for formal innovation, even though his powerful creative drive had waned. Many of his public statements, such as his Nobel acceptance speech, took on a lofty humanistic quality, praising the resolution of the human spirit, although this was far from the tortured, complex view of humanity in his novels of the 1920s and '30s.

Faulkner's private life remained a mess in his later years. Affairs with young women finally destroyed his marriage, and continued alcohol abuse ruined his health. Insisting on riding although unfit, he died of complications after a fall from a horse.

△ **HOWARD HAWKS**
Faulkner became great friends with Hollywood director Hawks, and the two worked together off and on for about 20 years. Their method was collaborative, with Faulkner providing entire scenes or sometimes just single ideas for Hawks to flesh out.

◁ **DESK AT ROWAN OAK**
Faulkner bought the Greek Revival house Rowan Oak in Oxford, Mississippi, in 1930, and spent much of his life restoring it. Visitors to the house today can view the study in which he wrote many of his most famous works.

▷ **BERTOLT BRECHT, 1927**
Brecht is pictured here at his piano in
his apartment in Berlin at the age of 29,
sporting his trademark leather jacket;
cropped hair; and big, fat cigar. It is,
according to some commentators,
a somewhat surprising image for a
bourgeois-loathing Marxist intellectual.

# Bertolt Brecht

## 1898–1956, GERMAN

Brecht wrote epic plays that explored social and historical issues
from a socialist perspective, and developed innovative theatrical
techniques that have influenced many later writers and directors.

Eugen Berthold Brecht was born in Bavaria, Germany, to middle-class parents and gained, from his devoutly Protestant mother, a knowledge of the Bible that was to influence his later writing. He was almost expelled from school for his anti-patriotic views, but in 1917 he enrolled at Munich University to study medicine (while also fueling his love of literature by attending theater seminars). He worked briefly in a military clinic, and began to write theater criticism. When the war ended, he took part in a political cabaret, before starting his own company with writer and director Arnolt Bronnen, changing the spelling of his own name to Bertolt, so that their two names rhymed.

## Berlin collaborations

Before long, Brecht began to write plays of his own, completing *Baal* in 1918 and *Drums in the Night* the following year, as well as producing verse influenced by traditional ballads, French chansons, and poets such as François Villon. In 1925, he moved to Berlin, which was becoming a vibrant cultural center under the Weimar Republic. Brecht met many other artists, writers, and musicians, and notably visited the groundbreaking art exhibition "Neue Sachlichkeit" (New Objectivity), described by its organizer as "new realism bearing a socialist flavor." Its new, objective take on the visual arts encouraged Brecht to be equally daring in his theatrical work: his writing became very matter-of-fact, and he began to use harsh lighting and in-the-round staging (influenced by the layout of a boxing ring).

His greatest collaborator in the Weimar period was the composer Kurt Weill. The pair produced a series of operas: *The Threepenny Opera* (an adaptation of British poet John Gay's *The Beggars' Opera*), *Happy End*, and *The Rise and Fall of the City of Mahagonny*. Weill supplied the music while Brecht (and his collaborators, who were often unacknowledged) wrote the words.

## Into exile

When the Nazis came to power in 1933, Brecht, left Germany to settle first in the US and later in Switzerland. After the war, he wrote the plays for which he is famous, including *The Life of Galileo*, *The Good Person of Szechuan*, and *The Caucasian Chalk Circle*. These works employed the principles of epic theater—a movement that addressed "contemporary existence" using an episodic structure of loosely connected scenes combined with the alienation effect (see box, right).

After World War II ended, Brecht moved to communist East Berlin, where he directed the Berliner Ensemble. He put on the plays that he had written in exile and classic dramas by Sophocles and Shakespeare. He continued to write poetry and produce works on dramatic theory until his death in 1956.

△ **EAST GERMAN STAMP**
When he moved to East Berlin in 1949, Brecht initially backed the policies of the German Democratic Republic, including its suppression of a popular uprising in 1953, but he later changed his views. He is remembered here on an East German stamp.

◁ **ON STAGE, 1930**
Brecht's satirical, nonrealist production of *The Threepenny Opera* demonstrates his intense opposition to naturalistic theater, whereby the audience "hang up their brains with their hats in the cloakroom."

> ## ON STYLE
> ### The alienation effect
>
> Brecht described his key theatrical technique in German as the *Verfremdungseffekt*, which translates to the alienation or estrangement effect. It is a way of distancing the audience from the theatrical action, so that they do not become emotionally involved in the play and are reminded that theater is an artificial experience. The alienation techniques that were adopted by Brecht included actors stepping out of character to summarize or comment on the action or to sing songs. He also used bare stage sets to make it obvious that the play was taking place in a theater. Brecht saw these techniques as ways of helping him explain the social and historical issues dramatized in his plays.

SONG IS USED IN BRECHT'S *MOTHER COURAGE AND HER CHILDREN*

" Society cannot share a common **communication system** so long as it is split into **warring factions**. "

BERTOLT BRECHT, *A SHORT ORGANUM FOR THE THEATER*

# Jorge Luis Borges

## 1899–1986, ARGENTINIAN

Borges is hailed as one of the best writers of his generation. His poetry and his genre-defying short stories haunt readers with their rich imagery and their combination of realism and the unexpected.

Jorge Luis Borges was born in 1899 in Buenos Aires. His father was part English in ancestry and grew up speaking English at home. His mother's family included heroes of the Argentine War of Independence in the early 19th century.

### Emergence as a poet

From an early age, Borges was encouraged to read both Spanish and English literature. He grew into a bookish child who consumed the contents of his father's library, which included works by Robert Louis Stevenson, Lewis Carroll, H. G. Wells, and G. K. Chesterton. From 1914 to 1921, the family lived in Europe, first in Geneva, Switzerland, where the young Borges went to school, leaving without graduating. They then moved to Spain, where Borges became involved in the avant-garde ultraist poetic movement, which was based in the capital, Madrid. The ultraists wanted to create poetry suited to the dynamism of 20th-century society by subverting traditional rhyme and meter, and by using metaphor, striking

### IN CONTEXT
### Argentine tradition

Many Argentine writers of the 19th and early 20th centuries evoked life in the pampas, celebrating the freedom of the gaucho in works that drew on José Hernández's epic poem *Martín Fierro*. Borges admired this work, but stepped back from using this tradition to create nationalist fiction. Leading by example, Borges showed that South American writers could be international in their outlook (open to influences as diverse as Anglo-Saxon poetry and Islamic writings) and similarly global in their appeal.

**GAUCHO WITH HIS HORSES, PATAGONIA, ARGENTINA**

◁ **BORGES, 1919**
Borges is photographed here, at the age of 20, while he and his family were living in Switzerland. His first collection of poems was published two years later.

visual imagery, and the innovative arrangement of words on the page. In 1921, Borges returned to Argentina and two years later he published *Fervor of Buenos Aires: Poems*, a collection of poems in an ultraist style (from which he later distanced himself for its "excesses"). Around this time, he also cofounded two literary journals, *Proa* and *Prisma*, in which he published some of his early work, translated numerous works by overseas poets for Argentinian readers, and wrote extensively and critically about poetry.

### Short stories

In the 1930s, Borges began to publish the short stories for which he is now known internationally, collaborating initially with his friend Adolfo Bioy Casares on fantasy tales and parodies of detective stories, which were published under the pseudonym H. Bustos Domecq. His first book of stories as the sole author was *A Universal History of Infamy* (1935), a collection of short fictional biographies of real criminals and adventurers. This was a breakthrough work, covering themes such as

"When **writers die** they become **books**, which is after all **not too bad** an **incarnation.**"

JORGE LUIS BORGES

△ **BORGES'S LABYRINTH, VENICE**
Borges's frequent use of the symbol of the labyrinth is celebrated in the maze built to honor the 25th anniversary of his death. The Labyrinth was created in 2011 in Venice by the Fundación Internacional Jorge Luis Borges and the Giorgio Cini Foundation.

identity and violence, for which the author would become famous. Slim volumes like this did not earn much money, however, and so Borges got a job as a librarian in Buenos Aires. More books of stories that followed in the 1930s and '40s included the volumes *Fictions* and *The Aleph*.

## Complex fantasies

Although diverse in subject, many of Borges's brief stories (most of them only a few pages long) share several distinctive aspects. They describe a world that is dreamlike, parodic, or fantastic; they play with concepts such as time; they make fun of pedantry and the world of scholarship; and they often present the reader with

mazelike complexity. Recurring motifs—notably labyrinths, libraries, and mirrors—give the stories a haunting quality that persists in the reader's memory. Much of the work is also humorous and paradoxical: famous images include the author who rewrites the Spanish classic *Don Quixote* word for word; the map that is at exactly the same scale as the county it depicts; and the "Library of Babel," which contains every possible book in the universe.

## Politics and Perón

Borges hated extremism of all kinds. During World War II, he supported the Allies against Hitler, but he also expressed his dislike for monolithic

communist states. His liberal views put him at odds with Juan Perón, the newly elected president of Argentina, who came to power in 1946. Perón began to transform the country into a one-party state, and handed key posts and sinecures to his loyal supporters, forcing Borges to resign from his library job.

With his eyesight failing as a result of an inherited condition, Borges continued to write fiction, while earning a living by lecturing, sharing his love of English literature. He also published essays on British writers.

When President Perón was removed from power in a coup d'état in 1955, Borges found himself appointed director of the Argentine National

## KEY WORKS

### 1935
In *A Universal History of Infamy*, Borges gathers together into one collection pieces that were first published in the journal *Crítica*.

### 1944
*Fictions*, Borges's most famous collection of stories, is published. In it, he explores the paradoxes and images for which he became best known.

### 1949
*The Aleph and Other Stories* includes fantasy tales on themes such as immortality.

### 1970
*Doctor Brodie's Report* is a collection of stories that are set in Buenos Aires, many of which feature vivid nightmares or violence.

### 1975
Stories that Borges wrote late in life—and that he considered to be his best works—are collected in *The Book of Sand*.

JORGE LUIS BORGES / 225

# "Let others **pride themselves** about how many pages they have **written**; I'd rather boast about the ones **I have read**."

JORGE LUIS BORGES

Library, as well as holding a post as professor of English and American literature at the University of Buenos Aires. By now he was totally blind, and "The poem of the gifts" describes the irony of his gaining his ideal job—custodian of the nation's books—just as he lost his sight.

## International reputation

Borges' academic and library appointments gave him an ideal platform from which to write and lecture. More volumes of stories appeared, and his work began to gain recognition abroad through translations of the collections *Fictions* and *Labyrinths*, published in Britain, North America, and France. In 1961, Borges was (jointly with Samuel Beckett) awarded the prestigious Prix Formentor, which further enhanced his international stature.

From 1967, Borges collaborated with the American translator and writer Norman Tomas di Giovanni, who helped bring his poetry and prose to an ever wider audience in the English-speaking world.

Borges continued to write, producing books of short stories in the 1960s and '70s. These later works, which appeared in collections such as *Book of Imaginary Beings*, *Doctor Brodie's Report,* and *The Book of Sand*, are compressed, poetic, and make extensive use of allegory. They were written with the help and support of Borges' mother (with whom he lived for much of his adult life, except for a brief, unsuccessful marriage in the 1960s to a widow, Elsa Astete Millán) as well as that of his personal assistant, María Kodama.

### Lecture tours

By the 1970s, Borges was well-known all over the world and traveled widely (often accompanied by Kodama) to give lectures and appear on television. He also wrote much more verse, saying that since he had become completely blind, he liked to write poems because he could hold an

entire work in his head at one time. After his mother's death at the age of 99, Borges continued living in the apartment that he had once shared with her, cared for by a housekeeper. He married Kodama in 1986 and died, at 86, a few months later.

### A remarkable legacy

Many critics have hailed Borges as the most important author to write in Spanish since Cervantes. His work connects the cultures of the Old and New Worlds, modernity with tradition, and popular fiction with philosophy. The influence of the imaginary, magical worlds of his stories can be seen in the blossoming of "magic realism" in Latin America—in the mesmerizing narratives of writers such as Gabriel García Márquez—as well as in the work of a new generation of writers in North America. His legacy is so strong that he has lent his name to a new genre—Borgesian literature.

◁ **THE ALEPH**
Borges's story *The Aleph*, shown here in its 1952 Argentinian edition, is—like much of his writing—about illusion, infinity, and the inadequacy of language to articulate human feelings.

## IN PROFILE
### Adolfo Bioy Casares

The Argentinian writer Adolfo Bioy Casares (1914–1999) became a long-standing friend of Borges in 1932. He is best known for his short novel *The Invention of Morel* (1940), the story of a fugitive who hides on a Polynesian island where he has several uncanny experiences, ranging from encounters with people who appear and disappear to the presence of two suns in the sky. Bioy Casares collaborated on numerous projects with Borges, including collections of stories and fantasies, several screenplays, and the joint editorship of a series of translations of English detective fiction.

**ADOLFO BIOY CASARES, 1991**

◁ **MARIA KODAMA**
Borges met María Kodama when he was 54 and she 16. She became his literary secretary in 1975, helping him with his writing after he lost his sight, and collaborating on a number of works. They married in 1986, just months before Borges died of cancer.

# Ernest Hemingway

**1899–1961, AMERICAN**

An icon of masculinity, drawn to war, violence, and death, "Papa" Hemingway was a modernist giant. His stark, athletic style of writing was radically new and was perhaps the most widely emulated voice in 20th-century literature.

◁ **OAK PARK HOME**
Hemingway's childhood home was in Oak Park, Illinois, just 10 miles (16 km) from Chicago but—as a conservative, religious, Midwestern town—very distant from the metropolis in its ethos.

While it is common for writers to draw to some extent on the events of their own lives for material, Ernest Hemingway did so more than most, so that his life and his work are intimately intertwined. Indeed, he lived his life like a character from one of his own novels, building up his famous hard-drinking, macho persona and writing his experiences into his work. Those experiences were often violent and extreme, and included bullfighting, big-game hunting, and war. From the time he burst onto the literary scene of the 1920s with *The Sun Also Rises*, it was clear that he was mining this action-packed life to create a new way of writing.

### Childhood interests

The second of six children, Ernest Miller Hemingway was born on July 21, 1899 in Oak Park, Illinois, a middle-class suburb of Chicago that he described as full of "wide lawns and narrow minds." His father, Clarence Edmonds Hemingway, was a respected local doctor, and his mother, Grace Hall Hemingway, a musician. He later maintained that he had hated his mother, and indeed for the first few years of his life she indulged in the somewhat bizarre habit of dressing him and his older sister, Marcelline, identically—often in dresses. Hemingway's aggressive masculinity may have stemmed from a need to compensate for this early ambiguity, and his animosity to his mother may have been at the root of his later treatment of women.

At school, Ernest took part—though without excelling—in several sports, including football and boxing. He was a good student; he shone at English and wrote for the school paper, *Trapeze*, and the yearbook, *Tabula*. Just as influential as his schooling were the summers that he spent with his family on Walloon Lake in Michigan, where his father taught him how to hunt, fish, and camp. These experiences instilled in him a love of adventure and the outdoors that stayed with him throughout his life.

On leaving school in 1917, instead of going to college, Hemingway took a job as a cub reporter for the

**FIRST EDITION OF HEMINGWAY'S**
*DEATH IN THE AFTERNOON*

> " All **good books** have **one thing** in common—they are **truer** than if they had **really happened.** "
>
> ERNEST HEMINGWAY

▷ **ERNEST HEMINGWAY**
Hemingway was a celebrity in his day, known for his rugged persona and outdoor exploits; he was even photographed writing outdoors. This was an image of himself that he scorned, saying "I don't work like this."

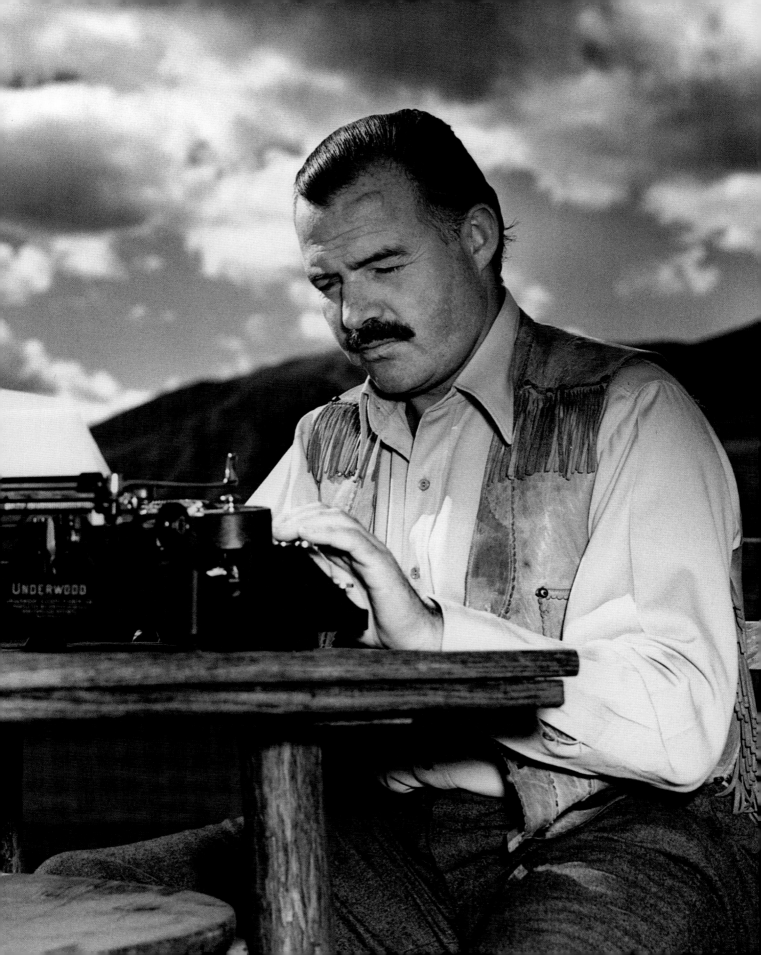

△ **ROYAL TYPEWRITER**
Ernest Hemingway would sometimes write standing up; his favored machine was the Royal. He reportedly told his friend, the actress Ava Gardner, that the only psychologist he would ever open up to was his typewriter.

*Kansas City Star.* Here, writing reports on police and emergency-room items, he learned and practiced the style that would become his hallmark, following the *Star*'s style guide, which began: "Use short sentences. Use short first paragraphs. Use vigorous English. Be positive, not negative." The essence of Hemingway's declarative, lucid, and deceptively simple style can be seen in those basic instructions.

### Wartime adventures

Hemingway only stayed at the *Star* for six months. World War I was raging, and he desperately wanted to join in what he saw as the great adventure in Europe. Turned down by the army because of faulty vision, he volunteered instead as an ambulance driver in the Red Cross and was sent to Italy. There, he experienced the blood and

△ **KEY WEST HOME**
Ernest and Pauline bought this large Spanish colonial house on the island of Key West, Florida, in 1931. The house is now a museum and a US-designated National Historic Landmark.

horror of war firsthand, and was wounded in the legs while helping Italian soldiers to safety: he was later awarded the Silver Medal of Valor. While recuperating in Milan, he fell in love with an American nurse, Agnes von Kurowsky, who jilted him for an Italian officer. Hemingway later drew on this relationship in his war novel *A Farewell to Arms*.

Back in North America and in low spirits, Hemingway worked as a reporter for the *Toronto Star*, first in Toronto and then in Chicago. A camping and fishing trip with friends in the backwoods of Michigan inspired the acclaimed short story "Big Two-Hearted River" (1924), featuring the recurring semiautobiographical character Nick Adams.

In Chicago, Hemingway met Hadley Richardson, a woman eight years older than him. He fell in love. They married in September 1921 and two months later sailed for Paris, Hemingway having secured the position of foreign correspondent for the *Toronto Star*.

### European travels

Paris in the 1920s was a creative hot spot, and Hemingway threw himself into the melee with gusto. His friends included James Joyce, Gertrude Stein, Ezra Pound, and F. Scott Fitzgerald—a group that Stein dubbed "the Lost Generation" (see box, left). Stein read and critiqued his drafts, while Pound's Imagist style of poetry (see page 198) was also influential as Hemingway honed his sparse, stripped-back style of writing.

Hemingway traveled around Europe writing articles for the *Toronto Star* and gathering material for his own short stories. In September 1923, the couple returned to Toronto for the birth of their son, John Hadley Nicanor (known as Bumby), but by January 1924, they were back in Paris.

---

IN CONTEXT
## The Lost Generation

A term first used by Gertrude Stein, the Lost Generation refers to the cohort of expatriate writers who came of age during World War I, many of whom congregated in Paris, and whom Hemingway wrote about in his novel *The Sun Also Rises*. They were "lost" in the sense of being directionless and confused after the changes wrought by the war—alienated from the values of a prewar world that no longer seemed relevant. Along with Hemingway, these writers included Archibald MacLeish, F. Scott Fitzgerald, John Dos Passos, e. e. cummings, and John Steinbeck— all of whom were hugely successful.

**FIRST EDITION OF HEMINGWAY'S**
*THE SUN ALSO RISES*, 1926

🍎 **THE SUN ALSO RISES** 🍎

**ERNEST HEMINGWAY**
*Author of*
"IN OUR TIMES" and "THE TORRENTS OF SPRING"

---

" The **world** breaks **every one** and **afterward** many are **strong** at the **broken places**. But those that will not break it **kills**. "

ERNEST HEMINGWAY, *A FAREWELL TO ARMS*

In the meantime, Hemingway's first book, *Three Stories and Ten Poems*, was published, and in 1925 his story collection *In Our Time*, came out in New York to critical acclaim.

## Key West

Hemingway's next work, *The Sun Also Rises* (1926), propelled him to fame. This novel—his first—centers on a group of expatriates wandering around bars and bullfights in France and Spain. It portrays in thinly fictionalized form—and in radically clean, spare prose—his own friends in the aftermath of the war: cynical, melodramatic, and given to excess.

While writing the novel, Hemingway began an affair with a wealthy American woman, Pauline Pfeiffer.

In 1927, he and Hadley were divorced and he married Pauline, with a haste that he later claimed to regret. In October of that year, he published another short story collection, *Men Without Women*, which contained several of his most praised stories, including "The Killers," "Hills Like White Elephants," and "In Another Country."

In 1928, with Pauline now pregnant, the couple moved to Key West, Florida, where their son Patrick was born. Later that year, Hemingway's father killed himself; devastated, the writer commented: "I'll probably go the same way." He spent much of the following year working on *A Farewell to Arms* (1929). This powerful novel depicted the war with austere lyricism, telling the story of a young American

ambulance driver in Italy who falls in love with an English nurse—clearly based on Hemingway's own war experiences. The book was a commercial and critical success.

## Animal passions

Now living in Key West with his family (his third son, Gregory, was born in 1931), Hemingway became restless and traveled extensively. In his beloved Spain he returned to the corrida that had so fascinated him a few years earlier, which resulted in the nonfiction work *Death in the Afternoon* (1932). In this encyclopedic examination of the tragic ritual of the bullfight, he delved into the nature of bravery and fear, saying: "Bullfighting is the only art in which the artist is in

▽ **BULLFIGHTING**
Hemingway had a passion for bullfighting and befriended many of Spain's most glamorous matadors. His description of the Pamplona bull run in *The Sun Also Rises* helped make the festival into a world-famous event.

> " Madame, **all stories**, if continued far enough, **end in death**, and he is **no true-story teller** who would keep that **from you**. "

ERNEST HEMINGWAY, *DEATH IN THE AFTERNOON*

△ **CAREER HIGH**
*The Old Man and the Sea* cemented Hemingway's reputation and his fortune. An excerpt of the story published in *Life* magazine (which sold five million copies) brought the work to wide public attention.

danger of death." In 1933, on safari in East Africa, he developed a passion for big-game hunting, which inspired two of his finest short stories, "The Snows of Kilimanjaro" and "The Short Happy Life of Francis Macomber," as well as the less well-received nonfiction work *The Green Hills of Africa* (1935). In 1934, he bought a fishing boat, the *Pilar*, with which he could indulge his love of another manly sport—big-game fishing.

### War correspondent

In 1937, Hemingway returned to Spain as a war correspondent to cover the Spanish Civil War. There, he often traveled with the American journalist Martha Gellhorn, whom he had met the previous year at his favorite Key West bar, Sloppy Joe's. The two began an affair. While staying with Gellhorn in a hotel in Madrid, Hemingway wrote his only play, the poorly received *The Fifth Column* (1937).

Hemingway reported on the war for two years, and was present at the catastrophic Battle of the Ebro (July–November 1938). His 1940 novel *For Whom the Bell Tolls* was the successful fictional result of his Spanish experiences, in which he focused on the comradeship that war creates despite its brutality.

On his return from Spain, Hemingway moved to Cuba with Gellhorn, setting up house on a property named Finca Vigía (Lookout Farm), outside Havana, where he cultivated his macho "Papa Hemingway" image, spending his time hunting, fishing, boxing, and drinking hard.

In 1940, he and Pauline were divorced and he married Martha. The following year, he accompanied her to China to cover the Chinese–Japanese war, an assignment he disliked. In 1944, the couple traveled again, this time to Europe to report on World War II, but by now their marriage was in trouble. In London Hemingway met Mary Walsh, a correspondent for *Time* magazine, and began an affair with her. They married in 1946.

In 1950, Hemingway published *Across the River and Into the Trees*, which was universally panned. He

▽ **THE HUNTER'S TROPHY**
Hemingway kneels while holding a pair of antelope horns. His safaris in Kenya and Tanzania helped him cultivate his image as a great outdoorsman and provided him with material for his writing.

△ **CUBAN HOME**
Hemingway wrote *For Whom the Bell Tolls*, *The Old Man and the Sea*, and his memoir, *A Moveable Feast*, in his study at Finca Vigía, his home in Cuba,

## Martha Gellhorn

Hemingway's third wife was a novelist and journalist who refused to be merely a footnote in the Hemingway story. One of the greatest 20th-century war correspondents, Martha Gellhorn (1908–1998) reported on all of the world's major conflicts over her 60-year career. She covered the Spanish Civil War and the Blitz in London, and was the only female correspondent at the D-Day landings in 1944; she reported on the liberation of Dachau, the Arab–Israeli conflict, and the Vietnam War. Her marriage to Hemingway was combative; she said that he was jealous and bullying, and she was the only one of his wives to leave him.

**MARTHA GELLHORN TALKS TO BRITISH TROOPS IN ITALY**

## Illness and decline

Although at a high point in his career, Hemingway was at a personal low point, and suffering from anxiety and ill health. Years of hard living had taken a toll, as had numerous accidents, including two plane crashes while on safari in 1954. At the end of 1956, in Paris, he discovered a cache of his old notebooks, and over the next few years worked them into the memoir *A Moveable Feast*. In 1960, he left Cuba and moved home to the US. Paranoid, depressed, and drinking heavily, he was hospitalized twice and subjected to electroshock treatments at the Mayo Clinic in Minnesota.

followed it up with *The Old Man and the Sea* (1952), a slim novel of epic breadth about a Cuban fisherman's struggle to hook a giant marlin, only for sharks to eat it on the way back to port. This book, which Hemingway called the "best I can write ever for all of my life," won the Pulitzer Prize in 1953, and was instrumental in Hemingway's being awarded the Nobel Prize in Literature in 1954.

In 1961, he was diagnosed with a genetic disease that prevented his body from processing excess iron. In July that year, he took his life with a shotgun. (There were five other suicides in his family: his father, two siblings, and a granddaughter.)

Hemingway's influence was vast. He created a new way of writing about nature and human experience that resonated through 20th-century literature. The posthumously published *The Garden of Eden* (1986), an exploration of gender, suggests that his aggressive masculinity may not have been as hard wired as he liked people to think.

## KEY WORKS

**1925**
*In Our Time*, the expanded US version of a collection of stories first printed in Paris the previous year, is published.

**1926**
*The Sun Also Rises*, Hemingway's first novel, is based on his own friends and real events, such as the Pamplona festival and Parisian café life.

**1929**
*A Farewell to Arms* is published and consolidates Hemingway's status as a major American modernist writer.

**1932**
*Death in the Afternoon* is the result of Hemingway's extensive research into bullfighting.

**1940**
*For Whom the Bell Tolls* is nominated for the Pulitzer Prize and sells half a million copies within a few months of publication.

**1953**
*The Old Man and the Sea*, written in eight weeks, is an overnight success and wins Hemingway the Pulitzer Prize.

**1964**
*A Moveable Feast*, Hemingway's moving memoir of his early Paris years, is published posthumously.

**1986**
*The Garden of Eden*, exploring gender fluidity in a relationship between a writer and his wife, is published in edited form.

# Kawabata Yasunari

## 1899–1972, JAPANESE

Kawabata's spare, lyrical writing expressed "the essence of the Japanese mind" and made him the first Japanese author to win the Nobel Prize in Literature.

Kawabata Yasunari's life was marked from an early age by experiences of loss, trauma, and loneliness. These would later find expression in the detachment frequently seen in his characters, and in his fascination with death. Kawabata was born in Osaka in 1899 and was orphaned at the age of four. While his sister was sent to live with an aunt, he was raised by his mother's parents. By the time he was 15, his sister and grandparents had died, leaving him essentially alone.

### Childhood influences

Kawabata began living in Tokyo in 1917, and studied at the city's Imperial University, graduating in 1924 with a degree in English. In Tokyo, he became engaged to a 14-year-old girl, Hatsuyo Ito, and was devastated when she left him after she was raped by a monk at the temple where she was staying. Characters based on Hatsuyo and their tragic relationship would later appear in his works, including in the short story that brought him attention, "The Dancing Girl of Izu" (1926)—a semiautobiographical piece about a melancholy student's infatuation with a young dancer. Other stories would echo his youthful experiences, exploring themes of impossible love, emptiness, and the search for comfort.

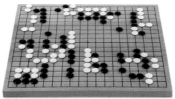

△ **THE MASTER OF GO,**1951
Kawabata's *The Master of Go* is a semifictional account of a legendary Go match that took place in 1938. The struggle between the two players is thought by some to be an allegory of World War II.

### Japanese Modernism

In the years after school, Kawabata cofounded the journal *The Artistic Age* as an outlet for Japan's Neosensualist writers. The movement, which had parallels with expressionism in the West, valued "art for art's sake" and rejected the prevailing idea that art should convey a moral message.

In 1934, he moved from Tokyo to Kamakura with his wife, Hideko, whom he had married in 1926. It was around this time that he began to produce his most famous works, albeit at a painfully slow rate: *Snow Country* was published in installments between 1935 and 1947; *Thousand Cranes* was begun in 1949 and never completed; and *The Sound of the Mountain* took six years to write. Kawabata left many works unfinished, partly because he was happy writing vignettes, but also because he did not want to confront endings. This passivity even carried through to his political opinions—he distanced himself from the militarism of World War II, for example, rather than voicing either protest against or support for it.

Kawabata was awarded the Nobel Prize in Literature in 1968. The melancholy that marked his work spilled into his acceptance speech, which touched on Zen, ikebana, and most tellingly, suicide. In 1972, Kawabata was found dead at his home, a gas hose in his mouth and an empty bottle of whiskey nearby—a surprisingly disorganized end for a man who had found such solace and inspiration in the precise formality of Japan's ancient traditions.

YUKIO MISHIMA PHOTOGRAPHED IN TOKYO, 1970

◁ **THE KAMAKURA MUSEUM OF LITERATURE**
Kawabata moved to the city of Kamakura, south of Tokyo, in 1934. At first, he socialized with the city's community of intellectuals, but he became increasingly reclusive with age. Today, the Kamakura Museum of Literature houses many of his effects.

▷ **YASUNARI KAWABATA, 1968**
Kawabata is photographed here in the year he received the Nobel Prize. His receipt of the award, exactly 100 years after the Meiji Restoration in Japan, signaled the emergence of Japanese literature on the world stage.

# Directory

## ▽ Edith Wharton

### 1862–1937, AMERICAN

Author Edith Wharton, born Edith Newbold Jones, is famous for her powerfully ironic novels that attack the privileged society to which she herself belonged. Although she wrote from an early age, her wealthy New York family discouraged her from pursuing writing as a career.

She endured an unhappy marriage to the socially acceptable Teddy Wharton, and did not publish her first novel until the age of 40. Success came after *The House of Mirth* was published in 1905. The story of a woman crushed by upper-class New York's hypocritical social mores, it was an immediate best seller. Her reputation was confirmed by the novella *Ethan Frome*, which focused on New England Puritanism. Divorced from her husband in 1913, Wharton spent the rest of her life in France. *The Age of Innocence*, the finest of her later novels, returned to a critical portrayal of the New York of her childhood. She was the first woman to win the Pulitzer Prize (1921).

**KEY WORKS:** *The House of Mirth*, 1905; *Ethan Frome*, 1911; *The Custom of the Country*, 1913; *The Age of Innocence*, 1920

△ EDITH WHARTON, c.1885

## Maurice Maeterlinck

### 1862–1945, BELGIAN

A symbolist dramatist, poet, and essayist who won the Nobel Prize in Literature in 1911, Maeterlinck was born into a prosperous French-speaking Flemish family in Ghent. His breakthrough as a writer came in 1889 with the play *La Princesse Maleine*, an adaptation of a tale by the Brothers Grimm.

Maeterlinck created a novel style of drama in which characters who are powerless against their fate drift toward their doom in an atmosphere saturated with symbolism. His gloom-ridden love story *Pelleas and Melisande* was made into an opera by Claude Debussy in 1902. Maeterlinck was also celebrated for his extended essays, notably *The Life of the Bee*, which used the natural world as the basis for mystic reflections on human existence. In the first decade of the 20th century, plays such as the fairy-tale drama *The Blue Bird* retained the prestige of the avant-garde. In later years, however, literary fashion turned against Maeterlinck's refined aestheticism and his creativity petered out.

**KEY WORKS:** *La Princesse Maleine*, 1889; *Pelleas and Melisande*, 1892; *The Life of the Bee*, 1900; *The Blue Bird*, 1908

## Gabriele d'Annunzio

### 1863–1938, ITALIAN

A flamboyant public figure, Italian author Gabriele d'Annunzio was as famous for his political gestures and love affairs as for his writings. He published his first book of poems, *Primo Vere*, at the age of 16 and quickly established a reputation as a poet and short-story writer of original talent. Beginning with *The Child of Pleasure* in 1889, he published torrid novels that reflected his own overheated emotional and sexual life—*The Flame of Life*, for example, was based on his highly publicized affair with actress Eleonora Duse. He also had success as a playwright, most notably with *Francesca da Rimini* (1901), written as a vehicle for Duse.

D'Annunzio was an aggressive nationalist who promoted Italy's entry into World War I. He fought for his county, achieving hero status, and lost an eye in combat. After the war, he briefly seized control of the contested city of Fiume (Rijeka), which he ruled as a personal dictatorship.

**KEY WORKS:** *Canto novo*, 1882; *The Triumph of Death*, 1894; *The Flame of Life*, 1900; *Francesca da Rimini*, 1902

## Constantine Cavafy

### 1863–1933, GREEK

The most influential Greek poet of the 20th century, Cavafy was born in Alexandria, Egypt. He spent part of his youth in England, where his family had business connections, but returned to live in Alexandria in 1885 and stayed there for the rest of his life. Working as a civil servant for 30 years, he wrote poetry in his spare time. He found his own style around the age of 40, eventually producing some 150 short poems that he considered acceptable.

Many of Cavafy's poems are set in ancient Greece and Rome, such as the celebrated "Waiting for the Barbarians" and "The God Abandons Antony." With great subtlety, he makes the ancient world reflect upon the present. He also wrote love poems poignantly evoking the intense but fleeting pleasures of casual gay sex. Partly because of this intimate subject matter, most of his poetry was not published until after his death.

**KEY WORKS:** "Waiting for the Barbarians," 1904; "Ithaka," 1911; *Poems of C. P. Cavafy*, 1935

## ▷ André Gide

1869–1951, FRENCH

Nobel Prize–winning author André Gide was born into a Protestant family, the son of a professor, and published his first fiction at the age of 21. In the 1890s, while visiting North Africa, he recognized his attraction to boys and embraced a Nietzschean paganism that found expression in the lyrical prose of *The Fruits of the Earth* (1897).

An established presence on the Parisian literary scene, he was a founder of the influential *Nouvelle Revue Française* magazine in 1909. His fiction included *The Vatican Cellars* (1914), which introduced the concept of the *acte gratuit*, an arbitrary exercise of freedom, and *The Counterfeiters*, a complex novel exploring notions of authenticity.

Gide defended homosexuality, attacked colonialism, and rejected Soviet communism. In 1947, he was awarded the Nobel Prize in Literature. His autobiographical writings—including *If It Die ...* (1926) and his *Journals*—are among his most interesting works.

**KEY WORKS:** *The Immoralist*, 1902; *Strait Is the Gate*, 1909; *The Pastoral Symphony*, 1919; *The Counterfeiters*, 1926

## Colette

1873–1954, FRENCH

One of France's best-loved writers, Sidonie-Gabrielle Colette was introduced to the world of letters by her first husband, author Henri Gauthier-Villars. Her first novels, the best-selling *Claudine* series, appeared under his name. After their separation in 1906, Colette earned a living as an erotic performer in music halls while using her life, including affairs with both sexes, as material for semiautobiographical novels, such as *The Vagabond*. A second marriage brought her the financial security to concentrate on writing.

△ *ANDRE GIDE*, PAUL ALBERT LAURENS, 1924

Love between a woman and a younger man became a recurrent theme of her fiction—notably in the much-praised *Chéri*—and of her life. She had an affair with her stepson, and her third and final husband was 16 years her junior. Colette's novels express a warm sensuality, an observant love of nature, and the shrewd sense of men's weaknesses that enabled her to flourish in a sexist world.

**KEY WORKS:** *The Vagabond*, 1910; *Chéri*, 1920; *The Ripening Seed*, 1923; *Gigi*, 1944

## Robert Frost

1874–1963, AMERICAN

The poet Robert Frost was born in California but moved to New England at the age of 11. For many years, he experienced depression and frustration: only a handful of his poems were published; his marriage was marred by his children's deaths; and an attempt at farming failed. In 1912, he moved to Britain, where he found a more sympathetic literary environment. Publication of his

first two collections, *A Boy's Will* (1913) and *North of Boston* (1914)—poems set in rural New England and reflecting the rhythms of ordinary speech—established his reputation. Returning to New England in 1915, he enhanced his standing with such notable verses as "The Road Not Taken" (1916) and "Stopping by Woods on a Snowy Evening" (1922). Indifferent to the pressures of literary Modernism, he continued to produce subtle, understated poetry throughout a long life and famously read "The Gift Outright" (1941) at John F. Kennedy's presidential inauguration in 1961.

**KEY WORKS:** *North of Boston*, 1914; *A Mountain Interval*, 1916; *New Hampshire*, 1923; *A Further Range*, 1936

## Rainer Maria Rilke

1875–1926, AUSTRIAN

An exalted lyric poet influential in the development of Modernism, Rilke was born in Prague, then part of Austria-Hungary. Despite his poetic nature, his parents forced him to spend five years in a military academy.

His early poems exhibited the dreamy mix of sensuality and spirituality that was typical of fin-de-siècle decadence. Starting in 1902, after coming under the influence of the French avant-garde, he developed his *Dinggedichte* (Thing poems), describing the experience of spiritual alienation in the modern world with intense, concrete imagery. He wrote the first of his renowned *Duino Elegies* in 1912, while staying at the Castle Duino in Trieste. World War I disrupted his life, and it was not until 1922, in a late burst of creativity, that he completed the *Elegies*, as well as writing his *Sonnets to Orpheus*. These late works express an idiosyncratic aesthetic mysticism in poems of exceptional beauty and obscurity.

**KEY WORKS:** *New Poems*, 1907; *The Notebooks of Malte Laurids Brigge*, 1910; *The Duino Elegies*, 1912–1922; *Sonnets to Orpheus*, 1923

## Hermann Hesse

1877–1962, GERMAN

The novelist and poet Hermann Hesse was the son of Protestant missionaries, and although he rebelled against his religious education, he retained a spiritual view of life. After the success of his first novel, *Peter Camenzind*, in 1904, he devoted himself to writing. During World War I, he experienced a spiritual crisis and endured a painful marital breakdown. He found salvation through Eastern philosophies and Jungian psychoanalysis (he later incorporated Jungian archetypes into his writing).

In the 1920s, his novel *Siddhartha* popularized Buddhism in the West, and the "magic theater" of *Steppenwolf* encouraged exploration of the wilder shores of the imagination. He worked on *The Glass Bead Game*, a utopian fantasy of a spiritually organized world, from 1932 until its publication in 1943. He spent the last years of his life in Switzerland, and was awarded the Nobel Prize in Literature in 1946. Hesse's novels won a large following in the counterculture of the 1960s.

**KEY WORKS:** *Demian: The Story of Emil Sinclair's Youth*, 1919; *Siddhartha*, 1922; *Steppenwolf*, 1928; *The Glass Bead Game*, 1943

## Robert Musil

1880–1942, AUSTRIAN

Novelist and short-story writer Robert Musil was born into a prominent family in the city of Klagenfurt. Destined for the army, he was educated at a military academy, a painful experience that formed the basis of his first novel, *The Confessions of Young Törless*.

Rejecting a military career, he studied engineering and philosophy while writing the stories that appeared as *Unions* in 1911. After serving as an officer in World War I, he built a reputation among literary insiders with his play *The Enthusiasts* (1921) and another book of short stories,

△ KATHERINE MANSFIELD

*Three Women*. The first volume of his monumental work *The Man Without Qualities*, set in the declining years of the Austrian Empire, appeared in 1930. Now regarded as a masterpiece of Modernist literature, it was not a commercial success. The final volume was never finished. Musil died in Switzerland, where he had fled with his Jewish wife to escape Nazism.

**KEY WORKS:** *The Confessions of Young Törless*, 1906; *Unions*, 1911; *Three Women*, 1924; *The Man Without Qualities*, 1930, 1932, 1942

## Nikos Kazantzakis

1883–1957, GREEK

Nikos Kazantzakis was born in Crete, which was then under the rule of the Turkish Ottoman Empire. He grew up against a violent background of Greek rebellion and Turkish repression. He published his first

novels and plays in his 20s, arguing for the use of everyday Greek, the spoken language of the people, as a literary language.

Kazantzakis traveled widely, and came under the conflicting influences of Buddhism and communism. Surviving financially by writing various translations, travel books, and school textbooks, he worked for many years on an epic poem, *The Odyssey: A Modern Sequel*, completed in 1938.

His most famous book, *Zorba the Greek*, was written during World War II, initiating a series of novels in which he expressed his fascination with Crete and his idiosyncratic version of religious faith. His controversial novel *The Last Temptation of Christ* was condemned by both the Orthodox and the Roman Catholic churches.

**KEY WORKS:** *The Odyssey: A Modern Sequel*, 1938; *Zorba the Greek*, 1946; *Christ Recrucified*, 1948; *Captain Michalis*, 1950; *The Last Temptation of Christ*, 1955

## ◁ Katherine Mansfield

1888–1923, NEW ZEALAND

The short-story writer Katherine Mansfield Beauchamp was born in Wellington, New Zealand, the daughter of a prosperous businessman. In revolt against the narrowness of her background, she left for England in 1908 to become a writer. She lived a bohemian life and had many complex relationships—her first marriage lasted just weeks. Her development as a writer was rapid: a prominent magazine began publishing her stories in 1910 and her first collection, *In a German Pension*, soon followed.

Inspired by the example of Anton Chekhov, Mansfield wrote sharp, observant fiction, which was recognized by her peers as being distinctively modern. She became connected with the Bloomsbury Group and in 1918 married the critic John Middleton Murray. Some of her best later stories, including "Prelude" and "The Garden Party," were set in the New Zealand of her childhood. After a long struggle against tuberculosis, she died in France at 34.

**KEY WORKS:** *In a German Pension*, 1911; "Prelude," 1918; "Bliss," 1920; "The Garden Party," 1922

## Fernando Pessoa

1888–1935, PORTUGUESE

An idiosyncratic Modernist poet, Pessoa grew up in Durban, South Africa, where his stepfather was Portuguese consul. He returned to his native Lisbon at 17 and stayed there for the rest of his life. A prominent figure in Portuguese literary circles, he was unknown to the general public. Aside from some poetry in English, the language of his early education, the only book of verse that he published in his lifetime (the remainder were published posthumously) was *Message*. Yet his creative activity was tireless. He invented a wide range of "heteronyms"—fictional characters in whose names he wrote poetry and prose of differing viewpoints and styles. His chief poetic heteronyms were Alberto Caeiro, Ricardo Reis, and Alvaro de Campos. His "factless autobiography," *The Book of Disquiet*, is attributed to an assistant bookkeeper, Bernardo Soares.

Poems written under Pessoa's own name show a melancholy obsession with boredom and nostalgia. His reputation has grown steadily since his death.

**KEY WORKS:** *Message*, 1934; *Poems of Fernando Pessoa*, 1942; *Poems of Alberto Caeiro*, 1946; *The Book of Disquiet*, 1982

## Boris Pasternak

1890–1960, RUSSIAN

Boris Leonidovich Pasternak was a poet and novelist who became the focus of political controversy on winning the Nobel Prize in Literature in 1958. Born into a cultured family in St. Petersburg (his father illustrated Tolstoy's work), he published his first volume of poetry in 1914. After the 1917 Revolution, he elected to stay in Russia. In the 1920s he published much-admired lyric verse showing the influence of symbolist Aleksandr Blok and futurist Vladimir Mayakovsky. However, during Stalin's dictatorship his creative output declined. In 1949, his lover, Olga Ivinskaya, was sent to a labor camp but Pasternak himself was left untouched.

In 1956, he completed the novel *Doctor Zhivago*, a love story set in the period of the Revolution. Although not overtly anticommunist, it was banned in the Soviet Union. When it was published in the West, it won Pasternak the Nobel Prize, but under pressure from the Soviet authorities he was forced to refuse the award.

**KEY WORKS:** *My Sister, Life*, 1922; *Themes and Variations*, 1923; *Doctor Zhivago*, 1956; *When the Weather Clears*, 1959

## ▽ J. R. R. Tolkien

1892–1973, ENGLISH

The father of modern fantasy fiction, John Ronald Reuel Tolkien was born in South Africa but grew up in the English Midlands. An orphan by the age of 12, he was placed under the guardianship of a Catholic priest. While serving as a junior officer in World War I, he began to elaborate the mythical world that was the setting of all his fiction. After the war he became professor of Anglo-Saxon at Pembroke College, Oxford.

Old English poetry, especially the epic *Beowulf*, was the major influence on his writing. *The Hobbit*, written for his children, was a success when published in 1937, encouraging him to begin the *Lord of the Rings* trilogy. Completed in 1948, the trilogy was published in the 1950s and became a huge international best seller in the following decade. His incomplete early work, *The Silmarillion*, appeared posthumously in 1977.

**KEY WORKS:** *The Hobbit, or There and Back Again*, 1937; *The Fellowship of the Ring*, 1954; *The Two Towers*, 1954; *The Return of the King*, 1955

## Federico García Lorca

1898–1936, SPANISH

Poet and dramatist Federico García Lorca was the son of a landowner in Granada, Andalusia. Studying in Madrid starting in 1919, he was part of a generation of aspiring writers and artists that included the young Salvador Dalí. His first book of verse appeared in 1921. Lorca's individual style, blending European Modernism with Andalusian folk traditions, found its most popular expression in the *Gypsy Ballads* of 1928. The following year, he visited America, writing the surreal verse of *A Poet in New York* (1940). In 1931, the new Republican government in Spain entrusted Lorca with running a traveling company that took theater to rural audiences. While touring, he wrote a series of major plays, including *Blood Wedding* and *Yerma* (1934), dramatizing the tragic dilemmas of women in Spain.

In August 1936, early in the Civil War, Lorca was murdered by nationalists. His body was never found.

**KEY WORKS:** *Songs*, 1927; *Gypsy Ballads*, 1928; *Blood Wedding*, 1932; "Lament for Ignacio Sánchez Mejías," 1934

△ J. R. R. TOLKIEN

MID-
20th
CENTURY

CHAPTER 5

# Vladimir Nabokov

## 1899–1977, RUSSIAN-BORN AMERICAN

Nabokov became notorious for his novel *Lolita*, shocking in its time and still contentious today. He was a dazzling master of English in an oeuvre that included novels, poetry, short stories, autobiography, and criticism.

The eldest of five siblings, Vladimir Nabokov was born into a life of privilege in Saint Petersburg in pre-revolution Russia. He grew up speaking Russian, English, and French, and claimed that he had "the happiest childhood imaginable." In 1919, after the Bolshevik Revolution, his father, a prominent opposition leader, took the family into exile, to London and then to Berlin; three years later, he was assassinated by a monarchist fanatic.

After studying at the University of Cambridge, Nabokov moved to Berlin. He had already published two volumes of poetry in Russia, and now began to establish a reputation as a poet in the Russian émigré community, writing under the name V. Sirin. In 1925, he married a Jewish-Russian woman, Véra Slonim, with whom he had one son, Dmitri, who was born in 1934.

### From Europe to the US

Nabokov published his first, strongly autobiographical, novel *Mashenka* (*Mary*) in 1926. This was followed by *King, Queen, Nave* (1928), which marked the beginnings of the stylistic innovations and wordplay for which he would become renowned. Over the next decade, he wrote prolifically in Russian, supporting his family by giving lessons in tennis, boxing, and languages, while his wife worked as a translator.

With the advent of war, the family fled to the US. Nabokov obtained a post as a lecturer at Wellesley College, Massachusetts, which allowed him enough free time to write and to indulge one of his passions—butterfly collecting (he would eventually publish 18 papers on entomology). His first book in English, *The Real Life of Sebastian Knight* (1941), drew on his experiences at Cambridge; his second, *Bend Sinister* (1947), was a story set in a totalitarian regime that ends with the appearance of the author himself.

In 1945, Nabokov became a US citizen, and in 1948 he was appointed professor of Russian literature at Cornell University, New York. Now financially secure, he embarked on the novel that would catapult him to international fame: *Lolita*. First published in France in 1955, this "timebomb," as he described it, was eventually published in the US in 1958:

it sold 100,000 copies in its first three weeks. Dealing with the middle-aged narrator's fatal obsession with a 12-year-old "nymphet," the novel was, and has remained, controversial for its subject matter. With *Lolita* came fame, acclaim, and a great deal of money.

Nabokov's novel *Pnin* (1957), the story of a Russian émigré professor in the US, although written after *Lolita*, was published before it to critical recognition. *Pale Fire* (1962) showed him playing with the novel form in a work that consists of a 999-line poem by a fictional poet and a commentary on it by a fictional critic.

Nabokov died in 1977, leaving behind an unfinished manuscript, *The Original of Laura*. The influence of his playful, precisely detailed, lyrically beautiful prose style resonates through later fiction, in such writers as Martin Amis, Thomas Pynchon, and John Updike.

△ **MOVIE ADAPTATION**
Nabokov's *Lolita* combined dark humor, erudite wordplay, and passages of great lyrical beauty that elevated it above gross eroticism. A tour-de-force study in overpowering obsession, it is also a sharp satire of 1950s US trash culture. The novel was adapted into a successful movie in 1962, directed by Stanley Kubrick.

◁ **LATER YEARS**
Nabokov is pictured here in Ithaca, New York, in 1958. Three years later, he moved to Montreux, Switzerland, where he lived with his wife, Véra, in the Montreux Palace Hotel for the rest of his life.

## IN CONTEXT
### Index cards

Nabokov wrote on index cards, using hundreds of cards for each novel. He started writing once the "pattern of the thing" was clear in his mind; rather than writing linearly he would "pick out a bit here and a bit there, till I have filled all the gaps on paper." He would rearrange the cards, and not until the work was finished would he number them; then he dictated them to his wife, who typed them in triplicate. His final, unfinished novel, *The Original of Laura*, published posthumously (against his wishes) in 2009, is an invaluable record of this technique in its raw state.

NABOKOV DICTATES TO HIS WIFE, VERA, FROM HIS INDEX CARDS, 1958

# John Steinbeck

## 1902–1968, AMERICAN

A giant of American letters, Steinbeck produced a searing portrait of the Depression that explored fate and injustice in the lives of ordinary families, and defined him as the conscience of the nation.

It was while working on beet farms during school breaks that John Ernst Steinbeck gained his first insights into the plight of migrant workers—a key theme in his social novels of the 1930s. He was born into a middle-class family in Monterey County, California, where his mother, a former teacher, fostered in him a love of books. He dropped out of Stanford University after erratic studies in literature and biology, then headed to New York, where he worked in construction and as a reporter. On his return to California, jobs on farms and in forests and fisheries helped support his writing.

His first three books sold poorly, but success eventually came in 1935 with *Tortilla Flat*, a story about wine-soaked Mexican-Spanish workers, inspired by the Arthurian legend of the Knights of the Round Table. It was followed by *Of Mice and Men*, an unfolding tragedy of two migrant workers—the childlike giant, Lennie, and his protector, George.

A storm broke over his epic work, *The Grapes of Wrath* (1939), hammered out over five months after Steinbeck traveled with the Okies—desperate migrant families escaping to California from the dust bowl (see box, right). At its peak it sold 10,000 copies a week, and it earned Steinbeck a Pulitzer Prize, but there was a backlash against his indictment of the American dream.

### Postwar years

During World War II, Steinbeck was a war correspondent for the *New York Herald Tribune*. During this period, he wrote *The Moon is Down* (1942), an exploration of the effects of war and occupation on a once peaceable village (a thinly veiled examination of the Nazi occupation of Norway).

Now a settled New York resident, Steinbeck returned to his roots with *Cannery Row* (1944), based in the sardine-packing district of Monterey, and the epic *East of Eden* (1952), for which he drew upon his own family history in Salinas. In the 1960s, he lost credibility as a liberal voice because of his support for the Vietnam War—both of his sons from his second marriage were army recruits.

*The Winter of Our Discontent* (1961), which is a penetrating study of moral degeneration in the US, was a return to form that contributed to Steinbeck's winning the Nobel Prize in Literature in 1962. The author died of heart disease in December 1968, having written nearly 30 books.

△ **THE GRAPES OF WRATH**
Biblical in tone, Steinbeck's novel was rooted in the homespun details of the lives of the Joad family. "I tried to write this book the way lives are being lived not the way books are written," he said.

## IN CONTEXT
### The dust bowl

After the financial crash of 1929, the US fell into a severe economic depression; by the mid-1930s, 25 percent of the population was unemployed. Crop prices fell by 60 percent, and a combination of overfarming, soil erosion, and drought reduced the fertile Great Plains to a dust bowl. Thousands of small farmers had their homes and plots seized by landowners and banks. They then migrated west, lured by the promise of work and sustenance on the farms in California's land of plenty, only to face animosity and rejection when they arrived.

A FAMILY TAKES SHELTER FROM A STORM IN THE DUST BOWL

> "What some people **find in religion** a writer may **find in his craft** ... a kind of **breaking through** to **glory**."

JOHN STEINBECK

▷ **STEINBECK, c.1939**
The author is pictured here in the year that his Pulitzer Prize–winning *Grapes of Wrath* was published. Soon after this, he escaped to the Sea of Cortez to collect marine specimens with his close friend, marine biologist Ed Ricketts.

# George Orwell

## 1903–1950, ENGLISH

Orwell penned darkly satirical works describing disaffection and foreboding in the wake of two devastating world wars. A committed socialist and moralist, he often put himself at risk in pursuit of the truth.

George Orwell was the nom-de-plume of Eric Arthur Blair. He was born in 1903 in Motihari (now Bihar) in colonial India, where his father served in the opium department of the Indian civil service, overseeing the legal export of opium. Orwell returned with his mother, Ida, to England at just one year old. Ida settled with her children in Oxfordshire, and the family was separated from their father for several years until 1912. Orwell later described the family's social standing as "lower-upper-middle class": descended from English gentry but with the family money running short.

### Private-school education

Orwell had a lonely childhood but found solace in writing stories and poems, some of which were published in the local press. At the age of eight, he was sent to a "snobbish" boarding school in East Sussex on a partial scholarship and it was here that he faced the realities of the English class system, observing the disparity between his poor treatment and that of the wealthier, "higher-born" boys.

Orwell won a scholarship to the prestigious private school Eton, where he was involved in the production of the college magazine, but failed to stand out academically. On finishing his studies, and unable to afford university,

△ **KATHA, MYANMAR**
A horse and cart pass in front of the police station in Katha, Myanmar (formerly Burma), where Orwell's novel *Burmese Days* is set.

he was accepted into the Indian Imperial Police service. He chose a posting in Burma (now Myanmar), where his grandmother lived. He describes his distaste for the job in an essay called "Shooting an Elephant," which opens with the bold statement: "In Moulmein, in Lower Burma, I was hated by large numbers of people—the only time in my life that I have been important enough for this

to happen to me." His mistrust of authority and disgust at imperial rule had been sparked, but his love of the country itself is conveyed in uncharacteristically florid prose in *Burmese Days* (1934).

### London and Paris

Orwell returned to England in 1928, determined to become a writer. With lodgings in West London, he ventured to the less salubrious East End of the city, eager to garner firsthand experience of working-class life. To do so, he created an alter ego: dressing himself in ragged clothes, he slept in "spikes" (the poorhouse) and rooming

◁ **ORWELL AT THE BBC**
Orwell is shown here broadcasting from the BBC in London in 1943, during World War II. He joined the corporation in 1941 as Talks Producer for the Eastern Service, but resigned in 1943.

> " **All animals** are **equal**, but **some animals** are **more equal** than **others**. "
>
> GEORGE ORWELL, *ANIMAL FARM*

△ **WIGAN PIER, 1939**
Wigan Pier, Greater Manchester, is shown here (on the right), next to the canal. Orwell's bleak novel *The Road to Wigan Pier* (1937) focuses on poverty and hypocrisy in class-ridden England.

△ **REPUBLICAN POSTER**
Orwell fought in the Spanish Civil War but eventually had to flee from Soviet-backed communists who were suppressing socialist dissenters.

houses, and even wound up in "the clink" (jail). He soon extended his research to Paris, where he could rely on the occasional support of his aunt, who lived there. He spurned the Parisian literary cliques, preferring to get under the skin of the city and its people, weaving his experiences into a manuscript that was part social commentary and part travel fiction.

The work, which included highly controversial accounts of rape and drug dealing, was initially rejected by the literary establishment. Orwell, much like his close contemporary, the English novelist D. H. Lawrence,

concluded that British publishers were a "gutless" crew. He did, however, find himself a literary agent, Leonard Moore, and in the summer of 1932 learned that Victor Gollancz Ltd. was willing to publish his memoir. The work appeared the following year under the title *Down and Out in Paris and London*.

## Poverty in the North

Working as a teacher by day, Orwell developed his first full-length novel, *Burmese Days* (1934). He left teaching and settled in Hampstead, northwest London, to work in a bookstore, and through his circle of friends met Eileen O'Shaughnessy, whom he married a year later. *Keep the Aspidistra Flying* (1935) gives a fictional account of this time, but the couple's relatively comfortable domestic arrangements were not to last long.

Prompted by his publishers to write about the depressed north of England, where millions faced poverty, Orwell hit the road again. He combined his observations of life in northern towns with his personal socialist manifesto in *The Road to Wigan Pier* (1937). This work attracted the attention of the British security services, who suspected him of being a communist, in part because he "dressed in a bohemian fashion;" he was placed under observation for over a decade.

## The Spanish Civil War

In 1936, Orwell decided to join the volunteers fighting General Franco's fascist uprising in Spain. On his way to Barcelona, he met the writer Henry Miller in Paris, who warned that any beliefs Orwell had about defeating fascism were "sheer stupidity." In reality, the many Republican

" **All issues** are **political** issues, and politics itself is a mass of **lies**, evasions, folly, **hatred**. "

GEORGE ORWELL

## KEY WORKS

**1933**
Down and Out in Paris records Orwell's time living in near destitution with tramps and casual laborers.

**1937**
The Road to Wigan Pier provides a bleak but compelling description of poverty in the industrial north.

**1938**
Homage to Catalonia describes Orwell's contribution to the Spanish Civil War.

**1939**
Coming Up for Air is an exercise in nostalgia, dwelling on the money-short past of Orwell's childhood.

**1945**
Animal Farm: A Fairy Story, a bleak vision of totalitarianism, is published to great acclaim.

**1949**
Orwell publishes Nineteen Eighty-Four—his nightmarish portrayal of life under a dictatorship.

factions spent much of their time fighting each other rather than the fascists. Orwell proceeded to the front, but his participation in the war was ended by a sniper's bullet, which hit him in the throat and almost took his life.

When he returned to England, Orwell recorded his experiences of the Spanish Civil War in *Homage to Catalonia*, published in 1938. The author's physical health, which had been fragile since his boyhood, deteriorated and he was diagnosed with tuberculosis. After spending the winter in French Morocco funded by an unnamed sponsor, Orwell wrote *Coming Up for Air* (1939), a novel full of nostalgia for an England that he considered blighted by development and commercialization.

### Postwar works

As war threatened, Eileen took a post in the censorship department of the Ministry of Information, London, while Orwell worked for the BBC, producing propaganda for the eastern British Empire. Embittered, he left to write for the democratic socialist magazine *Tribune*, where he became literary editor in 1943; and set to work on a novel, *Animal Farm*, an allegory of Stalin's betrayal of the Russian Revolution. The book was initially rejected by publishers and censored by the establishment, because—at the time—Stalin was Britain's wartime ally. However, after its publication in 1945, it became a huge success.

Late in the war, the Orwells adopted a baby—Richard Horatio—but their time together was tragically short

lived. Their home in London was destroyed by a German bomb, and then Eileen died under anesthesia during a hysterectomy. Orwell was thrust into the role of lone parent. Bereaved and in poor health, he launched himself into work, taking on essays and articles, and beginning what was to be his great classic, *Nineteen Eighty-Four*. He jumped at an offer from his patron, the newspaper owner David Astor, to stay at his isolated estate on the Hebridean isle of Jura. It was there that he completed his book—a chilling, dystopian vision of the consequences of state control under a dictatorial regime.

George Orwell died in January 1950 after a hasty marriage to Sonia Brownell. She donated her husband's work to academia.

---

### ON STYLE
#### Neologisms

One of Orwell's greatest contributions to literature was his introduction of neologisms, memorable new words, into the English language. In his novel *Nineteen Eighty-Four*, he merged everyday words to coin terms such as "thoughtcrimes," "doublethink," "goodthink," and "newspeak." Orwellian sound bites remain relevant today, and have considerable resonance in the modern era of mass communication. Orwell used neologisms to illustrate his belief that language is power. He was eager to show how citizens can become indoctrinated through language and media, and how regimes are able to control people by deliberately confusing them and undermining their sense of judgment.

**COVER OF THE FIRST BRITISH EDITION OF *NINETEEN EIGHTY-FOUR***

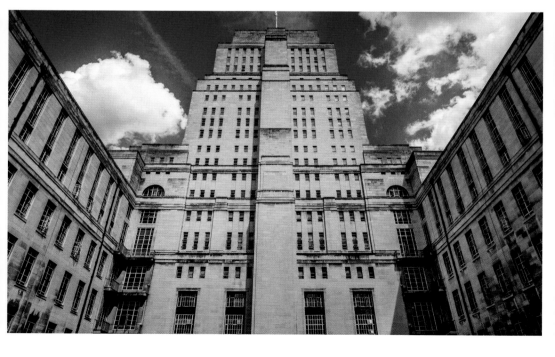

◁ **SENATE HOUSE**
Senate House, the administrative center of the University of London, inspired Orwell's chilling creation, in *Nineteen Eighty-Four*, of the "Ministry of Truth"— a body responsible for state propaganda and historical revisionism.

# Pablo Neruda

## 1904–1973, CHILEAN

The prolific Neruda left a rich and diverse body of work, encompassing tender and passionate love poems, epics, political verse, and the poetry of commonplace objects and animals.

Pablo Neruda—poet, diplomat, and politician—was born Ricardo Eliécer Neftalí Reyes Basoalto in the town of Parral, southern Chile. His mother, a teacher, died soon after his birth, and two years later his father, a railroad worker, moved to the town of Temuco, where he remarried. Neruda started writing poetry at the age of 10, despite the opposition of his father;

and from 1918 to 1920, he contributed various works to local magazines and newspapers, encouraged by Gabriela Mistral (see box, right). In 1920, he took the pen name Pablo Neruda (which he adopted legally in 1946) to avoid his father's disapproval.

Neruda moved to Santiago, the capital of Chile, in 1921, and enrolled at the university to study French, intending to become a teacher. Two years later, at just 18, he published his first volume of verse, *Book of Twilights*. This was followed in 1924 by *Twenty Love Poems and a Song of Despair*, a book of romantic, melancholy love poems that propelled him into the spotlight, causing a stir thanks to their frank sensuality; the first poem begins: "Body of a woman, white hills, white thighs, / You look like a world lying in surrender."

Neruda used original imagery and metaphors to trace the course of his love affairs, evoking and interweaving the sea, the weather, and the wild countryside of his home territory as well as the physicality of his passion.

### ▽ URUGUAYAN ESCAPE

Neruda's writing desk is shown here in a house at the resort of Atlántida, near Montevideo, Uruguay, where the author and his wife, Matilde, would often stay.

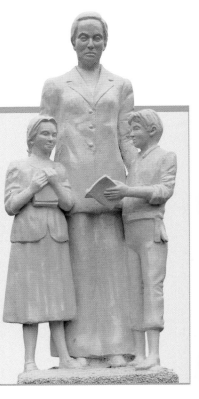

A third volume of poetry, *The Attempt of the Infinite Man*, followed in 1926, along with a novel, all of which helped to establish the author's reputation.

### Consular appointments

In 1927, Neruda accepted a post as honorary consul in Rangoon, Burma (now Myanmar), and for the next few years he moved from one diplomatic station to another, living in Ceylon (now Sri Lanka), Java, and Singapore. His was a very humble existence, since the post of consul was unpaid,

### ▷ NERUDA, c.1952

Neruda remains a towering figure in Chilean history and politics, but his full and adventurous life does not overshadow his writing; Gabriel García Márquez called him "the greatest poet of the 20th century in any language."

"No poet has any ... enemy other than his own **incapacity** to **make himself understood** by the most **forgotten** and **exploited** ..."

PABLO NERUDA, NOBEL LECTURE

## "There is **no such thing** as a **lone struggle**, no such thing as **lone hope**."

PABLO NERUDA, NOBEL LECTURE

and he was deeply affected by the deprivation he witnessed. His growing identification with the impoverished masses of Asia led to the publication of *Residence on Earth* (1933 and 1935). These poems, which established his international reputation, are entirely different in style from the traditional lyricism of *Twenty Love Poems*. Reflecting Neruda's sense of alienation, and his response to the chaos and senselessness of the world, they are surrealist in form.

It was in Java that Neruda met Maria Antonieta Hagenaar, a Dutch woman, whom he married in 1930. In 1932, the couple returned to Chile, and the next year Neruda was

appointed consul in Buenos Aires, Argentina, where he became friends with the Spanish poet and dramatist Federico García Lorca.

### Spanish Republicanism

In 1934, Neruda took the post of consul in Barcelona, Spain, then transferred to Madrid, where his daughter, Malva, was born. Through his friendship with García Lorca, he became part of a literary circle whose members were involved in leftist politics. With the outbreak of the Spanish Civil War in 1936, Neruda worked to mobilize support for the Republicans, and was further politicized when García Lorca was killed by a nationalist execution squad.

At this time, Neruda's poetry became less personal and was more socially and politically oriented, and in 1937 the publication of *Spain in my Heart*, a poem in support of the Republican movement, cost him his consular post. He was recalled to Chile and became involved in left-wing politics there. By now, Neruda had separated from his wife and was living with his lover, the Argentine painter Delia del Carril.

After a consular appointment in Paris, Neruda became consul general in Mexico City, where he and Del Carril married in 1943. That year, he visited Peru, climbing to the Inca citadel of Machu Picchu, which inspired him to write *The Heights of Machu Picchu* (1945), a lengthy, 12-part poem that

△ **PROTESTING AGAINST THE JUNTA**
The 1973 coup in Chile deposed Neruda's friend and comrade Allende, bringing an end to democratic rule. Left-wing groups protested against the military junta.

celebrates the ancient civilizations of South America. This work went on to form a major part of his *General Song*, an epic composition that he worked on intermittently beginning around 1938.

### Politics and exile

On his return to Chile in 1943, Neruda threw himself into national politics, becoming a senator and joining the Communist Party shortly afterward. He campaigned on behalf of the left-wing presidential candidate, Gabriel González Videla, who, after being elected in 1946, moved unexpectedly toward the right. Outspoken in his criticism of Videla's repressive measures, Neruda was expelled as a senator and eventually threatened with arrest. In 1948, he was forced into hiding, and after more than a year of living underground he went into exile, fleeing on horseback across the Andes into Argentina. For the next three years, he traveled around Europe, including a visit to the

▽ **LA SEBASTIANA**
Pablo Neruda's hilltop house gave him spectacular views over the colorful Chilean city of Valparaíso and the Pacific Ocean. He decorated the house playfully, painting the walls in bright hues to "make them dance." His study contained a life-size portrait of Walt Whitman, whom Neruda greatly admired.

## KEY WORKS

**1924**
*Twenty Love Poems and a Song of Despair* is published, later becoming the best-selling book of poems in Spanish.

**1935**
*Residence on Earth* is published in two volumes; a third volume follows in 1945.

**1945**
*The Heights of Machu Picchu*, celebrates the sacred city and its oppressed masses.

**1950**
*General Song* is published in Mexico, during Neruda's exile; an underground edition is published in Chile.

**1954–57**
*Elemental Odes* (three volumes) examines everyday objects, plants, and animals in simple, direct language.

**1959**
*Love Sonnets* is dedicated to his beloved third wife and muse, Matilde Urrutia.

**1964**
*Isla Negra: a Notebook* contains more than 100 reflective, autobiographical poems.

Soviet Union, whose dictator, Joseph Stalin, he greatly admired at the time. Neruda began an affair with a Chilean woman, Matilde Urrutia, who would be the great love, and greatest muse, of his life; they would marry in 1966.

Neruda continued working on *General Song*, which was finally published in Mexico in 1950; the culmination of his public poetry, it draws on his communist sympathies and his national pride. Around 330 poems are arranged into 15 cantos (sections) exploring both the past and the present of Latin America. They celebrate the natural world as well as the region's explorers and conquistadors, heroes and martyrs, and ordinary individuals.

## Works in Chile
In 1952, Neruda was able to return to Chile, where he lent his support to the (unsuccessful) presidential campaign of Salvador Allende, and brought out a book of love poems dedicated to Urrutia (*The Captain's Verses*), which

was published anonymously so as not to cause pain to Del Carril, to whom he was still married. In 1955, the pair separated for good and from then on, Neruda and Urrutia lived together.

By now Neruda was wealthy and famous, and his works had been translated into many languages. In his last two decades he wrote feverishly, publishing more than 20 books. In 1954, he published *Elemental Odes*, which marked a change in his style, with short lines focusing on small, everyday things described in simple terms—the language of the street. "Ode to Wine," for example, begins: "Day-colored wine, / night-colored wine, / wine with purple feet / or wine with topaz blood." His next major work was *Estravagaria* (1958), with its introspective poems, including some love poetry. During this period, he also wrote nature poetry, as well as personal, political, and public verse.

In 1970, the newly elected socialist president, Salvador Allende, appointed Neruda ambassador to France. The

following year, he was awarded the Nobel Prize in Literature. Diagnosed with cancer, and in extremely poor health, Neruda returned to Chile in 1972, and died there in 1973, just a few days after the military coup that saw the death of his friend Allende and the destruction of his hopes for his homeland. Mourning crowds at his funeral became impromptu public protests against the new dictatorship. Rumors that Neruda was murdered by the coup's leader, General Pinochet, persist to this day.

△ **MACHU PICCHU**
Considered to be one of Neruda's greatest works, *The Heights of Machu Picchu* sees the poet journey to the lost city of the Incas in the Peruvian Andes. He celebrates the achievements of the people who built the city and identifies with their suffering, reaching back in time for universal truths about the human condition.

## IN CONTEXT
## Communist sympathies

After the Spanish Civil War, Neruda remained a fervent communist for the rest of his life. As with numerous other idealist left-wing intellectuals of the time, he supported the Soviet Union and its dictator, Joseph Stalin. He wrote several poems in praise of the regime (such as "Canto a Stalingrado," 1942), and in 1953 was awarded the Stalin (later Lenin) Peace Prize. He wrote an ode to Stalin on his death that same year. He equally admired Lenin, calling him "the great genius of this century." Although Neruda never lost his faith in communism, he later renounced his support for Stalin.

A 1948 SOVIET AGITPROP POSTER PROCLAIMS "STALIN IS OUR BANNER!"

# Graham Greene

## 1904–1991, ENGLISH

The novelist, essayist, and playwright Graham Greene produced highly readable and popular work that addresses themes of great moral complexity, often from a Catholic viewpoint.

Henry Graham Greene was born in 1904 in Hertfordshire, England, into a large, influential family. He was bullied as a boarder at Berkhamsted School, where his father was headmaster, and attempted suicide several times, before being sent to a psychoanalyst at the age of 16. In 1926, a year after graduating from Oxford University, Greene (an atheist) converted to Roman Catholicism, having fallen under the influence of Vivien Dayrell-Browning, whom he married in 1927.

Greene's first novel, *The Man Within* (1929), was a "hopelessly romantic" story of smuggling and betrayal. Its favorable reception prompted him to quit his job as a copy editor at *The Times* to focus on freelance journalism and writing.

◁ **GRAHAM GREENE, c.1940**
The writer is pictured here in the year of publication of *The Power and the Glory*, often described as Greene's first great novel, and one of his own favorite works.

### Serious entertainment

Commercial success as a novelist came with *Stamboul Train* (1932), a fast-paced thriller that was the first of what Greene called his "entertainments" (deliberately populist work). *Brighton Rock* (1938), which became one of his most renowned novels, had elements of his entertainments—a thriller plot with a hunted protagonist—but also addressed more profound themes of morality and evil. In the year of its publication, Greene fled to Mexico to escape a court case; the result was his travel account *The Lawless Roads* (1939), and the novel *The Power and the Glory* (1940), which centers on a morally corrupt Catholic "whiskey priest" during the years of church suppression in Mexico.

A serial womanizer, Greene began an affair with Catherine Walston, a married Catholic woman, in 1946. The relationship ended in 1951 and inspired another of his best-known novels, *The End of the Affair*, published that year. Greene left Vivien in 1947, but the couple was never officially divorced.

### Wide travels

Greene traveled to the world's "wild and remote places" and used settings of conflict and war to intensify the moral ambivalence and ethical dilemmas faced by his characters. His stay in Haiti in 1954 inspired *The Comedians* (1966), a novel exploring the country's political suppression, while his visits to leper colonies in the Belgian Congo led to *A Burnt-Out Case* (1960), a tragedy about the possibility of personal redemption. Greene's travels in Cuba informed *Our Man in Havana* (1958), a black comedy set there just before Castro's revolution.

In 1966, Greene moved to Antibes, France, where he lived with his lover Yvette Cloetta; they relocated to Vevey, Switzerland, where the writer spent his final years. He was short listed for the Nobel Prize in 1966 and 1967. He continued writing until his death, with *The Honorary Consul* (1973) and *The Human Factor* (1978) being particularly notable. His clear writing style, realistic dialogue, and gripping plots, combined with the moral seriousness of his work, have ensured his place in the pantheon of 20th-century literary greats.

◁ **CITY HOTEL, FREETOWN**
Greene served as an intelligence officer in Sierra Leone. The City Hotel in Freetown (disguised as the fictional Bedford Hotel), shown here, came to symbolize the withering ambitions of an empire in decline in his novel *The Heart of the Matter* (1948).

## IN CONTEXT
### Screen adaptations

Greene's writing style was ripe for screen adaptation, and many of his thriller-type entertainments were made into movies. He produced the screenplay for Carol Reed's classic noir *The Third Man* (1949), writing a novella of the same name first to develop the setting, characterization, and atmosphere. For research, he visited postwar Vienna and was guided around the alleys, sewers, and nightclubs of the divided city, meeting army personnel and shady black-market hustlers. Greene's original happy ending differed from the movie's downbeat finale, but he later acknowledged that Reed had been "proved triumphantly right."

**POSTER FOR CAROL REED'S MOVIE** *THE THIRD MAN*

# Jean-Paul Sartre

## 1905–1980, FRENCH

Existentialist philosopher, novelist, and playwright, Sartre believed that humans were "condemned to be free." He spent his life grappling with the ideas of freedom and action, which informed his philosophy and writing.

◁ **CLASS OF 1922**
This portrait shows the preparatory humanities class for entrance to the Ecole Normale Supérieure. Sartre is seated in the first row, second from the right. Two places to the left is his friend the writer Paul Nizan.

After completing his military service, from 1929 to 1931, Sartre spent the next 14 years teaching philosophy at various high schools. He also studied in Berlin, where he encountered the phenomenological philosophy of Edmund Husserl, which would have a huge impact on his own thought.

Jean-Paul Sartre was born into a middle-class family in Paris. His father, a naval officer, died of yellow fever when Jean-Paul was not yet two years old, and his mother moved back to her parents' house in the Parisian suburbs. His grandfather, Charles Schweitzer, a respected intellectual (and the older brother of Nobel laureate Albert Schweitzer), tutored him at home and introduced him to classical literature.

### Education and influences
When Sartre was 12, his mother remarried and the family moved to La Rochelle on France's Atlantic coast.

He was bullied at the city's school, and transferred to a school in Paris at the age of 15. He excelled in his studies and in 1924 he was accepted into the Ecole Normale Supérieure, one of the most prestigious universities in France. There, he was renowned as much for being a great practical joker as for his intellectual abilities.

While he was preparing to qualify as a teacher of philosophy, he met Simone de Beauvoir, who would become his life companion, his "necessary love," the woman he was committed to beyond all others, despite the famous open relationship that the couple cultivated.

### An existentialist manifesto
In 1938, Sartre published his first novel, *Nausea*, a philosophical and partially autobiographical work influenced by phenomenology (the study of objects as we consciously experience them). In *Nausea*, the protagonist, Roquentin, is filled with hopelessness and despair, overcome with nausea as the meaninglessness of existence reveals itself. This is the human condition of freedom that—in his existentialist philosophy—Sartre believed could be relieved only by people taking responsibility for their own existence. He dealt with similar ideas in his short-story collection *The Wall*, published the following year.

THE OCTOBER 1970 ISSUE OF *LES TEMPS MODERNES*

> "**Man** is **condemned** to be **free**; because once **thrown** into the **world**, he is **responsible** for **everything** he does."

JEAN-PAUL SARTRE, *BEING AND NOTHINGNESS*

▷ **JEAN-PAUL SARTRE, 1946**
Sartre is pictured here at a production of his play *The Respectful Whore* at the Théâtre Antoine in Paris. The play explores racial divides and ideas of freedom in the US.

## KEY WORKS

**1938**
Sartre publishes his first novel, *Nausea*, which presents his existentialist philosophy in fictional form.

**1943**
The political drama *The Flies* avoids being censored in Nazi-occupied Paris.

**1943**
The monumental book *Being and Nothingness* is published and is seen as Sartre's most important philosophical work.

**1944**
Sartre stages *No Exit*, a play depicting an existentialist version of Hell, which includes the words "Hell is other people."

**1945**
*The Age of Reason* and *The Reprieve* are published. The two volumes are part of what was to have been a four-volume work.

**1948**
In the play *Dirty Hands*, Sartre investigates the motives for a crime that could be personal or political.

**1960**
*Critique of Dialectical Realism* is published. It is the philosophical work for which Sartre later says he wishes to be remembered.

▽ ***NO EXIT*, 1946 PRODUCTION**
Sartre's play, staged here in New York, has three characters locked up together in a room in Hell. Their mutual company serves as their eternal punishment for their sinful lives. The play was praised by US critics, with one reviewer calling it "a phenomenon of the modern theater."

At the beginning of World War II, Sartre was drafted into the French army. Captured by the Germans in 1940, he spent nine months in a prison camp—an experience that led to his political awakening. While his previous work had concentrated on ideas of individual freedom, little concerned with the affairs of the world, his later writings gave much more emphasis to social responsibility and political commitment.

In 1941, Sartre was released on health grounds and was given a teaching position in Paris. He became involved in the Resistance, but after the failure of an underground group that he had helped found, he decided that his pen was his best tool. In 1943, he wrote *The Flies*, a drama based on the myth of Electra. Staged in occupied Paris in largely empty theaters, the play managed to escape the German censors by using the symbolism of Greek mythology to cloak its message of resistance against oppression—as well as incorporating the existentialist themes of freedom and responsibility. On the opening night, Sartre met Albert Camus, who recruited him to a Resistance group, Combat. Sartre began contributing articles to the clandestine journal of the same name.

In the same year, Sartre published his monumental philosophical treatise *Being and Nothingness*. In it, he turned the traditional philosophical idea that "essence precedes existence" on its head, espousing the concept that "existence precedes essence" and extolling the importance of free will. In *No Exit* (*Huis Clos*), a one-act play staged in May 1944, he examined the concept of "the Other," through which an individual's consciousness of self is made concrete—a key idea in *Being and Nothingness*.

### Political engagement

Sartre founded *Modern Times*, a magazine that set out to publish existentialist literature—works of social and not just cultural value. The magazine was an outlet for Sartre's own works, as well as for those by other prominent postwar thinkers, such as Simone de Beauvoir and philosopher Raymon Aron (both of whom served on the editorial board), Jean Genet, and Samuel Beckett.

## IN PROFILE
### Simone de Beauvoir

Renowned novelist, essayist, existential philosopher, and feminist, Simone de Beauvoir (1908–1986) was Sartre's lifelong companion. De Beauvoir and Sartre never married or lived together, but they always read and commented on each other's work and certainly influenced one another's thought. Her personal life was turbulent and she had a number of lovers; she was fired from a teaching job for seducing one of her female pupils; and she and Sartre often shared female lovers. In 1949, de Beauvoir published the treatise *The Second Sex*, a cornerstone of feminist thought, which combines existentialist philosophy with feminist ideas. De Beauvoir died in Paris in 1986 and was buried next to Sartre at the Montparnasse Cemetery.

SIMONE DE BEAUVOIR AND JEAN-PAUL SARTRE, 1970

In 1945, Sartre published *The Age of Reason* and *The Reprieve*, the first two volumes of what would become the trilogy *The Roads to Freedom*. The third volume, *Troubled Sleep* (also translated as *Iron in the Soul*) was published in 1948. Partly autobiographical, the trilogy deals with Sartre's typical themes of commitment, freedom and responsibility, self-deception, and authenticity. *The Reprieve* is written in an experimental style with shifting viewpoints and loose punctuation, revealing the influence of the modernist techniques of John Dos Passos and Virginia Woolf.

As a whole, the trilogy shows the development of Sartre's views from his prewar focus on the individual to his postwar belief in the importance of action and engagement and his own growing politicization. He came to regard Marxism, rather than existentialism, as "the philosophy of our time." Although he initially supported the Soviet Union, he never joined the Communist Party.

Sartre's commitment to Soviet communism was shaken by the regime's invasion of Hungary in 1956 and by its oppression of writers, but he remained politically active, opposing anti-Semitism and colonialism, and campaigning against French rule in Algeria, which led to a bomb attack against him in 1961. A supporter of the Cuban Revolution, he traveled to Cuba with Simone de Beauvoir in 1960 and met Fidel Castro and Che Guevara, declaring the latter to be the "most complete human being of our age."

For the rest of his life, Sartre remained an ardent supporter of left-wing causes, including the May 1968 uprisings in France. Among other issues, he opposed the US involvement in Vietnam and the Soviet suppression of the Prague Spring, and campaigned for the rights of the Palestinians and of the Vietnamese boat people. Even in his later years, when he lived as a virtual recluse in Paris, he found time to mentor radical student groups and act as titular editor of left-wing publications

### Final years

In 1964, Sartre was awarded the Nobel Prize in Literature, but he refused the honor, not wanting to be "turned into an institution." That same year, he published *The Words*, a brilliant, witty autobiography that constituted his farewell to literature. With his eyesight failing, he gave up his writing in the mid-1970s, leaving unfinished a biography of Flaubert that he had begun in the 1960s.

Sartre died of edema of the lung at the age of 74. Fifty thousand people turned out to accompany his funeral cortege through the streets of Paris.

▽ **DIRTY HANDS, 1948**
In the play *Dirty Hands* (*Les Mains Sales*), Sartre explored political commitment, and in particular the use of political violence in revolutionary action.

" **Our responsibility** is much **greater** than we might have **supposed**, because it involves **all mankind**. "

JEAN-PAUL SARTRE, *EXISTENTIALISM AND HUMAN EMOTIONS*

# Samuel Beckett

1906–1989, IRISH

Beckett is celebrated for his bleakly absurdist plays but he was also a respected Modernist poet and novelist. He spent much of his adult life in Paris, and wrote many of his most important works in French.

◁ **TRINITY COLLEGE, DUBLIN, 1920s**
Beckett thrived at university, winning a gold medal upon graduation. As a lecturer there, he despaired at the pretensions of academia—the "loutishness of learning."

## Joyce and Beckett

Beckett loved Paris, but was frustrated by academic life. Fortunately, he found the stimulation he sought when he met James Joyce, an Irishman who had also made his home in the city. Joyce had gained notoriety as the author of the controversial novel *Ulysses*, and was now a prominent figure in Parisian literary circles. Taking the young Beckett under his wing, Joyce introduced him to other writers and artists and, recognizing his immense talent with language, asked him to help with research for his novel *Finnegans Wake*.

As Beckett began to take his own work more seriously, he worried that he would never emerge from his mentor's shadow: "it stinks of Joyce," he wrote about one of his short stories. The relationship between the two grew awkward when Beckett became embarrassed by the unwanted sexual advances of Joyce's daughter Lucia, and in 1930, he returned to Dublin. There, he taught French at Trinity College, but resigned the following year.

Like Oscar Wilde, George Bernard Shaw, and W. B. Yeats, Beckett was born into a middle-class Protestant family in Dublin. His father, a quantity surveyor, had built a large family house in the leafy suburb of Foxrock, where Samuel Barclay Beckett was born on April 13, 1906. He enjoyed the privileges and education expected by well-to-do Anglo-Irish families at that time, and was sent to Portora Royal School in Enniskillen. He was a good student and a natural athlete, taking an interest in sports—especially the quintessentially English game of cricket, which he played at almost a professional level, and which remained a lifelong passion.

In 1923, Beckett entered Trinity College, Dublin, to study Romance languages. After earning his BA in 1927, he pursued an academic career. He taught briefly in Belfast, and then took a post as a professor in English at the Ecole Normale Supérieure in Paris, moving to the city in 1928.

**SCENE FROM A NEW YORK PRODUCTION OF BECKETT'S *HAPPY DAYS*, 2008**

▷ **BECKETT, 1976**
Beckett's austere appearance helped build his reputation as a stern and forbidding character. According to friends and colleagues, however, he had a warm and humorous personality.

"**All** of old. **Nothing else** ever. Ever tried. Ever **failed**. No matter. **Try** again. **Fail** again. **Fail better**. "

SAMUEL BECKETT, *WORSTWARD HO*

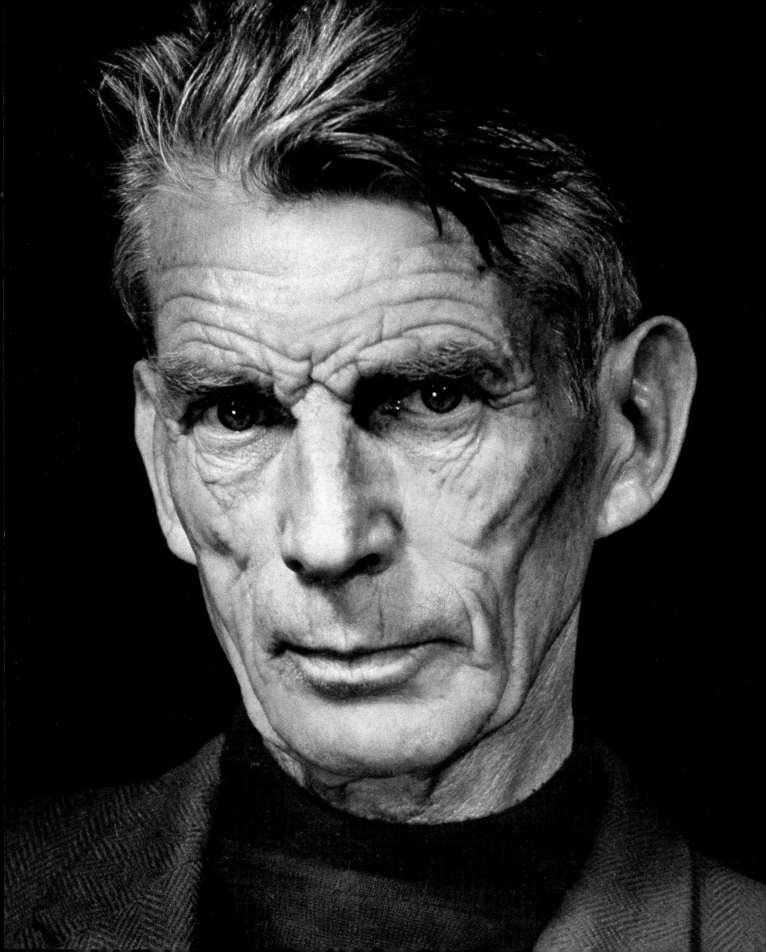

△ **WAITING FOR GODOT,** 1953
Beckett's seminal absurdist drama premiered in 1953 at the Théâtre de Babylone, Paris. Critic Vivian Mercier famously wrote of the two-act play that "nothing happens, twice."

Having turned his back on a career in academia, Beckett embarked on travels around Europe that were to last six years. During this time, he began writing in earnest, producing a volume of poetry, numerous short stories, and a novel, *Dream of Fair to Middling Women*, which failed to find a publisher in his lifetime but provided material for his collection *More Pricks than Kicks* (1934).

Beckett's beloved father died in 1933, provoking an existential crisis and anxiety attacks that the writer addressed with two years of psychoanalysis in London.

He drew upon this experience to create the dreamlike scenarios and tortured psyches that inhabit his later works. The time he spent in London informed Beckett's second novel, the absurdist masterpiece *Murphy*. This bleakly comic piece centers on a man who withdraws into a rocking chair after realizing that he cannot achieve contentment in the physical world.

## Residence in Paris
After traveling in Germany, Beckett returned to Ireland in 1937, but his homecoming was short-lived. There was conflict at home, and

arguments with his mother led to a serious rift between them. He then decided to leave Ireland for good and settle permanently in Paris.

Once back in France, he rejoined Parisian artistic society, renewed his friendship with Joyce, and began an affair with the immensely wealthy socialite Peggy Guggenheim. During his first winter in the city, he almost lost his life when he was stabbed in the chest by a pimp. After a period in the hospital with a perforated lung, Beckett confronted his assailant in court, asking why he had attacked him. The man's reply, "I don't know, sir. I apologize," struck a chord with Beckett, who dropped all charges. While recovering, Beckett was visited by Suzanne Deschevaux-Dumesnil, whom he had met some years earlier, and they began a relationship that was to last for the rest of their lives.

## War and resistance
German troops invaded Paris in 1940. As a citizen of Ireland, a neutral country, Beckett was allowed to stay in the city with Suzanne. Incensed by the occupation and the brutality of the Nazis, he joined the French Resistance, working as an undercover courier. He and Suzanne were forced into hiding in 1942, when members of his unit were arrested by the Gestapo, and the couple eventually fled to the village of Roussillon in unoccupied southern France. Recollection of their long and desolate journey south through the countryside is thought to have been the inspiration for the scenario of *Waiting for Godot*.

After the war, Beckett returned to Paris to resume his writing career. He visited Ireland to see his mother, and it was in his mother's bedroom that he experienced what he described as a "revelation" about the future

"They **give birth** astride of **a grave,** the **light gleams** an instant, then it's **night once more.**"

SAMUEL BECKETT, *WAITING FOR GODOT*

▷ **CROIX DE GUERRE**
Beckett worked for the Resistance in Paris and in southern France. After the war, he was honored with the Croix de Guerre and the Médaille de la Résistance.

direction of his work—that he should embrace the inner darkness that "includes folly and failure, impotence and ignorance." He began to write from a position of confusion and lack of knowledge, by subtracting words rather than adding them. He also wrote in French, which allowed him to write "without style," freed from his English literary inheritance. A period of prolific creativity followed, in which Beckett wrote a groundbreaking trilogy of prose narratives: *Molloy*, *Malone Dies*, and *The Unnameable*. These self-referential monologues lacked any plot or characterization and

are often seen as the literary equivalent of abstract paintings. Suzanne eventually succeeded in finding a publisher for *Molloy* in 1951, and its modest success secured publication of many of Beckett's other books.

## Dramatic works

In 1948, Beckett began work on a play that was to become his masterpiece. *En attendant Godot* (which was later translated into English by Beckett as *Waiting for Godot*) was a story of deliverance forever postponed, told through impenetrable clownlike characters. First staged in Paris in 1953, the play was hailed by some critics as a revolutionary moment in theater and its reputation soon spread. Beckett had not only achieved recognition as a writer, but also found the style and genre in which he felt comfortable. From then

on, he devoted most of his time and effort to drama, both as a playwright and a director. In the late 1950s, he branched out into writing for radio, and often spent time in London working for the BBC. There, he met a young, widowed script editor, Barbara Bray, and started an affair that would last for the rest of his life, despite having married Suzanne in a secret civil ceremony in 1961.

## Seclusion and late poetry

Beckett continued to live in Paris, but found the seclusion that he needed to work in a remote house in the Marne valley. He was a private man who avoided public appearances and refused to give interviews. When he received the news that he had won the Nobel Prize in Literature in 1969, he and Suzanne—who were vacationing in Tunisia at the time—went into hiding and sent a friend to Stockholm to receive the award on his behalf.

In old age, however, Beckett returned to writing prose and poetry. In 1986, having been diagnosed with emphysema, and possibly also suffering from Parkinson's disease, he moved into a nursing home. His wife, Suzanne, died in July 1989; five months later, on December 22, Beckett also passed away, at 83.

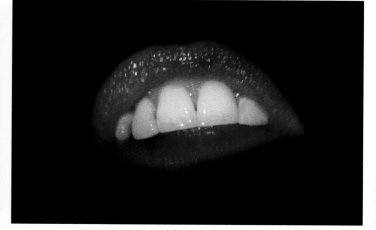

◁ **NOT I, 2014**
In Beckett's short play (the performance lasts just 14 minutes), nothing is visible of the actor but a disembodied mouth surrounded by darkness, from which issues a stream-of-consciousness monologue about a troubled life.

### ON FORM
### A master of media

Beckett came to theater relatively late but soon became a master of stagecraft. He adapted his skills to push boundaries in a range of media, especially in the dramas that he wrote for television, such as *Eh Joe* (1965). The Modernist experimentation in his TV work was typified by limited verbalization, minimalist sets, and a concentration on excessively slow physical action: at the end of *Eh Joe*, for example, the camera moves very gradually toward the character Joe, ending with an intense close-up of his face. Beckett's radio plays were similarly innovative, notably for the ingenious interaction of sound, music, and speech. He even made one short movie, starring Buster Keaton.

**1960s TELEVISION STUDIO CAMERA**

# KEY WORKS

**1934**
*More Pricks than Kicks*, Beckett's first full-length book, is published. It is a collection of short stories.

**1938**
*Murphy*, a novel, goes into print, after two years of rejection by publishers.

**1948–49**
Beckett works on *Waiting for Godot*, his first major work for the theater. It premieres in Paris in 1953.

**1951**
*Molloy*, the first of "The Trilogy" novels in French, is published. It is soon followed by *Malone Dies* and *The Unnameable*.

**1972**
The play *Not I* premieres at Lincoln Center, New York.

**1989**
The novellas *Company*, *Ill Seen Ill Said*, and *Worstward Ho* are published together as *Nohow On*.

▷ **MAHFOUZ IN CAIRO**
Mahfouz is pictured here in 1989
in the Gamaliya quarter of Cairo, where
he grew up. He was highly prolific,
publishing 34 novels and hundreds
of short stories. Several of his works
have been adapted into movies.

# Naguib Mahfouz

## 1911–2006, EGYPTIAN

Mahfouz was the first Arab writer to win the Nobel Prize in Literature.
He is best known for realist novels that paint a vivid portrait of life in
Cairo in the first half of the 20th century.

# "This man coming from the **Third World**, how did he find the **peace of mind** to write **stories**?"

NAGUIB MAHFOUZ, NOBEL PRIZE ACCEPTANCE SPEECH

Naguib Mahfouz was born in 1911 in Gamaliya, one of the oldest areas of Cairo, where narrow medieval streets and alleys housed a dense population following a traditional Islamic lifestyle. He was the youngest son of a civil servant, a rigidly old-fashioned man who imposed a strict Islamic code of conduct on his family. At the age of eight, Mahfouz witnessed the violent events of Egypt's 1919 Revolution (see box, right). Rising through the education system from the local Koran school up to university level, he emerged in the 1930s as a supporter of the anti-British nationalist Wafd party.

In need of financial security, Mahfouz took a job in the Egyptian civil service, where he made a successful lifelong career. But his true ambition was to write fiction. After experimenting with historical novels set in Pharaonic Egypt, he found his subject and style with *Midaq Alley* (1947). Set in old Cairo during World War II, the novel describes a society in which the only escape from poverty and frustration appears to be in the adoption of Western modernization. A dazzling cast of characters ranges from a gay drug dealer to a marriage broker and from a heartless beauty who prostitutes herself to foreign officers to a professional mutilator who maims poor people so they can beg for a living.

## Progressive ideas

*Midaq Alley* was followed by *The Cairo Trilogy*. This gripping saga, charting the lives of the Abd al-Jawad family from the 1910s through to the 1940s, made Mahfouz famous across the Arab world. The first volume, *Palace Walk* (1956), describes the world Mahfouz experienced as a child. The head of the family is a man who keeps his wife shut up in her home out of Islamic principle, while he indulges in extramarital affairs. The reaction of various family members to this patriarchal tyranny provides the book's central drama. The second and third volumes, *Palace of Desire* and *Sugar Street*, followed in 1957. They chart the course of Egypt's political and social conflicts in rapidly changing times, as well as the struggle for independence from British influence and military presence.

Mahfouz's later novels became more experimental in structure and often allegorical in nature. *Children of Gebalawi* (1959), in which the Prophet Mohammed appears as a character, was condemned by Islamic conservatives and banned in Egypt. In the Alexandria-based *Miramar* (1967), four narrators give different versions of the same events.

The unexpected award of the Nobel Prize in Literature in 1988 brought Mahfouz belatedly to the attention of the non-Arab world. His realist novels became best sellers in North America and Europe. In old age, he remained a controversial, politically engaged figure and in 1994 survived an assassination attempt by an Islamic fundamentalist. Mahfouz died in 2006, at 94.

## IN CONTEXT
### The 1919 Revolution

During World War I, Egypt became a British protectorate and military base. The rowdy Australian and British troops appalled the people of Cairo and soon after the war Egyptian nationalists, led by Saad Zaghlul, petitioned the British High Commissioner to end the protectorate. In 1919, ordinary Egyptian citizens staged widespread demonstrations calling for the foreigners to leave. Hundreds were killed by the British in the suppression of these disturbances. In 1922, faced with continuing resistance, Britain granted Egypt formal independence, but maintained a substantial presence in the country. The events of the 1919 Revolution appear in Mahfouz's novel *Palace Walk*.

**AUSTRALIAN INFANTRYMEN AT THE GREAT PYRAMID OF GIZA, 1915**

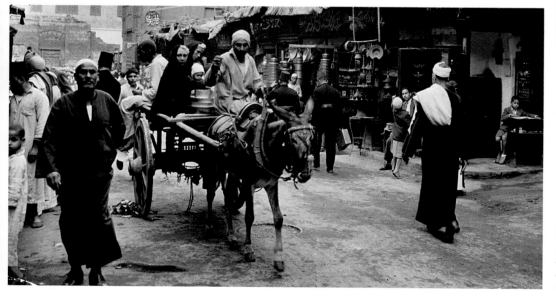

◁ **CAIRO BAZAAR**
Urban Cairo—shown here in the 1950s—formed the backdrop to most of Mahfouz's early fiction. His characters were ordinary people dealing with the clash between traditional society and increasing Westernization.

# Albert Camus

## 1913–1960, FRENCH

A key figure in the modernist movement and one of a group of radical intellectuals in Paris, Camus rejected the conventions of classical literary prose to fictionalize his philosophy of the absurdity of human existence.

"My mother died today. Or maybe yesterday, I don't know." The opening of Camus's first novel, *The Outsider*, captures the emotional detachment of the book's protagonist, Meursault, and encapsulates the author's philosophy of the absurd, in which all humanity must accept existence as meaningless and chaotic. Camus's simple, short, direct sentences shun metaphor and embellishment, instead reporting firsthand Mersault's thoughts and apparent motives.

### Early adversity

Camus was born into relative poverty in Mondovi (now known as Dréan) in French Algeria in 1913. The next year, his father, Lucien, died in battle during World War I, leaving his illiterate and partially deaf wife, Catherine, to raise their son in a poor quarter of Algiers. Camus was later admitted into the University of Algiers to study philosophy. There he joined the Communist Party and, with his fellow students, founded the Théâtre du Travail as a platform for left-wing political dramas. In addition to producing and directing, Camus co-wrote plays, including his first published drama, *Revolt in Asturia*. He had a lifelong passion for soccer, but was forced to abandon sports when he contracted tuberculosis in 1930. When later asked to choose between his love of theater and soccer (football), Camus replied, "Football, without hesitation."

Rejected by the army because of poor health, he wrote for magazines in Paris during the city's occupation by the Germans (1940–1944), before moving to Bordeaux to complete *The Outsider* and a nonfiction work, *The Myth of Sisyphus* (both 1942). He reduced his journalistic work to focus on writing a second novel, *The Plague* (1947), which used the allegory of a devastating plague in the Algerian city of Oran to probe the human condition. His output included numerous plays and essays through which he explored the concept of individual freedom in a hostile and incomprehensible world. He was awarded the Nobel Prize in Literature in 1957.

### Turbulent loves

Personal dramas exerted their own influence on Camus's work. He was a womanizer and serial adulterer. His first marriage, to Simone Hié, ended in divorce, and although he loved his second wife, Francine Faure, he publicly renounced the institution of marriage and fictionalized Francine's later mental breakdown in his confessional novel *The Fall* (1956).

Camus died in a car accident at the age of 46, along with his friend and publisher Michel Gallimard.

◁ **FRENCH ALGIERS**
Camus was a harsh critic of the French colonial authorities in Algeria. In the 1930s, he supported proposals to give Algerians full French citizenship.

THE CAFE DE FLORE, BOULEVARD SAINT-GERMAIN, PARIS, 1946

> " People **hasten to judge** in order not to be judged **themselves**. "
> ALBERT CAMUS, *THE FALL*

▷ **THE OUTSIDER**
Camus is considered a giant of French literature, but it was his Algerian birth and background that gave him his unique literary perspective. He is pictured here in 1947, the year of publication of his novel *The Plague*.

---

▷ **AIME CESAIRE, 1967**
Césaire is pictured here at the age of 54, during a period in which his literary work focused on politically charged "verse plays," in which the dialogue was written in verse form.

# Aimé Césaire

## 1913–2008, MARTINICAN

Césaire was a Caribbean poet and politician who cofounded the Négritude movement, urging colonized peoples to take pride in their heritage and reject the policy of assimilation under colonial rule.

# "I am on the side of those who are oppressed."

AIME CESAIRE

◁ **BASSE-POINTE**
A stamp printed in Martinique in the 1960s shows the town of Basse-Pointe, Aimé Césaire's birthplace.

Aimé Césaire was born in the French colony of Martinique, an island in the eastern Caribbean. The second of six children, he grew up in poor conditions in Basse-Pointe, a town that had been all but destroyed by the eruption of volcanic Mount Pelée a decade earlier. Césaire was a gifted student in high school, and earned a scholarship to study in Paris at the prestigious Lycée Louis-le-Grand, from where he moved on to the Ecole Normale Supérieure.

In Paris, he mixed with a group of black intellectuals and cofounded the journal L'Etudiant noir (The Black Student), in which he and various other thinkers developed new ways of responding to the innate racism and exploitative history of colonialism (see box, right). They devised the concept of Négritude: in broad terms, an appeal to the colonized peoples of the Caribbean to consider themselves unified by their mutual African heritage, and in so doing, to reject the secondary status that had been imposed upon them by white European colonizers.

## Return to Martinique

Newly married and with a young son, Césaire returned to teach at the Lycée Schoelcher in Martinique's capital, Fort-de-France, just before World War II. With his wife, Suzanne, he set up a literary journal, *Tropiques*, which championed Martinican identity and Afro-Caribbean poetry.

It was at this time that Césaire's groundbreaking work *Cahier d'un retour au pays natal* (*Return to My Native Land*) was published in a French literary magazine. In this book-length, partly autobiographical poem, Césaire invented his own language by combining dream imagery, colloquialisms, historical documents, and literary French; he used this revolutionary form of expression to explore black identity.

Césaire's work over the next decade was strongly influenced by the surrealist movement (he became a friend of André Breton), and he went on to write more collections of poetry, as well as drama and essays that chimed with his growing involvement in politics. Césaire was elected mayor of Fort-de-France in 1945 and aside from a brief hiatus, held the position for 56 years; he was instrumental in helping Martinique to gain the status of an overseas department of France.

Some commentators in later generations came to see Césaire as a somewhat conflicted figure because although he railed against European colonizers, he wrote in classical French and was accepted into the French pantheon; he was also influential in bringing Martinique closer to France.

▽ **FORT-DE-FRANCE**
Césaire drew inspiration from the landscapes of Martinique, and became mayor of the capital, Fort-de-France. The island's airport is named in his honor.

## IN CONTEXT
### Négritude

Césaire was one of the group of students who described the concept of Négritude, or black consciousness, in the literary review *L'Etudiant noir*. The group included the writer Léopold Sédar Senghor, who in 1960 became the first president of Senegal. They promoted the idea of a pan-African identity for all Caribbean colonized peoples and viewed Négritude as an historical phenomenon that had evolved from the shared experiences of the colonized—particularly slavery. Césaire became a mentor to the author Frantz Fanon, who argued for a far more radical rejection of colonialism, and who influenced such figures as Che Guevara in Cuba and Malcom X in the US.

**SENEGALESE INDEPENDENCE LEADER LEOPOLD SEDAR SENGHOR**

▷ **THOMAS IN 1936**
Thomas, photographed here in his early 20s, was flamboyantly theatrical and would read his works aloud in a musical Welsh lilt that emphasized the assonances and consonances in his highly crafted verse. He inspired many other poets to read their works in public.

# Dylan Thomas

**1914–1953, WELSH**

A Welsh writer of poetry and poetical prose with a gift for high-flown rhetoric and a sly sense of humor, Thomas was a prominent figure in mid-20th century literature. Heavy drinking curtailed his life.

> # "**Time** held me **green** and **dying** Though **I sang** in **my chains** like **the sea**. "

DYLAN THOMAS, "FERN HILL"

ACTORS SYBIL THORNDIKE AND RICHARD BURTON READING *UNDER MILK WOOD*

Dylan Thomas was born in Swansea, Wales, where his father taught English literature. Dylan's first name was derived from Welsh mythology, but he never learned to speak the Welsh language. Totally lacking his father's academic ability, he performed poorly at school. Spoiled by his overindulgent mother, he gained an early reputation for mischievous behavior. He also showed a precocious talent for poetry. Thomas began filling notebooks with poems at the age of 15 and by the time he was 19, had written some of his most famous works, including the poem "And Death Shall Have No Dominion." Perhaps as a consequence of his father being diagnosed with cancer, in his 20th year Thomas produced a series of intense, dark, surreal poems, including "The force that through the green fuse drives the flower" and "Light breaks where no sun shines." Published as *18 Poems* in 1934, these were hailed by critics as representing a powerful new voice in poetry. In 1936, he published a second volume, *25 Poems*, more than half of which were taken from his adolescent notebooks. Even at this stage in his life, new poems were slow to appear.

## London to Laugharne

Still in his early 20s, Thomas moved to London, becoming a familiar figure in Soho pubs frequented by writers and artists. In 1937, he married Caitlin Macnamara, a fiery Irish dancer and artist's model. They had three children in the course of a stormy relationship, which was marred by infidelities on both sides and by a constant shortage of cash. He began to publish short fiction and memoirs alongside his poems, notably *Portrait of the Artist as a Young Dog* (1940), which drew on his experiences growing up in Swansea.

Always in poor health, Thomas was found unfit for military service in World War II. During the war, he wrote scripts for documentaries and began a fruitful career writing for radio and broadcasting. He also recovered the inspiration to write poetry. His wartime poems included "Fern Hill," based on summer visits to an aunt's farm in rural Wales, and his Blitz poem "A Refusal to Mourn the Death, by Fire, of a Child in London." Publication of these and other poems as *Deaths and Entrances* in 1946 made Thomas a literary celebrity.

Starting in 1949, Thomas lived in the Boathouse in Laugharne on the Welsh coast. The village was the model for the fictional Llareggub, the setting for his celebrated voice drama *Under Milk Wood*, which was first performed on stage in 1954. In 1952, he prepared his *Collected Poems*, including "Over Sir John's Hill," inspired by Laugharne's scenery, and the famous poem in the form of a villanelle "Do not go gentle into that good night," addressed to his dying father. Beginning in 1950, Thomas made several trips to the US, where he enthralled audiences with his readings and appalled his hosts with drunken antics. It was in New York that he died of pneumonia in November 1953, at 39.

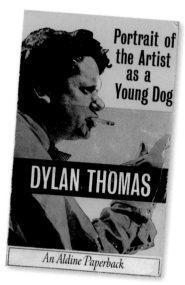

△ **AUTOBIOGRAPHICAL STORIES**
In *Portrait of the Artist as a Young Dog*, the dog is of course Thomas himself, who tells tales of his youthful adventures and loves, and of the odd characters whom he met in his early years in Wales.

▷ **WRITING SHED, LAUGHARNE**
Thomas's writing shed, above the Boathouse in Laugharne where he lived for four years, gave him inspiring views of four estuaries. The first poem he wrote here was "Over Sir John's Hill," in which he describes the vista.

# Marguerite Duras

## 1914–1996, FRENCH

Duras was a French novelist, playwright, scriptwriter, essayist, and experimental filmmaker whose work often blurred the line between fiction and autobiography, making her mercurial life hard to pin down.

◁ **HIROSHIMA MON AMOUR**
Memory and forgetfulness—explored within a long conversation between two lovers—are the key themes of this 1959 movie, for which Duras wrote the screenplay.

Her early experience of poverty, and of the violence and degradation she experienced at the hands of her mother and her eldest brother, often feature in her writing. She would later claim, too, that the story of *The Lover*, about an affair between a 15-year-old girl and a 27-year-old Chinese man, was autobiographical. The assertion made her a media star, but details of Duras's life would always be the subject of controversy—a confusion between fact and fiction that she was happy to exploit.

### Loves and politics
Duras went to college in Paris at the age of 18, and in 1939 she married the writer Robert Antelme: they had a son who died at birth. Duras began drinking heavily and took another writer, Dionys Mascolo, as a lover. Both Duras and Antelme joined the French Resistance during World War II; in her war memoir *La Douleur*, Duras describes nursing her husband back to health after he had been imprisoned in German camps.

The couple divorced and Duras married Mascolo, with whom she had a son. She joined the Communist Party in 1945 and was an active member for 10 years, before leaving in a disagreement over artistic freedom.

The novel *Les Impudents* (1943) was to be the first of many that she published under the pen name Duras. She also wrote screenplays, including that for the cult classic *Hiroshima Mon Amour*, and began to make her own movies, becoming a fixture in the glamorous world of French cinema. Duras was diagnosed with cirrhosis of the liver, detoxed—nearly dying in the process—and later recovered from a five-month coma. She finally succumbed to throat cancer in 1996.

Marguerite Duras was born Marguerite Donnadieu in Gia Dinh, in what is now Vietnam. When she was four, her father died and her mother, with Marguerite and her two brothers, moved to a small farm on the Cambodian coast. The land frequently flooded and was difficult to cultivate. The family was extremely poor.

◁ **DURAS IN 1955**
A provocative figure in both life and work, Duras was notoriously difficult with both directors and publishers, and once commented that she drank so much that it was "astonishing" that she managed to write.

▽ **THE MEKONG**
Duras spent part of her childhood in Sa Dec, a town on the Mekong Delta of Vietnam. It was here that she set her semiautobiographical novel *The Lover*.

" You have to be **very fond** of **men**. **Very, very fond**. You have to be **very fond** of them to **love** them. Otherwise they're **simply unbearable**. "
MARGUERITE DURAS

# Saul Bellow

## 1915–2005, CANADIAN-BORN AMERICAN

Essayist, novelist, and professor, Bellow delved into the madness and materialism of the modern world in search of sanity. He mixed high and low registers, humor and pathos, to devastating effect.

Bellow was born Solomon Bellows in Quebec, Canada, into a Lithuanian-Jewish family. When he was nine, they moved to Chicago—the city in which he would later set several of his novels. He graduated with degrees in sociology and anthropology from Northwestern University in 1935 and two years later married for the first time (of five). While serving in the merchant marine, Bellow wrote his first novel, *Dangling Man* (1944), an unsettling account of a man's restless wait to be sent to war. He later criticized this work for its imitation of European literary style.

### Urban literature

In the late 1940s and early 1950s, Bellow lived in New York, a city whose "trembling energy" fascinated him.

But his breakthrough novel was written in Paris on a Guggenheim Fellowship and set in Chicago: *The Adventures of Augie March* (1953) was exuberant and innovative, written in a loose, colloquial voice, and portrayed the Jewish community that Bellow knew from his childhood. It was a critical and commercial success and won a National Book Award.

In 1955, he married again and in the following year published the New York–based novella *Seize the Day*, which returned to the tightly written style of his earlier works. *Henderson the Rain King* (1959), set in Africa, was a sprawling, picaresque adventure about a middle-aged man in search of "higher qualities." The novel, which combined vigorous comedy with philosophical insight, was reportedly among the author's favorite works.

After teaching at the University of Minnesota in the late 1950s, Bellow moved back to Chicago with his third wife. His 1964 novel *Herzog* dealt with a troubled professor who manically writes (unsent) letters to a gamut of people—friends, philosophers, God—to try to make sense of his despair after his wife betrays him with his best friend (mirroring real-life events in Bellow's life). Despite its intellectual nature, this moving and darkly comic novel spent 42 weeks on the best-seller lists. Bellow was awarded the Pulitzer Prize for *Humboldt's Gift* (1975), which was a "comic novel about death," based on his relationship with the poet Delmore Schwartz, a self-destructive genius whose protégé Bellow had been.

### Mature style

In his later works, written after he won the 1976 Nobel Prize in Literature, Bellow perfected his highly distinctive style, which mixed "street smarts" with cultural sophistication, and a rich absurdist vein with emotional poignancy. Although Bellow resisted being pigeonholed as a Jewish writer, his introspective, intellectual, alienated heroes are almost all Jewish, and he himself typified the Jewish intellectual from an immigrant family made good.

In 1989, Bellow married for the fifth time; his fourth child and only daughter was born in 1999. His final novel, *Ravelstein*, was published in 2000, a thinly fictionalized portrait of his friend and colleague Allan Bloom (see box, right). Bellow died in 2005, the recipient of numerous honors.

**THE FIRST US EDITION OF SAUL BELLOW'S *RAVELSTEIN***

◁ **WINDY CITY**
Bellow acknowledged the influence of his home city in the first line of his novel *The Adventures of Augie March*: "I am an American, Chicago born—Chicago, that somber city—and go at things as I have taught myself, free-style, and will make the record in my own way ...."

▷ **BELLOW IN PARIS, 1982**
Bellow was a complex character. He could be charming and was very attractive to women, but he did not take criticism easily and was often drawn into spats with friends.

# Aleksandr Solzhenitsyn

## 1918–2008, RUSSIAN

Solzhenitsyn was a conservative moralist who painted a bitterly ironic picture of life in the communist Soviet Union and especially of its prison camps, of which he had firsthand experience.

Aleksandr Isayevich Solzhenitsyn was born at Kislovodsk in the Caucasus one year after the Russian Revolution. He was raised by his mother, and went on to study physics and mathematics at college, while always dreaming of being a writer. In World War II he served with distinction as an artillery officer in the Soviet Red Army.

In February 1945, Solzhenitsyn was arrested by the secret police for making disrespectful comments about Soviet dictator Joseph Stalin in private correspondence. He was sentenced to

**◁ SOLZHENITSYN IN EXILE**

After the publication of Solzhenitsyn's *Gulag Archipelago* in the West, Soviet leader Leonid Brezhnev declared that "This hooligan Solzhenitsyn is out of control." The writer was sent into exile in 1974, living for a while in Zurich with his wife Natalia and his children before moving to the US.

eight years in prison camps, and served part of this time at a special camp where college-educated inmates pursued scientific research on behalf of the Soviet regime—an experience that formed the basis for his novel *The First Circle* (1968). The rest of the time he suffered the hard manual labor and harsh conditions he would later describe in *One Day in the Life of Ivan Denisovich* (1962).

### Release and publication

Solzhenitsyn was released from prison in 1953, coincidentally on the day of Stalin's death, but was condemned to permanent exile in Kazakhstan. In 1956, the new Soviet leader, Nikita Khrushchev, denounced Stalin's reign of terror. Solzhenitsyn was restored to full citizenship but he did not at that time expect to see the works he was writing appear in print.

In 1961, however, *Ivan Denisovich* was accepted by *Novy Mir* magazine, and it was published with Khrushchev's approval the following year. Its direct, unvarnished account of prison-camp life caused a sensation in the Soviet Union. A short story collection, *For the Good of the Cause*, appeared in 1963.

A campaign of harassment against Solzhenitsyn followed Khrushchev's fall from power, and the writer's work could circulate in the Soviet Union only as underground "samizdat" literature, although it appeared in translation in countries in the West.

For years, Solzhenitsyn had also been working on a history of the Soviet prison-camp system, *The Gulag Archipelago*. Its publication in the West in 1973 was the final straw for the Soviet leadership. Sent into exile, Solzhenitsyn settled as a recluse in Vermont, shunning celebrity status while also denouncing the irreligious materialism of Western society. He had embarked on a vast novel cycle, *The Red Wheel*, intended as a Tolstoyan epic portrayal of modern Russian history. The first volume, *August 1914*, was published in 1971, but subsequently only a few more fragments appeared. He was able to return to Russia in 1991 and died there in 2008, a half-forgotten figure from an earlier era.

## IN CONTEXT
### The Gulag

Gulag is an acronym referring to the prison work camps set up in the early years of the Soviet Union and developed on a vast scale under Stalin from the 1930s to 1953. At least 14 million people were sent to the camps during the Stalinist period and millions died from the hardships suffered. In his three-volume work *The Gulag Archipelago*, Solzhenitsyn used islands as a metaphor for the secret camps scattered across the Soviet Union, weaving together his own experiences and those of hundreds of fellow prisoners to portray mass suffering and injustice.

**AN ITALIAN EDITION OF** *THE GULAG ARCHIPELAGO*

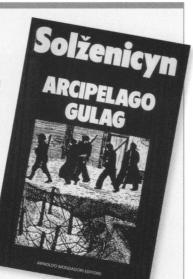

**▷ LIBERATION, 1953**

Solzhenitsyn is pictured here on the day that he was freed from the Gulag. At the time, he was fighting cancer, a struggle that was later reflected in his novel *Cancer Ward* (1966).

# Primo Levi

## 1919–1987, ITALIAN

Levi's account of his year in the abyss of Auschwitz concentration camp is widely recognized as one of the most profound and touching works in Holocaust literature.

Born in 1919, Primo Levi was a timid, studious child, homeschooled for a year because of illness. He and his younger sister Anna Maria were raised in a large family apartment on the Corso Re Umberto in Turin, a wedding gift to cement the marriage of his mother Ester (Rina), a middle-class intellectual, and his engineer father Cesare, 20 years her senior.

For Primo, being Jewish was a minor cultural concern confined to not having a Christmas tree, learning Hebrew for his Bar Mitzvah, and being forbidden to eat salami (but eating it anyway). There was tension between Primo's domineering mother and his extrovert father, but what the family shared was a passion for the arts and literature. Like his parents, Primo read widely. He joined the lyceum (high school) at age 14 and excelled in classics and literature, but focused on chemistry and biology after being captivated by *Concerning the Nature of Things*, an exploration of science based on the lectures delivered by Nobel laureate Sir William Bragg.

As was expected of all schoolboys in Mussolini's Italy, Levi joined the Avanguardisti movement for young fascists, but he opted for skiing in the mountains instead of gun practice.

◁ **TURIN HOME**
Although he was raised in Turin, Levi's heart belonged in the Piedmont Mountains above the city. He described the spiritual recovery provided by his hikes in the mountains.

In 1937, Levi enrolled at Turin University to study chemistry. His timing was most fortunate: when the Italian Manifesto of Race was introduced prohibiting Jews from attending state schools and universities, Levi was already a student and so was allowed to continue. The university was a safe haven from the mounting aggression against Jews. Levi graduated with high grades in 1941, with the words "of Jewish race" added to his diploma.

### Years of persecution

Following the German invasion of northern and central Italy, Levi was forced to assume a false identity in order to work. He found employment extracting nickel from asbestos-mine waste, and later worked for a Swiss chemical company in Milan.

The exportation of Jews to labor camps was gathering pace, and after the death of his father in 1942, Levi installed his mother and sister in a small hotel near the Swiss border in a bid to keep them safe.

He joined a disorganized resistance group but was arrested with two compatriots almost immediately. Faced with a choice between certain death as a partisan, or deportation as a Jew, Levi admitted he was a Jew.

**POSTCARD CELEBRATING THE "PACT OF STEEL"**

▷ **PRIMO LEVI, JANUARY, 1986**
Primo Levi is shown here in his study in Rome the year before his death. He produced more than a dozen works in his lifetime. These included memoirs, short stories, novels, poetry, and essays.

" Why is the **pain** of every day **translated** so **constantly** into our **dreams**, in the ever-repeated scene of the **unlistened-to story**? "

PRIMO LEVI, *IF THIS IS A MAN*

△ **A VISION OF HELL ON EARTH**
Nazi soldiers "grade" prisoners on the train concourse outside the entrance to Auschwitz-Birkenau in 1944. Most entrants were never put to work, but were sent directly to the gas chambers for extermination.

△ **THE DEFENSE OF THE RACE**
The manifesto of Italian racism was published in 1938. Its 10 points were developed by a group of university professors, under the auspices of the Ministry of Popular Culture. Its goal was for Italy to "avoid the catastrophic plague of the crossbred."

In February 1944, Levi was one of the 650 men, women, and children who were crammed into railroad cars at the village of Fossoli for the five-day journey to the complex of camps that made up Auschwitz concentration camp in Poland. With no water or sanitation on board, three people died en route. And of the remainder, 96 men and 29 women were deemed capable of work when they reached their final destination; the remaining women and children, the elderly and the frail were taken to gas chambers.

Levi was assigned to slave labor at Monowitz, which was servicing the Buna rubber factory. The slight 24 year old may have lacked physical strength but he found the spirit to survive a year of appalling hardship. He was sustained by a determination to record what he had witnessed, and, after the war, produced one of the defining works of Holocaust literature.

In *If This Is a Man*, Levi catalogs factually and without bitterness life in the *Lager* (camp): the stripping and head shaving; the tattooed number that reduced him to *Häftling* (prisoner) 174517; the thin, striped cotton suits and mismatched shoes; the nights spent head to toe in narrow bunks; and the dreaded call to work at 4 am. He describes the starvation rations of bread and watery vegetable stew, and

## KEY WORKS

**1958**
*If This Is a Man* is published internationally and heralded as a lucid account of a man's descent into hell.

**1963**
*The Truce* describes Levi's chaotic train trip home from Poland back to Turin.

**1975**
*The Periodic Table* takes different chemical elements as the starting point of 21 autobiographical stories.

**1978**
In *The Wrench*, the problem solving of a womanizing engineer provides the framework for a collection of short stories.

**1982**
*If Not Now, When?* is published. It is a fictionalized account of Russian, Polish, and Jewish partisans trapped behind enemy lines.

**1986**
*The Drowned and the Saved*, Levi's most despairing work, probes the mind-set of the oppressors and the oppressed.

# "There is **Auschwitz**, and so **there cannot be God**. I don't find a **solution** to this **dilemma**. I **keep looking**, but **I don't find it**."

PRIMO LEVI

the exhaustion from heavy labor in freezing temperatures. In the nearby Birkenau camp, dead bodies were burning day and night. After regular selections in which naked prisoners put a spring in their step to survive, the weak and old disappeared from Levi's camp to be gassed.

## Endurance and survival

Combining accurate testimony with an unerring moral stance, Levi's account affirmed the dignity of people trapped in the most inhuman project. Instead of an undefined mass of victims, he describes individuals who survived through resolution, wit, and luck.

The camp held prisoners of all nationalities, and many inmates had no understanding of the German commands that could seal their fate in seconds. Levi survived by trading bread for German lessons and through his close friendship with

a fellow Italian, Alberto Dalla Volta. There was also the simple kindness of an Italian civilian worker, Lorenzo Perrone, who regularly shared his rations. Levi wrote, "Thanks to Lorenzo, I managed not to forget that I myself was a man."

In January 1945, as the liberating Russian troops drew close, the camp prisoners were evacuated by the retreating Germans. Most, including Alberto, were marched to their death, but in a stroke of luck, Levi developed scarlet fever and was one of 800 sick men left behind in the infirmary.

## Return to humanity

In his follow-up book, *The Truce*, Levi recalls the days spent waiting to be rescued. Levi, along with 100 or so survivors, was taken by the Russians on a needless seven-month train trip, traveling deep into Belorussia (Belarus) before he arrived

in Turin in the fall of 1945. He was one of only three people from his original transport to return home.

## Literary success

Levi began writing within months of his return home, sharing his story with his first reader and editor, Lucia Morpurgo, who later became his wife. The first edition of *If This Is a Man* in 1947 made little impact and Levi went back to work as a chemist, then as the manager of a paint factory on the outskirts of Turin. In 1958 a new edition of the book was widely translated and became a best seller. It was followed by *The Truce* in 1963.

In 1975, Levi's reputation as one of the century's most gifted writers was confirmed by *The Periodic Table*, a life-affirming collection of short stories, each of which was associated with one of 21 elements from Mendeleev's Periodic Table.

Levi retired to devote himself entirely to writing, producing new collections of Auschwitz memoirs, poetry, and his Strega Prize–winning novel *The Wrench*—a celebration of technical work that is told through an Italian engineer's adventures.

In 1987, Levi toppled over the railing outside his apartment and was found dead at the bottom of the stairwell. A coroner's ruling of suicide confirmed for many that Auschwitz had finally claimed Levi; others, however, maintain that his fall was an accident.

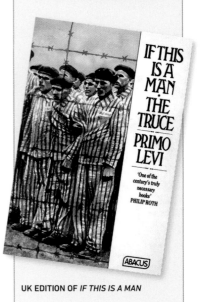

## ON STYLE
### Bearing witness

Levi describes Auschwitz in the language of a witness rather than that of a victim. He describes camp rituals, labor, and starvation factually, reserving philosophical discussion for his analysis of optimists, pessimists, collaborators, careerists, and Kapos (prisoners appointed as supervisors). His small anecdotes speak volumes about human nature: for example, a Kapo shows loss of all feeling as he wipes his soiled hand on a prisoner's shoulder; and Levi experiences a surge of happiness reciting Dante's *Canto of Ulysses* to a French inmate.

UK EDITION OF *IF THIS IS A MAN*

◁ **AUSCHWITZ-MONOWITZ, 1942**
Primo Levi was imprisoned in the Monowitz labor camp, which provided workers for the I G Farben factory, seen in this photo. The factory made many chemical products, including the poisonous gas Zyklon B.

# Jack Kerouac

### 1922–1969, AMERICAN

Often described as a spokesman for the 1950s Beat Generation, Kerouac was an idiosyncratic writer whose work charted a lifelong spiritual quest. He is best known for his fictionalized memoir *On the Road*.

# "... the **only people** for **me** are the **mad ones**, the **ones** who are **mad to live** ..."

JACK KEROUAC, *ON THE ROAD*

Jean-Louis Kerouac was born to French-Canadian parents in the decaying mill town of Lowell, Massachusetts. He grew up speaking French, and did not speak English fluently until adolescence. His father turned to alcohol when his printing business collapsed in the Great Depression, so Jack was brought up mainly by his mother. Talented at sports, he won a football scholarship to Columbia University in New York, but dropped out and worked for a time as a merchant sailor.

It was in New York in the mid-1940s that Kerouac first became associated with a group of aspiring writers that included poet Allen Ginsberg, William Burroughs, and Neal Cassady. They adopted a bohemian lifestyle, rejecting materialism and exploring drugs, mysticism, and free love. Kerouac later christened them "the Beats."

## Spontaneous prose

Kerouac's first novel, *The Town and the City*, was a fairly conventional work that attracted little attention when it was published in 1950. By that time, however, he had already begun writing in a radically different style that he would call "spontaneous prose," an improvisatory flow of words partly influenced by the example of modern jazz. In 1951, using this method, he wrote *On the Road*, a freewheeling account of his travels across the US with Neal Cassady. For six years, *On the Road* was just one of many unpublished manuscripts that he

carried around in his backpack. Kerouac moved west when the focus of the Beat movement shifted to San Francisco. Here he developed an interest in Buddhism under the influence of poet Gary Snyder. *The Dharma Bums*, written in 1957, is an account of a climbing expedition with Snyder in search of fresh air and enlightenment. In that same year, Kerouac's life was transformed when an abridged version of *On the Road*

◁ **ON THE ROAD, FIRST EDITION**
Blending fiction and autobiography, *On the Road* chronicles a hedonistic and often chaotic journey of self-discovery made by Sal Paradise (a character based on Kerouac himself) and his mystical friend Dean Moriarty.

was published to great acclaim. Hailed as the voice of a generation, Kerouac became a celebrity. His other works appeared in print in rapid succession: *The Dharma Bums* and *The Subterraneans* in 1958, *Doctor Sax* and *Maggie Cassidy* in 1959.

## The price of fame

Although the young loved Kerouac's writing, critics were woundingly scornful. Kerouac responded by descending into alcoholism; his writing suffered and became ever more intermittent. *Big Sur* (1962) charted his struggle with depression and addiction; *Vanity of Duluoz* (1968) returned to an account of his formative years. But mostly he drank and played cards, living with his mother in Queens, New York. His conservative political views, including support for America's Vietnam War, put him at odds with '60s radicals and hippies. He died as a result of long-term alcohol abuse at the age of 47.

▽ **SCROLLED SCRIPT**
To allow himself to write without interruption, Kerouac stuck sheets of paper together in a single scroll to feed through his typewriter. The manuscript of *On the Road* measured an astonishing 120 feet (36 meters).

▷ **ITALO CALVINO, 1984**
Calvino is pictured here at his home in Rome. His death a year later prompted messages of condolence from the pope and the president of Italy—such was his status and popularity in Italy. His playful wit and inventiveness distinguished him from his intellectual contemporaries.

# Italo Calvino

### 1923–1985, ITALIAN

Calvino's erudite yet playful postmodern stories have secured his position as one of the most important writers of the 20th century. His narratives subvert traditional expectations of form and content, author and reader.

Italo Calvino was born in Cuba in 1923 to Italian parents, both scientists. The family moved to San Remo, Italy, where Italo spent his childhood, and at the age of 18 he enrolled at the University of Turin (later transferring to Florence)—despite his love of literature—to study agriculture.

After World War II—during which he became a communist and joined the anti-fascist Resistance—he returned to study in Turin, graduating with a master's in literature. Politically committed, he took a job as a writer on the communist paper L'Unità, but left the Communist Party 12 years later, disillusioned by the invasion of Hungary by Soviet troops in 1956.

His experiences in the Resistance provided material for two of his fictional works: the neorealistic novel The Path to the Spiders' Nest (1947), which views the Resistance from the perspective of a boy, and the short-story collection Adam, One Afternoon and Other Stories (1949). In 1955, Calvino had a torrid affair with a married woman, Elsa De Giorgi. His steamy letters to the actress caused a scandal when they were published posthumously in 2004. An intensely private man, Calvino would have recoiled from this scrutiny of his private life.

## The craft of fiction

In the 1950s, Calvino's work turned to fantasy and allegory, with three tales in particular winning international recognition: The Cloven Viscount (1952), The Baron in the Trees (1957), and The Nonexistent Knight (1959). Starting at this time—in works that have clear echoes of Borges, Cervantes, and Kafka—Calvino jettisoned realism from his writing, along with the notion that the author controls meaning. Beginning in the 1960s—in the short-story collection t zero (1967), for example—his tales took the form of an elaborate game, in which the reader is encouraged to participate in the unfolding of the story.

Calvino married the Argentinian translator Esther Judith Singer in 1964. After moving to Rome, where their daughter Giovanna was born, he turned his attention to the short stories that would form the inventive, highly

**ITALO CALVINO**
**IL BARONE RAMPANTE**
EINAUDI

◁ **COMMUNIST POSTER**
After World War II, Calvino believed that the Italian Communist Party would lead an international renewal of communism.

acclaimed collection Cosmicomics (1965–c.1968). With references as diverse as Samuel Beckett, Lewis Carroll, algebra, astronomy, semiotics, structuralism, and Popeye comics, these tales set out to retell the creation and evolution of the cosmos.

Shortly before the revolution of 1968, Calvino moved to Paris with his family and joined the radical literary group Oulipo (see box, right). Invisible Cities followed in 1972—a beautifully written, intoxicating text that explores the idea that "meaning" is not stable, but endlessly shifts, negating the possibility of a single, unitary truth.

His most famous metafictional work, If on a Winter's Night a Traveler (1979), consists of 10 unfinished novels. It is a book about the act of reading and the literary process itself, with some passages written in the second person—addressed to "you" the reader, who becomes a central character in the text: "You are about to begin reading Italo Calvino's new novel If on a Winter's Night a Traveler. Relax. Concentrate. Dispel every other thought."

In 1980, Calvino returned to Rome; he published Mr. Palomar, his last work, three years later. He died in a hospital in Siena from a cerebral hemorrhage in 1985, at 61. At the time of his death, he was the most-translated contemporary Italian writer.

◁ **THE BARON IN THE TREES** (1957)
Calvino's enchanting fantasy tells the story of Cosimo, a boy of noble birth who climbs up into a tree and lives a full—and highly eventful—life without ever descending. It is a utopian tale of rebellion, escape, and separation.

## IN CONTEXT
### Oulipo

In the late 1960s, Calvino became an active member of the Paris-based experimental group of writers known as Oulipo, short for Ouvroir de littérature potentielle (Workshop of potential literature). Here, he met writers and theorists including Roland Barthes, Raymond Queneau, Claude Lévi-Strauss, and Georges Perec, who greatly influenced his theoretical approach to literature and writing. The group explored, among many things, the potential links between numbers, systems, and literature, and "the infinite potential of language for new forms."

**ROLAND BARTHES, PARIS, 1979**

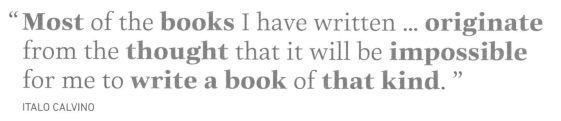

"**Most** of the **books** I have written ... **originate** from the **thought** that it will be **impossible** for me to **write a book** of **that kind.** "
ITALO CALVINO

▷ **VOICE OF A GENERATION**
Günter Grass, pictured here in 1981,
wrote close to 40 novels, memoirs,
short stories, poems, plays, and political
essays. He married twice, was father
to 8 children, and had 18 grandchildren.

# Günter Grass

## 1927–2015, GERMAN

Author, artist, and poet, Grass was described as "the conscience of a nation" after his novel *The Tin Drum* painted a darkly satirical portrait of ordinary Germans under the Nazi regime and their denial of the past.

> " Yet for **decades** I **refused** to **admit** to the **word**, and to the double letters (**SS**). "

GÜNTER GRASS, *PEELING THE ONION*

Born in 1927, Günter Wilhelm Grass was 11 years old when his home city of Danzig (now Gdansk, Poland) was annexed by Nazi Germany. Although Danzig was a free city of the League of Nations, many of its German citizens were loyal to the Reich. Growing up with his younger sister, his German father, and Kashubian mother, Grass witnessed creeping Nazification and the persecution of the city's minorities. He was a self-professed mama's boy, whose passion was art history, which he had learned from his cigarette-card collection of great works.

### Fighting for the fatherland

Grass became a member of the Nazi children's organization *Jungvolk* and, following compulsory military training, he joined the artillery of the feared Waffen SS when he was just 17. He came of age during the pitiless final years of the war, was wounded fighting the advancing Soviet army, and was recovering from his injuries in a sanatorium when US forces detained him as a prisoner of war.

In *Peeling the Onion* (2007), part of his trilogy of memoirs, Grass struggles to identify with this younger self, immune to the suffering of others during the rise of "Führer, Folk, and Fatherland." Newsreels of German heroes on the front played a part: "I was a pushover for the prettified black-and-white 'truth' they served up," he wrote. He regretted deeply that he had concealed his SS status for almost half a century.

### Success and controversy

After the war, Grass worked on farms and in a potash mine before pursuing his passion for art in Düsseldorf and Berlin. In Paris he joined the influential writers' group *Gruppe 47* (Group 47), and published poetry and plays, and his first novel, *The Tin Drum* (1959). The book prompted accusations of blasphemy and pornography in Germany, and was banned in Gdansk, the now communist city, where it was set. However, it earned its author worldwide acclaim, and, in 1999, the Nobel Prize in Literature.

Grass used his hero, the tiny, fierce figure of Oskar Matzerath with his tin drum and a scream that could break glass, to revisit memories of the war's atrocities and its complacent aftermath, and illuminate them with a mix of magic, fantasy, and hindsight. He continued to develop his writing style in *Cat and Mouse* (1961) and *Dog Years* (1963), which with *The Tin Drum* made up his Danzig Trilogy; and in *Crabwalk* (2002), which centered on the real-life sinking by a Russian submarine of the *Wilhem Gustloff*, a refugee ship carrying thousands of Germans.

An earnest moralist, Grass became a ghostwriter for politician Willy Brandt's Social Democrats, authored a collection of political works, and alienated many when he opposed the reunification of Germany in 1990, fearing that a united Germany would reinvent itself as an aggressive nation-state. He died at the age of 87, near his home in Lübeck, northern Germany.

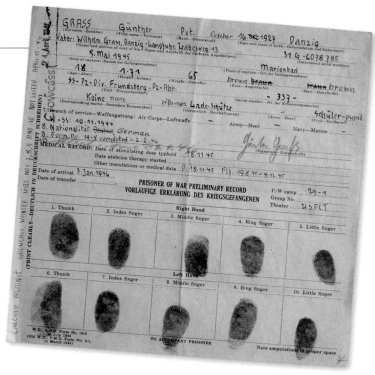

△ **WAR RECORD**
This registration form from US occupation forces in postwar Germany records Grass's membership of the Waffen SS. The writer claimed that he was drafted and that he never fired a shot in anger.

▽ **FLOUNDER IN HAND**
A talented sculptor, Grass made this bronze after the publication of his novel *The Flounder* in 1977. The book, loosely based on a fairy tale, became a best seller in Germany.

## ON STYLE
### Broadened reality

Grass's novels are often described as "magical realism" because of their interplay between historically accurate events and flights of fantasy and lyrical diversions. However, Grass preferred the term "broadened reality" for his style of writing. In *The Tin Drum*, he undermines expectations of realist writing with his "unreliable narrator" Oskar, who begins his story in a psychiatric institution. Grass slips from first- to third-person narration, and even hands over the pen to another character to provide a different perspective.

**THE COVER OF *THE TIN DRUM* WAS BASED ON GRASS'S OWN DESIGNS**

# Gabriel García Márquez

## 1927–2014, COLOMBIAN

One of the greatest Spanish-language authors of all time, García Márquez was a master of magical realism. His stories combine fantasy, folklore, and history to reveal the beauty and madness of Latin America.

In 1967, Gabriel García Márquez wrote the novel that would rescue his family from poverty and go on to sell more than 30 million copies worldwide. The 40-year-old writer produced *One Hundred Years of Solitude* in a frenzy of creativity, but its seeds were sown much earlier. García Márquez's masterpiece centers on a village called Macondo, surrounded by banana plantations, which he reimagined from his childhood in the small Colombian town of Aracataca.

On March 6, 1927, García Márquez was the first of 11 children born to Luisa Santiaga Márquez Iguarán and Gabriel Eligio García, a telegraph operator turned pharmacist. For his first eight years he lived with his grandparents in Aracataca. His grandfather, Nicolás Márquez Mejía, a retired army general who had fought for the liberals in Colombia's Thousand Days' War, became the center of his world and inspired many of his future characters. García Márquez soaked up the veteran's war stories and was also profoundly influenced by his grandmother, Doña Tranquilina Iguarán Cotes, who peopled the old house with ghosts, and delivered fantasies and premonitions with the conviction of truth. Reunited with his parents, the boy moved between Colombian

⊳ **TRUE TO TYPE**
García Márquez claimed that he could not "write in hotels or borrowed rooms or on borrowed typewriters." The machine he used has itself become a widely exhibited icon.

towns as his father struggled to make a living from homeopathy. Escape came in the form of a scholarship to a state-run boarding school outside Bogotá. Guaranteed three meals a day, "the kid from the coast" became a bookworm, poet, and star student.

The family hoped that their eldest son would pursue a respectable profession, so García Márquez set off to study law in Bogotá and then Cartagena. He continued to nurture his passion for writing, contributing articles to newspapers, and eventually abandoned his legal studies, certain that he wanted to become a writer.

### Early experiences

In his 20s, García Márquez lodged above a bordello in Barranquilla while he scraped together a living from journalism. In his autobiography, he claims that his first sexual encounter was with a prostitute when he was just 13; at 15 he was seduced by the wife of a steamship pilot; and he was

⊳ **BIRTHPLACE**
The house in Aracataca where Gabriel García Márquez grew up and absorbed the stories told by his grandparents has been transformed into a neat museum of the author's life.

⊳ **A LIFE IN WRITING**
García Márquez is pictured in 1982, the year in which he was awarded the Nobel Prize in Literature. He continued writing well into his 70s; his last novel, *Memories of My Melancholy Whores*, was published in 2004.

" All **human** beings have three lives: **public, private,** and **secret**. "
GABRIEL GARCIA MARQUEZ

> " **The truth** is that there's not a **single line** in all my **work** that does not have a basis in **reality**. The problem is that Caribbean reality resembles the **wildest imagination**. "

GABRIEL GARCIA MARQUEZ

△ **A SINGULAR FOCUS**
An obsessive worker and notorious chain-smoker, García Márquez reported that he "did not get up for 18 months" when he was working on *One Hundred Years of Solitude*.

later forced to play Russian roulette with a revolver after a police officer found him in bed with his wife. Outrageous sexual encounters and the generosity of prostitutes became prominent features of his writing.

The young reporter joined the Barranquilla Group of writers and journalists and became a voracious reader of Hemingway, Twain, Melville, and Faulkner, admiring the way the latter evoked the Deep South in the public's imagination. He also consumed Dickens, Tolstoy, Kafka, and Proust, and the internal monologues of Virginia Woolf and James Joyce. "I cannot imagine how anyone would even think of writing a novel without having at least a vague idea of the 10,000 years of literature that have gone before," he said in an interview.

### Early fiction writing

García Márquez's political affiliations hardened in the face of La Violencia, a 10-year period of civil war and repression in Colombia that led to as many as 300,000 deaths. In 1955, his first novella, *Leaf Storm*, was published, and in the same year he scooped a story about a sailor washed overboard from a naval vessel that was overloaded with contraband

goods. His articles, later published as *The Story of the Shipwrecked Sailor*, contradicted official accounts: now a marked man, he sought temporary refuge in Europe. He traveled to London, Paris, and Rome, and around Eastern Europe, before heading back to South America, to Venezuela. García Márquez worked for the Cuban news agency Prensa Latina, and became their correspondent in New York. In 1958, he returned to Colombia to marry Mercedes Barcha Prado, his elementary-school sweetheart. They explored the Southern states of the US, in the footsteps of Faulkner, before settling in Mexico City, where their two sons were born.

### Struggles and success

García Márquez continued to write fiction: a short story collection, *Big Mama's Funeral*, was set in the fictional town of Macondo (which resurfaced later in *One Hundred Years of Solitude*). *No One Writes to the Colonel*, the story of an impoverished army officer who bore a distinct resemblance to his grandfather, was his first literary hit. However, between the successes, there were also lean periods, when the family had to pawn their possessions to survive. And it was

△ **YELLOW SYMBOLISM**
The yellow butterflies that swarm around the character Mauricio in *One Hundred Years of Solitude* became an emblem of García Márquez himself.

after a tense four years of relative unproductivity that the first line of *One Hundred Years of Solitude* came to the writer on a drive to Acapulco: "Many years later, as he faced the firing squad, Col. Aureliano Buendía was to remember that distant afternoon when his father took him to discover ice." The novel was finished in August 1966, after 18 months of writing. The first print run of 8,000 copies sold out within a few weeks—an immense relief for the family, who by this time owed a year's rent.

### *One Hundred Years of Solitude*

In this novel, García Márquez reaches back to the deprivations of his childhood, the adult mysteries of the Aracataca house, the real-life massacre of banana plantation workers striking against the United Fruit Company, and his grandfather's

## KEY WORKS

**1967**
*One Hundred Years of Solitude*, translated into 25 languages, describes the 100-year span of the Buendía family in the town of Macondo.

**1981**
*Chronicle of a Death Foretold* is a solemn, fractured detective story told in reverse, that is based on an actual murder case.

**1985**
*Love in the Time of Cholera* is a romantic celebration of sex that centers on the passionate reunion of two former lovers.

**1989**
*The General in His Labyrinth* combines fiction and historical fact in an unflattering portrayal of the last days of Venezuelan leader Simón Bolívar.

**2002**
*Living to Tell the Tale* is an evocative memoir that reveals the influences and events that fueled García Márquez's first 25 years.

wartime experiences. He drew on lost traditions of magic, resurrection, and regeneration in his culture to forge a new kind of narrative—a metaphorical commentary on the centuries of oppression and Westernization in South America. As in Faulkner's creation of the Deep South, García Márquez had found a way to evoke South America and its complexity in the minds of readers.

## A culture hero

*One Hundred Years of Solitude* chimed with the revolutionary counterculture of the 1960s and it became the brightest flame in the explosion of literary creativity in South America known as the Latin American Boom. Magical realism was not invented by García Márquez, but his artistry inspired writers around the world,

including Isabel Allende in Chile and Salman Rushdie in Britain. The author feared that his future work would disappoint, but novels such as *Autumn of the Patriarch* (1975), *Chronicle of a Death Foretold* (1981), and *Love in the Time of Cholera* (1985) became best sellers. He went on to write 17 novels and short story collections and 8 nonfiction works, as well as screenplays for more than 20 movies.

◁ **A NEW BEGINNING**
*One Hundred Years of Solitude* was published in Spanish in 1967 to immense public acclaim. It went on to sell more than 30 million copies worldwide.

The author was a hero to the Latin American left but was denied entry to the US because of his political views. He received many honors in his life, notably the Nobel Prize in Literature in 1982, and counted presidents among his many friends; lifelong fan Bill Clinton lifted the ban on his entry to the US after three decades.

García Márquez wrote well into his 70s, publishing his memoir *Living to Tell the Tale* in 2002 and his last novel, *Memories of My Melancholy Whores*, in 2004. He died of lymphatic cancer at his home in Mexico City at the age of 87.

## IN CONTEXT
### Political engagement

The Latin American Boom was an explosion of literary creativity that gained worldwide attention for authors such as Gabriel García Márquez, Julio Cortázar, and Mario Vargas Llosa. These intellectuals were deeply engaged in the political struggles of Latin America and their writing was fueled by the energy of the 1960s counterculture. García Márquez was a lifelong friend and supporter of Fidel Castro, as well as a bitter opponent of the Chilean dictator General Augusto Pinochet.

**FIDEL CASTRO, 1998**

◁ **ARACATACA (MACONDO)**
García Márquez's hometown of Aracataca, Colombia, was the model for Macondo, which appears in several of the writer's books. In his time, it was a busy commercial hub, dominated by the financial muscle of American fruit companies.

▷ **MAYA ANGELOU, c.1976**
The author is pictured here a few years after the publication of her harrowing memoir *I Know Why the Caged Bird Sings*, for which she became so famous. According to Angelou, during the writing of the book she "stayed half drunk in the afternoon and cried all night."

# Maya Angelou

**1928–2014, AMERICAN**

Courageous and defiant, Angelou emerged from a childhood of abuse and neglect to become a legendary writer and a major figure of black empowerment. She was as dazzling in person as she was on the page.

As a child, Maya Angelou dreamed of becoming a real-estate agent; by the time of her death, she was acclaimed as a poet, playwright, essayist, movie director, entertainer, professor, and civil-rights activist. She served on two presidential committees, and received numerous honorary degrees, three Grammys for spoken-word albums, and the highly prestigious Presidential Medal of Freedom (2010). It had not, however, always been a charmed life.

### Early trauma

Angelou was born Marguerite Ann Johnson in St. Louis, Missouri. When her parents separated in 1931, she was sent by train—with a label around her wrist that read "To whom it may concern"—to live with her grandmother in rural Stamps, Arkansas. At the age of eight, after returning home to St. Louis, she was raped by her mother's boyfriend, who was later found dead. For almost five years after this, she refused to speak: "I thought, my voice killed him," she said. "I killed that man, because I told his name."

In her early teens, she dropped out of school to work in San Francisco as the first female, and black, streetcar conductor. The following year, she returned to education and became pregnant. Her only son, Guy Johnson, was born in 1945, soon after her graduation. She worked as a waitress,

⊲ **MISS CALYPSO**
In the 1950s, Angelou toured the US and Europe with her successful calypso-based stage act. This picture illustrated the cover of her album *Miss Calypso*, 1957.

a cook, and even a prostitute to support him, and in 1952 began a career as a dancer and singer in a San Francisco nightclub. At this time, she took the name Maya Angelou and embarked on the first of her three marriages.

After moving to New York in the late 1950s, Angelou became involved in the civil rights movement and joined the Harlem Writers Guild (a forum for African-American writers, founded in 1950), where she developed her skills in poetry writing and met several prominent black authors. In 1960, she went to Cairo, Egypt, as an editor for the *Arab Observer*, and later to Ghana as editor of the *Africa Review*.

### Literary breakthrough

Angelou returned to the US in 1964 and published prolifically for the next four decades. *I Know Why the Caged Bird Sings* (1970) was the first, and finest, part of her seven-volume autobiography. A candid account of the violence of racism and her childhood in the South, it was an immediate and resounding triumph,

praised for its innovative blend of autobiography and literary fiction.

Angelou was acclaimed as a poet, producing verse that won her cult status, as in the rousing "Still I Rise" and "Phenomenal Woman" (both 1978). Her various themes range from love and the indomitability of the human spirit to issues surrounding race, gender, and discrimination.

She was a charismatic performer of her own work, as evident at the inauguration of President Bill Clinton in 1993, when she read her poem "On the Pulse of Morning," with its celebration of diversity and strident message of hope: "History, despite its wrenching pain, / Cannot be unlived, but if faced / With courage, need not be lived again." When awarding Angelou the National Medal of the Arts in 2000, Clinton ventured that America owes her a "great debt" for her tireless insistence on presenting "the raw truth," but also for "keeping us looking toward the morning."

Angelou's final autobiographical book, *Mom & Me & Mom*, a tribute to her mother and grandmother, was published in 2013, the year before she died at her home in North Carolina.

△ **CAMPAIGN BUTTONS**
Through her civil rights work, Angelou met Malcolm X, with whom she planned the beginnings of the Organization of African-American Unity, and Martin Luther King, Jr., who inspired her to raise funds for the Southern Christian Leadership Conference.

### IN CONTEXT
## Literary influences

Some of Angelou's work continues a tradition initiated by African-American slave songs and slave narratives, including the extraordinary, seminal autobiography *Narrative of the Life of Frederick Douglass* (1845) by the escaped slave Frederick Douglass. She was also well versed in the work of 20th-century black authors such as Zora Neale Hurston, W. E. B. Du Bois, Paul Lawrence Dunbar, and Ralph Ellison. These writers were either influenced by or were active in the Harlem Renaissance, a flowering of African-American cultural pride that arose in New York in the 1920s and '30s and embraced literature, theater, music, and the visual arts.

*NARRATIVE OF THE LIFE OF FREDERICK DOUGLASS*, FRONTISPIECE, 1845

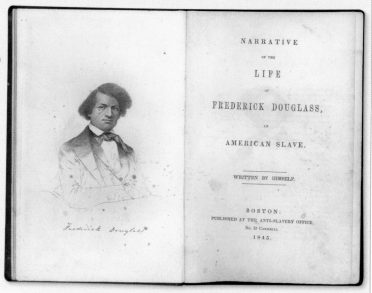

# Milan Kundera

## BORN 1929, CZECH–BORN FRENCH

Novelist and essayist Kundera is celebrated for his playful, erotic storytelling, which shined a spotlight on the political turmoil of his homeland, Czechoslovakia.

Milan Kundera has lived nearly half his life in France, in exile from his native Czechoslovakia (the Czech Republic). But most readers see him as Czech as a result of his two iconic novels, *The Book of Laughter and Forgetting* (1979) and *The Unbearable Lightness of Being* (1984), works that are laced with razor-sharp satire on the mid-20th-century invasions of his country.

### Liberty and oppression

Kundera was born in Brno in 1929, the son of a concert pianist and musicologist, and studied music before turning to writing. As a youth during World War II, he witnessed the devastation caused by the German invasion of Czechoslovakia. After the Communist Party seized power in 1948, he joined the party but was expelled while still a student for "anti-party activities." He studied literature and aesthetics in Prague before switching to scriptwriting and movie direction, and became a teacher of literature after graduating in 1952. He was readmitted to the Communist Party in 1956.

In the 1960s, under Alexander Dubček, Czechoslovakia saw a period of social liberty known as the Prague Spring. During this time, radical Czech writers, including Kundera and the playwright Václav Havel, attracted international recognition. Kundera turned from poetry and plays to a first novel, *The Joke* (1967), which evoked Stalinist-era Czechoslovakia. In the story, a subversive postcard sent to a serious-minded girlfriend unleashes a chain of consequences, including hard labor in the mines.

A Soviet-led invasion in 1968 resulted in a ban on the works of radical writers. Kundera was expelled from the party once again, and also from his university post. In 1975, he was allowed to immigrate with his wife of eight years, Věra Hrabánková, and began teaching at the University of Rennes in France.

### The French years

Kundera's next three novels focus on disempowered people at the mercy of external forces. *The Book of Laughter and Forgetting* is a loose narrative of personal and imagined stories on the denial of memory and the obliteration of historical truth—a practice of the Soviet regime, which would literally airbrush undesirable officials out of photographs. *The Unbearable Lightness of Being* skates across the lives of four intellectuals between the Prague Spring and the Russian invasion. It was followed in 1990 by *Immortality*, Kundera's last title written in Czech. In his recent novels in French, which include *The Festival of Insignificance* in 2014, and in his essays, Kundera is philosophically rather than politically engaged.

Although the Velvet Revolution in 1989 returned democracy to what has since become the Czech Republic and Slovakia, Kundera rarely returns to his homeland. He now identifies himself as a French writer and his work as French literature.

▷ **KUNDERA IN PARIS, 1979**
The author is pictured here in the year in which *The Book of Laughter and Forgetting* was published. The book is made up of seven separate narratives.

## ON STYLE
### Subverting realism

In Kundera's philosophical work *The Art of the Novel*, he deplores realist writing and pays tribute to the unfettered joyfulness of stories by Cervantes and Rabelais. In his own novels, the author often intrudes into the text to question the choice of words and actions. Characters are partially sketched, to be filled in by the reader's imagination. Political satire is mingled with eroticism and fun, but disturbing images of joyless sex and orgies suggest a commentary on humanity. Linear reading is often undermined by broken chronology and philosophical musings, but the development of various themes, such as "forgetting" and "angels," gives the text coherence.

**FIRST GERMAN EDITION OF** *THE JOKE*

◁ **INVASION, 1968**
Citizens of Prague surround Soviet tanks during the invasion of Czechoslovakia on August 20, 1968. The invasion was launched by the Soviet leader, Leonid Brezhnev, to curtail reforms and growing revolutionary fervor in the country.

# Chinua Achebe

## 1930–2013, NIGERIAN

Achebe is often hailed as the founding father of African literature. His postcolonial novels about Nigeria offered a voice to dispossessed people and inspired the development of a dazzling canon of global literature.

### ON STYLE
**Enriched English**

Achebe was raised speaking Igbo, but he wrote his novels in English because he felt that he could use the language of colonization as a powerful weapon in the struggle to retell his people's story. In his writing, he enriched standard English with pidgin, the cadence of Igbo speech, and elements of proverbs and myths from Nigeria's rich oral tradition. He wrote of *Things Fall Apart*: "I knew I couldn't write like Dickens or Conrad. My story would not accept that. So you had to make an English that was new. Whether it was going to work or not, I couldn't tell." His unique language propelled the book to critical success.

Novelist Chinua Achebe was born in his ancestral home of Ogidi, a small town in Igboland in southeast Nigeria, in 1930. He was christened Albert Chinualumogu Achebe by his parents, who were converts to the Protestant Church Missionary Society and had abandoned their tribal religion. Chinua attended Christian Sunday school and learned English at school but spoke Igbo at home, where traditional storytelling and ceremonies were integral to his childhood, which he shared with his five siblings. "We lived at the crossroads of cultures," recalled Achebe, who later dropped the tribute to Victorian England in his name. His was the last generation of Africans to hear from their elders what life was like before the white man came. The tension between tribal traditions and the disruptive power of colonialism became the bedrock of his writing.

### Academic promise

At 13, Achebe passed the entrance exams to the prestigious Government College in Umuahia, a colonial school set up to educate Nigeria's future elite. Modeled on the English private school, it imposed English as a common tongue on boys who spoke a variety of Nigerian languages. Achebe recalled being punished for using Igbo when he asked someone to pass him the soap.

Achebe won a scholarship to study medicine at University College in Idaban, but he changed to English literature. He pursued his interest in world religions and African cultures and read the classics, but found literary representations of Africa offensive. Irish author Joyce Cary's novel *Mister Johnson* was offered as a fine example of writing about Africa, but Achebe and his fellow students regarded its Nigerian hero as an "embarrassing nit wit" portrayed with an undercurrent of distaste. In his semiautobiographical *Home and Exile* (2000), Achebe maintains that Joseph Conrad's lurid descriptions of savages in *Heart of Darkness* typified the racist literature produced during 500 years of European presence in Africa.

### The African trilogy

After graduating, Achebe taught English in a ramshackle school in Oba, before moving to Lagos to help produce radio programs for the Nigerian Broadcasting Service. In 1956, he made his first trip to London as part of a British Broadcasting Corporation staff training program. He took with him a story that he was writing, in which his intention was to hand the narrative of the so-called dark continent back to its people. This story—*Things Fall Apart*—became the first part of a trilogy based on a fictional Nigerian village and its cataclysmic contact with English colonizers in the late

◁ **IGBO CULTURE**
Masked performances of dance, music, and drama are a key feature of Igbo culture. Achebe's stories draw heavily on Igbo song-tales, ballads, and fables.

**50TH ANNIVERSARY EDITION OF** *THINGS FALL APART*

▷ **CHINUA ACHEBE, NEW YORK**
Achebe is pictured here during his tenure at Bard College in New York. Through his writing, the author provided a new and liberating version of African history.

"There was a **writer** named **Chinua Achebe** in whose company the **prison walls fell down**."
NELSON MANDELA

△ **THE BIAFRAN CIVIL WAR**
In 1967, the Igbo people of eastern Nigeria established the new state of Biafra. The subsequent war with Nigeria caused the deaths of millions of Biafrans, mainly from starvation.

◁ *ARROW OF GOD*
The third part of what is now called Achebe's African Trilogy was first published in 1964. Its title references an Igbo saying in which an "arrow of God" is a person who delivers God's judgment.

19th century. With an intransigent, proud warrior called Okonkwo at its center, the novel describes a tribal society rich in commerce, culture, religion, and justice. It was written in English and showed the world that, in Achebe's words, "African people did not hear of civilization for the first time from Europeans." A novelist friend in London offered to help get the book published, but Achebe decided to continue working on the manuscript in Nigeria before sending his only copy to a London agency; the package was misplaced and lay in the corner of an office for months before it was eventually championed by an editor at Heinemann Educational.

Achebe borrowed the title for his novel from W. B. Yeats's poem "The Second Coming," which was written in the aftermath of World War I. The line "Things fall apart; the center cannot hold ..." aptly describes the effect of colonizers on tribal societies. Published in 1958, *Things Fall Apart* proved to have global relevance. It has been translated into 57 languages and remains the world's most widely read African novel. Nelson Mandela declared that the book was his solace during his 27-year imprisonment on South Africa's Robben Island.

**Corruption and colonialism**
Back in Lagos, a city teeming with migrants from the villages and in a state of flux as Nigeria approached independence, Achebe produced his second novel, *No Longer at Ease* (1960), which picks up the story of the grandson of Okonkwo making his way in a city mired in corruption.

"Those who **win** tell **the story**; those who are **defeated** are **not heard**."

CHINUA ACHEBE, *HOME AND EXILE*

## KEY WORKS

**1958**
*Things Fall Apart* deals with a fictionalized tribal village and its cataclysmic contact with colonizers.

**1960**
Set in the run-up to independence, *No Longer at Ease* centers on a man's struggle with bribery and corruption.

**1983**
In his polemic *The Trouble with Nigeria*, Achebe addresses the failure of his country's leadership.

**1987**
*Anthills of the Savannah* follows the lives of three friends oppressed by the military regime.

**2000**
*Home and Exile* discusses the power of stories to dispossess or empower, depending on who holds the pen.

**2012**
*There Was A Country: A Personal History of Biafra* reopens the discussion about the Nigerian Civil War.

The final novel in the trilogy, *Arrow of God* (1964), is based on a story that Achebe uncovered while working in radio—the history of an Igbo priest who was imprisoned for refusing to collaborate with British colonizers. During this period in Lagos, Achebe met Christie Chinwe Okoli, a student from Ibadan University; they married in 1961.

### An independent people

*A Man of the People* (1966) was written as a comic satire about a fictional coup, but when the breakaway region of Biafra sought independence from Nigeria, Achebe was treated with suspicion for his prescient tale. He fled to Igboland, where he embarked on peacekeeping missions that focused the world's attention on the starvation and slaughter of thousands of Igbo children in the Biafran Civil War. His own home was bombed and his best friend, the poet Christopher Okigwo, was killed. Achebe's collection of poems *Beware Soul Brother* (1971) and a volume of short stories *Girls at War and Other Stories* (1972) draw on these wartime experiences.

After the Nigerian government retook the region in 1970, Achebe taught at the University of Nigeria in Nsukka, and worked with Heinemann to establish a canon of literature by African writers. Throughout the 1980s,

Achebe split his time between political activity and teaching at universities in Nigeria and in the US. His novel *Anthills of the Savannah* (1987) reflects a Nigerian society that is bogged down by corruption, failed leadership, and subservience to foreign manipulation. One of his three protagonists, Ikem, describes the failure of rulers to make links with the poor and dispossessed of his country as "the bruised heart that throbs painfully at the core of the nation's being."

### In the US

Achebe had returned to Nigeria from the US in 1990 to celebrate his 60th birthday when he was involved in a car accident that left him paralyzed from the waist down. He accepted teaching posts that would ensure his future care at Bard College, New York, and then at Brown University, Rhode Island, but remained politically engaged with his homeland, commenting on the plundering of the country's wealth by the military dictator General Sani Abacha in the 1990s, and the more recent incitement of conflict between Muslims and Christians for political gain.

On a poignant trip back to his homeland in 2009, Achebe was greeted as a national celebrity and honored for his dedication to the myths and legends of his ancestors. Over his lifetime, Achebe wrote five novels, five books of nonfiction, and several collections of short stories and poems, winning the Man Booker International Prize for Fiction among numerous other awards.

Achebe continued to teach in the US until his death in 2013 at the age of 82. The writer was laid to rest in his home village of Ogidi.

△ **GENERAL SANI ABACHA**
Under Abacha's dictatorship (1993–1998), Nigeria's oil wealth was pocketed by the leadership, its infrastructure declined, and freedom of expression was curtailed—a move marked by the murder of the writer Ken Saro-Wiwa in 1995.

### IN CONTEXT
#### A lifetime in Nigeria

Achebe's life and novels are inextricably bound to the troubled history of Nigeria. The early tribal memories of his family, his colonial school days, and the contrast between his life as part of the intellectual elite and the poverty of the general population informed much of his writing. After 50 years of British rule, Nigeria's independence was dogged by coups and countercoups; assassinations of leaders, writers, and campaigners; and the presidential squandering of extraordinary wealth from its oil fields. In 1967, Achebe witnessed Biafra's failed bid for autonomy and a brutal civil war. Fifty years later, its anniversary was marked by protests and renewed demands for independence for his home territory.

THE BIAFRAN FLAG FLIES ON THE 50TH ANNIVERSARY OF THE BIAFRAN SECESSION

# Directory

## Louis-Ferdinand Céline

### 1894–1961, FRENCH

Céline was a novelist of the first rank whose reputation was damaged by his political attitudes. Of lower-middle-class origins, he was wounded in World War I, and after the conflict he became a doctor, choosing to practice in a rough district of Paris.

His novel *Journey to the End of the Night* was a stunning debut, a black comedy written in a colloquial style, replete with vulgarities. *Death on Credit*, a coming-of-age novel, extended the stylistic innovation by repeated use of ellipses, which became Céline's trademark.

In the 1930s, he published scurrilous anti-Semitic writings, and in World War II he associated with collaborators during the Nazi occupation. After the war he spent a year in a Danish prison. Allowed back to France, he published a series of fictionalized accounts of his experiences as an eyewitness of the collapse of the Third Reich, which were rambling hallucinatory monologues veering between bitterness, farce, and tragedy.

**KEY WORKS:** *Journey to the End of the Night*, 1932; *Death on the Installment Plan*, 1936; *Guignol's Band*, 1943; *North*, 1960

## Giuseppe Tomasi di Lampedusa

### 1896–1957, ITALIAN

Tomasi di Lampedusa is famous for a single novel that he did not live to see published. He was born into the declining Sicilian aristocracy and inherited the title of Prince of Lampedusa on his father's death in 1934. As a young man, he fought in World War I, but otherwise his life was not eventful. He tried to avoid trouble during Italy's fascist period, although his palace in Palermo was destroyed by Allied bombing in 1943.

He began work on his masterpiece, *The Leopard*, in the late 1940s, walking every day to a café where he sat and wrote. A sumptuous novel set in Sicily during the Risorgimento (the movement that saw Italy unified as a single state), it was rejected by the two publishers to whom he submitted it. Soon after his death, the book was published to great acclaim. His other works included a short story, *The Professor and the Mermaid*; some memoirs; and critical essays.

**KEY WORKS:** *The Leopard*, 1958; *Stories*, 1961

## Witold Gombrowicz

### 1904–1969, POLISH

Novelist and dramatist Gombrowicz was born into the nationalist Catholic landed gentry—a group whose social and cultural attitudes he subverted throughout his life. By the time he published his first book of stories, *Memoirs of a Time of Immaturity*, in 1933 he was an established figure in Polish literary circles.

His first novel, *Ferdydurke*, a grotesque satire about an adult transported back to adolescence, is now regarded as a Modernist masterpiece. At the outbreak of World War II, Gombrowicz became an exile in Argentina. He stayed there for 24 years, mostly living in penury. The postwar communist regime in Poland banned his works. Starting in the 1950s, however, his novels and plays began to attract attention in translation. Moving back to Europe in 1963, he lived chiefly in France, enjoying a modest celebrity. His eccentric *Journals*, published between 1957 and 1966, are regarded as being among his most interesting works.

**KEY WORKS:** *Ferdydurke*, 1937; *Yvonne, Princess of Burgundy*, 1938; *Trans-Atlantyk*, 1953; *Pornography*, 1960

## ▽ W. H. Auden

### 1907–1973, ENGLISH

Wystan Hugh Auden was a prolific poet who made technically adroit use of traditional verse forms. His early poetry, oblique and cryptic,

△ W. H. AUDEN

was haunted by the industrialized landscapes of the English Midlands where he had been raised. In the 1930s, he was viewed as the leader of a group of left-wing poets who had met at Oxford University.

Auden showed a firm commitment to the anti-fascist cause during the Spanish Civil War (1936–1939). His poems, however, expressed the frustrations of same-sex love and a generalized cultural malaise, rather than a specific political viewpoint. In 1939, Auden moved to the US, becoming an American citizen in 1946. He declared his opposition to committed verse, proclaiming that "poetry makes nothing happen." His later works reflected his Christian beliefs and pessimism about modern civilization. His most popular poems include "Miss Gee" (1938), "Funeral Blues" (1938), and "September 1, 1939" (1940).

**KEY WORKS:** *Poems*, 1930; *Look, Stranger!*, 1936; *The Age of Anxiety*, 1947; *The Shield of Achilles*, 1955

△ JORGE AMADO

---

## Alberto Moravia

1907–1990, ITALIAN

Alberto Pincherle, known by the pen name Alberto Moravia, was a novelist and short-story writer who chronicled the lives of the Italian bourgeoisie, laying bare their financial and sexual cravings, pettiness, and hypocrisies.

In childhood Moravia suffered bone tuberculosis, which he described as one of the two most formative experiences of his life—the other was living under fascist rule. He built his reputation as a writer during the Mussolini era; he published his first novel in 1929, worked as a newspaper journalist, and helped set up two literary review magazines. Several of his books were banned by the fascist authorities.

It was in the period after World War II that he established himself as a renowned popular novelist, writing in a straightforward, realist style but with a sharp eye for the murky psychological roots of Italy's new

consumer society and its flawed democracy. His writing began to decline in the 1960s. Late in life, he was elected as an Italian communist deputy to the European Parliament.

**KEY WORKS:** *Time of Indifference*, 1929; *The Conformist*, 1951; *Roman Tales*, 1954; *Two Women*, 1957

---

## Elizabeth Bishop

1911–1979, AMERICAN

One of the finest American poets of the 20th century, Elizabeth Bishop was born in Massachusetts but, after her father's death and her mother's confinement to a psychiatric institution, she spent much of her childhood with relatives in rural Nova Scotia.

She began writing poetry at Vassar College, New York, under the influence of poet Marianne Moore. Her work reflected a widely traveled life, with long sojourns in Paris, Florida, and Brazil. Nourished by precise observation and often employing traditional verse forms, her poetry

avoids the confessional mode, but nonetheless often obliquely relates to her frequent depression, alcoholism, and lesbian relationships.

A perfectionist, Bishop published just 101 poems in her lifetime. Although she received recognition from the 1950s onward, she only posthumously achieved the status her work deserved. Her most famous poems include "A Miracle for Breakfast" (1935), "The Fish" (1946), and "One Art" (1976).

**KEY WORKS:** *North & South*, 1946; *Questions of Travel*, 1965; *The Complete Poems*, 1969; *Geography III*, 1976

---

## △ Jorge Amado

1912–2001, BRAZILIAN

Novelist Jorge Amado was the son of a plantation owner in Bahia, northern Brazil. He published his first book at 18. Writing as a Marxist realist, he depicted the brutality and exploitation at the heart of Brazilian society. Under the rule of dictator Getúlio Vargas his books were burned

and he was forced into exile. Returning to Brazil in 1954, he turned to writing more relaxed novels rich in fantasy, humor, and sensuality. *Gabriela, Clove and Cinnamon*, the first work in his new style, was a best seller both in Brazil and abroad. The almost equally successful *Dona Flor and Her Two Husbands* came close to magical realism with its supernatural resolution of insoluble conflict.

Despite becoming a popular novelist, Amado remained controversial for his frank depictions of women's sexuality. Later in life, he continued to address major issues, such as the need to reconcile the European and African elements in Brazilian culture.

**KEY WORKS:** *Jubiabá*, 1935; *The Violent Land*, 1943; *Gabriela, Clove and Cinnamon*, 1958; *Dona Flor and Her Two Husbands*, 1966

---

## Octavio Paz

1914–1998, MEXICAN

Poet and essayist Octavio Paz was born into a family of intellectuals in Mexico City. He wrote poetry from an early age, publishing his first volume of verse in 1933. Although deeply concerned with his native country (his essay *The Labyrinth of Solitude* is a profound meditation on Mexican identity and culture), Paz was much influenced by European Modernism, especially the French surrealists.

Beginning in 1945, he served abroad as a diplomat. The poetry in his volume *East Slope* was inspired by his time in India, where he served as ambassador starting in 1962. In 1968, he resigned from the diplomatic corps in protest at a government massacre of students in Mexico City. Regarded as Mexico's leading intellectual figure, as well as a major poet, he was awarded the coveted Cervantes Prize in 1981 and the Nobel Prize in Literature in 1990.

**KEY WORKS:** "Between the Stone and the Flower," 1941; *The Labyrinth of Solitude*, 1950; "The Sunstone," 1957; *East Slope*, 1969

## Camilo José Cela

1916–2002, SPANISH

Novelist Camilo José Cela y Trulock used innovative literary techniques to present a harshly misanthropic vision of Spanish society, determined not "to disguise life with the mad mask of literature." Born in Galicia, Spain, he fought on the Francoist side in the Spanish Civil War. His sensational first novel, *The Family of Pascual Duarte*, depicted the brutalizing effects of poverty and backwardness through the death-row confessions of a callous and homicidal peasant.

Some of his books were initially banned in Spain, including *The Hive*, which is considered by many to be his masterpiece. Its bleak view of life in Madrid is presented through a cast of hundreds of characters followed over three days. Cela took experimentation to extremes in his later works. The novel *Christ Versus Arizona* (1988) is written as a single sentence over more than a hundred pages. He was awarded the Nobel Prize in Literature in 1989.

KEY WORKS: *The Family of Pascual Duarte*, 1942; *Convalescence Wing*, 1944; *The Hive*, 1950

## Carson McCullers

1917–1967, AMERICAN

The novelist Carson McCullers was born Lula Carson Smith in Columbus, Georgia. Although she spent most of her adult life in New York and Paris, the Deep South remained the territory of her imagination.

McCullers published her first short story, "Wunderkind," in 1936. Her most celebrated novels of the 1940s—*The Heart is a Lonely Hunter*, *Reflections in a Golden Eye*, and *The Member of the Wedding*—are powerful, sensitive studies in social exclusion, physical disability, and psychological disturbance.

McCullers herself led a troubled existence, plagued by severe illness and alcoholism. Her relationship to

△ HEINRICH BÖLL

Reeves McCullers, whom she married, divorced, and remarried, ended with his suicide in 1953. The novella *The Ballad of the Sad Café* was her last significant work. She wrote a play, *The Square Root of Wonderful*, in 1958 and a novel, *Clock Without Hands*, in 1961, but they did not achieve the success of her earlier work.

KEY WORKS: *The Heart is a Lonely Hunter*, 1940; *Reflections in a Golden Eye*, 1941; *The Member of the Wedding*, 1946; *The Ballad of the Sad Café*, 1951

## △ Heinrich Böll

1917–1985, GERMAN

The novelist and short-story writer Heinrich Böll came from an artistic Catholic family in Cologne. His key formative experience was fighting as a soldier in World War II under a Nazi regime that he loathed.

After the war, he articulated the ordinary German soldier's experience of the conflict, and of the disillusioned homecoming to a physically and morally ruined country. His early style, influenced by American writers such as Ernest Hemingway, was realist, direct, and sardonic. His work evolved in technical complexity as he became an outspoken critic of West German society, with its heartless materialism and amnesia about embarrassing historical facts.

Böll's work was often combative, taking on the Catholic Church in *The Clown* (1963) and the gutter press in *The Lost Honor of Katharina Blum*. He was the only West German writer widely read in communist East Germany. Böll was awarded the Nobel Prize in Literature in 1972.

KEY WORKS: *The Train Was on Time*, 1949; *Traveler, If You Come to Spa*, 1950; *Group Portrait With Lady*, 1971; *The Lost Honor of Katharina Blum*, 1974

## J. D. Salinger

1919–2010, AMERICAN

Author of the teenage classic *The Catcher in the Rye*, Jerome David Salinger was born into a Jewish family in New York City. He began to build a reputation as a writer after returning from service in World War II, publishing the story "A Perfect Day for Bananafish" in *The New Yorker* in 1948.

*The Catcher in the Rye* was an instant success when it appeared in 1951. Its themes of teenage alienation and rebellion, explored through the voice of its troubled protagonist, Holden Caulfield, ensured that its popularity with adolescents grew over the years.

After publishing his *Nine Stories*, including the highly regarded "For Esmé—with Love and Squalor," Salinger moved from New York to New Hampshire and became a reclusive figure, fiercely defending his privacy. His output declined, only four stories appearing in the decade from 1953, all concerned with the fictional Glass family of New York. Both critical and popular opinion hold that *Franny and Zooey* was his last truly successful work. From 1965 onward, he published nothing.

**KEY WORKS:** *The Catcher in the Rye*, 1951; *Nine Stories*, 1953; *Franny and Zooey*, 1961

## Doris Lessing

1919–2013, BRITISH

Born Doris May Tayler, Lessing grew up on a farm in Southern Rhodesia (now Zimbabwe) owned by her British-born parents. By the time she moved to England in 1949, she was a staunch communist and a committed anticolonialist, and had survived two divorces. Her early books were set in Africa, including her first novel, *The Grass is Singing*, and four of the five volumes of her semiautobiographical *Children of Violence* series.

In the 1950s she grew disillusioned with communism. Published in 1962, *The Golden Notebook* showed her turning away from politically driven realism toward psychological analysis and formal innovation. Between 1979 and 1983, she defied expectations by experimenting with the science-fiction genre in her *Canopus in Argos* series. *The Good Terrorist* of 1985 was an impressive return to political subject matter. Lessing was awarded the Nobel Prize in Literature in 2007.

**KEY WORKS:** *The Grass is Singing*, 1950; *The Golden Notebook*, 1962; *Shikasta*, 1979; *The Good Terrorist*, 1985

## Shusaku Endo

1923–1996, JAPANESE

Novelist Shusaku Endo was a Japanese Catholic, an oddity in his society. In the 1950s he studied in Lyon, France, coming under the influence of radical French Catholic

writers such as the novelist George Bernanos. At this time, he experienced the first of several prolonged illnesses (with the result that hospitals feature prominently in his books).

Returning to Japan, he published novels critical of Japanese society, which he denounced as a heartless "mudswamp" inaccessible to the Christian message of love. His most famous novel, *Silence*, is an anguished story of Catholic missionaries whose faith is tested by the indifference and cruelty of the Japanese. But Endo also criticized the authoritarian stance of the Catholic Church, believing in Jesus as a figure of compassion and shared suffering rather than of authority and judgment. Works like his late novel, *Deep River*, about a group of Japanese tourists visiting India, are suffused with a warm humanity.

**KEY WORKS:** *White Man*, 1955; *The Sea and Poison*, 1957; *Silence*, 1966; *Deep River*, 1993

## Yukio Mishima

1925–1970, JAPANESE

Kimitake Hiraoka, known by the pen name Yukio Mishima, was the most prominent Japanese cultural personality of the post-World War II era. He was born into the elite society of Imperial Japan but experienced a traumatic youth laced with sadistic discipline and the humiliation of Japan's defeat in war. His first novel, *Confessions of a Mask*, exposed his sadomasochistic homoerotic fantasy life and made him a celebrity at 23.

Combining the influence of Western Modernism with a romanticized view of Japan's samurai past, he became prominent not only as a novelist and short-story writer but also as a playwright, actor, and filmmaker. Politically, he was a right-wing extremist committed to restoring the traditional power of the emperor.

In 1970, Mishima committed *suppuku* (ritual suicide by disemboweling) after leading his personal militia in a failed attempted coup. Shortly

before his death, he completed his final work—the four-volume series *Sea of Fertility*, an epic on Japanese life in the 20th-century.

**KEY WORKS:** *Confessions of a Mask*, 1948; *The Temple of the Golden Pavilion*, 1956; *The Sailor Who Fell from Grace with the Sea*, 1963; *The Sea of Fertility* tetralogy, 1965–1970

## ▽ Sylvia Plath

1932–1963, AMERICAN

As famous for her troubled life as for her confessional poetry and prose, Plath hailed from Massachusetts. Her German-born father, a professor of biology, died when she was just eight. Plath published poetry and stories at a young age and graduated from Smith College in 1955.

By this time she had already made her first suicide attempt and undergone psychiatric treatment, including electroshock therapy. These events later formed the subject of her only novel, *The Bell Jar*.

After moving to study at the University of Cambridge in England on a Fulbright Scholarship, Plath married English poet Ted Hughes. Her first volume of poetry, *The Colossus*, attracted only limited attention. Plath and Hughes had two children, but in September 1962, Hughes's infidelity led to their breakup. Around this time Plath wrote her most famous poems, including "Daddy" and "Lady Lazarus," published posthumously in the collection *Ariel*. She committed suicide in February 1963.

**KEY WORKS:** *The Colossus and Other Poems*, 1960; *The Bell Jar*, 1963; *Ariel*, 1965; *The Collected Poems*, 1981

△ **SYLVIA PLATH**

# WRITING TODAY

**CHAPTER 6**

# José Saramago

## 1922–2010, PORTUGUESE

Saramago's deeply held political beliefs produced a challenging body of work that deals with themes such as religion, power, exploitation, corruption, and social disintegration, often through allegorical satire.

Toward the end of his life, José Saramago noted that the starting point for his work is "the possibility of the impossible. I ask the reader to accept a pact; even if the idea is absurd, the important thing is to imagine its development." And so his long, elegant, unconventional sentences—sparsely punctuated and paragraphed, and with just an initial capital letter to signpost dialogue—propel the reader on magnificently inventive allegorical journeys that intertwine history and fantasy, the realistic and the bizarre.

Imaginative leaps such as these are chronicled in, for example, the exploits of a maimed soldier, his clairvoyant lover, and a wondrous flying machine in *Baltasar and Blimunda* (1982); in the detachment of the Iberian peninsula from Europe in *The Stone Raft* (1986); and in a city reduced to savagery following a plague of blindness in the harrowing political parable *Blindness* (1995). The metafictional, magical realist, and chatty style of Saramago's novels has led to comparisons with authors such as Cervantes, García Márquez, Borges, and Kafka.

### A clerical error

Saramago was born into a poor family in the rural village of Azinhaga. His father's last name was de Sousa, but a clerk—in drunkenness or as a prank—registered the boy at birth as "Saramago" (which was his father's nickname). In his teens, he trained as a car mechanic and later scraped together a living as a translator and journalist. *Land of Sin*, his first novel, was published when he was just 24, in 1947, the same year as the birth of his daughter, Violante, from his marriage to Ilda Reis.

### Lifeblood

Between 1966 and 1976, Saramago produced three volumes of poetry, but became best known for his novels. In 1969, he joined the outlawed Portuguese Communist Party—the main opposition to António de Oliveira Salazar's fascist dictatorship—and remained a staunch communist and atheist all his life. In 1974–1975, after the Carnation Revolution brought down Salazar's successor, he served as editor of the revolutionary daily paper *Diário de Notícias*, but was fired for his hard-line approach—he is said to have ousted all noncommunists from the journal. The author's reputation as an austere, arrogant, somewhat steely man may have arisen in this period, when his political beliefs, unpopular in a country that had been long immersed in extreme right-wing ideology, were so clearly on display.

Saramago did not win international acclaim until he was 60, with the translation into English of *Memorial do convento* (*Baltasar and Blimunda*). A raft of successful works followed, and in 1998 he became the first Portuguese-language writer to win the Nobel Prize. He died in Lanzarote in 2010, after suffering from leukemia. More than 20,000 people attended his funeral, which was held in Lisbon, Portugal.

## IN CONTEXT
### Writer and militant

Saramago stated that he couldn't imagine himself existing "outside any kind of social or political involvement." His political and religious beliefs formed the beating heart of much of his fiction and have frequently attracted anger and controversy. *The Stone Raft*, for example (an allegory about Iberia set adrift from Europe), was published in 1986, coinciding with Spain's and Portugal's entry into the European Community. An indictment of that union, the book was criticized in Portugal and beyond.

Five years later, in 1991, *The Gospel According to Jesus Christ* rocked Catholic Portugal for its depiction of Jesus as a desiring, fallible being and God as a manipulative, power-hungry deity. The Portuguese government, pressured by the Church, banned the text and blocked Saramago's nomination for a European literary prize in 1992. And in 2002, the writer caused further outrage during his tour of the West Bank by equating the plight of Palestinians under Israeli occupation with the suffering of Jews in Auschwitz.

# Derek **Walcott**

## 1930–2017, ST. LUCIAN

Walcott navigates, often in passages of great lyrical beauty, the relationship between his region's brutal colonial past and its complex modern identity via issues of origin, belonging, landscape, and memory.

In 1990, Derek Walcott published *Omeros*, an epic poem of astonishing richness that catapulted him to international fame. Two years later, at the age of 62, he was awarded the Nobel Prize in Literature. Although global fame came late in life, his name was well known to Caribbean readers for a prior body of outstanding work.

### A colonial legacy

Walcott was born on St. Lucia, a tiny island of dazzling beauty. His father was a painter and poet, his mother a school principal who would frequently recite the classics. The family spoke English at home, even though the local French patois was used widely on the island. Walcott respected his "good English education," which included an immersion in the Western literary canon—Homer, Shakespeare, Dante, Milton, Eliot, Pound, Joyce, and Yeats became major influences.

His works often allude to the language and forms of this Western tradition, but always in order to explore his own unique associations, many of which focus on issues of colonialism and Caribbean and African identity. *Omeros*, for example, references Homer's *Odyssey* and *Iliad* in its examination of themes of displacement and exile in a modern Caribbean setting.

### Acclaim and controversy

While still a teenager, Walcott self-published his first poetry collection with $200 borrowed from his mother. Two years later, he wrote and staged his first play, which kick-started a theatrical career that included the award-winning *Dream on Monkey Mountain* (1970), *Ti-Jean and His Brothers* (1972), and *The Joker of Seville* (1978). He founded the Trinidad Theatre workshop (1959), and the Boston Playwrights' Theatre at Boston University (1981). However, he was best known for his poetry.

Walcott graduated from the University of the West Indies in 1953, then moved to Trinidad to work as a reporter and critic. A breakthrough came in 1969, when his poetry collection *In a Green Night* was published in the US. From the 1980s until 2007, he held positions at universities, including Harvard and Yale, where he taught poetry, creative writing, and theater. Among his many awards was the prestigious T. S. Eliot Prize for Poetry for *White Egrets* (2010), his final collection.

Walcott's life was often turbulent: three marriages ended in divorce; his friendship with author V. S. Naipaul turned to open hostility; and in 2009, he withdrew his application for the post of Oxford Professor of Poetry, becoming Professor of Poetry at the University of Essex from 2010 to 2013.

Walcott's friendships with, and mutual admiration for leading poets such as Seamus Heaney and Joseph Brodsky underlined his position as one of the most respected poets on the world stage. He nevertheless identified "primarily, absolutely," as a Caribbean writer and continued to live and work in St. Lucia. Walcott died on March 17, 2017, at his home. He was given a state funeral.

△ **WHITE EGRETS**

In his poetry collection *White Egrets*, published seven years before his death, Walcott chose the elegant white egrets that grace the Caribbean sky to represent his intimate reflections on friendship, mortality, and the passing of time. He likened the rapaciousness of these "abrupt angels" to his own intellectual curiosity: "my pen's beak, plucking up wriggling insects / like nouns and gulping them."

## IN CONTEXT
### Paradise lost

The Caribbean landscape—the sea in particular—is a powerful motif in Walcott's work. The author was a fierce critic of the tourist industry that is having a devastating impact on the region's fragile ecosystem, and of governments' greed and lack of respect for their national, cultural, and environmental heritage. In 2013, he was particularly enraged by the St. Lucian government's plan to build a prominent hotel at the foot of the island's spectacular pitons: "What can you say," he despaired, "when a country approves of its own disfigurement?"

**THE JAGGED VOLCANIC PITONS, A FAMOUS ST. LUCIA LANDMARK**

◁ **ARTIST AND WRITER**
Derek Walcott, pictured here in his study, initially trained as an artist. His watercolors of vibrant Caribbean scenes are reproduced on some of his book covers. One of his seascapes is visible top right in this photograph.

# Toni Morrison

## BORN 1931, AMERICAN

Morrison's novels are powerfully poetic explorations of black American history. Her intense and honest writing has won international acclaim and made her the first ever black female Nobel laureate.

△ **PRESIDENTIAL HONORS**
Morrison is a highly celebrated novelist. In 1993, she was awarded the Nobel Prize in Literature for work "characterized by visionary force and poetic import." She received the Presidential Medal of Freedom (above)—the highest civilian award in the US—in 2012.

Chloe Wofford was born in the small industrial town of Lorain, Ohio. In her youth she was known by her nickname, Toni, and was later published under the surname Morrison—that of her husband, Harold, whom she married in 1958 and divorced in 1964.

Morrison was the second child of George, a welder, and Ramah, a domestic worker, who had moved from Georgia to escape the racism and segregation prevalent in the South. Her mother, a Methodist, had a skill for music, singing, and storytelling, especially the ghost stories passed down from her own mother. Supernatural tales and song clearly informed Morrison's later themes, and helped shape her incantatory prose style and acutely observed dialogue.

### Student and teacher

Encouraged by her parents, Morrison excelled at school and found great inspiration in literature, devouring everything from drawing-room

△ **A DIVIDED SOCIETY**
A party at an Alabama plantation graphically shows the realities of discrimination and segregation in the southern US—injustices that Morrison addressed in her fiction.

comedies to the classics. In 1949, she enrolled at Howard University in Washington, D.C. There she mixed with some of the most distinguished black intellectuals of the era, but was also forced to confront the realities of living in a segregated city beset by a stifling racial hierarchy.

After an MA at Cornell University in New York, Morrison embarked on a career as an English professor. She returned to teach at Howard, and joined a creative writing group. It was at Howard that she developed a short story that formed the premise of what was to become her first novel, *The Bluest Eye* (1970), which explores the exclusion of black women from popular culture.

The majority of Morrison's novels are historical. Through her work, she sets out to reclaim aspects of the African-American story that she considers previously "untold and unexamined." Writing from within, the author seeks to liberate viciously silenced voices— an act described by the character Sethe in the novel *Beloved* as "rememory." Morrison continues to write fiction; her latest novel, *God Help the Child*, was published in 2015.

◁ **A MULTIFACETED CAREER**
Morrison, pictured here in 1977, has published 11 novels and nearly as many nonfiction titles. She is a prominent advocate of black rights and an accomplished educator. From 1989 to 2006 she held a chair at Princeton, where she is now a professor emeritus.

### IN CONTEXT
#### Publishing successes

Divorced and with two children, Morrison worked as an editor with the publisher Random House in New York starting in 1967, writing only in the early hours while her children slept. She was a champion of black writing, developing *Contemporary African Literature* (1972), a collection that showcases the work of Wole Soyinka, Chinua Achebe, and Athol Fugard, among others. She also published the controversial autobiography of Muhammad Ali and produced *The Black Book* (1974), documenting black life in the US from slavery onward.

NIGERIAN AUTHOR CHINUA ACHEBE, WHO WAS PUBLISHED BY MORRISON

" **Her story** was **bearable** because it was his as well—to **tell**, to **refine** and **tell again**. "

TONI MORRISON, *BELOVED*

# Alice Munro

## BORN 1931, CANADIAN

Nobel Prize–winning author Munro is celebrated for revealing the wondrous in the everyday, crafting the finest short stories out of the lives and thoughts of ordinary folk in her native Canada.

Born in 1931, Alice Ann Laidlaw grew up on her father's struggling mink and fox fur farm on the outskirts of Wingham, a rural town in Huron County, Ontario, Canada. Alice and her mother were not a natural fit in the community: a teacher turned farmer's wife, and a "too smart for her own good" child who invented stories on the long walk to school. When her mother developed multiple sclerosis, Alice kept house and took care of her younger brother and sister.

She won a scholarship to study English and journalism at the University of Western Ontario, but her funds ran out before she graduated. By the age of 21, she was married

to another student, James Munro, had moved to West Vancouver, and had given birth to her first baby. Over the next 15 years, she produced short stories for magazines and radio, writing frantically through her pregnancies—and then during her babies' naps, school hours, and into the night—for fear she would never get the time again. Munro had three more daughters but her second child died shortly after birth. Years later she said in her Nobel Prize interview: "I was desperately consumed when I was writing, but I always got lunch for my children."

### Mastering the story

Munro was 37 when her first anthology, *Dance of the Happy Shades* (1968), was published and won the Governor General's Award, Canada's highest literary prize. By this time, the family had moved to Toronto and opened a bookstore. Munro then tried to write a

coming-of-age novel, but reverted to her familiar short-story format halfway through, publishing the collection as *Lives of Girls and Women* in 1971. "That's when I learned that I was never going to write a real novel because I could not think that way," Munro recalled. A master of revealing rather than telling, Munro writes stories with little action but with the depth of novels. She paints rich and complex characters and has a genius for digging down into their very core to reveal what makes all lives remarkable and often wicked.

### Late works

Since the 1980s, Munro has published a short-story collection at least once every four years. She has won nearly 20 major Canadian, UK, and US awards for titles such as *Open Secrets* (1994), *The Love of a Good Woman* (1998), and *Runaway* (2004), including the Man Booker International Prize in 2009 and the Nobel Prize in 2013.

After her second marriage to geographer Gerry Fremlin, Munro moved to Clinton in rural Ontario, within 20 miles (30 km) of where they both grew up. She retired from writing in 2013 at 81, her last book, *Dear Life*, incorporating four "not quite stories" that were the "closest things that I have to say about my life."

▽ **HURON COUNTY**
Munro mined riches from her humble origins in Huron County, Ontario. Her stories return time and again to rural communities with their complexity of characters and whispered histories.

## ON FORM
### Nonlinear storytelling

Munro was an early innovator of nonlinear storytelling, which leapfrogs between the present, the past, and the future. Her stories are veiled and sometimes never fully revealed; a relic held in the hand conjures a memory from the past, or a secret surfaces in the present through a newspaper clipping or from the lips of an unreliable witness. A narrator's account of an event may later be reported by another character, shedding light on the act of storytelling itself. Munro describes her writing as "natural" but not an easy gift. Her handwritten jottings are transcribed and typewritten, and are subject to intensive revision to capture life's subtlety and complexity in crystalline prose.

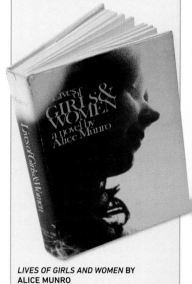

**LIVES OF GIRLS AND WOMEN BY ALICE MUNRO**

▷ **THE CANADIAN CHEKHOV**
Alice Munro was awarded the Nobel Prize in Literature at the age of 82—one of only 13 women to receive the award. Her work has been compared to Chekhov's—little happens but much is revealed.

# Nawal El Saadawi

**BORN 1931, EGYPTIAN**

El Saadawi has devoted much of her life to exposing the oppression of women in the Arab world and addressing issues of gender and class. Internationally acclaimed, she has been persecuted in her own country.

Nawal El Saadawi's writing is rooted in feminism, politics, and her experience as a doctor and psychiatrist in the Arab world. One of her best-known novels, *Women at Point Zero* (1975), tells the story of Firdaus, a proud, articulate woman condemned to death for killing a pimp. Banned in many Middle Eastern countries, the novel was based on a meeting that El Saadawi had with a woman, who was herself awaiting execution, in Egypt's notorious Qanatir Women's Prison.

El Saadawi was born in 1931 in Kafr Thala, a village on the banks of the Nile. Her political conscience developed early in life: in her autobiography, she records that when her grandmother told her that "a boy is worth 15 girls at least … Girls are a blight," she stamped her foot in rage. At the age of six, she underwent the horrific experience of female circumcision, which was commonly done in Egypt for religious and social reasons. "The pain was there like an abscess deep in my flesh," she wrote, and she never ceased to challenge the abusive practice in her work.

## Doctor, feminist, and activist

El Saadawi trained as a doctor at the University in Cairo and specialized in psychiatry. She returned to practice in her home village, where she witnessed first hand the brutalities inflicted on

**IN CONTEXT**
**Political activity**

El Saadawi has campaigned relentlessly against FGM and other forms of male oppression of women in the Arab world; in 1979–1980, she served as the UN Advisor for the Women's Program in Africa and the Middle East. She has opposed political Islam and has spoken out against Western imperialism and the class structure in Arab countries, which she holds to be forces that conspire to keep women second-class citizens. In 2011, she joined protests in Cairo's Tahrir Square that led to the fall of President Hosni Mubarak.

A WOMAN IN TAHRIR SQUARE DURING THE EGYPTIAN REVOLUTION, WHICH BEGAN AS A PROTEST AGAINST POLICE BRUTALITY

women, and wrote her first novel, *Memoirs of a Woman Doctor* (1958). In 1963, she was appointed Egypt's Director of Public Health but was fired following the publication of *Women and Sex* (1972), a critical discussion of female genital mutilation (FGM) and other oppressive practices. She came to be regarded by the authorities as a dangerous subversive, but continued to write prolifically.

In 1981, following her criticism of Egypt's President Sadat, El Saadawi was imprisoned in Qanatir for "crimes against the state." Here, she wrote *Memoirs from the Women's Prison—*

inscribing it on a roll of toilet paper using a smuggled eyebrow pencil. She was released three months later, after Sadat's assassination.

Increasing persecution and death threats prompted El Saadawi and her then husband to flee Egypt for the US where she held various academic posts. She returned to Egypt in 1996, and she continued to write and be politically active. Her recent works include *Zeina* (2009), a novel that follows the lives of two women, Bodour and her abandoned daughter Zeina, who confront patriarchal oppression in different ways.

> " **Danger** has been part of **my life** ever since I picked up a **pen** and **wrote**. Nothing is more **perilous** than **truth** in a world that **lies**. "
> NAWAL EL SAADAWI

▷ **A FORCE OF NATURE**
Nawal El Saadawi is a prolific author and fervent activist. Despite official censorship and censure, she has published more than 50 books, and recently claimed that she was "becoming more radical with age."

▷ **JOHN UPDIKE, 1991**
At the time that this photograph was taken, Updike was living in Beverly, Massachusetts, with his second wife, Martha Ruggles Bernhard, whom he had married in 1977.

# John Updike
## 1932–2009, AMERICAN

A remarkably prolific short-story writer and novelist, Updike stayed at the top of his profession for his entire career. His gift was to describe the business of everyday life in exquisite, sensuous, revelatory prose.

> "My **only duty** was to **describe reality** as it had **come to me**, to give **the mundane** its **beautiful due**."

JOHN UPDIKE, *EARLY STORIES*

John Updike was born in Reading, Pennsylvania, in 1932. Although his parents were poor, he achieved remarkable grades at school, earning a scholarship to Harvard, where he became editor of the *Harvard Lampoon*. He wanted to become a cartoonist, but before he could nurture that career, he was already earning good money as a writer.

By the mid-1950s, married and with a pregnant wife, Updike briefly lived in New York City. As a young contributor to the prestigious *The New Yorker* magazine he was edited by the great William Maxwell, who fostered the careers of many leading 20th-century authors, including J. D. Salinger, Eudora Welty, and John Cheever. In 1957, Updike moved with his family to the country, where he felt he belonged. He settled in Ipswich, Massachusetts, where his neighbors—hardworking, churchgoing, middle-class suburban folk—would provide the subject

◁ **THE NEW YORKER**
Updike was a regular contributor to *The New Yorker* magazine throughout his life, writing fiction, poetry, essays, and criticism.

matter for his novels for years to come. As a young writer, Updike was so prolific, and his work was in such high demand, that he was able to support his family with his writing at the age of 24.

### Chronicles of suburbia

In 1959, Updike published his first novel, *The Poorhouse Fair*, and followed it a year later with *Rabbit, Run*—the first in the "Rabbit" sequence that was to make him one of the America's foremost writers, and the book that many still consider to be his greatest achievement. A sequence of four novels and a novella follow Harry "Rabbit" Angstrom, an ordinary middle-class man in Brewer, Pennsylvania, from his youthful

aimlessness through to his wealthy (albeit unhappy and dissatisfied) middle age, and then death. The sequence is distinguished by Updike's extraordinarily rich prose, in which he makes every detail of ordinary life shine with beauty and significance. It is also notable because Updike aged at the same rate as his character, producing the books at roughly 10-year intervals. The series (1961–2000) won him two Pulitzer Prizes, and stands as an artistic monument to the loneliness, waywardness, and despair at the center of America's postwar economic boom.

Updike wrote about the decline of 1950s Christian morality and the effects on society of the sexual revolution of the 1960s in his novel *Couples* (1968). The book stirred up controversy for its detailed descriptions—which some critics thought overwrought—of adultery and carnality among a group of suburban professionals who use sex to mask their existential fears.

Updike's productivity and curiosity remained undiminished as he grew older, and later in life he experimented with a variety of subjects, writing novels about African dictatorship (*The Coup*, 1978), a postapocalyptic future (*Toward the End of Time*, 1997), and a prequel to *Hamlet* (*Gertrude and Claudius*, 2000), among many others. He died in a Massachusetts hospice following a battle with lung cancer.

◁ **POLLY DOLE HOUSE**
This charming historic house in Ipswich, Massachusetts, parts of which date back to 1680, is where John Updike and his first wife, Mary, raised their four children. The couple divorced in 1974.

---

## IN CONTEXT
### Recurring characters

Literary novelists such as John Updike and his contemporary Philip Roth (who wrote nine novels about his alter ego Nathan Zuckerman) became well known for writing series of books following one protagonist. Such series allow the author to chart the development of a character over time and explore the changing political and social backdrop in a way that is impossible in a single volume. Familiarity clearly also confers commercial advantages: readers like to follow a character's progression, and authors enjoy returning to themes. For Updike, writing about Rabbit was "like coming home every ten years and paying a visit."

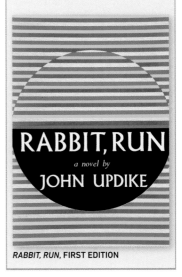

*RABBIT, RUN*, FIRST EDITION

# Cormac McCarthy

**BORN 1933, AMERICAN**

One of the most enigmatic living American writers, McCarthy has also become one of the most popular, thanks to his bleak and powerful novels about men struggling to survive in harsh landscapes.

Cormac (born Charles) McCarthy was born in Rhode Island but raised in Knoxville, Tennessee. His father worked at the Tennessee Valley Authority, and part of his job involved removing people from the hills they had lived in for generations so that the areas could be flooded. This seems to have had an effect on the young McCarthy, who maintained a sympathy and fascination for these rural folk, taking inspiration for his first four novels from their lives and situations.

### American Gothic
In the 1950s, McCarthy attended the University of Tennessee, before spending four years in the US air force. He then chose not to finish his degree but to try to make his way as a writer. His first four novels, beginning with *The Orchard Keeper* in 1965, were well reviewed, winning McCarthy enough awards and grants to let him continue writing, but their subject matter was often gruesome—including child murder, incest, corpse mutilation, and necrophilia. None of

the books made it into a second printing, so McCarthy was often short of money. In the mid-1980s—now twice divorced—he moved to El Paso, Texas, so that he could better research the material he needed for *Blood Meridian*, the semihistorical and extremely violent "anti-Western" novel that marked a new maturity in his work. His career was transformed by the success of *All the Pretty Horses* (1992), which won the National Book Award. This was the first volume in the Border Trilogy, which charts the lives of two young men coming of age in the American Southwest and Mexico.

McCarthy writes about men who struggle in a pitiless world, confronting their own capacity for evil in the midst of landscapes that are equally bleak.

△ **SOUTHERN STYLE**
McCarthy is known for his tales of twisted morality, set firmly in the southern states of the US. He uses these landscapes to subvert traditional representations of the heroic cowboy in American folklore.

His work has been called a serious contribution to the genre of Southern Gothic, alongside that of William Faulkner and Flannery O'Connor. He has also added a dark dimension to the American genre of the Western.

In 1997, McCarthy married Jennifer Winkley, his third wife, with whom he has a son (his second). He has said that it was being a father that led him to write *The Road*—the best-selling story of a man's journey with his son across a postapocalyptic landscape.

◁ **CORMAC McCARTHY**
This photograph shows the reclusive author in 1991. McCarthy is seldom seen in public, and he shocked the literary world when he appeared on the *Oprah Winfrey Show* in 2007.

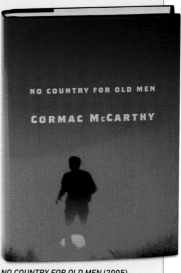

*NO COUNTRY FOR OLD MEN* (2005)
**EXEMPLIFIES McCARTHY'S STYLE**

" **My perfect day** is sitting in a room with some **blank paper**. That's **heaven**. That's **gold**, and **anything else** is just **a waste of time**. "
CORMAC McCARTHY

# Seamus Heaney

## 1939–2013, IRISH

Heaney was one of the great modern elegiac poets as well as a notable literary critic and translator. His work—exploring ancient texts, Northern Ireland's Troubles, and love in its many forms—has universal appeal.

△ **DERRY AND THE RIVER FOYLE**
Northern Ireland forms the backdrop to Heaney's life and work. His childhood was blessed with familial love and firmly rooted in his local community.

*NORTH* (1975), COLLECTION OF POEMS BY SEAMUS HEANEY

Seamus Justin Heaney was born in 1939, the first of nine children of cattle trader Patrick and his wife, Margaret. He grew up Catholic on his family's farm in County Derry, rural Northern Ireland, and began his education at Anahorish primary school, near his home village of Bellaghy. He later recognized the values instilled by the school, and was proud to have been educated in its "tin huts." To this day, he is lauded by the people of County Derry as a "humble Bellaghy man."

Many of Heaney's poems share a reverence for the past, drawing on his childhood and on the values and traditions of his local community, often focusing on the micro details of existence. In "Sunlight," for example, he reminisces about his aunt baking; and in "The Forge" about the work of the village blacksmith (which is also a metaphor for the craft of the poet). But as a boy growing up during World War II, he was also witness to maneuvers at a nearby US airbase that gestured to a very different world beyond the security and familiarity of Bellaghy. It was these early influences that formed Heaney's personal, cultural, and national landscape, and that later fed into his poetry.

### Heaven and hell

In 1951, Heaney earned a scholarship to a Catholic boarding school in Derry, 40 miles from his home. Here, he studied Latin and Irish, languages that were central to his development as a poet. He has referred to this first relocation as a shift from "the earth of farm labour to the heaven of education," but he had not been in the school long

> "And **the poet** draws from his **word-hoard** a **weird tale** / Of a **life** and a **love balked**. "
>
> SEAMUS HEANEY, "ON HIS WORK IN THE ENGLISH TONGUE"

▷ **SEAMUS HEANEY, 1995**
A popular, gregarious man, Heaney was a charismatic teacher and broadcaster and a superb reader of his own work. He is pictured here in the year in which he received the Nobel Prize in Literature.

## IN CONTEXT
### Literary collaboration

Heaney's literary network included many towering figures, such as Derek Walcott, Robert Lowell, and Joseph Brodsky. He worked particularly closely, however, with the English writer Ted Hughes (1930–1998), whose memories of the atrocities of war had, as for Heaney, informed much of his verse. Together, the two poets compiled and edited *The Rattlebag* (1982) and *The Schoolbag* (1997)—eclectic, compendious anthologies of verse in English that have been widely used by educators throughout the world in the teaching of poetry.

TED HUGHES, 1970

△ **STREETS OF DERRY, AUGUST 1975**
The British occupying forces, armed and with riot shields, are shown here policing the streets of Derry during the height of the Troubles in the 1970s.

when his brother Christopher, four years old, died in a car accident. Heaney describes the loss in sparse verse in "Mid-Term Break": "He lay in the four foot box as in his cot. / No gaudy scars, the bumper knocked him clear. / A four foot box, a foot for every year."

After leaving school, Heaney studied at Queen's University Belfast, earning a degree with honors in English. He remained in the city, training as a teacher at St. Joseph's (now part of University College), then teaching at St. Thomas's secondary school. The principal there was the established Irish writer Michael McLaverty. He became a mentor for Heaney (whose poem "Fosterage" is dedicated to McLaverty), introducing him to a number of poets, including Patrick Kavanagh. In Belfast, Heaney also discovered a writers' workshop known

as the Group, set up by Philip Hobsbaum, who taught at Queen's, and sought out the work of other contemporaries, notably citing Ted Hughes's "Lupercal" (1960).

### A letter from God

By 1962, Heaney was a published poet. Over the next few years, various leading publications, including *The Irish Times* and the *New Statesman*, promoted his work. His big breakthrough, however, came in 1964, when Northern Irish-born Charles Monteith, a director of the prominent UK publishing house Faber & Faber, wrote to Heaney asking to see his work. Heaney said he was transfixed by the request; it was "like getting a letter from God the father." Two years later, Faber published Heaney's first major collection of poetry, *Death of a Naturalist* (1966), which won four

awards, including the Somerset Maugham Award and the Geoffrey Faber Prize. Heaney dedicated the collection to Marie (Devlan), whom he had married in 1965. The 34 poems in the volume range in focus from the description of love and anticipation of a life together, to childhood, family, nature, rural Ireland, and war.

When hostilities in Northern Ireland escalated at the end of the 1960s, Heaney's work became more politically engaged and more critical of the British presence, and increasingly addressed the turbulence and violence of his homeland (see box, p.318).

## KEY WORKS

**1966**
*Death of a Naturalist*, Heaney's first poetry collection, is published to instant critical acclaim.

**1975**
*North* is published. It is the first collection of Heaney's to tackle violence and political unrest in Northern Ireland.

**1980**
*Preoccupations*, the first of Heaney's prose publications, includes essays on Yeats, Wordsworth, and Hopkins.

**1984**
In *Station Island*, a verse collection, Heaney focuses on the relationship between history and current affairs.

**2000**
*Beowulf*, Heaney's translation of the Anglo-Saxon epic, is published. It goes on to win several prestigious awards.

**2004**
*The Burial at Thebes*, the second of two plays by Heaney, compares Creon, ruler of Thebes, and George W. Bush of the US.

**2010**
*Human Chain*, Heaney's final poetry collection, is published. It is thought by many to include some of his finest work.

> "Between **my finger** and my **thumb**
> **The squat pen** rests; **snug as a gun**."

SEAMUS HEANEY, "DIGGING"

Heaney sometimes expressed ambivalence about becoming a spokesman for Northern Ireland, yet his poetry acknowledges the tragic loss of life and invites analysis and commentary. He also continued to write about domestic life and landscape, defending the poet's right to celebrate the parochial.

### Escape from civil strife

In 1970, Heaney and his family found some respite from the Troubles by spending the academic year at the University of California, Berkeley, where Heaney took a teaching post.

On his return to Northern Ireland in September 1971, he resigned from Queen's in Belfast and, in 1972, took the significant step of moving to the Republic of Ireland, on what was once the estate of the playwright J. M. Synge in Glanmore, Wicklow. At the end of his verse collection *North* (1975), Heaney refers to his situation as "Escaped from the massacre." He loved the remote location. Glanmore became almost muselike for Heaney: he lived there without a telephone, often writing into the small hours of the night in a trancelike state.

Some commentators consider Heaney's next collection, *Field Work* (1979), to be a move away from direct political engagement, while others, such as American poet Joshua Weiner, view it as "a growing commitment to stay engaged, but ... maintaining the long view, which asks questions more than it assumes positions."

By the end of the 1970s, Heaney had won global recognition for his work, particularly in the US. In 1979, he spent a semester teaching poetry at Harvard University. He also won two honorary doctorates from universities in New York. In 1981 he returned to Harvard, where he would teach for one semester a year until 1997.

Also in the 1980s, Heaney worked with playwright Brian Friel and actor Stephen Rea to set up the Field Day Theatre Company in Derry, following the tradition of Yeats and the Abbey Theatre in Dublin. His poetry turned to the subject of grief; he had lost both his parents within two years of each other. *The Haw Lantern* (1987) includes a sonnet cycle called "Clearances," dedicated to his late mother. He also translated Irish poetry in "Sweeney Astray" (1984), and ended the century on a high note with his prizewinning translation of *Beowulf* (2000), which was considered a masterpiece—a groundbreaking modernized epic.

Heaney won the Nobel Prize in Literature in 1995 for what the judges described as "works of lyrical beauty and ethical depth." In accepting the award, he joined eminent fellow Irish writers Yeats, Shaw, and Beckett, commenting that it was like "being a little foothill at the bottom of a mountain range." The following year brought another accolade, when his collection *Spirit Level* won the Whitbread Book of the Year Award.

Heaney's late poetry addressed the theme of mortality. He reworked Virgil's *Aeneid* in his collection *Seeing Things* (1991), referring to the afterlife: "At any rate, when the light breaks over me ... I'll be in step with what escapes me." A stroke in 2006, which rendered him "on the brink," inspired his last collection, *Human Chain* (2010). Heaney died at 74 in Dublin, but chose to be buried in Bellaghy, in the soil he describes his father and grandfather laboring over in "Digging," one of his first poems.

△ **HUMAN CHAIN**
Heaney's last collection of poems, *Human Chain*, finally won him the Forward Poetry Prize—one of Britain's most prestigious poetry awards—after two narrow losses.

▽ **HEANEY'S GRAVE, BELLAGHY**
The poet's headstone reads: "Walk on air against your better judgement," which is a line from his poem "The Gravel Walks" (1992). Heaney also quoted these words in his Nobel Prize acceptance speech.

# J.M. Coetzee

## BORN 1940, SOUTH AFRICAN

Author, linguist, essayist, and translator, Coetzee has won multiple literary awards, including the Nobel Prize, for compelling, complex works that have taken novel writing into new imaginative territory.

◁ **CAPE TOWN UNIVERSITY, 1985**
Students and teachers attend a mass protest against the strictures of apartheid, which included racial quotas for admission to the university.

Now in his 70s, John Maxwell Coetzee is South Africa's most celebrated writer, who has built his reputation with a series of novels that blur the distinctions between fiction, essay, and autobiography. Despite his fame, he is an intensely private man, and insights into his own life are largely confined to his three fictionalized autobiographical narratives, all of which are written in the third person: *Boyhood: Scenes from Provincial Life* (1997), *Youth* (2002), and *Summertime* (2009).

Coetzee was born in 1940 to Afrikaner parents, Zacharias (Jack) and Vera. His father was an attorney, whose malpractice and alcoholism would plunge the family into chaos and poverty; while he was away during World War II, Vera, a schoolteacher, struggled to take care of John and his baby brother, David, in a series of temporary homes. Jack's return was an intrusion into an intense, matriarchal family unit.

### An academic path

The Coetzees were liberal English speakers, out of step with the hard-line South African government that imposed racist apartheid laws. Yet they tacitly accepted the way that society operated; and while living in Cape Town they employed a seven-year-old "colored" boy named Eddie. A move to a new housing development on the edge of Worcester in the Western Cape had the sole advantage of being closer to his uncle's farm in the Karoo desert. It was a place of freedom that became a site of longing for Coetzee.

### European culture

At school, Coetzee was a loner who clung to his Englishness because he did not want to be allocated to Afrikaans classes. His education left a lasting mark; in his 1990 novel *Age of Iron*, he describes Afrikaner politicians as "the bullies in the last row of school-desks, raw-boned, lumpish boys, grown up now and promoted to rule the land." While at a Catholic secondary school in Cape Town, Coetzee continued to develop his passion for European culture, drawn to the Modernist poets T. S. Eliot and Ezra Pound and the music of Bach.

The University of Cape Town, where Coetzee went on to study mathematics and English, was a hotbed of left-wing protest against an increasingly authoritarian government. Coetzee watched from the sidelines because masses of people together aroused in him "something close to panic."

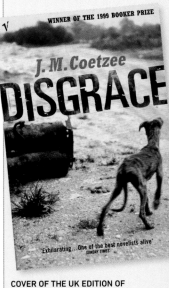

WINNER OF THE 1999 BOOKER PRIZE

J.M. Coetzee

DISGRACE

'Exhilarating...One of the best novelists alive' SUNDAY TIMES

**COVER OF THE UK EDITION OF COETZEE'S NOVEL *DISGRACE***

▷ **J. M. COETZEE**
Coetzee has written 13 novels, three volumes of fictionalized biography, seven pieces of short fiction, nine collections of literary theory, criticism and letters, and produced numerous translations of Dutch poetry.

> "I'm afraid I make it a **rule not to discuss** my **own works**."
>
> J. M. COETZEE

△ **COETZEE'S KAROO**
Coetzee spent long periods of his childhood in South Africa's Karoo and developed a profound love of the region's arid landscapes. The Karoo was the setting for his second novel, *In the Heart of the Country*, the story of an Afrikaner woman on an isolated farm.

A professor at Coetzee's university remembers his former student as being so unobtrusive that he was practically invisible. Coetzee was absent on graduation day because he had set sail for Southampton, England, to avoid compulsory military service.

### London and the US
After moving to London, Coetzee worked briefly as a computer programmer while completing his master's dissertation on the English Modernist writer Ford Madox Ford. In *Youth*, Coetzee recalls affairs and failed relationships with a lingering shame, but omits any mention of Philippa

Jubber, the drama student whom he met in Cape Town, and his brief return to South Africa to marry her.

Six years of study and teaching in the US fired Coetzee's imagination. His doctorate at the University of Texas included Germanic languages, linguistics, and a computer analysis of the works of Samuel Beckett. Echoes of Beckett's misanthropic monologues can be found in Coetzee's *In the Heart of the Country* (1977), in which the unmarried, virginal Magda rehearses competing versions of her own history on a remote South African farm.

Coetzee continued his life in academia, taking a post at the University at Buffalo in New York,

where he taught a class on South African Literature. He was eager to stay in the US, where his children Nicolas and Gisela had been born, but his application for residence was refused, partly because of Coetzee's involvement in a demonstration against the Vietnam War.

### Reluctant homecoming
Coetzee returned to South Africa in 1971 with the beginnings of a first novel, *Dusklands*, which drew parallels between the moral degeneration of 17th-century colonizers in South Africa and the US atrocities in Vietnam. He took a teaching post at the University of Cape Town and over 30 years he

" What passes between us now is **parody**. I was born into a **language** of **hierarchy**, of distance of **perspective**. It was my **father-tongue**. "

J. M. COETZEE, *IN THE HEART OF THE COUNTRY*

## KEY WORKS

**1974**
*Dusklands* juxtaposes a story of a Boer's revenge on a Khoikhoi tribe with napalm bombing in the Vietnam War.

**1977**
*In the Heart of the Country* chronicles a spinster's descent into madness through fantasies about sex and death.

**1980**
*Waiting for the Barbarians* examines complicity with regimes that ignore justice and decency.

**1983**
*Life & Times of Michael K* follows the desperate journey of a man carrying his dying mother back to her homeland.

**1999**
*Disgrace*, with its bleak story line, runs contrary to national optimism after South Africa's first free elections.

**2007**
*Diary of a Bad Year* mixes the author's professorial musings with the story of an aging lecturer's obsessions.

rose to the position of Distinguished Professor of Literature. He began his novel *Waiting for the Barbarians* (1980) during sabbatical periods of teaching and study in the US, introducing themes of torture, interrogation, and violence in an imaginary empire at an unspecified time. For this work, Coetzee won the James Tait Black Memorial Prize and gained international recognition.

### Beyond history

A succession of meticulously crafted novels placed Coetzee at the forefront of writing against apartheid, but he regarded himself as an experimental storyteller rather than an activist. He wanted his novels to stand apart from history—at some distance from their immediate subject matter, such as class conflict and race. So while the works of many other modern South African writers were banned, ironically, Coetzee's highly complex postmodern narratives offered some protection: the censors struggled to detect sexual or political offense in his generalized settings and decided that his "difficult" books were unlikely to be popular reads.

### Booker awards

In *Life & Times of Michael K*, Coetzee tells the story of a gardener with a cleft lip who sets out to take his ailing mother back to the Karoo in a wheelbarrow, and achieves a level of freedom after repeated imprisonment and starvation. Harsh, haunting, and astonishing, it won the Booker Prize in 1983.

Coetzee's second Booker-winning novel, *Disgrace* (1999), which was published five years after the first free elections in South Africa, was a stark contrast to the optimistic postapartheid "honeymoon" literature of the period. Despite a violent story line, for which the book received some criticism, it is a finely balanced work that explores historical and ongoing states of disgrace. Coetzee had a reputation for being difficult with journalists and critics because of his repeated refusals to answer questions about the meaning of his work. In the late 1980s and '90s, his writing focused on literary criticism and theory. *White Writing: On the Culture of Letters in South Africa*, for example, examines the work of modern South African writers "who are no longer European but yet are not African."

### Personal philosophies

A vegetarian since his 30s, Coetzee is a passionate advocate for animal rights, both in person, and through his fictional alter ego, Elizabeth Costello, in *The Lives of Animals* (1999). After moving to Australia with the author Dorothy Driver, he became an Australian citizen in 2006. In 2012, he cooperated with Afrikaans biographer John Kannemeyer on *J.M. Coetzee: A Life in Writing*, a biography that verifies details of his early years and reveals a string of sadnesses: the accidental death of his son at the age of 23; his daughter's debilitating illnesses; and the loss of his brother and his ex-wife, Philippa. Coetzee may have mellowed socially in his later years, but he has continued to push the boundaries with his philosophically themed novels, *The Childhood of Jesus* (2013) and *The Schooldays of Jesus* (2016).

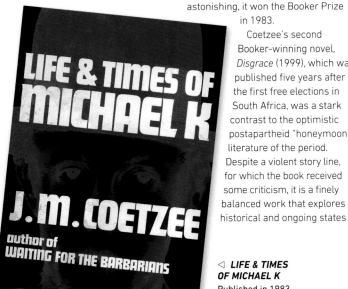

◁ **LIFE & TIMES OF MICHAEL K**
Published in 1983, Coetzee's novel is an account of a man's struggle for survival and search for dignity in a country brutalized by civil war.

**NELSON MANDELA CELEBRATES HIS ELECTION VICTORY ON MAY 2, 1994**

# Isabel Allende

**BORN 1942, CHILEAN**

One of the most beloved Latin American authors, Allende uses magic realism to express the indomitable strength of her characters in the face of political oppression and emotional upheaval.

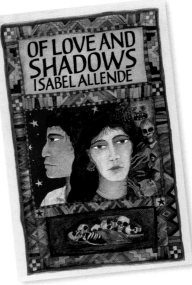

△ *OF LOVE AND SHADOWS*
Allende's second novel, first published in 1985, is a story of love, sacrifice, and betrayal, set in a country in which terror and repression reign.

A writer who has championed the outsider and the underdog, Isabel Allende, perhaps surprisingly, was very much part of the establishment in her early adulthood. During the 1960s and early '70s in her native Chile, she enjoyed success as a journalist and television host, and her father's cousin, Salvador Allende, was president. Then came the event that was to shape both her and her country's lives: the US-backed coup in which the democratically elected socialist Allende was ousted in favor of General Pinochet (see box, right), who imposed a military dictatorship.

### A tale of the generations

Isabel Allende fled to Venezuela, where she stayed for 13 years. She began what was to be her first and most famous book, *The House of Spirits*, in 1981, as a letter to her dying 100-year-old grandfather, who had helped bring her up after her father absconded. Her intention was to show him that he would always live on in the hearts of those he left behind. The text grew into a multigenerational tale of a Chilean family, however, told via the struggles of its women. Published in 1982, it established Allende's reputation as a major force in Latin American literature. Since then, she has written more than 20 books,

including collections of short stories, memoirs, and children's books, and has sold more than 50 million copies. In 1989, she moved to California, where she continues to write.

### Magic realism

Allende is often thought of as a writer of magic realism: in her work, supernatural events—such as clairvoyance, levitation, and the appearance of ghosts—take place within an otherwise mundane and realistic setting. She uses such magical happenings to elaborate upon events or ideas that are so terrible or so wonderful that they take on an almost surreal complexity. Although Allende often stretches beyond the confines of realist narrative, she also achieves an intense emotional engagement with her subjects, and her writing has consistently focused on the untold stories of the oppressed (often women), showing their fortitude and emotional resilience, and also the victory of love. In *The House of the Spirits*, for example, the youngest woman in the story is imprisoned, tortured, and raped, but survives and overcomes her trauma. And in her memoir *Paula*, Allende presents a passionate account of the tragic death of her daughter at the age of 28 from complications of porphyria.

Allende has declared that she has no political intentions for her work, but simply wants to tell the human story. This commitment to compelling and emotionally truthful storytelling is the key to her popularity, and will almost certainly be her legacy.

▷ **ISABEL ALLENDE, 2004**
The author is pictured here in the year of publication of her novel *Kingdom of the Golden Dragon*. She remains productive; her most recent work appeared in 2017.

## IN CONTEXT
### The Chilean "revolution"

The "revolution" of 1973 in Chile that overthrew socialist Salvador Allende was supported by the CIA, which saw the spread of socialism as a threat to stability in the US. Allende was replaced by military dictator General Pinochet, under whom thousands of political enemies were executed or "disappeared," and tens of thousands more tortured. In response to international pressure, Pinochet legalized opposition parties in 1987, which led to his being voted out of power in a 1988 plebiscite. His arrest in 1998 was the first time that a former head of state had been held accountable for his crimes, although he never saw prison, dying in 2006 before the case came to court.

GENERAL AUGUSTO PINOCHET (CENTER) IN SANTIAGO, CHILE , 1983

# Peter Carey

**BORN 1943, AUSTRALIAN**

One of the world's most successful literary novelists, Carey is a writer of great energy and fantastical sensibilities who also engages with important issues of Australian history.

Peter Carey has forged a career as a best-selling literary novelist and is one of just four writers to have won the prestigious Booker Prize twice. He was born in 1943 in the village of Bacchus Marsh, near Melbourne, to a working family who saved money to send him to one of the country's best boarding schools, Geelong Grammar. He later observed that being sent away at a young age was the reason that so many orphan characters appeared in his fiction, something that was also true of Dickens. Later, as a subversive tribute to Dickens, Carey wrote *Jack Maggs*, an informal sequel to *Great Expectations*.

## Literary success

After dropping out of college and going to work in an advertising agency, Carey discovered his love of literature, and began to write. During the 1970s, he produced numerous short stories that appeared in magazines and in a 1974 collection, but had his first novel (*Bliss*) published only in 1981, at the relatively advanced age (for a career

◁ **AT HOME IN NEW YORK, 2007**
Carey moved to New York in 1991, and still lives and teaches there. While he is best known as a novelist, his work also includes short stories, travelogues, movie scripts, and a children's book.

novelist) of 38. Carey did not have to wait long for success. He won the Booker Prize in 1988 with his third novel, *Oscar and Lucinda*, a feat that he repeated in 2001 with *The True History of the Kelly Gang*.

Carey was involved in a scandal in 2006, when his ex-wife accused him of writing an unfavorable version of her in his novel *Theft: A Love Story*, in which the narrator's ex-wife, referred to as "The Plaintiff," is portrayed as a shallow spendthrift. Carey denied this was the case, although many noted at the time that the narrator in question was, like him, born in 1943 in Bacchus Marsh, Victoria.

◁ **NED KELLY**
Carey's *The True History of the Kelly Gang* gives voice to the colonial outlaw Ned Kelly, who terrorized northeast Victoria in his quest for freedom. He survived a shoot-out by wearing homemade armor, only to be hanged shortly afterward.

The themes of authenticity, deception, and fraudulence recur in Carey's work. His second novel, *Illywhacker* (1985), is named from the Australian slang for a carnival trickster and tells the story of a con artist who claims to be 139 years old; the novels *Theft* and *My Life as a Fake* both concern frauds in different sectors of the art world.

Carey also engages with Australian history, addressing the crimes of Australia's colonial past in *A Long Way From Home* (2017), the mid-1970s collapse of government in *Amnesia* (2014), and the story of Australian outlaw and hero Ned Kelly in *The True History of the Kelly Gang*.

Carey is known for his immense skill in creating different, and compelling, narrative voices, perhaps best seen in the ungrammatical, difficult, and wildly expressive vernacular he invents for Ned Kelly. Reviewers often remark that Carey is restless, exuberant, inventive, very curious about people in different times and places—and notoriously difficult to pin down.

## IN CONTEXT
### Literary inspiration

Although much of Carey's work is about quintessentially Australian subjects, some of his novels take direct inspiration from the literary history of Great Britain and the US. *Jack Maggs* (1997) follows the character of Magwich from *Great Expectations* after he is sentenced to be transported to Australia; and *The Unusual Life of Tristan Smith* (1994), is a variation on a theme of Laurence Sterne's *Tristram Shandy*. *Parrot and Olivier in America* (2010)—a fictionalized version of the life of Alexis de Tocqueville, a French nobleman who wrote *Democracy in America*—is an influential study of manners and politics in the US.

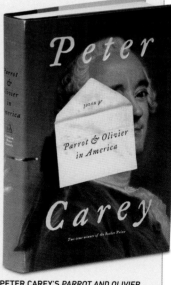

**PETER CAREY'S *PARROT AND OLIVIER IN AMERICA***

> " I have never **begun a novel** which wasn't going to **stretch me further** than I had ever stretched before. "
PETER CAREY

▷ **HWANG IN PARIS, 2005**
Hwang Sok-yong's transition from
political dissident to nationally celebrated
and best-selling author has spanned a
turbulent period in his country's history
and involved great personal sacrifice.

# Hwang Sok-yong

BORN 1943, SOUTH KOREAN

The foremost Korean author of the postwar generation, Hwang
has chronicled in his novels and short stories the lives of people
in a region torn apart by war and political power play.

# " Unless we **find** a way to **forgive one another**, **none of us** will ever be able to **see** each other **again**. "

HWANG SOK-YONG, *THE GUEST*

Hwang Sok-yong was born in Hsinking in China, where his family lived in exile until 1945 when their native Korea was liberated from Imperial Japanese rule. They returned to a country divided and occupied by the Soviet Union and the US (see box, right).

Hwang grew up in South Korea, and studied philosophy at Dongguk University in Seoul, but the shadow of the Cold War division was ever-present, as was the feeling of a loss of national identity. As a result, he became politically active, protesting against the control of his country from outside, despite its supposed independence. His activism led to brief imprisonment in 1964, but it was after military service during the war in Vietnam in the late 1960s that he channeled his energy into writing.

Living under a repressive dictatorship, Hwang began to take an active part in resistance movements, which culminated in 1980 in the Gwangju uprising against military rule. He was more circumspect in his writing, publishing the collection of stories *On the Road to Sampo* in 1974, and the serialized epic *Jang Gilsan*, using parables to indicate the injustices of the dictatorship and thereby evade censorship. Hwang became more outspoken throughout the 1980s, in novels including *The Shadow of Arms* (1985) about the Vietnam War, and in his direct criticism of the government.

## Rough justice

A committed democrat, Hwang hoped to unite Korea by building bridges between artists in the North and South, and in breach of the law he traveled via Japan and China to Pyongyang in North Korea. Rather than return to Seoul to face justice, he then went into voluntary exile in the US, where he lectured at Long Island University. He also spent some time in Germany.

The pull of his homeland was too strong to resist, however, and Hwang returned to South Korea in 1993. He was jailed for seven years for his breach of national security, and was denied writing materials and generally treated badly while in prison.

Hwang responded by going on a hunger strike, an action in which he was supported by human rights organizations, including Amnesty and PEN America. In 1998, pressure on the newly-elected president Kim Dae-jung led to his release and pardon after serving five years of his sentence.

The author's broad-ranging historical and political writing continues to give voice to feelings of "homelessness": the loss and isolation caused by war and occupation, and the alienation and disappearance of traditional values caused by modernization.

◁ **CONFLICT FICTION**
Hwang's experiences of "cleaning up" evidence of massacres in the Vietnam War informed his short story "The Pagoda," published in 1970. In the same year, he finished his first novel, *Mr. Han's Chronicle*, the story of a doctor separated from his family by the Korean War.

△ **MODERN SEOUL**
In the more liberal atmosphere of 21st-century South Korea, Hwang has continued to highlight the abuses of his divided country in novels such as *The Guest* (2001) and *Familiar Things* (2011).

## IN CONTEXT
### The 38th Parallel

Until 1945, Korea was united under Japanese rule, but the end of World War II saw the country divided by a border running along the 38th parallel. The North was occupied by the Soviet Union, the South by the US, and during the subsequent Cold War, it proved impossible to reunite the country. Instead, the Republic of Korea was established in the South in 1948 and the communist Democratic People's Republic of Korea in the North. Each claimed rights over all of Korea, which led to the Korean War of 1950–1953. Since then, a demilitarized zone roughly following the 38th parallel has separated the two parts of the peninsula.

**CROSSING THE 38TH PARALLEL DURING THE KOREAN WAR, 1950**

# W. G. Sebald

## 1944–2001, GERMAN

The German academic Sebald wove together autobiography, travelogue, meditative essay writing, and history to create his unique and powerful prose. Tragically, he died at the height of his creative powers, at 57.

◁ **BAVARIAN ALPS**
Sebald grew up at the foot of the Alps in a village of 1,000 or so inhabitants that was snow covered for much of the year. He described it as "a silent place."

◁ **W. G. SEBALD, 1999**
Sebald lived in England for many years: he was particularly attached to the old Norfolk rectory that was his home, as well as to the English sense of humor.

Winfried Georg Sebald was born in the Bavarian village of Wertach im Allgäu, southern Germany, in 1944, just months before the country suffered defeat in World War II. His parents were from Catholic, working-class, farm-labor backgrounds, although his father, Georg Sebald, had been elevated to the status of captain in the army. He was, however, held in a French prisoner of war camp until 1947, so the young Sebald was largely brought up by his kindly grandfather, who became a major figure in his life.

### Generational silence

Although raised in Germany in the immediate aftermath of the war, Sebold was not exposed to images of persecution in the German concentration camps until he was 17 years old, when he was shown a documentary about Belsen. "Somehow," he said, "we had to get our minds around it—which of course we didn't." The 1950s was the time of the so-called conspiracy of silence around the persecution of Jews and minority groups. German citizens—scarred by the horrors of the war and doubtless riddled with guilt and shame—made no reference to this immense aspect of their history, and so, astonishingly, Sebald and his entire generation grew up in complete ignorance of it. In his

view, the Holocaust had become "a secret that bound all Germans together." It took years, he said, to find out what had really taken place. This deeply troubled relationship with the past later resulted in anger for many Germans of his generation.

### Restlessness and "exile"

By the early 1960s, Sebald had secured a place at the University of Freiburg to study German and English literature. He graduated in 1965, and the following year moved to Manchester, England, for three years, to work as a university lecturer. He had a Jewish landlord, who later inspired the character of Max Ferber in his novel *The Emigrants* (1992). The Ferber section of the book has a confessional tone: the narrator depicts a personal awakening regarding the impact of the Holocaust on German-Jewish Ferber and his family. In Manchester, Sebald reflected on his sheltered life in provincial Bavaria, where he had little experience of diversity, and certainly no contact with Jewish culture.

**JEWISH CHILDREN ARRIVE IN ENGLAND ON A *KINDERTRANSPORT*, 1939**

"To **my mind** it seems **clear** that those who have **no memory** have the much **greater chance** to lead **happy lives**."

W. G. SEBALD

△ **UNIVERSITY OF EAST ANGLIA**
Sebald taught at the university from 1970 until his sudden death in December 2001. This view of the university's brutalist campus in Norwich, Norfolk, is from across a lake known simply as the Broad.

## KEY WORKS

### 1990
*Vertigo*, Book 1 of Sebald's trilogy, recounts episodes in the lives of Stendhal, Kafka, Casanova, and Sebald himself.

### 1992
*The Emigrants*, Book 2 of the trilogy, explores the lives of four German emigrants living in England or the US.

### 1995
In *The Rings of Saturn*, the final book in the trilogy, the narrator meditates on truth, art, and history.

### 2001
In *Austerlitz*, the main character was once an infant refugee who had been saved from a concentration camp.

In 1967, Sebald married Ute, his Austrian-born partner. Two years later, during a somewhat nomadic stage in his life, he tried living in Switzerland, with a view to remaining there as a teacher, but he felt unsettled and moved to England, taking a post as a lecturer at the University of East Anglia (UEA). Sebald lived in England for the rest of his life, but he never felt completely at home there—or, by all accounts, anywhere.

He completed his PhD on the German author Alfred Döblin in 1973. Sebald's creativity was undoubtedly affected by Döblin's eclectic approach to writing, which included travelogue, philosophical treatises, science fiction, and historical novels. Sebald also cited the Austrian novelist Thomas Bernhard as a major influence on his writing; and, in *The Emigrants* and *The Rings of Saturn* (1995), he refers to the work of Borges, Kafka, and Nabokov.

In 1987, Sebald was appointed chair of European literature at UEA, and remained a professor of modern German literature there for the rest of his academic career. He founded the British Centre for Literary Translation in 1999, which continues to support UEA's MA course in the subject and other similar academic programs. The center now holds annual Sebald lectures in tribute to the influential author and academic. For almost 20 years, Sebald wrote exclusively academic texts. He was a formidable critic of German and Austrian writing, publishing studies and collected essays.

### Cult status
In his mid-40s, however, having adapted to life in Norfolk with Ute and their daughter, Anna, Sebald began writing prose in his native tongue, in a style and rhythm that resembles 19th-century German prose and the work of the English essayists such as De Quincey. Sebald's long, formal sentences are sparse in descriptive language, but draw on various sources (see box, left). He claimed to feel self-conscious about writing in English: "Unlike Conrad or Nabokov," he said, "I didn't have circumstances which would have coerced me out of my native tongue altogether."

*The Emigrants* (published in English in 1996) was his first work to be translated from the German, by Michael Hulse, who went on to translate much of Sebald's work into English. *The Emigrants* was a literary coup, winning the Berlin Literature Prize, the Literature Nord Prize, and the Johannes Bobrowski Medal. The book both confounded and dazzled critics, and Sebald achieved cult status.

Two other extant works in German were translated by Hulse: *The Rings of Saturn* and *Vertigo*. In her review of *Vertigo*, cultural critic Susan Sontag

## ON STYLE
### Literary techniques

Written in German, Sebald's prose tends toward long sentences, with multiple clauses and infrequent paragraphing. The narratives range across centuries and interweave diverse topics and apparently unrelated historical, personal, and literary references, including vivid—albeit imperfect—memories, travelogues, and visits to historic sites. Sebald used his own black-and-white photographs to illustrate his books: the captionless images, which fascinate and puzzle the reader, serve to disrupt meaning and certainty in the text. Melancholic and epiphanic in style, his work has sometimes been compared to that of Marcel Proust.

**USE OF IMAGES IN *THE RINGS OF SATURN***

> " And so they are **ever returning** to us, **the dead.** "
>
> W. G. SEBALD, *THE EMIGRANTS*

△ **THE RINGS OF SATURN**
In this 1995 novel—which employs Sebald's characteristic blend of fiction, history, and travelogue—an unnamed narrator tours Suffolk, England, on foot.

praised the "passionate bleakness" of Sebald's "restless, chronically dissatisfied mind."

## Recovering silence

With success came an appetite and demand for more books. In the late 1990s, however, Sebald worked on a nonfiction project, *On the Natural History of Destruction* (1999)—a collection of essays on German literature that focuses on the Allied bombings of German cities in World War II (translated posthumously and published in 2003). It departs from the prose-memoir works in that it explores literary depictions of the suffering of German citizens rather than Holocaust persecution. But

this nonfiction title shared the same authorial determination as his fiction to recover a silenced moment in history and expose the inadequacy of written accounts to accurately describe human loss and devastation.

There was great excitement about the publication of *Austerlitz*, which turned out to be Sebald's final novel. He had just made a move to Penguin from a smaller publishing house, and also had a new translator, Anthea Bell. Sebald's book was inspired by a haunting BBC documentary about a three-year-old Jewish child, Susi Bechhöfer, who was evacuated from Germany in 1939; when she arrived in Britain, she was adopted by a Welsh minister and his wife. In adulthood,

Bechhöfer discovered that her biological mother had perished at Auschwitz and her father had been a Nazi soldier. The book came out in November 2001, but tragically, just a month later, Sebald died after suffering an aneurysm that caused him to swerve in front of a truck near his home in Norfolk. His daughter, a passenger, survived the crash.

*Austerlitz* won the National Book Critics Circle Award, although Sebald's greatness was already established and he was regarded as a candidate for the next Nobel Prize. Obituaries mourned the loss of an author who had enriched European culture and challenged how we write about memory and the past.

▽ **ALLIED PLANES OVER KIEL, 1944**
Sebald's *On the Natural History of Destruction* criticizes postwar German writers for remaining silent about the loss of hundreds of thousands of civilian lives following bombing raids by Allied forces on German cities.

# Lorna Goodison

## BORN 1947, JAMAICAN

One of the finest Caribbean writers of the postwar generation, Goodison is an author of great imaginative power, whose poems and short stories explore language, history, family, gender, and racial identity.

Lorna Gaye Goodison explains that when she was born in Kingston, Jamaica, in 1947, her mother dipped her finger in sugar and "rubbed it under my tongue to give me the gift of words." She attributes her love of poetry, however, to the colonial education she received at primary school, where the curriculum was imported from the "motherland," focusing on English male writers such as Shakespeare, Keats, Eliot, and Lawrence, whose cultural references often had little meaning or relevance in the islands. It was, says Goodison, Wordsworth's famous daffodil poem that "irritated" her into writing poetry reflective of her own culture.

After leaving school, she worked as a librarian and then as an advertising copywriter. But from an early age, she dreamed of becoming an artist, and so in 1967 she enrolled at the Jamaica School of Art, and later at the Art Students League of New York. At various times since then she has taught art and worked as a designer and illustrator; her art has also been widely exhibited and appears on many of her book covers.

It was in New York, while she was still in her 20s, that poetry took hold of Goodison like a "dominating, intrusive tyrant." Her first collection, *Tamarind Season*, with its poems embracing themes of struggle, survival, family, and national and gender identity, kick-started her career. It was published in 1980, the year in which Goodison gave birth to her son, Miles. Three years later, she became a visiting writer at the University of Iowa, where she gained a reputation as an impressive performer of her own work. In 1986, her second volume, *I Am Becoming My Mother*, included reflections on the Caribbean woman as miracle worker ("she would make a garment from a square of cloth / in a span that defied time") and the tensions, such as self-sacrifice and denial, that resulted. It was arguably, however, *Roses: Poems* (1995) that confirmed Goodison as one of the finest West Indian poets of the postwar generation.

### Painterly writing

Goodison likens her writing technique to chiaroscuro (light and dark) in art: "All these light images I place in relief to dark historical facts or hold them up as talismans against the sense of hopelessness and despair which can overwhelm us as human beings." But her poetry appeals to almost all the senses in its frequent tributes to the everyday: sensuous descriptions of eating a mango, or the smell of mint, of washing, or of Sunday lunch, for example. Goodison is also skilled at capturing the distinctive cadences of Jamaican speech, and in combining different voices (Standard English, Jamaican Creole, Rastafarian "Dread Talk") in just a line or two of poetry.

Professor Emerita at the University of Michigan, she has learned to live her life in several places at once, dividing her time between Jamaica and North America, where she has held various university posts during her distinguished career.

△ **THE ART STUDENTS LEAGUE**
Goodison enrolled at this New York art school in her early 20s. Her talent as a painter resonates in her writing, producing vibrant, richly textured literary landscapes.

### IN CONTEXT
### Ancestral history

Goodison's first full-length prose work, *From Harvey River* (2007), is an exquisitely written, evocative, and tender memoir of the author's forebears. It interweaves a history of Jamaica with a mesmerizing family narrative, introducing the reader to a cast of extraordinary characters. The book's title refers to Goodison's great-grandfather, William Harvey, an Englishman who gave his name to the small village and adjacent river in Jamaica's northwestern parish of Hanover that was to become his family's home. *From Harvey River* has won widespread acclaim, and British Columbia's National Award for Canadian Non-Fiction (2008).

*FROM HARVEY RIVER*

" **Good poetry** is like **effective prayer**, it feeds the **human spirit**, it **nourishes**, it puts us in touch with **forces** far greater than **ourselves.** "
LORNA GOODISON

▷ **LORNA GOODISON, 2017**
In the year that this photograph was taken, Goodison was chosen as Jamaica's second ever poet laureate, a post she will hold until 2020.

▷ **HARUKI MURAKAMI, 2004**
Haruki Murakami, photographed here
at the age of 54, is famous worldwide,
but revered in his home country. As
Japan's most prominent intellectual,
he often engages in public debate about
the state of the nation. He is also an
experienced long-distance runner, and
a translator of other authors' works.

# Haruki Murakami

## BORN 1949, JAPANESE

Murakami is a best-selling author and essayist, whose cult fiction
combines elements of surrealism and magic realism to explore
universal questions of what it means to be human.

# "Memories warm you up from the inside. But they also tear you apart."

HARUKI MURAKAMI, *KAFKA ON THE SHORE*

Born in US-occupied Kyoto to two teachers of Japanese literature, Haruki Murakami always felt himself to be an outsider in his native land. He grew up mainly in the port city of Kobe, where he immersed himself in Western and Russian literature—particularly hard-boiled detective stories—and jazz. He claims that he rejected Japanese literature because if he had read it, he would have had to discuss it with his father, which he had no desire to do. Yet Murakami was clearly also attracted to the visions of alternative lives offered by Western culture.

## Rebellion and writing
After studying drama at Waseda University in Tokyo, where he met his wife, Yoko, Murakami rebelled against a future as a corporate "salaryman," grew his hair, and took a job in a record store (a path shared by Toru Watanabe, a character in Murakami's 1987 meditation on love and youth, *Norwegian Wood*). Having saved some money, he opened a jazz bar in a Tokyo suburb, furnishing it with an upright piano to stage live music.

In his introduction to *Wind/Pinball: Two Novels* (2015), Murakami explained how he began his writing career. He reports experiencing an epiphany as he sat drinking beer and watching a baseball game in Tokyo between the Yakult Swallows and the Hiroshima Carp in 1978. At the precise moment that Dave Hilton, an American player, hit a double, Murakami was suddenly overwhelmed by a desire to write a novel. After the game, he went straight out and bought a pen and paper. Using the countercultural works of Kurt Vonnegut and Richard Brautigan as inspiration, over the next 10 months he wrote *Hear the Wind Sing* (1979), which won a prize for new writers. Murakami never looked back. He sold his jazz club, which he had run for 10 years, and began writing full time.

## Physical discipline
*Norwegian Wood* (1987) was popular with Japan's youth, sold millions of copies, and turned the author into a superstar. Murakami was extremely uncomfortable with the attention, and in 1986 he left Japan to settle in the

### ON STYLE
#### Jazz fiction
One of Japan's most experimental novelists, Murakami often blends humor, pop culture, and elements of magic realism in his works. A recurring structure is a realistic first-person narrative, littered with references to Western culture, and interspersed with surreal elements (levitating clocks, talking cats, and exploding dogs) and—as in *Sputnik Sweetheart* (1999)—parallel worlds. Through these frequently funny realist and symbolic worlds, he explores themes of loss, memory, and alienation.

**MURAKAMI'S *SPUTNIK SWEETHEART***

US. Since then, he has divided his time between homes in Hawaii and Japan, while sticking to a notoriously regimented routine designed to facilitate his writing: waking at 4 am to write for five or six hours, before swimming and running long distances, then retiring at 9 pm. In 1996, Murakami finished his first ultramarathon in Hokkaido, Japan, and he described the importance of running to him in his memoir *What I Talk About When I Talk About Running* (2007).

In 2017, he was widely touted to be in line for the Nobel Prize in Literature, but—having once said, "I don't want prizes. That means you're finished"—was perhaps relieved when the award went instead to fellow Japan-born writer Kazuo Ishiguro.

◁ **MUSIC AND WRITING**
Murakami's passion for jazz was ignited in 1964 at a concert in Kobe by Art Blakey and the Jazz Messengers. Jazz shaped his destiny and also his improvisational writing style—he claimed that he never knew exactly what the next page of his writing would be.

# Orhan Pamuk

## BORN 1952, TURKISH

Aside from three years in New York, Pamuk has spent his entire life in the same district of his home city, Istanbul. The tensions between East and West, ancient and modern, are often reflected in the themes of his novels.

When the Republic of Turkey, founded by Kemal Atatürk in 1923, replaced the old Ottoman state, the country underwent a period of rapid modernization. The new secular constitution looked to the West as a model for society as a new middle-class emerged, enriched by industrialization. Orhan Pamuk's grandfather was a member of this elite, having made his fortune building railroads in Turkey.

### Education and early work

By the time Pamuk was born in 1952, his family's wealth had dwindled, but he was nevertheless brought up in one of the most chic districts of Istanbul, Nişantaşı, on the European side of the Bosphorus. Pamuk was expected to follow in the family tradition of becoming a civil engineer, but he dreamed of becoming an artist instead. After graduating from the American Robert College in Istanbul, he succumbed to family pressure and enrolled at Istanbul Technical College to study architecture. Unhappy, he abandoned his architecture studies after three years and transferred to

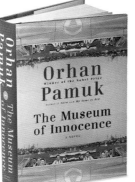

◁ **OBSESSIVE LOVE**
Pamuk's novel *The Museum of Innocence* explores attitudes to love and sex in Istanbul through the story of a man's infatuation with his young cousin.

Istanbul University, where in 1976 he graduated with a degree in journalism. Starting at 23, Pamuk lived with his mother and devoted himself to writing novels. The first of his works to be published was *Cevdet Bey and His Sons* (1982), a tale of three generations of a well-to-do family in Nişantaşı. The novel was well received by critics, winning two notable Turkish literary prizes, and its success allowed Pamuk to leave home and get married.

### East to West

A year later, he published *Silent House*, and in 1985 *The White Castle*—an examination of the relationship between master and slave, set in 17th-century Istanbul. That year, he moved to New York, where he took a position at Columbia University as a visiting scholar, but he returned home in 1988 to continue his career as a novelist. *My Name is Red* (1998), as

with many of Pamuk's works, reflects cultural tensions between the old, Islamic world and Western values, this time through a story of intrigue between artists in the Ottoman court of Sultan Murat III.

Pamuk's inventive language and his use of a range of postmodern literary devices, such as multiple and unusual narrators (including a dog and a corpse), won him international acclaim, and the Turkish government offered him the prestigious title of "state artist"—an honor that Pamuk declined. He did, however, accept the Nobel Prize in Literature in 2006, and continues to live and work in his apartment in Nişantaşı.

▽ **BOSPHORUS VIEW**
Pamuk writes at a desk with a view over the Bosphorus in Istanbul. The city, the former Ottoman imperial capital, is the setting for much of his work.

◁ **ORHAN PAMUK, 1992**
Photographed here in Istanbul, Pamuk is Turkey's most successful novelist, though he is a controversial figure in his home country. His 10th novel, *The Red-Haired Woman*—the story of a well digger and his apprentice—was published in 2016.

# Mo Yan

## BORN 1955, CHINESE

Known for his darkly humorous novels, Mo Yan has developed a highly original voice, blending socialist realism, magic realism, and Chinese literature and folklore to give a surreally satirical view of life in China.

The "Northeast Township" in which many of Mo Yan's novels are set is a fictionalized version of his home town, Gaomi, in Shandong Province, northeastern China. His parents were farmers there when he was born (with the given name Guan Moye) and during the "Great Leap Forward"—a period between 1958 and 1962, when the policies implemented by Chairman Mao to modernize China's agrarian economy led to a widespread famine.

In 1966, in the later years under Mao's governance, Guan Moye, aged 11, left school to work on the land. Seven years later, he took a job in a cotton factory, and while working there became interested in literature. During this time, his reading was restricted to social realist books approved by the authorities, and only later did he discover the Chinese classics and translations of foreign authors. While he still admired the social realism of Chinese writers such as Lu Xun, he found the works of William Faulkner and Gabriel García Márquez a revelation.

Guan Moye enlisted in the People's Liberation Army (PLA) but devoted much of his spare time to reading and writing. One of his short stories was published in a literary journal, under the pen name Mo Yan, in 1981. His early stories displayed the beginnings

of a distinctive style, influenced by Márquez's magic realism and traditional Chinese literature, but also mindful of Mao's dictum that a writer's duty is to politics before art.

### A growing reputation

To further his ambitions as a writer, he enrolled at the PLA Academy of Art for a two-year course in literature in 1984. While there, he published short stories, including "Transparent Red Radish" and "Explosions," that were well received by critics, but it was his first novel, *Red Sorghum*, which was set during the brutal years of the second Sino-Japanese War, that earned him a national, and later international, reputation. Its five parts were originally serialized in magazines in 1986, but their popularity led to publication in book form that same year, and to a

movie of the novel in 1987. Many of Mo Yan's later works extended the blend of myth and realism that he used to great effect in *Red Sorghum*. *The Republic of Wine* (2000), for example, moves away from realistic narrative, and borrows from genres as diverse as detective noir and traditional Chinese supernatural tales to make sarcastic comment on Chinese society. While his works are experimental in structure and are seen as postmodern from a Western perspective, Mo Yan points to Chinese folklore and the country's traditional storytelling traditions as his inspirations.

In 2012, he was awarded the Nobel Prize in Literature, becoming the first Chinese writer to receive the honor. The variety and innovation of his work have made him one of the most respected authors in his homeland.

△ **RED SORGHUM**
Mo Yan's *Red Sorghum* tells the story of a Gaomi family in turbulent years of the 20th century. The book was adapted into an award-winning movie by Zhang Yimou.

◁ **MO YAN, 2006**
Pictured here at a French book fair, Mo Yan has built an international reputation. His pen name, which means "don't speak," was possibly a warning given to him while growing up in Mao Tse-tung's China.

### IN CONTEXT
### Traditional storytelling

A significant influence on Mo Yan's literary imagination was pingshu, the traditional Chinese art of storytelling, which dates back at least 2,000 years. Its practitioners learned their art (which included memorizing lengthy passages of text) through a long apprenticeship to a master, and would embellish their stories with a few simple props – the opening of a fan, for example, representing the drawing of a sword. Pingshu's tales of brave soldiers and incorruptible officials (such as the saintly Lord Bao, the champion of justice) provided templates for desirable social values that entered the folklore of the Chinese people.

A STAMP FROM 2015 SHOWS LORD BAO, A FIGURE FROM CHINESE FOLKLORE

# Arundhati Roy

**BORN 1961, INDIAN**

Roy's first—and for 20 years her only—novel won the Booker Prize and was a commercial success. A determined activist for environmental and political causes, Roy has frequently been threatened with imprisonment.

Suzanna Arundhati Roy was born into an unconventional life. Her mother, Mary, was a Syrian Christian, while her father was a Bengali Hindu. When she was two her parents divorced, and Roy moved for a while with her mother and brother to her grandfather's house. The family then relocated to Kerala, southern India, where Mary set up a school (originally with just seven children, two of whom were her own) and began to make a name for herself as a human-rights activist.

Roy's early life was shaped by the influence of her nonconformist mother and by the lack of paternal oppression. Growing up, she refused to conform to what was expected of an Indian woman. At 16, she left her home village of Ayemenem to study architecture in Delhi, where she lived with her then boyfriend.

After a stay in Goa, Roy returned to the capital, and met the filmmaker Pradip Krishen, who gave her the lead role in his award-winning movie, *Massey Sahib* (1985). The two married, but later separated.

◁ **ARUNDHATI ROY, 2017**
Roy has featured on *Time* magazine's list of the 100 most influential people. The publication of her second novel, after a 20-year hiatus, has sparked renewed interest.

**Commercial success**
At the age of 31, Roy began working on her first novel, *The God of Small Things*, a semiautobiographical tale of an Indian family fading into decline, pulled apart by serial tragedies and scandals. It took more than four years to complete, but was a commercial sensation when published in 1997. In addition to success, the book also created trouble for Roy, since charges of obscenity were brought against her in her home state of Kerala.

◁ **SCHOOL DAYS**
A girl in the school that was set up by Roy's mother. Roy helped out at school, later saying that this turned her off children for life.

## Writing and activism
Since the late 1990s, Roy has written dozens of essays and nonfiction books; made documentaries; and engaged in various protests against US foreign policy in Afghanistan, India's nuclear test program and dam building, globalization, and Hindu nationalism. Her efforts have landed her in prison, and left her facing a stone-throwing mob and fighting charges of sedition. In 2016, she even had to briefly flee India in fear for her life. Her politics are frequently at odds with India's drive for modernization, but she has given a voice to those left behind by India's economic rise.

In 2017, Roy finally released a second novel, *The Ministry of Utmost Happiness*, having allegedly asked her own characters to decide which publisher should have the book; as spirited and uncompromising as their creator, they chose one offering half as much money as the other bidders.

ON STYLE
### Creating a language

In *The God of Small Things*, Roy explores her experiences of life in postcolonial India, deconstructing the English language on the way—partly as a form of resistance to British colonial domination. Her writing breaks the rules of grammar and is playful, colorful, and inventive: for example, she capitalizes certain words and invents unusual phrases and compound words. She was praised by the US writer John Updike for creating her "own language."

*THE GOD OF SMALL THINGS*

"That's what **careless words** do. They make people **love you a little less**."

ARUNDHATI ROY, *THE GOD OF SMALL THINGS*

# Directory

## Roald Dahl

1916–1990, BRITISH

In his lifetime, Dahl became one of the world's most beloved children's authors. He was born in Wales to Norwegian parents, attended boarding school in Derbyshire—an experience he found brutalizing—and worked briefly in the oil industry. He served as a fighter pilot in World War II, crash-landing in Libya and gravely injuring himself. His wartime exploits inspired his earliest published work.

Dahl's children's books are peopled by grotesque villains, eccentrics, and other characters observed in fiendish detail. His short stories for adults also gained great popularity. They are constructed around the delivery of diabolical plot twists, and have been widely adapted for the stage and television. Dahl also wrote two popular volumes of autobiography.

**KEY WORKS:** *James and the Giant Peach*, 1961; *Charlie and the Chocolate Factory*, 1964; *Tales of the Unexpected*, 1979; *Matilda*, 1988

## Philip Roth

BORN 1933, AMERICAN

Roth is an intensely autobiographical novelist whose long and successful career saw a remarkable late-life burst of creativity. Born in Newark, New Jersey, to first-generation Jewish immigrants, Roth's childhood and upbringing—as well as his sexual relationships with women—have served as hugely important source material for his fiction.

He won the National Book Award of America for his first book, *Goodbye, Columbus* (1959), and 10 years later became internationally famous for *Portnoy's Complaint*, the novel that

seemed to sum up his generation's anguished attitudes toward love and sex. In his mid-career works, Roth sought to blur the line between fiction and reality, often writing novels that included a fictional narrator called Philip Roth. After surviving cancer in the 1990s, he experienced a startling renewal, writing a host of novels regarded as masterpieces, several narrated by his fictional alter egos Nathan Zuckerman and David Kapesh.

**KEY WORKS:** *Goodbye, Columbus*, 1959; *Portnoy's Complaint*, 1969; *Sabbath's Theater*, 1995; *American Pastoral*, 1995

## Kenzaburo Oe

BORN 1935, JAPANESE

One of the most innovative writers of postwar Japan, Oe was born in 1935 on the smallest and most distant of the main four Japanese islands, Shikoku. As a college student, his natural shyness was compounded by his embarrassment of both his rural accent and his stutter, so he shunned company and instead worked at night on his literary career.

This shyness perhaps contributed to the inward-looking nature of Oe's fiction, which was greatly influenced by the philosophy of existentialism. Oe's life was transformed in 1960 by the birth of his first son, Hikari, who had serious learning disabilities. Oe formed an intense bond with his son and the difficulties of communication between the two became a key element of his novels and short stories. In 1994, Oe became only the second Japanese author to be awarded the Nobel Prize in Literature.

**KEY WORKS:** *Nip the Buds, Shoot the Kids*, 1958; *The Catch*, 1958; *A Personal Matter*, 1964

△ **ANNIE PROULX, 2003**

## △ Annie Proulx

BORN 1935, AMERICAN

Proulx is a novelist, short-story writer, and critic who was born in Norwich, Connecticut. She graduated from college at the age of 34, by which time she had been married and divorced three times, and had four children. Always drawn toward the outdoors, after completing an MA in 1973, she lived in a cabin in the Vermont woods and supported her children by writing journalism about hunting, fishing, and self-sufficiency.

Proulx received favorable attention for her short stories but had no ambition to write a novel. She was, however, forced to do so by a clause in her publishing contract and she surprisingly found the longer form easier, and became famous with her second novel, *The Shipping News*. Her work, rich in social observation, has received many prestigious awards

and is particularly notable for its gritty portrayal of the harsh realities of American rural life.

**KEY WORKS:** *The Shipping News*, 1993; *Accordion Crimes*, 1996; "Brokeback Mountain," 1997

## Mario Vargas Llosa

BORN 1936, PERUVIAN

Vargas Llosa was born into a middle-class family in Arequipa, Peru. His parents divorced before he was born and he grew up pampered by his mother's family. When he was 10 years old, his parents reconciled and he was sent by his father, who disapproved of his literary ambitions, to be educated at a military academy. Vargas Llosa drew on this experience in his first novel, *The Time of the Hero*, in which he attacked repression in both public and private spheres; this criticism of the Peruvian establishment caused controversy at the time. He lived in Paris, London, and Madrid for periods, but his fiction remained rooted in Peruvian life, exposing (often with great comic invention) the corruption of the church and the dictatorship.

Vargas Llosa was a part of what became called "El Boom"—the rapid evolution of Latin American literature (much of which carried a political charge) in the 1960s. First a leftist, later a democratic centrist, he has involved himself in Peruvian politics, running for president in 1990. He was awarded the Nobel Prize in Literature in 2010.

**KEY WORKS:** *The Time of the Hero*, 1965; *Conversation in the Cathedral*, 1969; *Aunt Julia and the Screenwriter*, 1977

## ▷ Georges Perec

1936–1982, FRENCH

Born into a Polish-Jewish family in France, Georges Perec lost both his parents in World War II—his mother in Auschwitz. He was brought up by relatives, and by the age of 20 was showing great interest in experimental writing. His first novel, *Things*, which had the structure of a sociological case study, proved to be a great success, as did the next two.

Then, feeling at a creative impasse, he joined the Workshop of Potential Literature, which was founded by the novelist Raymond Queneau and mathematician François Le Lionnais, and sought to create a synthesis of mathematics and literature. Thriving under these constraints, Perec wrote *The Disappearance* (also called *A Void*), a novel that entirely omits the letter "e." Several more experimental works followed, including a 5,000-word palindrome (which reads the same backward and forward) and *Life: A User's Manual*, before Perec's premature death in 1982.

**KEY WORKS:** *Things*, 1965; *The Disappearance*, 1969; *Life: A User's Manual*, 1978

## Thomas Pynchon

BORN 1937, AMERICAN

One of the most enigmatic of all American literary novelists, Pynchon was born on Long Island and educated at Cornell University. He served two years in the US Navy, and after the publication of his first novel, *V.*, when he was just 26 and working as a technical writer for Boeing, he went to great lengths to escape from public view. His mysterious private life helped his work gain a cult following, and because his novels are rooted in the paranoia of 1960s counterculture, some wild theories have coalesced around the writer and his works. All that is really known is that Pynchon has lived in Mexico, California, and New York, and married his literary agent, with whom he has a son. In recent decades, he has drifted toward

△ GEORGES PEREC, 1965

lengthy, discursive historical novels set as far apart as the 19th-century Mason/Dixon expedition and the late '90s dot-com bubble, and experimented in genre pastiche.

**KEY WORKS:** *V.*, 1963; *The Crying of Lot 49*, 1966; *Gravity's Rainbow*, 1973

## Raymond Carver

1938–1988, AMERICAN

Carver is one of the greatest of all American short-story writers. Born in Oregon, he was married with two children by the age of 20. He worked at various jobs to keep the family together and came to writing after attending a creative-writing workshop.

Carver dropped out of college twice, and his career as a teacher and a writer developed slowly: his genius was fully appreciated only around the time of his death from lung cancer at the age of 50. Carver's bleakly poetic stories chronicle the anguish of relationships, and the struggles of his characters to communicate and to withstand lives of adversity (his own life was dogged by alcoholism).

There was controversy in the 2000s, when it became clear how drastically Carver's editor had reworked his best stories, elevating them to greatness. Nevertheless, he retains his place in the canon of short-story writers.

**KEY WORKS:** *Will You Please Be Quiet, Please?* 1976; *What We Talk About When We Talk About Love*, 1981; *Cathedral*, 1983

## Ngũgĩ wa Thiong'o

BORN 1938, KENYAN

Novelist, playwright, essayist, and critic Ngũgĩ was born in Kamirithu, Kenya. His family was caught up in the Mau Mau war of the 1950s, during which his mother was tortured.

In 1964, Ngũgĩ earned a scholarship to Leeds University in northern England, where he wrote *The River Between*, a novel about the Mau Mau rebellion, which is now on the syllabus in Kenyan schools. In 1967, he rejected Christianity, the English language, and his birth name (James), choosing to write in Gikuyu or Swahili. He later became renowned for creating a new type of theater that, with its extensive use of improvisation and audience interaction, was more accessible to nonbourgeois audiences.

In 1977, he was imprisoned in Kenya for a year for the political message of his play *Ngaahika Ndeenda* (*I Will Marry When I Want*), before being freed and fleeing the country for the US. In his adopted country, he has taught at Yale and at the University of California, Irvine, and is considered a likely recipient for the Nobel Prize in Literature.

**KEY WORKS:** *The River Between*, 1965; *A Grain of Wheat*, 1967; *Ngaahika Ndeenda*, 1976

△ ALICE WALKER

## Margaret Atwood

BORN 1939, CANADIAN

Atwood is a prolific and multi-award-winning novelist and poet. Born in Ottawa, Ontario, she spent her childhood summers exploring the wilderness of the bush country of Quebec, and as a teenager she became interested in painting and designing clothes, before dedicating herself to writing. At the University of Toronto she was closely mentored by the critic Northrop Frye, who encouraged her poetry. Several volumes of her poems, beginning with *Double Persephone* (1961), have been published to great acclaim, but it is as a novelist that Atwood has achieved her greatest success.

She is best known for her historical novels and for her science fiction (she prefers the term "speculative fiction"), in which she uses the genre to explore environmental degradation, people's connections with nature, and, especially, the themes of misogyny and women's place in society. In what is now her most famous work—*The Handmaid's Tale*—she presents a bleak view of patriarchy set in a totalitarian dystopia, located in New England. *The Handmaid's Tale* was the number one literary text taught in American schools in 1995 and has been adapted for a movie and television.

**KEY WORKS:** *Surfacing*, 1972; *The Handmaid's Tale*, 1985; *Alias Grace*, 1996; *The Blind Assassin*, 2000

## △ Alice Walker

BORN 1944, AMERICAN

Walker is a Pulitzer Prize–winning author who almost single-handedly created the field of African-American women's studies. Born to a family of sharecroppers in Georgia, and half-blinded by an accident when she was eight, Walker was a shy and studious child. Encouraged by her mother, she earned a scholarship to Spelman College in Atlanta, where she discovered, and became inspired by, the works of the African-American writer and folklorist Zora Neale Hurston (1891–1960).

Walker was involved in the Civil Rights Movement, taught at several universities, and produced many novels, short stories, and works of poetry before winning a huge audience with *The Color Purple* (1982), an epistolary novel about an abused, uneducated girl from Georgia, which was made into an Oscar-winning movie.

She now lives in California, remains politically active, and continues to write about the American South and the lives of African-American women.

**KEY WORKS:** *Meridian*, 1976; *The Color Purple*, 1982; *Possessing the Secret of Joy*, 1992

## Paul Auster

BORN 1947, AMERICAN

Born in South Orange, New Jersey, Auster developed a love of literature from delving into the library of his uncle, the translator Allen Mandelbaum. He studied at Columbia University, earning an MA in 1970, soon after which he moved to Paris and then to Provence, where he found a job as the caretaker of a country house. He moved back to the US in 1974.

In the 1970s and the early '80s, Auster survived as a poet, essayist, and editor with the help of several prestigious grants, before writing his breakthrough work, *The New York Trilogy*—three short novels that explored identity and illusion in brilliant and unexpected ways.

Auster's books commonly feature paradoxes or Kafkaesque puzzles that affect the main protagonist—who is often a writer. His works are at once intellectually challenging and highly readable, with an appeal that has taken him to the top of international best-seller lists. Auster lives in Brooklyn, New York.

**KEY WORKS:** *The New York Trilogy*, 1985–1986; *The Book of Illusions*, 2002; *The Brooklyn Follies*, 2005

## Salman Rushdie

BORN 1947, BRITISH

Rushdie is best known for his prize-winning magical realist novels that confront the troubled issues of postcolonialism and Islam.

Born to a wealthy Muslim family in Mumbai, Rushdie was educated in India and England and worked as an advertising copywriter in London while writing his first two novels. His second, *Midnight's Children*, has the unique distinction of winning the Booker Prize three times: first in 1982, and then in two retrospective "Best of Booker" awards given in 1993 and 2008.

Rushdie's life was turned upside down in 1989, when a fatwa—death sentence—was issued against him by Ayatollah Khomeini, Iran's spiritual leader, for perceived insults to the prophet Muhammad in his novel *The Satanic Verses*. Rushdie lived for years in secret with armed guards, and although the fatwa was described as "finished" by Iranian officials in 1998, it has never been lifted. Rushdie has married four times, and now lives in New York.

**KEY WORKS:** *Midnight's Children*, 1981; *The Satanic Verses*, 1988; *The Moor's Last Sigh*, 1994

## Javier Marías

BORN 1951, SPANISH

Novelist and translator Marías was born in Madrid, the son of the famous Spanish philosopher Julián Marías,

who was imprisoned for opposing the Spanish dictator General Franco. Marías spent part of his childhood with his father in the US but then returned to the University of Madrid, where he began translating some of the world's greatest literature into Spanish. This included works by Updike, Nabokov, Faulkner, Conrad, and Hardy. He received a national award for his translation of *Tristram Shandy*.

His fiction is also concerned with translation. His protagonists are mostly translators or interpreters, who donate or renounce their own voices in various ways, showing how fiction can affect fact and vice versa. His most ambitious work on this theme is *Your Face Tomorrow*, a trilogy completed in the 2000s. In 2006, he was elected to the eminent Real Academia Española, although on his investiture he stated that he found writing fiction "pretty childish."

**KEY WORKS:** *A Heart So White*, 1992; *Dark Back of Time*, 1998; *Your Face Tomorrow*, 2002, 2004, 2007

## ▷ Kazuo Ishiguro

BORN 1954, BRITISH

One of the English-speaking world's most decorated authors, Kazuo Ishiguro was born in Nagasaki; his parents brought him to England in 1960, when he was just five.

After graduating from the University of Kent, Ishiguro became one of the earliest graduates to emerge from the illustrious creative writing course at the University of East Anglia, studying under Malcolm Bradbury and Angela Carter.

Although his first two novels, *A Pale View of Hills* (1982) and *An Artist of the Floating World* (1986), were set in Japan, Ishiguro later admitted that this was an imaginary land to him, since he had not visited the country of his birth since he left in his childhood. He became a British citizen in 1983, although he now says that he has in fact always considered himself

to be a Japanese artist. His fiction is usually written in the first person, often by characters who reveal themselves to be flawed or imperfect witnesses as the work gradually unfolds. His "novels of great emotional force" won him the Nobel Prize in Literature in 2017.

Ishiguro has co-written songs for the American jazz singer Stacey Kent, and describes himself as a serious cinephile. He lives in London.

**KEY WORKS:** *The Remains of the Day*, 1989, *The Unconsoled*, 1995; *Never Let Me Go*, 2005

## Michel Houellebecq

BORN 1956, FRENCH

Houellebecq is an author, critic, and screenwriter. He was born on the island of Réunion in the Indian Ocean, abandoned by his parents at the age

of six, and sent to live with his grandmother in the Parisian suburbs. In the 1990s, he embarked on the novels that made him internationally famous: bleak, cynical portraits of the emptiness of modern life. Often nihilistic, obscene, and fiercely critical of liberal orthodoxy, his works have attracted praise and criticism in equal measure.

During his publicity tour for his novel *Platform* in 2001, Houellebecq was accused of inciting religious hatred after allegedly insulting Islam. The controversy has boosted sales of his books, but at times necessitated security measures to ensure his safety. By coincidence, a cartoon of Houellebecq was on the front page of the French satirical magazine *Charlie Hebdo* on the day in 2015 that its offices were attacked by a subdivision of Al-Qaeda.

**KEY WORKS:** *Whatever*, 1994; *The Elementary Particles*, 1998

△ **KAZUO ISHIGURO, 1995**

# Index

# Acknowledgments

Cobalt id would like to thank Helen Peters for indexing. The publisher would like to thank the following for their kind permission to reproduce their photographs:

(Key: a-above; b-below; c-center; l-left; r-right; t-top)

**2 Getty Images:** Stock Montage / Contributor (c). **3 Alamy Stock Photo:** maurice joseph (c). **5 Getty Images:** ullstein bild Dtl. / Contributor (c). **12 Getty Images:** Fine Art / Contributor (ca). **12 Alamy Stock Photo:** ART Collection (crb). **13 Getty Images:** UniversalImagesGroup / Contributor (c). **14 Getty Images:** DEA / G. DAGLI ORTI / Contributor (bl). DEA / A. DAGLI ORTI / Contributor (tr). **15 Alamy Stock Photo:** Alexei Fateev (tl). **15 Getty Images:** De Agostini Picture Library / Contributor (cr). **16 Alamy Stock Photo:** Hemis (bl). **16 Getty Images:** Heritage Images / Contributor (crb). **17 Getty Images:** Leemage / Contributor (c). **18 Alamy Stock Photo:** Art Collection 3 (cb). jamesjagger / StockimoNews (crb). **19 Alamy Stock Photo:** Classic Image (c). **20 Getty Images:** UniversalImagesGroup / Contributor (tl). Fine Art Photographic / Contributor (bl). **20-21 Getty Images:** David Goddard / Contributor (tr). **21 Bridgeman Images:** © Christie's Images (cr). **22 Alamy Stock Photo:** Hemis (cla). ART Collection (crb). **23 Bridgeman Images:** Chateau de Versailles, France (c). **24 TopFoto:** Roger-Viollet (tl). **24 Getty Images:** Heritage Images / Contributor (tr). DEA / V. PIROZZI / Contributor (bl). **25 Getty Images:** DEA / J. E. BULLOZ / Contributor (br). **26 Getty Images:** Christophel Fine Art / Contributor (c). **27 Alamy Stock Photo:** Hemis (bl). **27 Getty Images:** Culture Club / Contributor (br). **28 Getty Images:** Leemage / Contributor (ca). Culture Club / Contributor (br). **29 Alamy Stock Photo:** Granger Historical Picture Archive (c). **30 Getty Images:** ullstein bild Dtl. / Contributor (tl). CURTO DE LA TORRE / Stringer (tr). Photo Josse/ Leemage / Contributor (br). **31 Alamy Stock Photo:** robertharding (br). **32 Alamy Stock Photo:** DavidCC (cla). **32 Getty Images:** Scott Barbour / Staff (crb). **33 Getty Images:** Fine Art / Contributor (b). **34 Alamy Stock Photo:** Falkenstein / Bildagentur-online Historical Collect (tc). North Wind Picture Archives (cl). **35 Alamy Stock Photo:** Hirarchivum Press (t). **36 Getty Images:** Print Collector / Contributor (cl). DEA PICTURE LIBRARY / Contributor (tr). **37 Alamy Stock Photo:** ART Collection (tr). Michael Brooks (b). **38 Bridgeman Images:** National Portrait Gallery, London, UK (c). **39 Getty Images:** Culture Club / Contributor (cla). De Agostini Picture Library / Contributor (cr). Universal History Archive / Contributor (br). **40 Getty Images:** DEA PICTURE LIBRARY / Contributor (b). **41 Getty Images:** PHAS / Contributor (tr). **41 Alamy Stock Photo:** PjrStatues (bl). parkerphotography (br). **42 Alamy Stock Photo:** Lebrecht Music and Arts Photo Library (tr). **42 Getty Images:** Photo Josse / Leemage / Contributor (br). **43 Getty Images:** Photo Josse / Leemage / Contributor (c). **44 Alamy Stock Photo:** Artokoloro Quint Lox Limited (c). **45 Bridgeman Images:** London Metropolitan Archives, City of London (tr). **45 Alamy Stock Photo:** Peter Horree (br). **46 Alamy Stock Photo:** PersimmonPictures.com (bl). JTB MEDIA CREATION, Inc. (crb). **47 Getty Images:** Apic / RETIRED / Contributor (c). **48 Getty Images:** Stock Montage / Contributor (c). **49 Getty Images:** Print Collector / Contributor (tl). **49 Alamy Stock Photo:** Peter Horree (br). **50 Alamy Stock Photo:** Florilegius (tc). **50 Getty Images:** Culture Club / Contributor (bl). **51 Alamy Stock Photo:** AF Fotografie (tr). **51 Getty Images:** MARTIN BERNETTI / Staff (b). **52 Alamy Stock Photo:** Ian Dagnall (tr). **53 Alamy Stock Photo:** Ian Dagnall (bl). AF Fotografie (cra). Chronicle (br). **54 Getty Images:** Photo Josse / Leemage / Contributor (c). **55 Bridgeman Images:** Wallace Collection, London, UK (c). **55 Getty Images:** AFP / Stringer (br). **56 Alamy Stock Photo:** Classic Image (bc). **57 Getty Images:** Christophel Fine Art / Contributor (tl). **60 Alamy Stock Photo:** Heritage Image Partnership Ltd (c). **61 Alamy Stock Photo:** Novarc Images (bl). **61 Getty Images:** Ulrich Baumgarten / Contributor (br). **62 Alamy Stock Photo:** FALKENSTEINFOTO (cl). **62 Getty Images:** Heritage Images / Contributor (br). **63 Getty Images:** DEA PICTURE LIBRARY / Contributor (tl). **63 akg-images:** Joseph Martin (br). **64 Alamy Stock Photo:** Simon Whaley Landscapes (cl). **64 Getty Images:** Culture Club / Contributor (crb). **65 Alamy Stock Photo:** Granger Historical Picture Archive (c). **66 Alamy Stock Photo:** SuperStock (tl). Richard Allen (clb). **66 Getty Images:** Olaf Protze / Contributor (br). **67 Alamy Stock Photo:** nobleIMAGES (ca). Paul Fearn (cb). **67 Alamy Stock Photo:** Pictorial Press Ltd (crb). **68 Alamy Stock Photo:** Peter Titmuss (bl). **68 Getty Images:** Culture Club / Contributor (tc). DEA PICTURE LIBRARY / Contributor (br). **69 Bridgeman Images:** Private Collection (c). **70 Alamy Stock Photo:** Ruby (tl). **70 Bridgeman Images:** Private Collection / The Stapleton Collection (bc). **71 Alamy Stock Photo:** Steve Vidler (l). **71 Bridgeman Images:** British Library, London, UK / © British Library Board. All Rights Reserved (br). **72 Getty Images:** Heritage Images / Contributor (c). **73 Getty Images:** DEA / G. DAGLI ORTI / Contributor (bl). **73 Alamy Stock Photo:** Everett Collection Inc (crb). **74 Alamy Stock Photo:** Glyn Genin (bl). Paul Fearn (crb). **75 akg-images:** Pictures From History (c).

**76 Alamy Stock Photo:** Peter Horree (tr). **77 TopFoto:** ©Roger-Viollet (tr). **77 akg-images:** Erich Lessing (bl). **77 Bridgeman Images:** Musee de la Ville de Paris, Maison de Balzac, Paris, France / Archives Charmet (br). **78 Getty Images:** Photo Josse / Leemage / Contributor (c). **79 Getty Images:** Apic / RETIRED / Contributor (c). Mondadori Portfolio / Contributor (br). **80 Getty Images:** Photo Josse/Leemage / Contributor (clb). **80 Alamy Stock Photo:** age fotostock (bc). **80 TopFoto:** Roger-Viollet (tr). **81 Getty Images:** Christophel Fine Art / Contributor (t). Popperfoto / Contributor (c). **83 Getty Images:** Bettmann / Contributor (tr). **83 Alamy Stock Photo:** Chronicle (bl). **83 Dorling Kindersley:** Dreamstime.com / Thomas Barrat / Tbarrat (br). **84 Getty Images:** Bettmann / Contributor (tl). **85 Getty Images:** Culture Club / Contributor (tl). Barry Winiker (bl). **85 Alamy Stock Photo:** BFA (br). **86 Bridgeman Images:** Charles Dickens Museum, London, UK (tr). **86 Getty Images:** Culture Club / Contributor (br). **87 Getty Images:** Historical Picture Archive / Contributor (c). **88 Alamy Stock Photo:** Entertainment Pictures (bl). **88 Getty Images:** Culture Club / Contributor (tc). Epics / Contributor (br). **89 Alamy Stock Photo:** VIEW Pictures Ltd (t). **90 Getty Images:** Culture Club / Contributor (tl). **90 Alamy Stock Photo:** Paul Fearn (b). Mondadori Portfolio / Contributor (t). **92 Getty Images:** Fine Art / Contributor (c). **93 Alamy Stock Photo:** Steve Morgan (cr). **93 Getty Images:** Rischgitz / Stringer (br). **94 Alamy Stock Photo:** Granger Historical Picture Archive (t). **94 Bridgeman Images:** Bronte Parsonage Museum, Haworth, Yorkshire, U.K. (bl). **95 Alamy Stock Photo:** Paul Fearn (tl). Virginia Velasco (cr). **96 Alamy Stock Photo:** darryl gill (t). **96 Bridgeman Images:** Bronte Parsonage Museum, Haworth, Yorkshire, U.K. (bl). **97 Getty Images:** Culture Club / Contributor (tr). Fine Art Photographic / Contributor (br). **98 Getty Images:** Mondadori Portfolio / Contributor (bl). **99 Alamy Stock Photo:** GL Archive (tl). **100 Getty Images:** Print Collector / Contributor (tr). **101 Getty Images:** Print Collector / Contributor (br). **104 Getty Images:** DEA PICTURE LIBRARY / Contributor (c). **105 Getty Images:** Culture Club / Contributor (tr). **105 Alamy Stock Photo:** Chronicle (bl). **106 Alamy Stock Photo:** David Lyons (cla). **106 Getty Images:** Michael Nicholson / Contributor (crb). **107 Getty Images:** Bettmann / Contributor (c). **108 Getty Images:** Apic / RETIRED / Contributor (c). **109 Alamy Stock Photo:** Randy Duchaine (ca). Premium Stock Photography GmbH (crb). **110 Getty Images:** Otto Herschan / Stringer (clb). Library of Congress / Contributor (cra). **111 Library of Congress:** (tr). **111 Getty Images:** GraphicaArtis / Contributor (b). **112 Getty Images:** De Agostini Picture Library / Contributor (cla). Photo 12 / Contributor (crb). **113 Getty Images:** Apic / RETIRED / Contributor (c). **114 akg-images:** arkivi (tl). **114 Bridgeman Images:** Tallandier (tr). **115 Getty Images:** De Agostini Picture Library / Contributor (tr). Christophel Fine Art / Contributor (br). **116 Alamy Stock Photo:** Lebrecht Music and Arts Photo Library (c). **117 Getty Images:** Hulton Archive / Stringer (cla). adoc-photos / Contributor (crb). **118 Bridgeman Images:** Tallandier (tl). **118 Getty Images:** Photo Josse/ Leemage / Contributor (b). **119 Getty Images:** Culture Club / Contributor (tl). **119 Alamy Stock Photo:** Granger Historical Picture Archive (crb). **120 Getty Images:** De Agostini Picture Library / Contributor (b). Heritage Images / Contributor (br). **121 Getty Images:** Fine Art / Contributor (c). **122 Alamy Stock Photo:** Paul Fearn (t). **122 Getty Images:** UniversalImagesGroup / Contributor (bl). **122 TopFoto:** RIA Novosti (br). **123 TopFoto:** RIA Novosti (tr). RIA Novosti (crb). **124 Getty Images:** Culture Club / Contributor (tr). **125 Alamy Stock Photo:** Paul Fearn (tr). **125 Getty Images:** Robbie Jack / Contributor (br). **126 Getty Images:** Bettmann / Contributor (c). **127 Getty Images:** Bettmann / Contributor (tr). **127 Alamy Stock Photo:** Alexey Zarubin (bl). Art Collection 3 (tl). **128-129 akg-images:** Elizaveta Becker (tl). **128 Alamy Stock Photo:** SPUTNIK (bl). **129 Alamy Stock Photo:** SPUTNIK (cra). **129 Getty Images:** Elliott & Fry / Stringer (crb). **130 Alamy Stock Photo:** Granger Historical Picture Archive (tr). **131 Getty Images:** Universal History Archive / Contributor (tr). Hulton Archive / Stringer (br). **132 Alamy Stock Photo:** Norman Eggert (bl). Granger Historical Picture Archive (cr). **133 Alamy Stock Photo:** IanDagnall Computing (c). **134 Getty Images:** Buyenlarge / Contributor (b). Historical Picture Archive / Contributor (cr). **135 Getty Images:** Hulton Archive / Staff (c). **136 Alamy Stock Photo:** International Photobank (cla). **136 Getty Images:** Universal History Archive / Contributor (crb). **137 Alamy Stock Photo:** Granger Historical Picture Archive (c). **138 Alamy Stock Photo:** Pictorial Press Ltd (cl). **138-139 Alamy Stock Photo:** David Noton Photography (tr). **139 Bridgeman Images:** British Library, London, UK / © British Library Board. All Rights Reserved (bl). **139 Alamy Stock Photo:** Chronicle (br). **140 Getty Images:** Christophel Fine Art / Contributor (c). **141 Getty Images:** Photo 12 / Contributor (tr). DEA PICTURE LIBRARY / Contributor (br). **142 Alamy Stock Photo:** IanDagnall (c). **143 Alamy Stock Photo:** Tim Jones (cb). **143 Getty Images:** Bettmann / Contributor (cr). **144 Getty Images:** Universal History Archive / UIG (tr). **145 Getty Images:** DEA / A. DAGLI ORTI / Contributor (tl). PHAS / Contributor (cra).

**145 Lebrecht:** Tristram Kenton (br). **146 Getty Images:** Heritage Images / Contributor (c). **147 Getty Images:** DEA / J. L. CHARMET / Contributor (cla). Mondadori Portfolio / Contributor (cr). **147 Alamy Stock Photo:** Hemis (br). **148 Alamy Stock Photo:** Heritage Image Partnership Ltd (tr). **149 Alamy Stock Photo:** Paul Fearn (bl). **149 Bridgeman Images:** British Library, London, UK / © British Library Board. All Rights Reserved (tr). **149 Alamy Stock Photo:** Pictorial Press Ltd (br). **150 Alamy Stock Photo:** ART Collection (bl). Everett Collection Inc (cr). **151 Alamy Stock Photo:** Granger Historical Picture Archive (c). **152 Getty Images:** API / Contributor (tl). Universal History Archive / Contributor (tr). **152 Alamy Stock Photo:** Chronicle (bl). **153 Getty Images:** Caterine Milinaire / Contributor (t). **154 Alamy Stock Photo:** Peter Brown (bl). **154 Bridgeman Images:** Private Collection / The Stapleton Collection (cr). **155 Getty Images:** DEA PICTURE LIBRARY / Contributor (c). **156 Bridgeman Images:** Tretyakov Gallery, Moscow, Russia (c). **157 TopFoto:** SCRSS (tr). **157 Alamy Stock Photo:** Heritage Image Partnership Ltd (crb). **158 Alamy Stock Photo:** ITAR-TASS News Agency (tl). **158 Getty Images:** SVF2 / Contributor (b). **159 Getty Images:** Heritage Images / Contributor (ca). **159 TopFoto:** SCRSS (bl). **159 Alamy Stock Photo:** Heritage Image Partnership Ltd (br). **160 Getty Images:** Estate of Emil Bieber / Klaus Niermann / Contributor (tr). **161 Alamy Stock Photo:** volkerpreusser (bl). Xinhua (cr). **162 Getty Images:** De Agostini Picture Library / Contributor (tr). **163 Alamy Stock Photo:** Granger Historical Picture Archive (br). **164 Alamy Stock Photo:** Art Collection 3 (br). **165 Getty Images:** Imagno / Contributor (tr). **168 Alamy Stock Photo:** George Munday (bl). **168 Bridgeman Images:** Private Collection / Photo © Christie's Images (crb). **169 Getty Images:** DEA PICTURE LIBRARY / Contributor (c). **170 Getty Images:** Edward Steichen / Contributor (tr). **171 Getty Images:** Universal History Archive / Contributor (cl). Evans / Stringer (cra). **171 Alamy Stock Photo:** ITAR-TASS News Agency (br). **172 Alamy Stock Photo:** JTB MEDIA CREATION, Inc. (bl). **172 Getty Images:** Popperfoto / Contributor (br). **173 TopFoto:** TopFoto.co.uk (c). **174 Alamy Stock Photo:** Masterpics (c). **175 Getty Images:** FRANCOIS GUILLOT / Staff (tr). **175 TopFoto:** The Granger Collection, New York (clb). **175 Getty Images:** Leemage / Contributor (br). **176 Getty Images:** GAROFALO Jack / Contributor (tl). **176 akg-images:** Catherine Bibollet (bl). **177 Getty Images:** Apic / RETIRED / Contributor (bl). **177 TopFoto:** Roger-Viollet (br). **178 Getty Images:** New York Times Co. / Contributor (tr). **179 Alamy Stock Photo:** Michael Snell (bl). Paul Fearn (crb). **180 Getty Images:** Edward Steichen / Contributor (c). **181 Alamy Stock Photo:** Keystone Pictures USA (cr). AF archive (bl). INTERFOTO (br). **182 Getty Images:** Bettmann / Contributor (tr). **183 akg-images:** Pictures From History (cla). **183 Alamy Stock Photo:** SPUTNIK (cr). Henry Westheim Photography (cb). **184 Getty Images:** Photo 12 / Contributor (c). **185 Alamy Stock Photo:** Alain Le Garsmeur James Joyce Ireland (tl). ART Collection (br). **186 TopFoto:** Fine Art Images / Heritage Images (cl). **186 Getty Images:** Hulton Deutsch / Contributor (br). **187 Getty Images:** Bettmann / Contributor (tl). **187 Bridgeman Images:** Private Collection / Courtesy of Swann Auction Galleries (cr). **188 Alamy Stock Photo:** IanDagnall Computing (c). **189 Alamy Stock Photo:** Christopher Nicholson (bl). **189 Getty Images:** Culture Club / Contributor (cr). **190 Alamy Stock Photo:** INTERFOTO (tl). Art Collection 3 (bl). **190 Getty Images:** Hulton Deutsch / Contributor (br). **191 Alamy Stock Photo:** The National Trust Photolibrary (tr). **191 Getty Images:** Lenare / Stringer (cr). **192 akg-images:** Archiv K. Wagenbach (tr). **192 Getty Images:** Three Lions / Stringer (br). **193 Getty Images:** Private Collection / Prismatic Pictures (c). **194 Alamy Stock Photo:** Lebrecht Music and Arts Photo Library (b). **195 Getty Images:** Mondadori Portfolio / Contributor (tl). **195 Alamy Stock Photo:** INTERFOTO (bl). **195 akg-images:** Archiv K. Wagenbach (br). **196 Getty Images:** Historical / Contributor (tr). **197 Getty Images:** Bettmann / Contributor (bl). **197 Alamy Stock Photo:** Paul Fearn (crb). **198 Alamy Stock Photo:** Art Kowalsky (b). **199 Getty Images:** David Lees / Contributor (tc). **199 Alamy Stock Photo:** Granger Historical Picture Archive (clb). **199 Getty Images:** Print Collector / Contributor (crb). **200 Alamy Stock Photo:** Granger Historical Picture Archive (cla). **200 Getty Images:** Central Press / Stringer (crb). **200 Lebrecht:** Lebrecht Music & Arts 2 (br). **201 Getty Images:** Hulton Deutsch / Contributor (c). **202 Getty Images:** John Springer Collection / Contributor (bl). **202 Cobalt id:** (crb). **203 Alamy Stock Photo:** Pictorial Press Ltd (c). **204 Mary Evans Picture Library:** IDA KAR (tr). **205 Alamy Stock Photo:** Granger Historical Picture Archive (cr). **205 Getty Images:** Picture Post / Stringer (br). **206 Bridgeman Images:** Pearl Freeman (tr). **207 Getty Images:** Bettmann / Contributor (ca). **207 Alamy Stock Photo:** Darryl Brooks (bl). **207 Cobalt id:** (br). **208 Bridgeman Images:** © Tobie Mathew Collection (cla). **208 Alamy Stock Photo:** PRISMA ARCHIVO (crb). **209 Alamy Stock Photo:** Paul Fearn (c). **210 Getty Images:** Oli Scarff / Staff (cla). **210 Alamy Stock Photo:** Everett Collection Inc (crb). **211 Alamy Stock Photo:** Everett Collection Historical (c). **212 Getty Images:** Bettmann / Contributor (t). Culture Club / Contributor (clb). **213 Getty Images:** Hulton Archive / Stringer (cra). **213 Alamy Stock Photo:** Hemis (bc). **214 Alamy Stock Photo:** Pictorial Press Ltd (c). **215 Alamy Stock Photo:** Bhammond (bl). **215 Getty Images:** Chicago History Museum / Contributor (br). **216 Getty Images:** Transcendental Graphics / Contributor (tr). Photo 12 / Contributor (b). **217 Getty Images:** Bettmann / Contributor (tc). **217 Royal Books, Inc:** (br). **218 Getty Images:** John D. Kisch / Separate Cinema Archive / Contributor (tl). Popperfoto / Contributor (crb).

**219 akg-images:** Olivier Martel (bl). **219 Getty Images:** John Springer Collection / Contributor (cra). **220 Getty Images:** ullstein bild Dtl. / Contributor (tr). **221 akg-images:** ullstein bild (tr). **221 Getty Images:** Imagno / Contributor (bl). Robbie Jack / Contributor (br). **222 Alamy Stock Photo:** MARKA (c). **223 Getty Images:** DEA / P. JACCOD / Contributor (cra). **224 Alamy Stock Photo:** Greg Wright (t). **225 akg-images:** Album / Kurwenal / Prisma (ca). **225 Getty Images:** Rafa Samano / Contributor (bl). Ulf Andersen / Contributor (crb). **226 Getty Images:** Raymond Boyd / Contributor (cla). Herbert Orth / Contributor (crb). **227 Getty Images:** Lloyd Arnold / Contributor (c). **228 Alamy Stock Photo:** Cosmo Condina (tl). Brian Jannsen (tr). Granger Historical Picture Archive (clb). **229 Getty Images:** Europa Press / Contributor (b). **230 Lebrecht:** Lebrecht Music & Arts 2. From *The Old Man and the Sea* by Ernest Hemingway, published by Jonathan Cape, London. Reproduced by permission of The Random House Group Ltd. ©September 2018 (tr). **230 Getty Images:** Hulton Archive / Stringer (bl). **231 Alamy Stock Photo:** john norman (tl). **231 Getty Images:** Keystone / Stringer (cr). **232 Getty Images:** Mondadori Portfolio / Contributor (cr). John S Lander / Contributor (bc). **233 Getty Images:** The Asahi Shimbun / Contributor (c). **234 Alamy Stock Photo:** The Granger Collection (bl). **235 Alamy Stock Photo:** Archivart (ca). **236 Alamy Stock Photo:** Paul Fearn (ca). **237 Getty Images:** Haywood Magee / Stringer (br). **240 Getty Images:** Carl Mydans / Contributor (c). **241 akg-images:** (tr). **241 Getty Images:** Carl Mydans / Contributor (br). **242 Alamy Stock Photo:** Granger Historical Picture Archive (tr). **242 Getty Images:** Arthur Rothstein / Contributor (br). **243 Getty Images:** Hulton Archive / Stringer (c). **244 Alamy Stock Photo:** Granger Historical Picture Archive (c). **245 Alamy Stock Photo:** Julio Etchart (c). **245 Getty Images:** Hulton Deutsch / Contributor (br). **246 Getty Images:** Kurt Hutton / Stringer (t). Hulton Archive / Stringer (clb). **247 Alamy Stock Photo:** Scott Sim (bl). Granger Historical Picture Archive (crb). **248 Getty Images:** MIGUEL ROJO / Stringer (bl). **249 Getty Images:** Keystone-France / Contributor (c). **250 Alamy Stock Photo:** Sueddeutsche Zeitung Photo (clb). World History Archive (tr). **251 Getty Images:** Justin Setterfield / Contributor (t). Heritage Images / Contributor (br). **252 Alamy Stock Photo:** Everett Collection Historical (c). **253 Alamy Stock Photo:** Philip Dunn (bl). Everett Collection Inc (crb). **254 Getty Images:** RDA/RETIRED / Contributor (cla). **254 Bridgeman Images:** PVDE (crb). **255 Getty Images:** Lipnitzki / Contributor (c). **256 Getty Images:** Horst P. Horst / Contributor (bl). **257 Getty Images:** STF / Staff (tr). **257 TopFoto:** (br). **258 Getty Images:** Hulton Archive / Stringer (cla). Hiroyuki Ito / Contributor (cr). **259 Getty Images:** ullstein bild / Contributor (c). **260 Getty Images:** Lipnitzki / Contributor (tl). **261 Dorling Kindersley:** Gary Ombler / Wardrobe Museum, Salisbury (tl). **261 Lebrecht:** John Haynes (clb). **261 Alamy Stock Photo:** ClassicStock (crb). **262 Magnum Photos:** Chris Steele-Perkins (tr). **263 Getty Images:** Frederic Lewis / Staff (bl). Paul Thompson / FPG / Stringer (cr). **264 Alamy Stock Photo:** John Frost Newspapers (tr). Old Paper Studios (bl). **264 Getty Images:** Keystone-France / Contributor (br). **265 Getty Images:** Kurt Hutton / Stringer (c). **266 Getty Images:** Lipnitzki / Contributor (tr). **267 Alamy Stock Photo:** Neftali (tl). **267 Getty Images:** Andia / Contributor (bl). Hulton Deutsch / Contributor (br). **268 Getty Images:** Hulton Archive / Stringer (tr). **269 Getty Images:** Evening Standard / Stringer (cl). **269 Alamy Stock Photo:** Antiques & Collectables (tr). Aled Llywelyn (br). **270 Getty Images:** Lipnitzki / Contributor (c). **271 Alamy Stock Photo:** Everett Collection, Inc. (cla). ERIC LAFFORGUE (br). **272 Getty Images:** Bettmann / Contributor (bl). **272 Cobalt id:** (crb). **273 Getty Images:** Ulf Andersen / Contributor (c). **274 Getty Images:** James Andanson / Contributor (c). **275 Getty Images:** Mondadori Portfolio / Contributor (bl). Apic / RETIRED / Contributor (br). **276 Alamy Stock Photo:** Zoonar GmbH (clb). **276 Bridgeman Images:** Peter Newark Military Pictures (cr). **277 Getty Images:** Gianni GIANSANTI / Contributor (c). **278 Alamy Stock Photo:** Shawshots (t). **278 Getty Images:** Fototeca Storica Nazionale. / Contributor (bl). **279 akg-images:** ullstein bild (bl). **279 Lebrecht:** Lebrecht Music & Arts 2. *If This Is a Man* by Primo Levi, Little, Brown Book Group (br). **280 Bridgeman Images:** Prismatic Pictures (tr). **281 Alamy Stock Photo:** AF Fotografie (ca). **281 Getty Images:** Ted Streshinsky Photographic Archive / Contributor (cr). **281 Bridgeman Images:** © Christie's Images (br). **282 Getty Images:** Gianni GIANSANTI / Contributor (tr). **283 Alamy Stock Photo:** MARKA (bl). **283 akg-images:** Fototeca Gilardi (tr). **283 Getty Images:** Ulf Andersen / Contributor (br). **284 akg-images:** Marion Kalter (tr). **285 Getty Images:** Sean Gallup / Staff (tr). Bloomberg / Contributor (bl). **285 Alamy Stock Photo:** dpa picture alliance archive (br). **286 Getty Images:** Bettmann / Contributor (c). **287 Getty Images:** EITAN ABRAMOVICH / Staff (ca). **287 Alamy Stock Photo:** Xinhua (bl). StellaArt (br). **288 Alamy Stock Photo:** Everett Collection Inc (cl). Organica (tr). **289 akg-images:** Album / Oronoz (tc). **289 Alamy Stock Photo:** dpa picture alliance (bl). **290 Alamy Stock Photo:** Everett Collection Historical (tr). **291 Getty Images:** Gene Lester / Contributor (tl). The Frent Collection / Contributor (tr). **291 Bridgeman Images:** Newberry Library, Chicago, Illinois, USA (br). **292 Getty Images:** Sovfoto / Contributor (bl). **292 Alamy Stock Photo:** INTERFOTO (crb). **293 TopFoto:** Roger-Viollet (c). **294 Alamy Stock Photo:** PRAWNS (bl). Jonny White (cr). **295 Lebrecht:** Hollandse Hoogte (c). **296 Getty Images:** Romano Cagnoni / Contributor (t). **296 Lebrecht:** Lebrecht Music & Arts 2 (bl). **297 Getty Images:** ISSOUF SANOGO / Stringer (tr). STEFAN HEUNIS / Stringer (br). **298 Getty Images:**

ADALBERTO ROQUE / Stringer (cr). Erich Auerbach / Stringer (br). **299 Getty Images:** Ulf Andersen / Contributor (ca). **300 Alamy Stock Photo:** dpa picture alliance (tr). **301 Alamy Stock Photo:** Granger Historical Picture Archive (br). **304 Getty Images:** Ulf Andersen / Contributor (c). **305 Alamy Stock Photo:** Martin A. Doe (tr). Martin A. Doe (bl). **306 Getty Images:** Brooks Kraft / Contributor (c). **307 Alamy Stock Photo:** Brian Jannsen (br). **308 REX/Shutterstock:** SNAP (c). **309 Alamy Stock Photo:** Science History Images (ca). dpa picture alliance archive (tr). **309 Getty Images:** Eliot Elisofon / Contributor (br). **310 Alamy Stock Photo:** Christopher Stewart (bl). **310 Getty Images:** Rene Johnston / Contributor (crb). **311 Marion Ettlinger:** (c). **312 Getty Images:** FILIPPO MONTEFORTE / Staff (cra). David Levenson / Contributor (c). **314 Getty Images:** Boston Globe / Contributor (tr). **315 Getty Images:** Apic/RETIRED / Contributor (tl). Boston Globe / Contributor (bl). **315 Alamy Stock Photo:** The Protected Art Archive (br). **316 Marion Ettlinger:** (c). **317 Getty Images:** Education Images / Contributor (ca). Christian Science Monitor / Contributor (br). **318 Alamy Stock Photo:** scenicireland.com / Christopher Hill Photographic (cl). Helen Thorpe Wright (crb). **319 Getty Images:** Richard Smith / Contributor (c). **320 Bridgeman Images:** British Library, London, UK / © British Library Board. All Rights Reserved (cl). **320 Alamy Stock Photo:** Alain Le Garsmeur "The Troubles" Archive (tr). **321 Getty Images:** Tara Walton / Contributor (tr). **321 Alamy Stock Photo:** Paul McErlane (br). **322 Getty Images:** Bernard Bisson / Contributor (cla). **322 Lebrecht:** Lebrecht Music & Arts 2. From *Disgrace* by J. M. Coetzee, published by Vintage, London, 2000. Reproduced by permission of The Random House Group Ltd. ©September 2018 (cr). **323 Getty Images:** Micheline Pelletier Decaux / Contributor (c). **324 Alamy Stock Photo:** AfriPics.com (t). **325 Lebrecht:** Lebrecht Music & Arts 2. From *Life & Times of Michael K* by J. M. Coetzee, published by Sacker & Warburg. Reproduced by permission of The Random House Group Ltd. ©September 2018 (bl). **325 Getty Images:** Per-Anders Pettersson / Contributor (crb). **326 Lebrecht:** Lebrecht Music & Arts 2. From *Of Love and Shadows* by Isabel Allende, published by Jonathan Cape, London 1987. Reproduced by permission of The Random House Group Ltd. ©September 2018 (tr). **326 Getty Images:** ILA AGENCIA / Contributor (br). **327 Getty Images:** The Sydney Morning Herald / Contributor (c). **328 Getty Images:** Ulf Andersen / Contributor (c). **329 Alamy Stock Photo:** GL Archive (c). **329 Getty Images:** Rick Madonik / Contributor (br). **330 Getty Images:** Raphael GAILLARDE / Contributor (tr). **331 Getty Images:** ED JONES / Staff (t). Dominique BERRETTY / Contributor (bl). **331 Alamy Stock Photo:** Science History Images (br). **332 Getty Images:** Gina Ferazzi / Contributor (c). **333 Getty Images:** ullstein bild Dtl. / Contributor (cla). Popperfoto / Contributor (crb). **334 Alamy Stock Photo:** Jim Laws (tl). **334 Cobalt id:** (bc). **335 Cobalt id:** (tr). **335 Alamy Stock Photo:** Photo 12 (b). **336 Alamy Stock Photo:** Sam Kolich (tr). **336 Cobalt id:** (br). **337 Alamy Stock Photo:** GARY DOAK (c). **338 Alamy Stock Photo:** INTERFOTO (tr). **339 Getty Images:** Imagno / Contributor (bl). **339 Lebrecht:** Lebrecht Music & Arts 2 (tr). **340 Lebrecht:** Ulf Andersen/Aurimages (c). **341 Getty Images:** Steve Russell / Contributor (cla). **341 Alamy Stock Photo:** MARKA (br). **342 Getty Images:** Ulf Andersen / Contributor (c). **343 Cobalt id:** (tr). **343 Alamy Stock Photo:** zhang jiahan (br). **344 Getty Images:** Hindustan Times / Contributor (c). **345 Alamy Stock Photo:** Ruby (c). **345 Cobalt id:** (crb). **346 Getty Images:** Fairfax Media / Contributor (tr). **347 Getty Images:** DEUTSCH Jean-Claude / Contributor (bc). **348 Getty Images:** Harcourt Brace / Stringer (t). **349 Getty Images:** David Levenson / Contributor (br).

**Endpaper images:** *Front:* **Alamy Stock Photo:** Andrejs Pidjass; *Back:* **Alamy Stock Photo:** Andrejs Pidjass

All other images © Dorling Kindersley. For more information see:
**www.dkimages.com**

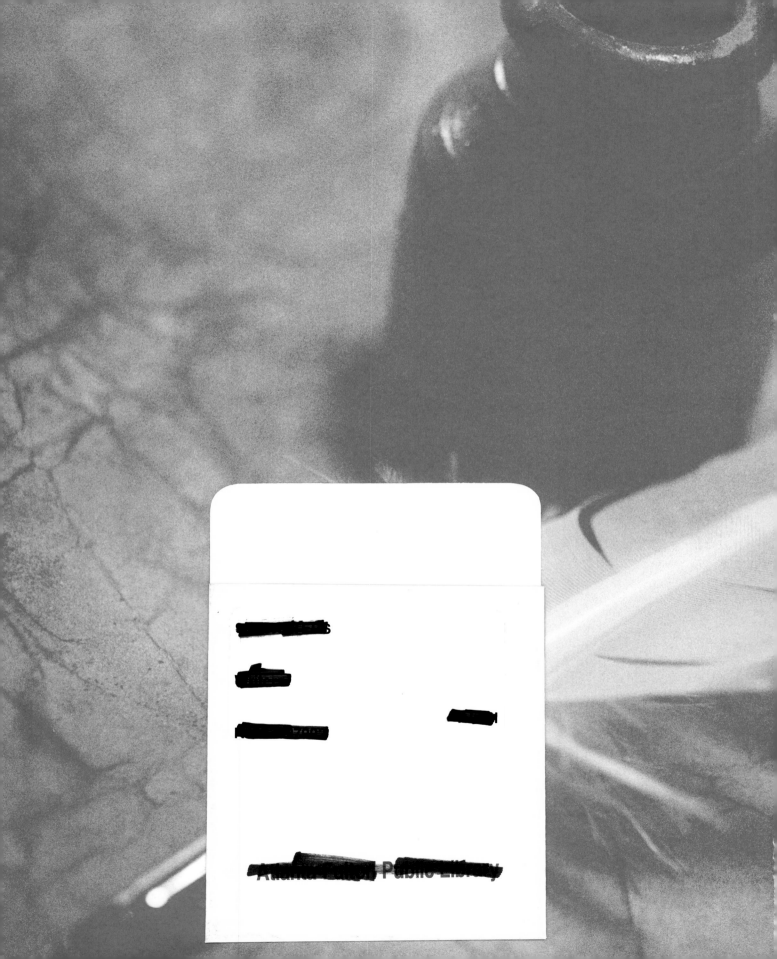